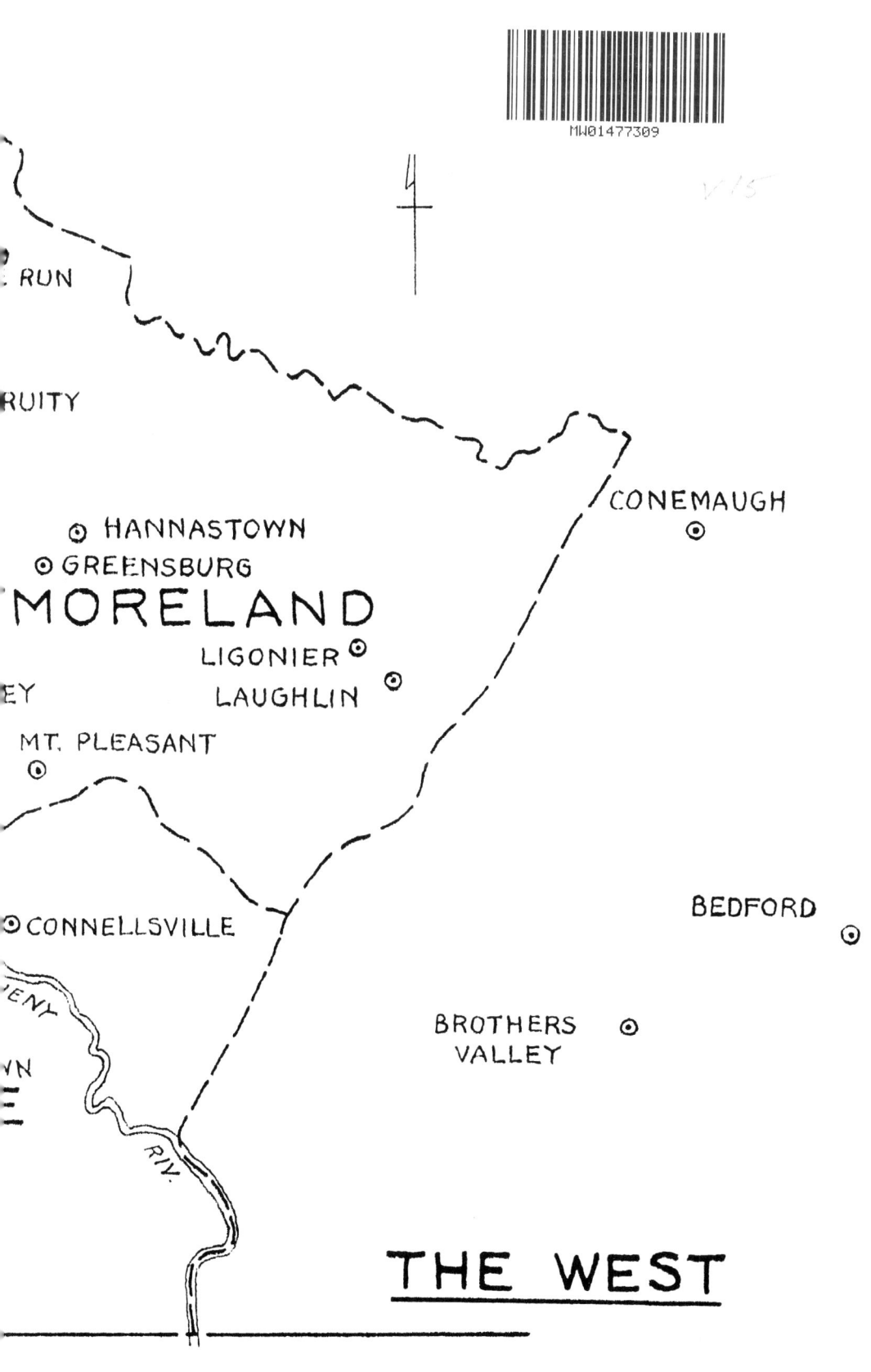

JOHN MCMILLAN

John McMillan is one of a list of books in the cultural history of western Pennsylvania—made possible through a grant-in-aid from The Buhl Foundation of Pittsburgh.

Expences for the year 1822.

Jan. y. 7th to snuf for Dido	.25
to Coffee & snuf for Jane McMillan	.37½
14th for two of the everlasting tapes	.12½
Feb. y. 9th for two yards of flanel to Dido	1.
16th to Samuel McMillan	.50
20th to Samuel McMillan for repairing axes	1.75
for snuf for Dido	.25
for an hancircheif for Dido	3.
March y. 4th to a spelling book for Hannah	.25
to T. Leatherman for Dido	.25
10th to Ritchie for a pound of tobaco	.12½
to Ritchie for a pound of Coffee	.37½
April y. 2d paid for road taxes	2.50
15th for snuff for Dido	.25
17th for transcribing minutes of P.b.y	.50
for a snuff box for Dido	.25
27th for snuff for Dido	.25
May y. 8th for the Pittsburgh Recorder	2.
22d for glass for School house	.25
27th to Ritchie for a pound of tobaco	.12½
June y. 1st gave to Isabella McMillan	.50
3d gave to Peggy Neil	5.
10th gave to Jane Harper for interest	32.50
12th to Watson for shoing my horse	.25
to Ritchie for shaving soap	.25
28th for snuff for Dido	.25
July y. 19th gave to McFadden for John Neil	20.
August y. 6th gave to James Shiw for taxes	12.75
to Ritchie for two pounds of lead	.25
to collection for missionary purposes	4.
7th to Ritchie for dido 3 yards	3.37½
15th to a Presbyterian magazine	2.50
to repairing a watch	1.
27th to snuff &c for Dido	1.
to a dress Isabella McMillan	2.25
September to two pounds of feathers for Dido	.50
to a pair of shoes for Dido	1.50
to collection	.25
	102.00

Page from John McMillan's Expense Account
(See Appendix B, page 258)

JOHN MCMILLAN

Oil portrait, courtesy of Helen A. Wragg
great, great, great granddaughter of John McMillan

John McMillan

The Apostle of Presbyterianism in the West

1752 - 1833

by

DWIGHT RAYMOND GUTHRIE
SAMUEL P. HARBISON PROFESSOR OF BIBLE
GROVE CITY COLLEGE

UNIVERSITY OF PITTSBURGH PRESS

Copyright, 1952
UNIVERSITY OF PITTSBURGH PRESS
Printed in the United States of America

Contents

Foreword	v
To the Reader	vii
Maps	ix
I. Beginnings	**1**
The Scotch-Irish	1
Traits and Characteristics	3
The Parents of John McMillan	5
Earliest Youth	9
Fagg's Manor	10
Pequea Academy	11
II. Mission	**17**
College of New Jersey	17
Entering the Ministry	20
The Presbytery's Appointment	21
McMillan's Decision	27
To the West	30
III. Home	**37**
Housekeeping	37
The Neighborhood	40
The Family	42
Ministers, Laymen, and Students	48
IV. Church	**57**
Chartiers and Pigeon Creek	57
Other Churches	62
The Pulpit	65
Revivals	66
McMillan's "Medulla"	70
Theological Seminary in the West	74
V. Education	**80**
Log Cabin School	80
Academies and Colleges	88
Washington Academy Chartered, 1787	88
Canonsburg Academy Founded, 1791	89
Washington College Chartered, 1806	91
Canonsburg Academy Chartered, 1794	94
Jefferson College Chartered, 1802	95
Washington and Jefferson College Chartered, 1865	96

VI.	Presbytery	101
	History	101
	History of the Presbytery	102
	Men of the Ohio Presbytery	103
	John Clark (1718-1797)	104
	John Brice (1760-1811)	107
	James Hughes (1766-1821)	110
	Joseph Patterson (1752-1832)	113
	Presbytery Matters	117
	Barr Case	118
	Taylor Case	132
	Birch Case	134
	Kerr Accusation	144
	Gwinn Case	146
	Salaries	148
	The Duty of Zion's Watchmen	151
VII.	Politics	158
	The Whiskey Rebellion	159
	The Congressional Election of 1794	166
	The Jay Treaty 1794-1796	169
	Campaign of 1808	172
VIII.	Personality	178
	Preaching	178
	Old School	181
	Blunt Speech	183
	Humor	185
	Practicality	186
	Reading	188
	Feeling	191
	Retirement	196

Appendix A—The Journal	202
Part I	202
Part II	211
Part III	237

Appendix B—Expense Account	258

Appendix C—Letter from the Late Rev. Dr. McMillan to President Carnahan	273

Bibliography	277
Index	288

Foreword

JOHN McMILLAN, a son of Scotch-Irish immigrants to Chester County, Pennsylvania, has been called by many the "Apostle of Presbyterianism in the West." His life and work have proved his right to the title.

To choose his life for my study and my writing was natural for me. I was born and reared in western Pennsylvania. My Scotch-Irish heritage has been similar to John McMillan's, and so has my choice of vocation. Our common interests have made the search into his life enjoyable.

Several institutions and many individuals have helped me in the gathering of material.

The librarians of many local institutions have been very kind and helpful: the University of Pittsburgh, Carnegie Library of Pittsburgh, Western Theological Seminary, Washington and Jefferson College, Princeton Theological Seminary, Western Pennsylvania Historical Society, and the Department of History of the Presbyterian Church in the United States of America.

Mrs. Helen Wragg, a great-great-great granddaughter of John McMillan, has been very gracious in making available her treasure-trove of original sources.

The Reverend Frank D. McCloy of the Western Theological Seminary Library unearthed several original sources recently and thoughtfully called them to my attention.

Among the individuals I should like especially to thank are members of the teaching staff of the University of Pittsburgh: Dean Samuel P. Franklin, Dr. Russell J. Ferguson, Professor Demas Barnes, Dr. John W. Oliver, Dr. Alfred P. James, and Dr. Laurence C. Little. My wife, I thank for hours of typing and much encouragement.

It is a pleasure to acknowledge those named, and many others unnamed, with these too few words of gratitude. Without the assistance of any of them this work could not have been completed.

One man, especially, I wish to thank, although the help and guidance he has given me are beyond the reach of mere thanks. Percival Hunt, formerly professor and head of the department of English at the University of Pittsburgh, has given this book any live and literary qualities it may merit. To him goes my deepest gratitude.

DWIGHT R. GUTHRIE
December, 1952

To the Reader

FOR any reader, but especially for any reader not familiar with Presbyterian terminology or the organization of the Presbyterian Church, some words and phrases used in this book may need explaining and defining. These words and phrases to me, as to John McMillan and to many others of our Church, are everyday language. Yet, since they are, in this book, often used with special meanings, I have thought it well to tell what these meanings are.

Apostle is the English equivalent of the Greek word *apostolos* and means "a messenger charged with a high mission." There is in the word, too, the connotation: "first missionary who plants the Christian faith in any region" or "the one among the first who by virtue of his outstanding character, superior leadership, and years of service outdistances all of his associates."

Presbyterianism, as used in this book, means any one of several branches of the Church that follows in general the doctrines of the Westminster Confession of Faith, the Catechisms, the Directory of Worship, and the form of Government that has Calvinistic lines,[1] for instance, the Associate Presbytery (or Seceders), the Reformed Presbytery, and the Cumberland Presbyterians. They were those branches of the Church of the West that paralleled McMillan's denomination, which was the Presbyterian Church in the United States of America.[2]

West, as of 1752-1833, the approximate period of McMillan's life, meant the country lying immediately on the west side of the Allegheny Mountains. Southwestern Pennsylvania was the first area to which large numbers of white people came for settlement, and so it was referred to as "the West" or "the Western Country."

The *session* is the body of ruling elders, elected by the congregation, that governs and regulates the affairs of a particular church. It is responsible to the congregation, which in turn is responsible to the *presbytery*. The regularly installed pastor is the moderator of this body. The session has certain powers of discipline that were more commonly used in John McMillan's day than in our own. One of the paramount duties of the session is to promote the peace and spiritual progress of the Church.[3]

The *presbytery* supervises the individual churches under its jurisdiction. The ministers who have pastorates within its bounds, other such ministers as it may enroll, and one ruling elder from each congregation make up its membership. All communications sent to it by the higher courts of the church must be acted upon. Appeals or complaints from sessions or ministers are received and issued; members of individual churches may appeal a decision of a church session to the presbytery; the erection, union, division, or dissolution of congregations at the request of the proper people lie within its jurisdiction; and, in general, the presbytery is empowered "to order whatever pertains to the spiritual welfare of the churches under its care."[4]

The *synod* stands immediately above the presbytery in supervision and jurisdiction. A minimum of three presbyteries is necessary to constitute a synod and these bodies are responsible to it. An equal number of ministers and elders from the presbyteries are elected. Any seven ministers thus elected and as many elders as are present constitute the synod.[5] The powers of this body are limited, but its specific responsibilities may be grouped as follows: the consideration of all appeals that are sent up from the presbyteries, an occasional check on the presbyteries to make sure that the Constitution of the Church is being followed, an approval or censure of the records of the presbyteries, and "to decide finally in such cases all questions that do not affect the doctrine or Constitution of the Church."[6]

"The *General Assembly* is the highest judicatory of the Presbyterian Church."[7] It represents, in one body, all the particular churches of the denomination. It stands to the constituent elements thereof somewhat as the United States government to the states, counties, municipalities, and citizens. Again, the presbyteries must elect an equal number of ministers and elders from their respective bodies and all so elected constitute the Assembly for that year. The affairs of the whole Church are its immediate concern. If a minister, a layman, or a church has not had satisfaction in the lesser courts of the Church, he or it may appeal to this body for its consideration. A specific duty is that the records of its synods be submitted for approval or censure.

A *Call* is a formal request by a congregation for the pastoral services of an ordained minister. The Call is presented to the minister through the presbytery that has supervision over the congregation concerned.[8] After the presbytery is satisfied with the minister's credentials and answers, and very often, not until a separate inquiry of his background has been made by a special committee, the Call is put into his hands for acceptance or rejection. The Call as thus presented has certain terms written therein and becomes a contract between the congregation and the minister. It is signed by representatives of the congregation.

THE MAPS

Three maps are in the book. The one printed on the endpapers shows the territory known as the "West" in John McMillan's time. It gives the location of Chartiers and of many other places throughout Western Pennsylvania mentioned in his study. The map on page x shows Southeastern Pennsylvania, with Fagg's Manor, Pequea, and other places associated with the earlier part of McMillan's life. The third map, printed on page 16, enables the reader to trace the course of the first three of McMillan's journeys as he recorded them in his *Journal*. These maps are here for those who are not familiar with the location of places, some of them nonexistent today.

CONESTOGA WAGON

NOTES *(To the Reader)*

1. Guy S. Klett. *Presbyterians in Colonial Pennsylvania*. 2.
2. Robert E. Thompson. "A History of the Presbyterian Churches in the United States," *American Church History*. VI. 46-57, 61-63,
3. Cleland B. McAfee. *The Ruling Elder*. 58-59.
4. *Manual of Presbyterian Law for Church Officers and Members*. 191.
5. *The Constitution of the Prebyterian Church in the United States of America*. 347.
6. *Ibid*. 347-348.
7. *Ibid*. 349.
8. *Ibid*. 361.

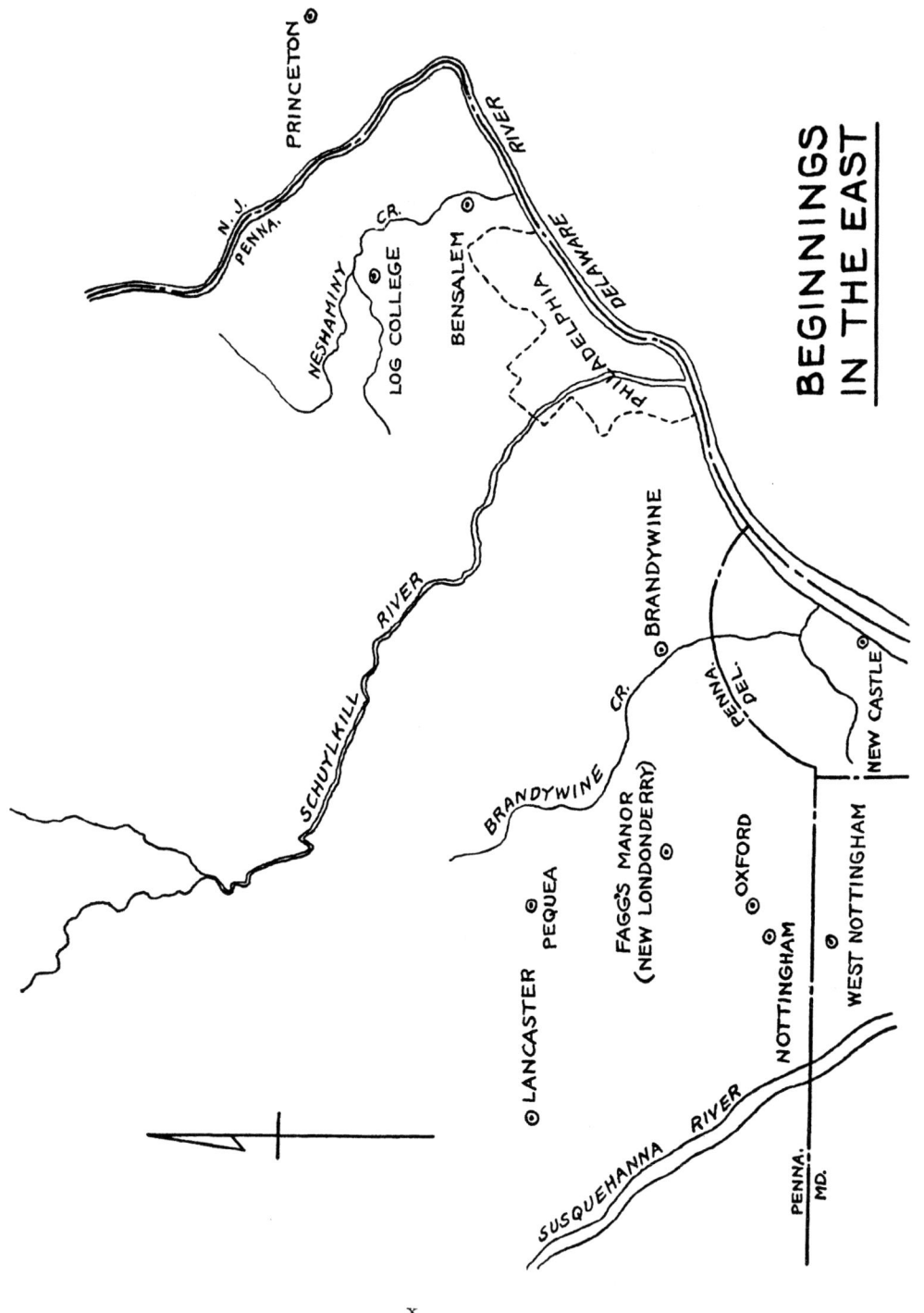

I. BEGINNINGS

JOHN McMILLAN, "the father of Presbyterianism in western Pennsylvania,"[1] was born of Scotch-Irish parents. To understand his life one must go back into the history of the people who, a century before his birth in 1752, went first from Scotland to settle in northern Ireland and then to English colonies in America. John McMillan, a frontier minister for fifty-eight years, apostle to the settlers beyond the western mountains in the valley of the Ohio, was a true son of his Scotch-Irish forebears. Their struggles among unfriendly neighbors in Ireland and against hard living and despotic rule developed in their character a religious security and a rugged independence that became his strength in the wilderness of a new world.

THE SCOTCH-IRISH

The story of John McMillan must go back to James I, who in the early seventeenth century confiscated the estates of the Irish lords and settled them with people he thought would be more loyal to the English Crown.[2] Before him Queen Elizabeth had reduced the northern provinces of Ireland to the lowest and most abject conditions of misery in punishment for their rebellion against her laws. James I, her successor, planned to extend English law and custom over all parts of the kingdom. His first move in Ireland was to curtail the powers of the Irish lords by declaring illegal the whole system of tanistry and gavelkind under which they had governed their own land. The Irish lords fled the country, either because they anticipated even more rigorous interference, or, as some have held, because a definite plot of rebellion instigated by them had been discovered.[3]

Whatever the truth may be, James I then ordered their estates confiscated to form a part of a great Plantation of Ulster. No less than six counties were confiscated and planted with English and Scots.[4] The plan established the whole of north Ireland as a governmentally controlled colony for settlement. By 1610 James had appointed the so-called "undertakers" and divided among them the Irish estates. These new supervisors were forbidden to rent or sell the lands to native Irish.

Most of the new settlers in the north of Ireland were from Scotland, and most of them were Presbyterians led by their own parish clergy. For a time Presbyterianism thrived. As William Blackwood has said, in *A History of the Presbyterian Church* by Richard Webster: "A remarkable revival of religion followed the labours of these devoted servants of God, and the cause of divine truth began to prosper in a remarkable way in Ulster."[5]

But all this did not come about without travail and persecution. The Scotch-Irish, as they were called in Ireland, were subjected to the same tyranny that had driven out the Irish lords. Persecution ebbed and flowed throughout the seventeenth century.

William Laud, made archbishop of Canterbury by Charles I (who followed James I to the throne) in his zeal to promote the Church of England, persecuted and encouraged others to persecute the Presbyterian congregations. Some of the ministers fled back to Scotland; members of their congregations were arrested and imprisoned.[6] The Scotch-Irish were compelled to swear that they would never oppose the King and would not enter into covenants and oaths contrary to the wishes of the crown. Fighting broke out, but fortunately the regiments came in time to restore peace in North Ireland. Under Cromwell (1649-1658) conditions improved somewhat, although ministers were still called upon to declare their acceptance of the King's law. Many of them went to prison rather than accept government control of the Church.

It was the hope of the Scotch-Irish that Charles II, who became king in 1660, would permit Presbyterianism to grow unmolested. But he had committed himself to a policy of supervision over religion through prelates. They, following the example of Jeremy Taylor and other leaders, stripped Presbyterian ministers of their pastorates. Under Charles II both Presbyterians and Catholics had to support the English Church and were subjected to the jurisdiction of the Bishop's courts in such matters as wills, marriages, divorces, and the like.[7]

James II's (1685-1688) tolerance of the Roman Catholics only made the situation more difficult for the Presbyterians.[8] There was now not only the established church to oppose the Calvinists but the tolerated Catholic church as well.

When William and Mary came to the throne, in 1688, the Presbyterians, ministers and laymen, who had supported them in the civil war which placed them on the throne, hoped for friendliness at court. And, indeed, William's reign (1688-1702) was one of moderation for the nonconformists. The Ulster Presbyterians benefited by his lenient policy and increased rapidly in numbers. Around Londonderry there were congregations as large as one thousand.

By 1702 there were 120 churches formed into nine presbyteries, with three sub-synods, and a general synod that met annually. By 1717 there were 140 congregations with a membership of two hundred thousand.[9]

But there were still difficulties for the Scotch-Irish. The Toleration Act which was passed in 1689 did not apply to Ireland. Furthermore, the great landholders of Ireland were Episcopalians who forbade the erection of Presbyterian churches on their lands.[10] They exacted a higher rental from Presbyterians and forbade them to hold certain civil offices. In the meantime many Presbyterians had been encouraged to come in from Scotland, even though Irish laws were not kindly toward nonconformists.

When the situation did not improve under George I (1714-1727), emigration to America became the talk of the land. The English government, alarmed at the migration talk, grew lax in administering oppressive statutes, but the damage had been done.

TRAITS AND CHARACTERISTICS

Among the many thousands who left the north of Ireland in the early eighteenth century were the parents of John McMillan.

The personality and the characteristics which William and Margaret Rea McMillan and their neighbors brought with them to the new world are recognizable even today among the descendants of these early American Presbyterians. Out of persecution came soundness of doctrine, intelligence of faith, and steadfastness to conviction.[11] Back in Ulster the Presbyterians had not mixed socially with the native Irish. The children of Ulster had been taught that intermarriage with the Irish was never to be considered.[12] They were a people deeply religious, earnest, and sincere. Life was not a holiday nor a frolic. It was a serious business.[13] They were rough, hotheaded, and determined people who had accepted the lands of the Irish rebels as their right—almost as if they were a chosen people. They had never expected or received consideration from the hostile population among whom they worked hard to build their homes.[14] They practiced the closest economy; never to waste was a habit taught them by necessity. Although they were antisocial in their relations to other groups, they were friendly with their own people. Bitter experience had taught them the value of owning land and of having no neighbors but their own kind. In America as in Ireland they stayed together in self-sufficient groups, largely so that they could have their own minister and their own school for their children.[15] They were not unlike the children of Israel, who surrounded like them by enemies challenging their religious integrity, grew stronger in their own beliefs and in their separation. The Hebrews sojourned in Egypt; the Scotch-Irish in Ireland. Canaan was the promised land for one; America, for the other. Both have used the word *exodus* to describe their migration.[16]

Besides a strong respect for land owning, the Scotch-Irish people had a great hunger for education. The hunger for learning began in Scotland, two or three centuries before the migration to Ulster. For generations the Scottish parliament required families "to send their oldest sons to school until they had a competent knowledge of Latin and a sufficient familiarity with jurisprudence to distribute justice among their people."[17] The three great Scottish universities, St. Andrews, Glasglow, and Aberdeen, were set up even before Calvin and then Knox laid so much emphasis on the importance of learning. Poor boys with some promise were given, free, an education for which the sons of nobility had to pay.[18] Wherever the Scotch-Irish went the School stood second only to the Kirk. The ability to read and write was to them a part of goodness or at least a road to it. The rapid spread of education in early America has often been attributed to the zeal of the children of Ulster.[19]

The Scotch-Irish brought with them, too, a zeal for industry. Wherever they settled in Ireland and in America, as soon as the lands were plowed and the crops harvested, industries and industrial centers sprung up.[20] In their later years, in Ireland, oppressive legislation against their industrial production curtailed its development and became another reason why the Scotch-Irish were willing to seek the lands offered in America. In the new world, they thought, they might be as industrious as they pleased without restrictions from anyone.

The Scotch-Irish who came to America were strongly political-minded; they insisted on ruling where they lived and made a living, and they were willing to die if necessary to make this ruling possible.[21]

The religion of the Scotch-Irish unites all their characteristics. They would have preferred the name *Calvinists* or *Knoxites* rather than the title *Scotch-Irish*. Calvin's emphasis of Augustine's doctrines of original sin and total depravity became the core of their belief. The theories of election and predestination were equally important to them. The Westminster Assembly convened in 1643, and when the Confession of Faith came to the Church in Scotland from the Westminster Assembly, in 1647, they saw the one true way of life made certain. In it was a set of religious beliefs that thoroughly fired and animated the Scotch-Irish. They became minutely, intensely, and strenuously theological. Dinsmore, one of their biographers, has said, "A congregation might be very drowsy of a warm Sabbath afternoon, but an Arminian squint or a heretical suggestion in the sermon would rouse them like a pistol shot."[22] The word of God as expressed in the Scriptures and interpreted by the Presbyterian Church became their only infallible rule of faith and practice. Theirs was a stern and uncompromising faith that permitted bigotry and cruelty toward those who did not abide in it. New doctrines in theology, new agencies in the church, and new forms of worship they always discouraged. Family worship was a necessary part of the Christian experience. Dinsmore has made a statement that sums up the religious characteristics of the Scotch-Irish: "With them it was a matter of small moment, comparatively, how one stood with men, but it was of infinite moment how one stood with God."[23] And they were very sure they had found the way to Him.

THE PARENTS OF JOHN McMILLAN

The Rea and McMillan families, the ancestors of John McMillan, had been reared in this strict and individualistic background. The union of the two families in the marriage of William McMillan and Margaret Rea passed on this unique heritage to their son.

In a manuscript written by McMillan, January, 1832, we learn something of his parents:

My father's name was William McMillan; my mother's maiden name was Margaret Rea; they were both born and lived in the parish of Carmony, in the county of Antrim, Ireland. They emigrated to America, about the year 1742, and settled in Fagg's Manor, in Chester county, Pennsylvania. My mother died in the year 1768. My father married again, and during the time of the Revolutionary War he sold his property in Chester County and removed to the western country, where he died on the second of July, 1792, aged seventy-five. His remains were buried at Chartiers. My parents had but six children who grew up to be men and women, viz: three sons and three daughters. . . . Before my birth my parents had some children, I think two sons, who died while they were young.[24]

There is nothing positive known of John McMillan's parents before they came to this country. Since they came before the Scotch-Irish had set up many factories in Ireland, it is reasonable to believe that they were farmers. It is probably only a coincidence that there was, around the beginning of the eighteenth century, a John

McMillan active as a Presbyterian clergyman in Scotland who was a leader of the first group of seceders, later to be known as the Covenanters.[25] There is no record that he was related to the family of William McMillan.

A description of County Antrim in Ireland, which John McMillan says was his parents' early home, describes the climate as temperate and the soil as varying greatly in arability throughout the district.[26]

At any rate, we are sure that William and Margaret survived the turbulent years in Ulster and that they were at least of the fourth or fifth generation beyond the earliest Scottish emigration to northern Ireland. We know that William was born in 1717, but we have no birth date for Margaret. The parish of Carmony, where they both lived, was not large, and they probably had known each other all their lives. Their wedding date, too, is not exactly known, but it is known that their son Thomas was born in 1740, before they came to America.[27] They left County Antrim in 1742, when the tide of emigration following increased rents and barren seasons was in full swing.[28] William was then twenty-five years old.

They probably landed at Philadelphia or one of the Delaware River ports, as did most of the Scotch-Irish. New England was not hospitable to the Scotch-Irish, and so most of them came to Pennsylvania or went farther south.[29] The McMillans traveled westward as far as Fagg's Manor in Chester County, a region which was already the home of several thousand who had left County Antrim. They bought a farm from the original patentee, whose name was Pinkerton. He had been issued the patent by William Penn's grandson.[30]

What manner of people they were, the home they lived in, their neighbors, their way of life we may know much about from letters and chronicles of other Scotch-Irish who settled in southeastern Pennsylvania at the time the McMillans settled there.

The dress, home crafts, and customs of the McMillans of Chester County were, so far as we know, those of other Pennsylvania colonists.[31] It was practical to adopt many customs of the Pennsylvania colonists in the middle of the eighteenth century. Joseph Doddridge has given a description of pioneer society that may be accepted as characteristic of Pennsylvania frontier conditions before the coming of factories and railroads. He says:

The hunting shirt was universally worn. This was a kind of loose frock reaching half way down the thighs, with long sleeves, open before, and so wide as to lap over a foot or more when belted. The cape was large and sometimes handsomely fringed with a raveled piece of cloth of a different color from that of the hunting shirt. The bosom of this dress served as a wallet to hold a chunk of bread, cakes, jerk, tow for wiping the barrel of a rifle, or any other necessity for the hunter or warrior. . . . The shirt and jacket were of common fashion. A pair of drawers, or breeches and leggins, were the dress of the thighs and legs; a pair of moccasons answered for the feet much better than shoes. They were made of deerskin. . . . The women usually went barefooted in warm weather. Instead of the toilet, they had to handle the distaff or shuttle, the sickle or weeding hoe, contented if they could obtain their linsey clothing and cover their heads with a sunbonnet made of six or seven hundred linen. The coats and bedgowns of the women, as well as the hunting shirts of the men, were hung in full display on wooden pegs round the walls of their cabins, so while they answered in some degree the place of paper hangings or tapestries, they announced to the stranger as well as neighbor, the wealth or poverty of the family in the articles of clothing.[32]

Doddridge goes on for many pages with a description of the hominy block and the hand mills, the grater, the water mill, the use of sifters, weaving by the women, the tanning of leather, tailoring, and shoemaking.

Into this kind of community the William McMillans cast their lot, with those who were settling the western section of Londonderry township, near the source of the Big Elk River. The first task was to get shelter. A friend or neighbor would certainly house the new arrivals while the men of the area set a day for chopping and trimming the trees to their proper length. The trees would then be dragged by the horses to the site selected for the cabin. Care had to be taken in selecting a straight-grained tree for splitting the wood for roof clapboards and flooring. The greater part of this work was generally finished in a couple of days, and the men who had helped returned to their own farms and dwellings. A few would stay around another day or two to hew out and construct a table, stools, and the necessary beds. When everything was attended to, even to the placing of pegs in logs for the display of coats and garments, a date was set for the *Housewarming*.[33]

So it may well have been when the McMillans began housekeeping at Fagg's Manor. An old springhouse still stands on the farm where the first cabin was built. "No one knows its age, but framing and roofing timbers are hewed white oak, which for Chester County, would date it before the Revolution and possibly back to John McMillan's boyhood."[34] So says Welsh in his account of the early Scotch-Irish settlers.

Religion was so much a part of the Scotch-Irish that the family's religious activities followed close upon the establishment of the home. The William McMillans had anticipated this and had procured a farm adjoining the Fagg's Manor church on the west.[85] In November of 1739 Samuel Blair had become the pastor of this church and was installed in April of 1740. It may well be that his impression on the parents was one of the earliest influences urging John McMillan to the ministry.

Samuel Blair was born in the north of Ireland in 1712. He came to this country at an early age and entered William Tennent's Log College at Neshaminy, Pennsylvania, in 1730. "He remained in college five years, taking there, as was customary, both his literary and theological courses."[86] After serving four years at Shrewsbury, New Jersey, he was called to the Fagg's Manor Church as its first pastor. He had been there but a few months when he organized a classical school and theological seminary similar to that of the Log College. The blessings and influence of this school began at once to radiate in an ever widening circle.

While the Fagg's Manor school and seminary were getting under way, in 1739 the local church experienced one of the greatest revivals of that time. Blair wrote to a friend in Boston, thus:

Our Sabbath assemblies soon became very large, many people from all parts around inclining very much to come where there were such appearances of the divine presence and power. I think there was sarcely a sermon or lecture preached here through that whole summer but there were manifest evidences of impressions on the hearers and many times the impressions were very great and general: several would be overcome and fainting; others deeply sobbing, hardly able to contain themselves; others crying in a most dolorous manner; many others were silently weeping; and a solemn concern appeared in the countenances of many others.[87]

Into this setting, in the summer of 1742, less than three years after the arrival of Samuel Blair, came William and Margaret McMillan. It is not beyond the bounds of possibility that the McMillan or Rea family had known the Blair family in Ireland. The parents may have suggested that the young couple find a home in the Blair parish. Whether by premeditation or only by chance, a better pastor could not have been found. The McMillans enjoyed nine years of the best preaching and pastoral care in America before death brought to an early end the life of Samuel Blair. His passing must have made a profound impression on the McMillans, for their son John, born the following year, was given to the Lord. It has been written in a Presbyterian *Repository:* "John McMillan, like Samuel of old was the child of parental vows. His parents having lost an infant whose name was John, vowed to the Lord that, if he would give them another son, they would devote him to the work of the ministry."[38] Thus the one who was destined to be an apostle of his faith in the Western Country was consecrated, before his birth. His parents were committed to use every instrument in their power to bring about his conversion. Young John was a consecrated child, and it is possible to look upon his youth and to watch his parents' promises unfold.

EARLIEST YOUTH

The McMillan letter to Dr. James Carnahan written in March, 1832 makes a few references that fit into this period. Altogether it is silent about details of home training. We know William McMillan told his son that before he was born he had been dedicated to the Gospel ministry.[39] We know, too, that John was first carried and later led to the services in the Fagg's Manor church, where the parents and possibly John himself were reminded of the promise of God.

When John was old enough to talk and to memorize, the training began with a purpose and a will. The parents seem to have been wise enough to know that all might be lost if they were over zealous. They knew that they must find the happy medium between blind enthusiasm for their holy cause and seeming indifference to their sacred promise. These methods of childhood education had been used in Scotland and Ireland and were thought worthy of continuance in the New World.[40] Scriptural verses, as was the custom, were taught at first, and then longer passages of Scripture. Such Psalms as the first, the eighth, the nineteenth, the twenty-third, the Lord's Prayer, the Beatitudes, John 3:16, and other passages were committed to memory. A little later came the learning of the Shorter Catechism.

It may be taken for granted that John was sent to a school of some kind when he was a boy. Free schools, subscription schools, or parochial schools were considered a necessity in every Scotch-Irish settlement. John Knox (1505-1572) had advocated a system of education that included a school in every parish, and his plans were considered very much the order of the day by all Presbyterians.[41] The school was generally near the church. The minister's home often was the school until adequate arrangements could be made. Many of the subjects taught were simply an advanced portion of the materials used in the home training. Calvin (1509-1564) had insisted that the children be trained at home by Christian parents, and for such training he prepared, in 1541, *The Catechism for Children.* This work provided catechetical instruction for one year, with special portions of the Bible assigned for each Sabbath.[42] The catechism and selections from the Bible were used in the reading and grammar courses. *The New England Primer* was introduced and soon became the popular textbook in all the colonies, and the most widely used in America.[43] This unusual volume included the best selections of the *Hornbook,* the *A B C Manual,* and other primers. It also included new material. The little book was based on the Bible text. The teachers soon realized that they could teach spelling as well as reading from *The New England Primer.* About 1750, another textbook, *Dillworth's Speller,* was distributed among the colonies. It contained reading selections, a little elementary grammar, and many words to spell. It was not wholly a biblical text. There were easy sentences and words for the beginners, longer sentences and longer words for the more advanced, and illustrated fables and selections from the *Psalter.*[44]

Such books did not at first supplant the materials and technique brought from Ireland and Scotland, but many schools, and probably that attended by John McMillan, used one of the primers along with earlier accepted books. Henry Barnard writes, "One has only to examine the curriculum of the early colonial schools and he will find that until the time of the American Revolution, the Bible and the Catechism constituted the bulk of materials used."[45] Evidently no new approach to religious education was permitted during the pre-revolutionary days. Nothing in education took major emphasis away from the catechism. As Klett puts it: "It is found by Experience, that there is more Knowledge diffused among the Ignorant and Younger Sort by one Hour's Catechising, than by many Hours of Preaching."[46] The minister frequently catechised each family in his congregation and thus tested and supplemented the work of the schools. Having completed several years of such study John McMillan was considered ready for the next step of his education and was sent to Fagg's Manor Academy.

FAGG'S MANOR

John Blair, the younger Blair brother, had charge of the Academy at Fagg's Manor when McMillan "having made the necessary proficiency in English studies,"[47] entered that celebrated institution in his native town. John Blair was not less distinguished than Samuel, who had founded the Academy. He, like his brother, had been born in Ireland and had taken his theological training at William Tennent's Log College. Samuel had done great service by training Samuel Davies, Alexander Cumming, John Rodgers, James Finley, Hugh Henry, Robert Smith, and others who were to become ministers and leaders in the church. John Blair's gifts were equally great, and his success as a teacher equalled his brother's. His scholarship and his knowledge were, it is said, beyond that of almost any other man of his age.[48] Besides, as Archibald Alexander has explained, "His disposition was uncommonly patient, placid, benevolent, disinterested, and cheerful. He was too mild to indulge bitterness or severity; and he thought that the truth required little else but to be fairly stated and properly understood."[49] Under this wise and kindly man John McMillan received his classical education.

Schools like Fagg's Manor are often called "grammar schools." They were more than that. Some of their advanced students were introduced to the Greek classics. Latin held the leading place in the curriculum, but other classical and scientific studies were given increasing prominence. In the Nottingham Academy, founded by Samuel Finley, another Log College graduate, the students in 1759 were studying Latin, Greek, logic, arithmetic, geography, and "part of Ontology, Natural Philosophy, in a more cursory manner, as far as Opticks in Martin's Order."[50] Since the schools were sister academies, their curricula were probably about the same. Because of such curricula, institutions like Fagg's Manor had more solid worth than many of the larger schools of that day. Joseph Smith has said that their education "was far more valuable than that which had the sanction of the 'Facultates Artium,' and the 'Sigillum curatorum' of many colleges and universities of pompous pretension, in our day."[51] McMillan must have benefited from his years at this sort of study.

John McMillan studied in the Fagg's Manor Academy until 1767, when he was fifteen years old. At that time John Blair was called to the College of New Jersey. He had been offered the vice-presidency and the chair of moral philosophy and theology until John Witherspoon could arrive from Scotland.

PEQUEA ACADEMY

McMillan's training up to this point had been considered most fortunate. His parents knew well that the dearth of capable ministers made it likely the vacancy in the church and academy would not be filled for some time. They also presumed that a man of Blair's ability could not be found. And so young McMillan enrolled the next term at the Pequea Academy where Robert Smith was the principal. Pequea Academy was several miles to the north and west of Fagg's Manor.

Robert Smith had lived there as a student and was, naturally, well known to McMillan's parents. After his graduation, in 1750, he married Betsy Blair, the daughter of his instructor, and then removed to his first pastorate at Pequea. A short time later he started an academy like the one at Fagg's Manor. "Both were on the model of Log College."[52] Smith was to serve as preacher and teacher just as Samuel Blair and William Tennent had done and just as John McMillan, following his example, was to do one day. When Smith was fifteen or sixteen years old he "was made a subject of God's special grace, through the instrumentality of the preaching of Whitefield."[53] His classical and theological instruction under Blair prepared him for a rich and fruitful ministry. He was in the very prime of his career when McMillan came to him seeking knowledge and guidance.

It is fortunate that a record of the educational methods used at Pequea in the days of McMillan has been preserved. Frederick Beasley, intimate friend and former pupil of Robert Smith, says in his introduction to a volume of Stanhope Smith's sermons:

It was the custom of the school to require the pupils not merely to dip into the Latin and Greek classics, or pass in rapid transition from one to the other, by which means a very superficial knowledge of any is obtained, but when once they had commenced an author, to read carefully and attentively the entire work.... Latin was the habitual language of the school.... When any class had advanced in its course beyond the Metamorphoses of Ovid and the Bucolics of Virgil, the members of it were permitted to enter into voluntary competition for pre-eminence.[54]

These methods had been used in Ireland and had been known to bring the desired results in scholarship and mental discipline. The insistence of Robert Smith upon the complete mastery of the subject produced such men from Pequea as Samuel Stanhope Smith and John Blair Smith, David Caldwell, John Francis Armstrong, James Dunlap, John Linn, John Springer, Nathaniel W. Semple, John McMillan, and others who became prominent men of the Presbyterian church.

McMillan had his first deeply religious experiences at the Pequea Academy, which he entered in 1767. He knew that he had been dedicated to the Gospel ministry, and this knowledge served to prepare his mind for the peculiar experiences that were to come to him.

During his stay at Pequea a revival converted most of the pupils in the school. McMillan has told this part of his life story:

While there the Lord poured out of his spirit upon the students: and I believe that there were but few who were not brought under serious concern about their immortal souls: some of whom became blessings in their day, and were eminently useful in the Church of Christ, but they are all gone now to rest. It was here that I received my first religious impressions; though, as long as I can remember, I had some checks of conscience, and was frequently terrified by dreams and visions in the night, which made me cry to God for mercy: but these seasons were of short duration; like the morning cloud and the early dew, they quickly passed away. I now saw that I was a lost, undone sinner, exposed to the wrath of a justly offended God, and could do nothing for my own relief. My convictions were not attended with much horror; though I felt that I deserved hell, and in all probability that must be my portion: yet I could not feel that distress which I ought to feel, and which I thought I must feel before I could expect to obtain relief. I felt also much pride and legality, mingled with all the duties which I attempted to perform.[55]

This statement is an acknowledgment of a conversion. Heretofore McMillan had taken for granted his religion. Now there was a purpose to his life. It was a distinct privilege for him to have not only the advantages of this fine literary and scientific training offered by the Pequea School, but also to sit at the feet of the capable and consecrated Robert Smith.

When McMillan first came to Pequea, his finer qualities were not easily apparent. Smith soon was able, however, to see the moral worth and potential strength of his pupil. He often said of McMillan, "he is better than he looks."[56] Qualities of leadership grew. His teacher found that McMillan had a mind of a high order, holding promise of wise discernment. His body was massive and there was every indication that good health and great vigor would be among the many gifts of grace visited upon him. His tendency to be shy became the seed out of which genuine humility before God was to grow. It was evident then that his voice, though devoid of gentleness, would be heard by even the farthest listener. Smith was very kind and understanding and his teaching soon brought results. The growth of McMillan's abilities was slow, but in a few years they stood out, towering over the usual commonplaces of frontier life.

One incident during the Pequea training must have had great effect upon so young a man. In his manuscript he says of it simply, "My mother died in the year 1768."[57] This was about a year after he enrolled at Pequea. There is no evidence that the parents had seen, previous to his conversion experience, any strong desire on his part to give himself wholeheartedly to the Lord. Whether his mother was alive when the revival touched him is not certain. The revival, it is known, was either just before or shortly after her death. She had done her work well, but undoubtedly there were moments when his parents watched him with much solicitude. And undoubtedly, too, it was a difficult business to raise a family and educate one of the sons for the ministry:

> The pecuniary circumstances of McMillan's father were only moderate; and to defray the expenses of his son's education, he was often straitened and subjected to considerable difficulty. Even his sisters much to their honor, engaged in the labors of the field to help forward their brother in obtaining his education.[58]

And so, it was with great satisfaction that the Fagg's Manor household received the news of stirring things happening at Pequea, and of their son's being in the midst of them. They were encouraged to work the harder when they knew he was eager to enter the College of New Jersey at Princeton and prepare in earnest for the ministry. The mission of his life seemed beginning to unfold before him. They were confident he would hold his belief that God, in due time, would show him what his life's work was to be.

I. NOTES

1. L. J. Halsey. "Great Preachers and Pastors," *North Western Presbyterian.* November 14, 1868.
2. Sidney G. Fisher. *The Making of Pennsylvania.* 161.
3. William E. H. Lecky. *Ireland in the Eighteenth Century.* 1, 21, 22. See also Henry G. Ford. *The Scotch-Irish in America.* 20.
4. Ford. 11.
5. William G. Blackwood. Introductory article in *A History of the Presbyterian Church in America* by Richard Webster. 52.
6. Charles A. Briggs. *American Presbyterians.* 51, 52.
7. Robert E. Thompson. "A History of the Presbyterian Churches in the United States," *American Church History.* VI. 5.
8. Guy S. Klett. *Presbyterians in Colonial Pennsylvania.* 13.
9. William S. Sweet. *Religion in Colonial America.* 249.
10. Klett. 13.
11. Thomas Murphy. *The Presbytery of the Log College.* 26.
12. John W. Dinsmore. *The Scotch-Irish in America.* 16.
13. *Ibid.* 47
14. Fisher. 165.
15. James Veech. "The Secular History," *Centenary Memorial.* 295.
16. S. J. and E. H. Buck. *The Planting of Civilization in Western Pennsylvania.* 124.
17. Ford. 534.
18. James Stalker. *John Knox, His Ideas and Ideals.* 242, 243.
19. George Bancroft. *History of the United States.* II. 464. Note Bancroft's heading, "Progress from Calvinism."

20. Thomas Croskery. *Irish Presbyterianism.* 22.
21. Dinsmore. 39.
22. *Ibid.* 62.
23. *Ibid.*
24. Joseph Smith. *The History of Jefferson College.* Appendix, 413, 414. This manuscript was apparently prepared by McMillan with great care. It was left with the *Journal* and other writings that were bequeathed to a daughter, Catherine, but has not been seen for many years. The celebrated letter to James Carnahan, written two months later, omitted several portions of it, altered some passages, and enlarged other parts of it. See Smith's comments on these documents, 413.
25. Thompson. 4.
26. *Encyclopedia Britannica.* 11th ed. II. 153.
27. Daniel M. Bennett. *Life and Work of Rev. John McMillan, D. D.* 150.
28. *Ibid.* 43-63.
29. Sweet. 252.
30. Bennett. 7. This is quoted from an article by Edgar B. Welsh.
31. Ford. 277.
32. Joseph Doddridge. *Notes on the Settlement and Indian Wars of the Western Part of Virginia and Pennsylvania.* 91-93.
33. *Ibid.* 106-108; Buck. 318-321; cf. Klett. 122.
34. Bennett. 6, 7.
35. *Ibid.*
36. Murphy. 87.
37. *Ibid.* 88.
38. *Presbyterian Education Repository, Home, the School and the Church.* Edited by C. Van Rensseler. VI. 20.
39. See Appendix of Smith's *History of Jefferson College.* 414, and McMillan's Letter to Carnahan in Appendix C of this book.
40. Klett. 198.
41. Stalker. 240-243.
42. John Calvin, *Preface to the Catechism of the Church of Geneva.*
43. Oliver P. Chitwood. *A History of Colonial America.* 258.
44. Edwin G. Dexter. *History of Education in United States.* 214.
45. *American Journal of Education.* XIII (1863). 746. Cf. Frank G. Lankard. *A History of the American Sunday School Curriculum.* 17.
46. *Shorter Catechism* (1744). P. iii. Cf. Klett. 198.
47. Joseph Smith. *Old Redstone.* 167.
48. Murphy. 92, 93.
49. Archibald Alexander. *Biographical Sketches of the Founder and Principal Alumni of Log College.* 199.
50. Klett. 207. Klett quotes this material from Simon Gratz's book, *Autograph Collection, Colonial Ministers.*
51. *Old Redstone.* 168.
52. Murphy. 89.
53. *Ibid.* 169.
54. Jacob H. Beam. "Dr. Robert Smith's Academy at Pequea," *Journal of Presbyterian Historical Society.* VIII, No. 4.
55. *History of Jefferson College.* 414.
56. Lemuel F. Leake. "Early Life of Dr. John McMillan," *Presbyterian Advocate.* VII, No. 52.
57. *History of Jefferson College.* 413.
58. *Old Redstone.* 172, footnote.

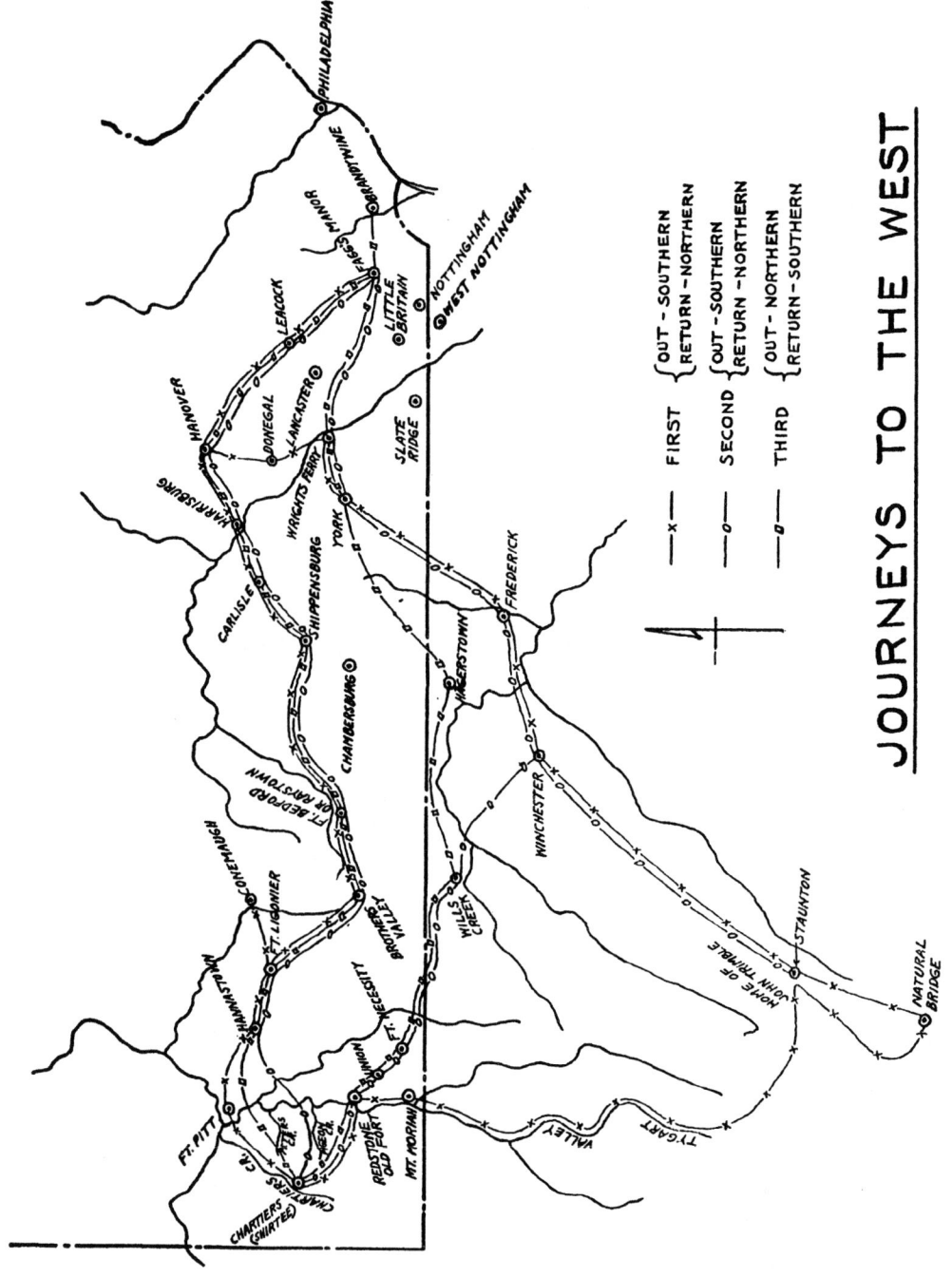

II. MISSION

McMILLAN'S mission was to go out as an apostle to the settlers beyond the mountains in southwestern Pennsylvania and to give them the fullest benefit of the preaching and teaching he had learned from such noted divines as John Blair, John Witherspoon, and Robert Smith. The assignment proved to be one of the longest and most exacting ever undertaken by a Christian missionary. The Apostle of the West[1] did not yet know the full nature of his mission. He did know, however, that he must have a college and theologic education before the great steps in his life's mission could be revealed to him, or even the Presbytery's appointment could be made. Ahead of him was the discovery that God's will for him was a long life of service in the West.

In his letter to James Carnahan, McMillan wrote, "In this situation I continued until I went to college in the spring of 1770."[2] *This situation* refers to his conversion under Smith at Pequea Academy. The experience had profoundly impressed the young man, now eighteen years old and ready to enter the college at Princeton.

COLLEGE OF NEW JERSEY

Again, to understand the career of John McMillan, we must know more about early influences. John Witherspoon was president of the College of New Jersey when McMillan entered. Samuel Davies, who had been president from 1759-61, was the most brilliant preacher thus far of the Presbyterian Church, but his term of office ended too quickly to realize the expectations his election had roused.[3] Samuel Finley, who came from academic and religious success at Nottingham Academy, was president from 1761 to 1766.

In 1768, when John Witherspoon became president, the College entered one of the brightest periods of its history.

Witherspoon was a lineal descendant of John Knox[4] and had already made a name for himself in the Scottish church. His three volume edition of *Essays and Doctrinal Sermons* had brought him popularity at home and had started him to fame abroad. The appearance of his *Ecclesiastical Characteristics,* a part of the fuller *History of a Corporation of Servants,* added to his prestige and made natural his selection as president of the college at Princeton. A call was given him by the trustees of the College of New Jersey in a letter dated November 19, 1766. Mrs. Witherspoon was reluctant to leave Scotland; the invitation was declined. Benjamin Rush, a graduate of the American college and a medical student at Edinburgh, kept the matter open by visiting the Witherspoon manse at Paisley, Scotland. He seems to have talked away Mrs. Witherspoon's fears;[5] for when the college renewed its call to Witherspoon, in a letter dated December 9, 1767, he accepted, and on May 18, 1768 he and his family took ship for America.

Better to understand this great man and the influence that he had on McMillan, it may be well to read the only contemporary description of him:

> I have dined and supped frequently with him here in Edinr; and am charmed with his Behavior. He appears Mr. Davies and Dr. Finley revived in One man. in point of Genius he is equal to the first, and in Knowledge I believe him superior even to Dr. Finley himself, more especially yt.Branch of Knowledge which is now a days so much admired viz: the Belles-Lettres. I have heard him preach twice, and can truly say he exceeds any preacher I have heard since I came to Scotland—indeed I have heard few Preachers in ye Course of my Life that were equal to him. his Voice has much of that melody in it wch we used so much admire in the late Mr. Bostwick. his appearance in the pulpit is solemn and graceful, his Sermons are loaded with good Sense, and adorned at ye same time with all the Elegance and Beauty that Language can give them. And what above all enhances these Accomplishments in him as a Preacher is, that he never carries a Note with him in the Pulpit, so that I am in hopes shd. he go to the College he will by his Example put an end to the too common Practise of Reading Sermons in America, more especially among our young ministers.[6]

About two years after Witherspoon came to Princeton McMillan entered. He remained there for two and one-half years. Joseph Smith, the author of *Old Redstone,* observes that the mind of the instructor could scarcely fail to impress something of its character on the mind of the pupil.[7] Many years later McMillan wrote to James Carnahan;

> I had not been long here until a revival of religion took place among the students, and I believe at one time, there were not more than two or three who were not under serious impressions. On a day which had been set apart by a number of the students as a day of fasting and prayer, while the others were at dinner, I retired to my study, and while trying to pray, I got some discoveries of divine things which I had never had before. I now saw that the divine law was not only holy, just, and spiritual, but that it also was good; and that conformity to it would make me happy. I felt no disposotion to quarrel with the law, but with myself, because I was not conformed to it. I felt that it was now easy to submit to the gospel plan of salvation; and felt a calm and serenity of mind to which I had hitherto been a stranger. And this was followed by a delight in contemplating the divine glory in all His

works; and in meditating on the Divine perfections, I thought that I could see God in everything around me.[8]

At Princeton McMillan felt, as he had at Pequea, the power of God in his life. Divine grace was at work fashioning his mind, he was sure, through the influence of men like Robert Smith and John Witherspoon. His mission in life had begun its revelation, but there were for him yet many steps before he could see it clearly.

The curriculum of the college was simple and yet exacting. The Latin and Greek he had learned at Pequea entered him into the sophomore class at Princeton.[9] At Princeton the classics were continued, but introductory or advanced courses of geography, logic, mathematics, and rhetoric were added to the schedule.[10] The next year brought courses in natural and moral philosophy, metaphysics and chronology, higher mathematics and Hebrew. Almost all the senior year was given to review. Classics, arts, and sciences were restudied, and President Witherspoon taught a course in Latin and Greek which served to give a finishing touch to the student's knowledge of these languages.[11] During the senior year came many more curricular activities. Public disputings each Saturday and *oration day* once each month let the seniors develop their ability as speakers.

The daily routine began for John McMillan and his classmates with the rising bell at five. Each student was expected to be in the chapel for morning prayers at five-thirty. At chapel services seniors took turns in showing their knowledge of Hebrew and Greek by reading in English a chapter out of the original language.[12] It was customary also for the president to comment briefly on some portion of the lesson. Since breakfast was not served until eight, some time for study came between early chapel and the morning meal. Classes ran from nine until one, and the afternoons were for study. At five came vespers, and dinner was at seven. Curfew rang at nine each evening. Of this regime Dr. Collins writes:

Of spare time there was little; of athletics none. The high purpose of a college education in those sterner days precluded reference to sports in the accounts of college life; in fact, the records, official or private, antedating the Revolution mention this frivolous subject only once. But the tacit official disapproval of sports did not deter students from working off superfluous energy in childish pranks which were the contemporary substitutes for better forms of exercise, and of which an instructive catalogue has been left to curious posterity by Philip Vickers Fithian of the Class of 1772.[13]

McMillan completed his course at Princeton in the class of '72 with Philip V. Fithian to whom reference has just been made. It is difficult to believe he engaged in the "childish pranks" catalogued by Mr. Fithian. The first degree in arts was conferred upon him by the College of New Jersey at the Commencement in the fall of 1772.

John McMillan was now ready for the training he needed to become a minister of the Gospel.

ENTERING THE MINISTRY

Witherspoon was an accredited professor of theology, but there were reasons why McMillan planned a return to Pequea to finish theological training. His family had made many sacrifices to send him to the College of New Jersey. At Pequea the plain and simple living, the nearness to Fagg's Manor, the opportunity for self-help all lightened the family's financial burden. Besides these practical reasons, McMillan had others. He had taken his preparatory work under Robert Smith and, it appears, had become attached to him in no small degree. Joseph Smith says in *Old Redstone* that since regularly organized seminaries did not exist in that day it was the usual procedure for theological students to put themselves under the direction of

some intelligent, judicious and devoted pastor, with the privilege of access to a library, which though moderate in size, was well selected; their opportunities were less splendid and the form of their preparation was less imposing; yet in some important respects their real advantages were superior.

The personal touch about such training would have been lost at Princeton.

At Pequea McMillan learned better how to think for himself and to turn the theoretical into the practical. In a very real sense he was serving an apprenticeship and receiving the necessary book learning to give him a firm and wide intellectual foundation. One who looks at the whole picture cannot doubt the wisdom of his decision to return to Smith, one of the most able theologians and convincing preachers of his age. There is evidence of an unusual touch of warmth and feeling in McMillan toward his Pequea experiences. According to his teacher he regarded his theologic training one of the happiest and most important providential arrangements of his whole life.[15]

That there were misgivings in McMillan's mind in 1772 when he began his advanced study at Pequea is revealed in a letter he wrote to Carnahan years later:

I had great difficulties in my own mind about undertaking the work of the gospel ministry. I at last came to this determination, to leave the matter wholly with God; if he opened the way, I would go on; if he shut it, I would be satisfied; and I think if ever I knew what it was to have no will of my own about any matter, it was about this.[16]

All doubts, however, were dispelled after he came to Pequea. His state of mind was that of many true and sincere servants of the Lord in all ages. Amos, Isaiah, Paul, and an exceedingly great host have experienced a shrinkage back when God's call to service has come. McMillan had a spirit of godliness and a piety that made him see the magnitude of the step he was about to take. He was conscious of his shortcomings as he faced God's requirements. That Witherspoon and Smith were spiritual giants made him humble. But once the battle was fought and won in his own mind no task was too great for him. From the day of that decision until his death in 1833 there was no turning back; God's will was supreme in his life.

The next two years he spent with Smith preparing for the ministry. Once his misgivings were over he began to plan earnestly for the ministry. Sometime in the fall of 1772 or the spring of 1773 the Presbytery of New Castle received him under its care. On October 26, 1774, at East Nottingham, he felt prepared to come before that reverend body and stand for licensure.[17] The minutes of the Presbytery of New Castle for that date read as follows:

Mr. John McMillan, having with Approbations, passed thro ye usual Trials for Licensure in this Presbytery and declared his Acceptance of the Westminster Confession of Faith, & Directory for Worship & Government and promised Subjection to this Presbytery; we judge we have sufficient clearness to license him Accordingly with a solemn Charge given him by the Moderator to diligence, Faithfulness & Prudence, we do hereby license him to preach the everlasting Gospel.[18]

THE PRESBYTERY'S APPOINTMENT

After the Presbytery had licensed him to preach McMillan proved his missionary zeal by setting out under the appointment of the Presbytery to visit vacant churches in the Presbyteries of New Castle and Donegal.

The first entry in McMillan's *Journal* reads: "Being licensed to preach the everlasting Gospel of Christ Jesus, accordingly attempted it at the following places, viz. at Fag's Manor ye 4th Sunday of Oct."[19]

It was with fear and misgiving that he entered the pulpit hallowed by such men as Samuel Blair and John Blair. His father and his other relatives and friends undoubtedly came to hear him preach his first sermon as a licensed minister. The family had mingled prayers with self sacrifice so he might enter this life, and now they were happy and proud. McMillan and his family would have thought of the absent mother, who would have been proudest of all.

The second preaching appointment was at Middle Octorara, the third at Little Brittain, the fourth at Pequea.

The Pequea assignment, like the first, was a great occasion. In this community he had for five years taken academic and theological training. From this place had come to him his first great religious experience. In this pulpit had stood for many years that matchless preacher, teacher, and friend, Robert Smith. For this hour he had been trained; there was no faltering or turning back.

Later, he visited West Nottingham, Pencader, Soldiers Delight, Slate Ridge, Chaunceford, Carlisle, Monaughany, Big Spring, Hanover, Conowaga, Georgetown, Deer Creek, East Nottingham, Leacocks, North Mountain Meeting House, Tinhting Spring, Cummins', and perhaps other places. At some of these he preached on two or more consecutive Sabbaths. Others, such as Fagg's Manor and Pequea, he revisited.

The winter and spring following his licensure he spent thus, for the most part supplying the vacancies of New Castle and Donegal Presbyteries. He has made no comment on how he felt or how the congregations received him. Probably, he began in those days to put into practice the method he had learned from Robert Smith. The scores of sermons in his own handwriting that are still preserved testify to "a writing out and memorizing" habit which he began at that time.[20] Such writing was slow labor, but it built character and personality and trained him in expression.

In the summer of 1775 McMillan determined to go farther afield, and he set off for the settlements of Virginia. On a Monday of July, following a preaching service at Bottlecourt Court House, he made his way up the forks of the James River in company with a man named Newsberry. When they were in the vicinity of Cedar Bridge, now called Natural Bridge, they turned out of their way to visit "that stupendous piece of Nature's workmanship." At this point the *Journal* changes from a mere listing of preaching appointments to a detailed description of the Natural Bridge. The composition of the rock, the formation of the arch, and the height of the bridge above the water surface are all mentioned. Within the concavity of the arch were a multitude of swallows. Not satisfied with a view from the creek level the two crawled to the top and looked at it from every angle. When they finally were ready to resume their journey, they discovered that McMillan's horse had tried to free himself from the saddle and bridle. McMillan says with dry humor that "great patience and composure of mind" were used in getting the saddle and bridle back on the horse. The night was spent at Hugh Berkly's.

The tour through the settlements of Virginia brought McMillan to the homes of James Gilmer, John McKee, William McKee, and others.

One Thursday he preached to a large congregation in the woods near Buflers Creek, and on the next Sabbath to a crowded audience at Hall's meeting house. These settlers who, for the most part, were Scotch-Irish had no regular preaching services; they were hungry to hear a message from the Book. The next Monday McMillan was in the saddle again and on Tuesday he set off on a journey to Fort Pitt. There is no suggestion that the original plan of a tour through Virginia had Fort Pitt as its destination. John Trimble, his host on Monday and his real friend, went with him for ten miles on his journey. John Henderson overtook him soon thereafter and rode with him to Tygart's Valley.

The journey north and west to Fort Pitt was in mountainous country most of the way. There were paths and trails but no well traveled roads. In a day's travel of thirty-five miles they passed only one house and that was probably only a hut. The two men met privations and difficulties but they kept on to North Mountain, Warm Spring Mountain, Back Creek Mountain, Naps Spur, Thorny Branch Mountain, Green Briar Mountain, Allegheny Mountain, Elk Mountain, and Cheat Mountain. This brought them to the head of Tygart's Valley. Word was sent out to the surrounding area that there would be preaching, and on the fifth Sabbath of July, 1775, McMillan did preach to a small but attentive audience at Charles Wilson's in Tygart's Valley. On Tuesday, August 1st, he preached to "a pretty large number of people" at the home of Jacob Westfall, and then he rode on with some others toward Laurel Hill and the home of William Barker. The next portion of the *Journal* is rich in description:

Here my company left me and Mr. Barker who had promised to accompany me to ye next house, which was about 30 miles distant, not having his horse at home, I was forced to tarry there till 5 o'clock when the horse coming home we set off. Nothing remarkable happened by the way, save that Mr. Barker shot a doe. . . . We then kindled a fire, roasted a part of our venison and took our supper, about 10 o'clock we composed ourselves to rest, I wrapped myself in my great coat and laid me on the ground, my saddle bags served me for a pillow. . . . The night being very dark and rainy I therefore resolved to return to the forenamed cabin. . . . Finding it impossible to open the door, I climbed the wall and went in at a hole in the roof, which served instead of a chimney. I then opened the door, brought in my saddle, kindled a fire, and soon after I had ordered affairs as well as possible, I laid myself down on a sort of bed and slept very comfortable to morning. . . . Saturday traveled about 16 miles to John McDowell's on Shirtee Creek where I tarried till Monday morning. The 4th Sabbath of August preached at said John McDowells. . . . The 2nd Sabbath preached at Ft. Pitt and rode about 7 miles to Thos. Ross where I tarried till Tuesday.

McMillan, though he did not realize it, had come into that part of the Western Country where he was to spend a ministry of nearly sixty years. The *Journal* tells of many preaching appointments in the Monongahela, Youghiogheny, and lower Allegheny river valleys: at Pentecost's, at the Forks Meeting House, at John McDowell's, at Arthur Forbus', at Thomas Cook's, at a meeting house on the banks of the Monongahela, at David Andrews', at Josiah Richards', at Fort Pitt, at Long Run, at Hannastown, at Conemaugh, at Proctor's Tent, and at Ligonier.

In commenting on the situation at Pentecost's, he wrote: "The people had been dilatory and had not given proper warning." Of the meeting on the Monongahela he wrote, "but the day being very wet I had a few hearers." When he visited Hannastown there was double confusion, for he rode some ten miles to preach on Wednesday and found that notice had been given that preaching was to be Thursday. On Friday a minister named Slemons was to preach but "Mr. Slemons not coming in time, I was forced to preach myself." He writes that Conemaugh is "a place in the woods nigh Wm. Dunlaps where they have agreed to build a meeting-house." McMillan, it seems, even so early in his life, was urging the establishment of congregations and churches. We know the Presbytery had made the founding of churches and schools its parting instruction to him.

On the afternoon of August 23 he came to the house of his brother-in-law, John McElhenny, where he spent the next two days "visiting friends and acquaintances." This visit shows his desire to include the Western Country in his missionary travels. McElhenny had married John's older sister Janet and, as the *Journal* implies, had gone out to western Pennsylvania some time before August, 1775.[21] The *Journal* refers, too, to McMillan's taking a seven mile trip from Fort Pitt to visit Thomas Ross.

Now the family records show that an older brother, Thomas McMillan, was married to Thomas Ross' sister Jane, and the *Journal* of November, 1776, mentions a visit to the Thomas McMillan home on Peter's Creek. This visit was a part of McMillan's third western journey. The implication is that Thomas had been married to Jane Ross back in the East and that they had moved to Peter's Creek after John's second western journey, for it is reasonable to assume that the *Journal* would have mentioned a visit to Thomas' home on the first or second trips had he then been living in the West. The *Journal* records his stopping at his brother William's in Brothers Valley, Somerset County, during the late September of 1775, just before his return to the East. The ties of blood and friendship, it seems evident, had some part in McMillan's going to the country beyond the mountains. He went, of course, chiefly as a missionary preacher, but he did take opportunities to be among his own people.

The journey homeward he began in October of 1775. McMillan tells of it in few sentences. He left Laughlin's near Ligonier the first Monday morning of October, crossed the Laurel Hill, and spent the first night at John Miller's, near the foot of the Allegheny Mountains; the second night he spent with the William McCombs at Bedford; the third at Burds in Lyttleton; and the fifth with Coopers in Shippensburg. On his mountain crossings he took time for a Sabbath's preaching at Big Spring, a visit to Carlisle, and a preaching at Hanover, Dauphin County.

On the fourth Sabbath of October he preached at the Pequea Church again. The whole journey from Ligonier to Pequea was made on horseback, through wilderness roads and paths, and was taken in easy stages. A good day's journey for him seems to have been about thirty miles. Variations in the day's ride may be explained by the wish to end at some convenient lodging place.

The Presbytery of New Castle heard McMillan's report of his long trip through Virginia and western Pennsylvania, and it gave him "fresh orders to Augusta and Westmoreland," and so after short visits and preaching appointments in Pequea and Fagg's Manor he was again on the trail.

This time he went through York, Lyttleton, and Tarrytown in Pennsylvania before he rode south to Winchester by way of Fredericktown. In the *Journal* the cost of lodgings and incidentals is set down carefully. On the night he stayed at Robert Wilson's near Winchester he wrote simply, "spent 4,4": Wilson received four shillings and four pence from him. Next a familiar name appears:

"and then rode to John Trimble's." The Trimbles, it seems, were friends of the family. It was from Trimble's home that he set out on his first journey to Fort Pitt, and it was the elder Trimble, who like a father had gone ten miles with him on the road before turning back. That McMillan writes later, "rode to John Trimble's," "continued at Mr. Trimble's," "came again to Mr. Trimble's," "lodged at Mr. John Trimble's," "called at Mr. Trimble's," shows he had a more than casual friendship with the family. Not many miles from the Trimbles he visited an uncle on Back Creek and "found them all well." This is the first proof that his father or mother had relatives in America.

The *Journal's* reference to "a number of my old acquaintances" in Staunton gives additional reason for his going into Virginia. On this trip it seems he forgot or mislaid his shoes, and he had to have another pair made at the cost of eight shillings. The boots, he comments, "were inconvenient to walk in." He spent about six weeks in those parts. On January 1, 1776, he preached a farewell sermon to a large assembly at Peter Hanger's. A purse of nearly nine pounds was presented to him. This is the first reference to his receiving money, although, of course, it has been assumed he had received payment for his many services.

Then, for the second time, the long journey to western Pennsylvania was begun. He revisited Winchester and, in the company of others, soon left behind Petticoat Gap and Hog Creek. Twenty-two miles were made the second day, though the roads were covered with ice and it was necessary for the men to walk most of the way. The North River and the Little Kepher were running high and were difficult to cross, and though he crossed them, he deemed it best to stay at Samuel Turk's a few days. But the week showed little easing of the traveling conditions.

The rest of the journey over the mountains brought exposure and suffering. Let the *Journal* tell this story:

Wednesday, ye 17th. This morning proved very cold and snowy, however, we made out to travel 28 miles and lodged at Mr. Rices' spent 4 S. Thursday ye 18th though the snow fell very fast yet we started to the road. On the Laurel Hill my company left me. While alone my feet got very cold, and getting down to walk awhile, I left my horse walk before me as usual. We had not walked very far until he taking some mad notion or other started off the road, broke past me at the full gallop, my saddle bag broke and fell off. I followed him near a mile but could not come in sight of him it being now after sundown and not knowing how far it was to a house, I gave over the pursuit, took my saddle-bags in my arms, and after walking between 2 and 3 miles I came to a poor cabin where one Wm. Decas dwelt. It being now after dark I determined to tarry until morning, my bed was a parcel of husks on the floor. Travelled 28 miles. Spent 2 S. Friday ye 19th, 1776, early this morning my landlord set off in search of my horse. I, in the meantime mended my saddlebags, went over to Thomas Gest, where I tarried all day. In the evening Philips Bachus came back with my horse for which I gave him 7 S 6 P. Saturday ye 20th. This morning after riding 3 miles I came to David Allen's, where I continued until Monday, spent 3 S. The 3rd sabbath of Jan. 1776 preached at David Allen's to a pretty numerous assembly. This evening it snowed very fast, 14 S. 6 P. Monday ye 22nd. This morning set out in company with John Carmichael to go over to Shirtee, but learning the river could not be crossed, we stopped at Hugh Laughlins after travelling 6 miles. Tuesday ye 23rd of Jan. 1776 crossed the river upon the ice, and after riding 18 miles I came to James Wherry's.

McMillan was now for the second time in the region of Pigeon Creek and Shirtee.[22] He revisited his sister and her family and his old friends. He may have made some tentative arrangements with these two congregations about accepting their call before he returned to the East in 1775, for he preached at Pigeon Creek on the first Sabbath after his return and the next Sabbath at Chartiers. Whatever these arrangements, they had not prevented his preaching in many other places: at Henry Newkirk's, at Thos. Edherton's, at Jacob Long's, at John Munn's, at McKibbon's, at David Allen's, and at a Baptist meetinghouse. While he was at the Scott home on Pigeon Creek "the distressing tidings of my brother's death" came. This brother was William McMillan of Brothers Valley in Somerset County, who died on January 24, 1776, after two weeks and three days of illness.

Until toward the end of March McMillan divided his time between Pigeon Creek and Chartiers. Then he went back to Fagg's Manor by way of Hannastown and the Allegheny mountains and so was able to visit with the family of his deceased brother. This second visit to the Western Country had more than accomplished its purpose; the *Journal* frequently mentions the many services and the interest of the worshippers. It also makes clear that McMillan at last had decided where he would do his life's work.

MCMILLAN'S DECISION

By the time John McMillan returned from his second journey beyond the mountains he had made his all-important decision to settle in the West. As the *Journal* shows, he had determined toward the end of his second western journey to accept calls from Chartiers and Pigeon Creek. The successive steps and the causes that brought him to this decision are fairly clear in his *Journal*.

The Presbytery had instructed him that, as a newly licensed candidate, he should itinerate among the vacant churches of New Castle and Donegal Presbyteries. In giving this instruction the Presbytery had a double purpose. Many churches had no minister though the settlers were eager to hear the spoken Word. At first McMillan would serve as a missionary; later, he, as the licensee, would wish to settle in a charge, and the Presbytery felt that the missionary work would let him look over the field. Such arrangements were made with the consent of the candidate and perhaps at his request. A winter's itineration among the churches would be sufficient. When McMillan continued the visitation into the summer and determined to go farther afield, the Presbyters realized he was taking full time for his choice and that he had not, as yet, found the place which satisfied him.

McMillan had shown no wish for a city church, nor had he wished to settle where people of Dutch, Quaker, or Episcopal churches predominated. His people were the Scotch-Irish; that probably largely governed his choice. It was essential, too, that he find a place where he could start the log cabin school which he had in mind. His remembering of Robert Smith's instruction "to look out for some pious young men, and educate them for the ministry,"[23] indicates that from the first he was intent in carrying on the Tennent-Blair-Smith tradition. Running like a crimson thread through the thinking of those three men, was the conviction that teaching of ministers should parallel preaching of the Word.

None of the places McMillan visited during his first winter journey seemed to be the place he was seeking. It is important to keep in mind his idea of Divine assistance. When he entered the ministry he became completely willing to abide by God's will. Smith encouraged this attitude during McMillan's last two years in his school. And so when the important choice was to be made, his feeling that he must carry out his Heavenly Father's will was urgent. Until, then, the Lord should speak clearly to him, he must keep seeking in other fields. He had, as he wrote, "In the summer of '75," taken "a tour through the settlements in Virginia between the North and South Mountains."[24] He had, at that time, visited many churches and settlements, but he had felt no compulsion for encouraging any of them to issue him a Call.

Then came the decision to go on to the region about Fort Pitt. A line in the *Journal* about this time reads, "This morning wrote a letter to Pequea". The *Journal* goes on: "about 9 o'clock set off on my journey toward Fort Pitt." It is possible that McMillan had talked with Smith, when he preached at Pequea a few weeks earlier, about his not having accepted a church. He may have agreed to write Smith if he decided to take a trip into the Western Country. And—again, perhaps—his sister and some friends already living near Fort Pitt may have encouraged him to explore that country before he accepted any Call.

McMillan preached at many places in the Fort Pitt region. Something made him prefer Chartiers and Pigeon Creek to Peter's Creek, Cross Creek, Fort Pitt, Hannastown, Ligonier, or any other place. The large Scotch-Irish settlement at Chartiers and Pigeon Creek may have counted toward this choice. Washington County was from the first dominated by the Scotch-Irish.[25] Then, too, a rural parish with the need for a log cabin school appealed to him. The Divine Voice within him seemed to will that the ministry should be in these parishes. Other churches, no doubt, approached him, even as these two, but for the first time in his missionary journeys he was interested in a Call. The churches were probably told that he would return East and then would decide.

After he had recrossed the mountains he visited four important places: Fagg's Manor, Brandywine, Pequea, and a meeting of the Presbytery. What did his father and other members of his family think about his removing to the West? What did a young woman named Catherine Brown in Brandywine have to say about living in the backwoods country? What did Robert Smith think about McMillan's usefulness on the frontier? McMillan must have talked about his impending decision with all these friends, and apparently they agreed he should plan seriously to accept a wilderness Call. The Presbytery, however, suggested that he revisit the churches of Augusta and Westmoreland.

In those days many, even Presbyters, had scant appreciation of the Western Country. The Presbytery may have thought his talents would be wasted there, and so rather have had him choose eastern Pennsylvania or Virginia. McMillan seems to have told the Presbytery he wished to settle in the West; but to make sure it was the Spirit which led him to the choice, the Presbytery had him spend nearly two months visiting churches around Augusta.

The *Journal* says that a large assembly came to hear him at Peter Hanger's on New Year's Day, Monday, in 1776. Yet a certainty urged him on his way. The next entry reads: "This day I set out on my journey to Shirtee." Now, it seems, he was sure of God's will. He does not say, as he had said of his first trip, that he set out "to Fort Pitt." "Shirtee" or Chartiers he had chosen as his home.

The *Journal* gives the impression that once there he encouraged the Chartiers and Pigeon Creek people to offer him separate Calls. Those Calls were in his hands when a few weeks later he went back to meet with the Presbytery.

TO THE WEST

The Presbytery of New Castle met on April 22, 1776, and they heard not only McMillan's report of his travels but also his statement that the churches of Pigeon Creek and Chartiers wanted him to become their regularly installed pastor. These Calls having been presented in the proper fashion, it was next in order that he be dismissed as a licentiate to the Presbytery of Donegal. Boundaries were uncertain in those days; "the Presbytery of Donegal included the whole territory west of the mountains, and of course embraced the congregations of Chartiers and Pigeon Creek."[26] Along with the certificate of dismission, Donegal Presbytery received a recommendation that McMillan be ordained and that he deliver a discourse on Romans 5:20 as a part of his ordination trial.[27] This would give the candidate time to prepare his sermon before the next meeting of Donegal Presbytery. On May 25, 1776, Donegal Presbytery held a *pro re nata* meeting in Philadelphia and received McMillan. The record of the Presbytery reads:

Mr. McMillan a Licensed Candidate appeared and produced a regular Certificate from the Pby of New Castle, Signifying that they had Dismissed him that he might put himself under the care of this Pby in Consequence of his having accepted a Call from Chartiers and Pigeon Creek, near Fort Pit, accordingly McMillan is received and taken under our Care.

The Presbytery then proceeded to the ordination trials. It agreed with the recommendation that the candidate be permitted to give a discourse on Romans 5:20: "Moreover the law entered, that the offense might abound. But where sin abounded grace did much more abound." McMillan's sermon was heard on the floor of the Presbytery. The Presbytery gave its unanimous approval and voted to accept his discourse as part of the ordination trials. It gave him a further assignment. He was to prepare a sermon on Matthew 7: 21: "Not everyone that saith unto me, Lord, Lord, shall enter into the kingdom of Heaven," "to be delivered at our next meeting in June." The Presbytery agreed to proceed to his ordination at the June meeting if the way was still clear. And it arranged for "Mr. Cooper to preach the ordination sermon and Mr. King to preside in the ordination and give the charge."

The Presbytery of Donegal met on Tuesday, June 18, 1776, at the Falling Spring Church, Chambersburg. This meeting was opened with a sermon by McMillan from Matthew 7:21, as had been planned the previous month. The Records of Donegal Presbytery for 1775-1776 tell that it then "proceeded to consider Mr. McMillan's discourse and unanimously agreed in sustaining it as a part of the Trials." A further examination was conducted, and at its end the Presbytery was so convinced he was fully qualified for the Gospel ministry that it agreed to proceed to his ordination the next day. During the evening meeting public notice was given that all objections to McMillan's "being set apart to the office of ye Gospel Ministry" must be presented before nine o'clock in the next morning. No objections were presented.

The ordination service took place on June 19, 1776. Cooper chose for his text, "Who then is a faithful and wise servant, whom his Lord hath made ruler of his household, to give them meat in due season? Blessed is that servant, whom his Lord when he cometh shall find so doing" (Matthew 24: 45, 46). So, all the necessary and preliminary steps having been taken in accordance with the rules of the church, "Mr. John McMillan was solemnly set apart by prayer and Imposition of the Hands of the Presbytery, to the Gospel ministry." King presided at this ceremony and gave the charge as appointed. The charge was followed by *the Right Hand of Fellowship*, extended to him by the members of the Presbytery. James Finley and John Carmichael, who had planned to visit the regions of western Pennsylvania in the fall, one or both, were commissioned by the Presbytery to install McMillan as the regular pastor over the Pigeon Creek and Chartiers churches.

After his ordination McMillan preached in the vicinity of Fagg's Manor until October. These preaching assignments included Long's Meeting House, Marsh Creek, Fagg's Manor, Little Brittain, St. George, Slate Ridge, Brandywine, Hanover, Big Spring, John Jack's, and John Brown's.

Between the Sabbaths of his Slate Ridge and Brandywine preachings McMillan was married to Catherine Brown. In the *Journal* he writes: "Tuesday ye 6th of August 1776, I was married to Miss Catherine Brown, in troublous times, by Mr. Carmickel." In a short autobiography, dated January 1832, fifty-six years after he had made the *Journal* entry, he writes:

Having now determined to remove to the western country and take charge of the congregations of Chartiers and Pigeon Creek, I thought it my duty to take with me a female companion. Accordingly on the 6th of August, 1776,

I was married to Catharine Brown, a young woman with whom I had long been acquainted, and who, I believed, was a dear child of God. She was the youngest child of Mr. William Brown, a ruling elder in the congregation of Upper Brandywine, Chester County, Pennsylvania. He was a very pious man, and lived to a great age, being about ninety when he died.[28]

The marriage was solemnized by John Carmichael of Brandywine, one of the two ministers who were going into the Western Country and who were to install McMillan that fall. The *Journal*, in addition to the brief telling of his marriage speaks of "troublous times."

The summer of 1776 was, indeed, a troublous time. Lexington, Bunker Hill, and other battles had been fought; the Declaration of Independence had been signed; the Revolutionary War had begun. A commentary on the "troublous times" has been given by D. X. Junkin, from what the daughter of John Carmichael told him. The Brandywine minister had just paid a visit to Washington's Camp at Valley Forge. After hearing Washington's complaint of the lack of bandages, he had gone back to Brandywine and on the next Sabbath had "made an appeal to the patriotic women in charge, asking them to spare three or four inches from the lower end of a certain garment."[29] The response was surprising. "I have no doubt," he says, "that the young bride, Catharine McMillan (for she was still at home) contributed her full share to the stores of the surgeons."[30]

McMillan did not because of the wedding interrupt for long his preaching schedule. If the Presbytery had arranged his appointments in advance, probably the wedding was set for a time when he could be near Brandywine.

The *Journal* or *Diary* changes form after the marriage and lacks some of the details included earlier. He writes merely a record of places where he had preached and in some instances the fee he received, though here and there some comment is added. On one Sabbath, August 4th, he preached at Slate Ridge. On Thursday, following his wedding on Tuesday, he preached again at Brandywine. On Wednesday, August 14, he took his wife to Pequea, perhaps to present her to his friends and relatives. He does not give Fagg's Manor the high emphasis he gives Pequea, but this may be explained by its being near Brandywine and, perhaps, by the supposition that Fagg's Manor relatives were guests at the wedding.

McMillan took his business of being minister seriously. For the next Thursday the entry reads: "left her Pequea and went to fulfill my various appointments." He seems determined to avoid the *New*

Testament situation in which a man said, "I have married a wife, and therefore I cannot come."[31]

On the last Sabbath of September, 1776, McMillan preached at Brandywine and on Thursday "set off on my journey to the back woods." His wife of less than two months he left at her home in Brandywine. The comment in the Carnahan letter is: "It being the time of the revolutionary war, and the Indians being very troublesome on the frontiers, I was prevented from removing my family to my congregation until November, 1778."[32]

McMillan returned to the West by way of Hanover, Dauphin County. There he preached, the first Sabbath of October. The next Tuesday the Presbytery met in Shippensburg, a great distance westward, but McMillan made the long ride and attended that meeting. He next preached at Bedford and, next, at Long Run (near Irwin), where he baptized fourteen children. At long Run his horse broke out of the pasture on Saturday night and, before it was stopped, went back along the trail as far as Hannastown three miles northeast of Greensburg. This detained him until Wednesday but did not interfere seriously with his plans. The last part of the journey across to John McDowell's on Chartiers Creek was punctuated with a brief visit to his older brother's home on Peter's Creek. After that Sabbath—the fourth Sabbath of October—he preached at Chartiers, and the following Sabbath, at Pigeon Creek. He remained one month with his congregation, preaching on three Sabbaths at Chartiers and on two at Pigeon Creek. He baptized several children at each church and at Peter's Creek, Thomas Cook's, and James Breadon's on Ten Mile, where he preached at services held between Sabbaths. On the last Monday of November he started back east, over the southern route that followed the Forbes' Trail through Virginia (West Virginia).

Of the journey he records several experiences—a stop-over with a man named Vance, a preaching engagement at Rock Creek on the first Sabbath of December, attendance at a Presbytery meeting in Elk Branch, and his preaching on the second Sabbath of December at Marsh Creek, where an aunt lived. He was back at Brandywine on Wednesday of that week in a snow fall, the weather "cold and and cloudy."

He gives no reason for his having stayed only one month in the West, though possibly his plans had included infrequent returns until he had an established home at Chartiers. This supposition is strengthened by his not returning to the West until the next August (1777) and then staying only one month. McMillan explains this shortness of his visit in this way: "I however visited them as often as I could, ordained elders, baptized their children, and took as much care of them as circumstances would permit."

There is no mention in the *Journal* or the letters of an installation service ever taking place. Finley or Carmichael could have installed him on one of McMillan's short stays, or the shortness of his stays could have delayed the ceremony. It is probable, however, that his minister friends, James Power and Thaddeus Dod and Joseph Smith, installed him after he had settled permanently in his pastorate.

A few things need to be said of the *Journal* for these three years. It is dull reading, yet here and there a word or two sparkles with human meaning. McMillan was capable of warm friendship. John Carmichael of Brandywine, in addition to being Catherine McMillan's pastor, appears to have become a fast friend of John McMillan. On the first Christmas following his marriage McMillan wrote in his *Journal:* "My wife and I went to Mr. Carmichael's." Many times he preached for Carmichael at Brandywine. McMillan was interested in changes of season and weather. The weather is mentioned in many entries, especially cold, rain, or snow. He felt human ties. In May, 1777, there are two significant entries: The first tells of two trips to Fagg's Manor because of the illness of his "mother" (his step-mother, Sarah McMillan), and the other announces the birth of his first child, a girl, on Saturday, May 31 at 7:30 P.M., presumably at Brandywine. The name Jean was given her. In August, 1777, McMillan and his father began the journey to Chartiers and Pigeon Creek. The out of the way stop at an "Aunt's at Marsh Creek" may have been to visit a sister of his stepmother. It is, though, more probable that another of the Reas or McMillans had come to Pennsylvania from Ireland. There are no other references to the father on this early trip save the ambiguous "we." Yet the father undoubtedly visited his son and daughter beyond the mountains and returned home with McMillan in September. That the West made a favorable impression seems certain, for some time later he sold his property in Chester county and went to the Western Country.[33]

The only other item of interest in the *Journal* for this period is the variance of the offerings in the different congregations. He received fifteen shillings at his sister-in-law's in Brothers Valley and twelve pounds at Leader Spring: There was a payment of ten pounds and ten shillings, another of ten pounds, but the average fee was two or three pounds. These fees, for the most part, were moneys given as free-will offerings.

In November, 1778, he took his family to the "back woods." McMillan says that he did not preach the second or third Sabbaths of October, 1778, "my time being taken up in preparing to move to Shirtee." The time had come for John, Catherine, and Jean McMillan to move into the Western Country.

Then the mission began in earnest for this man who had felt divinely led to go into the Western Country, there to spend a long lifetime preaching, teaching, and ministering.

WESTWARD

II. NOTES

1. Moses Allen. "Rev. John McMillan, D.D.," *Centennial Address*. 2.
2. McMillan's Letter to James Carnahan. See Appendix C.
3. Robert E. Thompson. "A History of the Presbyterian Churches in the United States," *American Church History*. VI. 46.
4. George P. Hays. *Presbyterians*. 119.
5. Varnum L. Collins. *President Witherspoon*. 85, 86.
6. *Ibid*. 84.
7. Joseph Smith. *Old Redstone*. 174.
8. See Appendix C.

9. "Biographical Sketch of John McMillan, D.D.," *Presbyterian Education Repository, Home, the School and the Church.* Edited by C. Van Rensseler. IV. 204.
10. Collins. 107.
11. *Ibid.*
12. *Ibid.*
13. *Ibid.* 107, 108.
14. *Old Redstone.* 176.
15. *Ibid.* 177.
16. See Appendix C.
17. *Ibid.*
18. Minutes of the Presbytery of New Castle, 1774-1795. 104.
19. The *Journal* of John McMillan. See Appendix A. Much of the material in this chapter is from Parts I and II of the *Journal*.
20. There are 135 of these sermons in the possession of Mrs. Helen Wragg, 1133 Lancaster Street, Pittsburgh, Pennsylvania.
21. See D. M. Bennett's *Life and Work of Rev. John McMillan, D.D.* 133.
22. "Chartiers" is the more common name.
23. See Appendix C.
24. *Ibid.*
25. Henry G. Ford. *The Scotch-Irish in America.* 44.
26. *Old Redstone.* 185.
27. Records of Donegal Presbytery. III. 336. The material on the following page is also taken from these Records.
28. Joseph Smith. *The History of Jefferson College.* 416.
29. David X. Junkin. "The Life and Labors of the Rev. John McMillan, D.D.," *Centenary Memorial.* 26.
30. *Ibid.*
31. Luke 14:20.
32. See Appendix C.
33. *History of Jefferson College.* 413, 414.

III. HOME

HOME had great importance in the life of the Apostle of the West. Home, to him, seemed more than the building of a house in which his family life might run its course. Home for licentiate McMillan must be a center from which his aims and ambitions as a minister, teacher, and presbyter would range wide in service and growth.

After he had visited the West in the summer of 1775[1] he felt that his new home should be in southwestern Pennsylvania. Several thousand Scotch-Irish had rushed to these western lands when they were opened to settlement in 1769. McMillan determined to make his home among his own people.

Later, McMillan's father, two of his sisters, and two brothers were to settle near him. His wife and seven children were with him for many years. And several of the neighboring ministers and many students who were about his home were to contribute immeasurably to his everyday living. Providence was kind to McMillan.

HOUSEKEEPING

McMillan's decision to settle on the American frontier was announced at a meeting of the New Castle Presbytery on April 22, 1776 and at a *pro re nata* meeting of the Donegal Presbytery on May 25, 1776.[2] There is, too, a record that John McMillan purchased a farm through the kindly offices of John McDowell. This farm contained 313.4 acres and in the record is referred to as the Thomas and Cook property. It was on the eastern branch of Chartiers Creek in the county of Yohogania, Commonwealth of Virginia. The old deed, dated September 9, 1777, states that the price paid was 195 pounds, 15 shillings, and 6 pence.[3] Western land was being settled so rapidly in 1776 that the first arrangements were made for the purchase, it is thought, before the young missionary told his intentions to the Presbytery. Indian disturbances on the frontier prevented for many months the McMillan family's going to that farm.

McMillan, his wife, and their baby made the journey to Chartiers in late October and early November of 1778. In the *Journal* the entry for the "first Sabbath" of November is defective but it seems to be "at ye new field of labor."[4] The second Sabbath is listed as "at Shirtee," the third, "at Pidgeon Creek," the fourth, "at

Shirtee," the fifth, "at Pidgeon Creek." An interesting account of the first few weeks is given in the letter to Carnahan.

> When I came to this country the cabin in which I was to live was raised, but there was no roof on it, nor any chimney or floor. The people, however, were very kind, assisted me in preparing my house, and on the 16th of December I moved into it. But we had neither bedstead, nor tables, nor stool, nor chair, nor bucket. All these things we had to leave behind us; there being no wagon-road at that time over the mountains; we could bring nothing with us but what was carried on pack-horses. We placed two boxes on each other, which served us for a table, and two kegs answered for seats; and having committed ourselves to God in family worship, we spread a bed on the floor, and slept soundly till morning. The next day, a neighbor coming to my assistance, we made a table and a stool, and in a little time had everything comfortable about us. Sometimes, indeed we had no bread for weeks together, but we had plenty of pumpkins and potatoes, and all the necessaries of life; as for luxuries, we were not much concerned about them. We enjoyed health, the gospel and its ordinances, and pious friends. We were in the place where we believed God would have us to be; and we did not doubt but that he would provide for us everything necessary; and (glory to his name!) we were not disappointed.[5]

The establishing of the new home required great effort. McMillan was strong; he was able to endure more than most men could endure. "The circumstances in which he was placed, required him to 'work with his own hands' in handling the axe, and other implements of the sturdy laborer, in the new country."[6] That there were six weeks between the arrival of the McMillans in Chartiers and their occupancy of the cabin, implies that McMillan himself did much of the work on the cabin. After the family had moved to their new home a great deal still had to be done. A barn, a spring house, a smoke house, and a shed were needed. So were work horses, cattle, and chickens. In the first winter potatoes, pumpkins, whatever meat was available would need to be got through donation or purchase. These would be stored in a small cellar excavated under the kitchen part of the cabin. That first winter was the McMillan's most difficult time. When the spring of 1779 came McMillan put in extensive crops.

The general poverty of his people kept his salary around 100 pounds, 260 dollars in Pennsylvania currency of the time. Part of this was often paid in tallow, paper, corn, wheat.[7] Because of these conditions McMillan supervised the planting and harvesting of crops and himself worked part of the land.[8] Yet the McMillans saved money and 1796 had increased their acreage to 989.5 acres. A new, two-story log house soon was built a short distance from the first log cabin. In this "mansion," as it was sometimes called, he raised his family and lived out his long and fruitful life. The new house had a stone foundation, although only under the left portion was there excavation for a cellar. The logs of the walls were hewed exactly and were fitted skillfully at the corners. The rafters and joints were all hewed oak; one-inch cherry boards of different widths made the flooring; the wood trim was black walnut, the moulding handworked; mud and stones tightly packed filled the spaces between the logs. At a later time the outside was sheathed in weather boarding. A visitor to the log manse in March, 1932 wrote:

A hall ran through the center as you entered the front. A door to your left opened into the living room which was of a good size and well lighted, and very cheerful, the room in rear of this was the Doctor's study, size 9x18. On the right side of the hall, was a door opening into the room on the one story side. About half way back in the hall was where the stairs started that led to the second floor; at the rear of the hall was a door out on to the back porch, also one of the Doctor's study. On the second floor were three nice size bed rooms.[9]

There is now in the college building at Canonsburg a high backed wooden tablet-chair from McMillan's study. The tablet on the right arm of the chair is about one and one half feet in diameter. It is believed McMillan was among the first to construct this convenient help to writing and study.

The McMillans lived in utmost simplicity and plainness. Friends were always welcome, but they were offered the McMillans' usual fare, and they heard no apology for this food.

Once I remember, there were two ministers from east of the mountains called at his house. They heard of him and the great work he was doing in the new settlements, and were very anxious to see him. When dinner was served, we all sat down at the table together; and this was the bill of fare: potatoes boiled in their jackets, as he called it, pumpkins stewed and prepared in milk; lamb's-quarter greens gathered in the pasture in front of the door: with great bowls of fresh milk, cool and nice from the spring house at the foot of the hill. This was the entire meal; plenty of everything, and everything of the best: and when the strange guests sat down, everything on the table was passed to them, but not one word of apology was offered, nor felt to be necessary. There were the fruits of the land, he and his boys lived in this way, and his guests were no better than they.[10]

The home was not without its servants or slaves. These helpers probably were part of the household as soon as the McMillans were able to afford keeping them. McMillan in his personal expense account 1820 to 1833,[11] names Dido as a worker around the house. The way in which the name Dido is used may indicate she was or had been a slave. Later McMillan seems to have taken a stand against slavery. Entries for 1825 and thereafter show that small sums of money were paid to Dido "for past services."[12] Such entries may not contradict the insistence of the McMillan descendants that "they had always understood that Dr. McMillan had slaves in his home."

One aim of the McMillan home was to help some others outside the family. This help was mainly through giving boarding and lodging to theological students. But in many other ways McMillan gave assistance. Once he was established in his ministry McMillan used part of his savings to help indigent young men who were preparing for the ministry. Among other references to such loans is one in a letter from John Watson at Princeton. The letter is dated May 13, 1796, and reads in part: "I believe with the strictest economy I cannot finish my studies here with less than twelve or fifteen pounds but I think this will do."[13] The money was always lent, not given, with the suggestion that the receiver repay it when he could so that the money might help others. Carnahan writes: "I have reason to believe that, in the latter part of his life, he gave, for benevolent purposes, more than he received from his congregations."[14]

THE NEIGHBORHOOD

When the McMillans came to western Pennsylvania, conditions there were somewhat much as those east of the Appalachians had been one hundred years earlier. This land, the American frontier, was in transition from savagery and conflict to order and independence.

Only a very few years before, Iroquois and Delaware and Shawnee Indians had used western Pennsylvania as their hunting ground. They were slow to leave the region, and they remained a constant threat to the settlers for years after the McMillans had built their home. And, too, the French had long claimed the upper Ohio Valley. It was territory which united their Canadian and Louisiana possessions. The English challenged this claim of the French and began to plan ways of making the valuable hinterland their own. The Ohio Company was one means of doing this. The Ohio Company had a double aim: to settle the land and to trade with the Indians. To accomplish this it opened, in 1753, a road from Wills Creek (Cumberland, Maryland) "by way of a line nearly coincident with the old National Road, to the mouth of the Redstone or Brownsville, on the Monongahela."[15] Efforts were made about this time to persuade the Pennsylvania Dutch to go to the West, and if Laurence Washington had been able to get the state of Virginia to remove the Episcopal parish taxes imposed, the Dutch and Germans would probably have migrated west.[16] But, as it fell out, the land was not settled by white men until the Scots and Scotch-Irish came nearly two decades later. An English victory over the French seemed the signal for the former Ulstermen and their children to occupy in great numbers the western lands.

In 1769 the land having been ceded by the Indians, all of southwestern Pennsylvania was thrown open to settlement, and in the next ten years more than 25,000 people were living in the territory now comprising the Counties of Westmoreland, Allegheny, Fayette, and Washington.[17]

With these settlers came visiting clergymen — James Maclagan, Charles Beatty, George Duffield, David McClure, and Levi Frisbee.[18] They preached throughout the settlements; yet the greatest effects came out of the reports they brought back to synods, presbyteries, and to those in the East who wished to go beyond the mountains. Beatty and Duffield made their visit at the request of the Synod of New York and Philadelphia.[19] As a result of their reports, this synod and its presbyteries drew up a missionary program to help their fellow Presbyterians beyond the mountains. The Beatty and Duffield report to Donegal Presbytery was in part: "That they found on the frontiers numbers of people, earnestly desirous of forming themselves into congregations."[20] The Indians were also considered a field for missionary endeavor.

The frontier settlements were not free from Indian uprisings until near the turn of the century. Horses and cattle were stolen from the settlers, their crops were destroyed, their houses and barns burned. Many were taken prisoners and not a few were murdered.

For many of the frontier inhabitants the summer of 1782 was a time of great trial. Indians raided all of what is now Westmoreland and Allegheny counties. Danger might be anywhere. For instance, James Power, of the Sewickley and Mount Pleasant fields, narrowly escaped injury or possibly death in the raid that laid waste Hannastown on July 13 of that year. He had left his home in the morning to attend some meeting or keep an appointment over toward Hannastown. Fortunately the Indians did not come upon him. His wife and family got news of the burning of Hannastown before he was back at his home; there had been for his family hours of intense agony.[21]

The people in the most populated districts built forts for protection. These often were so large that several families could live in them. A fort might consist of cabins, blockhouses, and stockades, or it might be a single blockhouse. "A large folding gate, made of thick slabs, on the side nearest the spring closed the fort. The stockades, cabins, bastions, and blockhouse-walls were furnished with port-holes at proper heights and distances."[22] In all probability, more than once the McMillans dropped everything and took refuge in the nearest fort. Reports from other farms and towns harried by Indians must have kept them fearful of attack in their first years at Chartiers.

The region about Chartiers was settled by religious-minded Scotch-Irish who had come from east of the Alleghenies. Yet to the Western Country came many persons who did not accept the discipline either of the church or of the settled community. They had crossed to America because they were adventurous and many were outside any church. Finding the East conservative, and knowing the freedom of the Indian country, they had gone over the mountains westward. Many of them were harsh, irascible, intolerant, and restless. "They found the life of the hunter or the solitary farmer ideal, especially since they were also courageous, self-reliant, aggressive, and hardy."[23] Partly because of them, and partly because any frontier is primitive, life in the new West was often crude and vulgar. Most farms and hamlets had little of what we call culture.

The comforts of civilization were unknown, not to speak of its luxuries, and there was little effort to observe the amenities of life. The houses were rude makeshifts, the domestic utensils few and crude; clothing was homespun and there were not many changes of raiment at that; food was coarse but usually plentiful; amusements were boisterous, vulgar, and often brutal.[24]

The frontiersmen had their shortcomings. Against these faults must be set, as credits, their quick hospitality and their capacity for warm and lasting friendships. Yet they were revengeful, and they held their resentments.[25]

Naturally conditions improved as into western Pennsylvania came people of more substance and greater culture. That McMillan, when he came on his earlier journey, found many who wanted to have resident pastors shows improvement.

THE FAMILY

After he came to Chartiers McMillan kept close contact with others of his family.

His father, William, sold his property in Chester County and moved to western Pennsylvania "during the time of the Revolutionary war."[26] He and his second wife, Sarah McClelland McMillan, lived on a 210 acre tract he bought in Mifflin Township (now Jefferson Township), Allegheny County. This farm lay about fifteen miles east of Chartiers and was, it seems, a second home for John McMillan. On it William lived until his death July 2, 1792, at the age of seventy-five years. His will shows that his wife and a stepdaughter, Sarah McClelland, were living at the time of his death.[27]

John McMillan's eldest brother, Thomas, had moved to the Western Country some time before McMillan set up his home at Chartiers. The farm of 196½ acres which Thomas owned lay east of Chartiers, in the vicinity of his father's farm. McMillan visited his brother on Peter's Creek the first Monday of November, 1776.[28] Thomas lived to be eighty. He died on February 7, 1820 and was buried in Mingo cemetery.

The second older brother, William, left the Fagg's Manor home before 1775. McMillan writes in the *Journal* that he visited William in Brothers Valley, Somerset County, in late September or October of that year. He records in a later entry that "distressing tidings" of his brother's death on January 24, 1776,[29] had reached him. He visited his sister-in-law whenever he was near Brothers Valley, and later he took his nephew, William III, into his home while the young man was being educated.

Mary, the eldest sister, married Samuel Ferguson and lived in Hanover, Dauphin County, Pennsylvania. The *Journal* shows that McMillan preached in Hanover. The entry for October, 1775, reads: "Tuesday after having rode about 22 miles I came to Samuel Ferguson's in Hanover, where my leg, being very sore, I continued that week."[30] In 1778 at least a dozen preaching appointments at Hanover are listed. Each of these meant a visit with his sister Mary, who may well have been a favorite with him. The will of William McMillan stipulated that "Mary Ferguson" was to share equally with her sister Janet, who married John McElhenny, and her brother Thomas in what remained of "all the property" after the legatees had been paid and the step-mother, Sarah, had died.[31]

Janet McMillan and her husband, John McElhenny, were living in the Western Country in August of 1775 when McMillan made his first visit to the Fort Pitt area. The McElhennys lived on Peter's Creek not a great distance from Thomas McMillan or the site of the future church at Chartiers. There are several references in the *Journal* to visits in the McElhenny home. The general reference is "to my brother-in-law's" with no mention of "Janet." Presumably Janet died around 1800. Later John McElhenny must have married Mary, the widow of John Ferguson, for the will of John McElhenny, Sr., made May 8, 1823 and proved August 3, 1824, reads in part: "To my wife Mary, my son Adam, my son Samuel, my son Robert and my son John Ferguson McElhenny ... Mary, my wife, to have the benefit of her share. ...."[32] This seems to mean that Janet McMillan, the wife of John McElhenny, had died as had Samuel Ferguson, Mary's husband. Mary must have moved to the Western Country and later married John McElhenny there. The son, John Ferguson McElhenny, mentioned in the will, is evidently the son of Samuel Ferguson and Mary, and had been adopted by John McElhenny, Sr. Nine heirs are mentioned in John McElhenny's will but, except John Ferguson McElhenny, it is not shown which of the children were Janet's and which Mary's.[33]

The last of the brothers and sisters of John McMillan was Margaret. She was the youngest of the family. Less is known of her than of any of the others. She married John Torbit and lived at Leacock in Lancaster County, Pennsylvania. The *Journal* gives several such references as "Lodged at John Torbit's in Leacock."[34] Leacock was not far from Hanover or Fagg's Manor; probably Margaret visited occasionally her parents and her sister as long as they lived in the East. The will of William I left ten pounds to Margaret and ten pounds to her daughter Sarah.[35] After Mary married John McElhenny and moved to Peter's Creek, it is probable that Margaret was the only one of the family living east of the mountains.

John and Catherine Brown McMillan had seven children. The *Journal* lists each child as he came into the world in this fashion: "Saturday the 31st of May at half past seven o'clock past meridian Jean McMillan was born, 1777." "Wednesday the 2nd of June, 1779, about seven o'clock past meridian, William McMillan was born." "Thursday ye 28th of June, 1781, Margaret McMillan was born between eleven and twelve o'clock at night." "Thursday, September 11th—83, Mary McMillan was born about eleven o'clock A.M." "Saturday the 28th of May—85, Catherine McMillan was born about 9 o'clock A.M." "Thursday ye 9th of October about half past four o'clock John McMillan was born (1787)." "Saturday the 5th of December, 1789, Samuel McMillan was born about two o'clock P.M."[36]

Jean, John McMillan's oldest child, was born at her mother's old home in Brandywine, Pennsylvania. When she was a year old, in November, 1778, she was taken to western Pennsylvania. At twenty-three she married William Morehead, a minister who had studied theology under her father. Many writers point out that McMillan married his daughters Jean and Margaret to two young ministers, William Morehead and John Watson, on the same day, and that by a remarkable coincidence these two, besides marrying sisters on the same day, "took sick on the same day, died on the same day, and were buried in the same grave."[37] Their grave, at Hill Church near Canonsburg, is marked with a table stone into which is cut the Bible verse: [They] were lovely and pleasant in their lives, and in their death they were not divided. John McMillan may have selected the epitaph. Jean remained a widow until 1811, when she married Samuel Harper, a widower with several children who lived near Carmichael, Greene County, Pennsylvania. There were four children by her second marriage. Her home was in Carmichael until her death, February 3, 1857, at the age of eighty years. Jean was active in the church, beloved by all, and greatly missed at her death.[38] She is buried in New Providence Cemetery, near Carmichael. The tombstone bears the name Jane. It is possible that she went by that name, though she had been given the name Jean.

The eldest son, William, was born at the manse at Chartiers in 1779. Little is known about him other than that he married Sarah Morehead, and that he went, while a young man, to Mercer County. In the history of the old Neshannock Church (Mercer County) is a record of John McMillan's coming to that community in 1796 and of his helping to organize the Neshannock church in 1802. William is mentioned in John McMillan's will:

To my beloved son William I give and bequeath, beside what I have already given him, all that tract of land lying in Mercer County near to the state line in the fourth donation district No. 656, containing 100 acres, to him, his heirs and assigns now forever."[39]

The reference here to "donation district" leads to the conclusion that John McMillan had received these one hundred acres as a Revolutionary War grant. He had belonged to the 6th Class of Captain James Scott's Company of the Third Battalion of Washington County Military and was eligible for such a grant.[40] These one hundred acres lay near New Wilmington, not far from the Neshannock Church. Like other pioneers, William and his wife Sarah first lived in a log cabin. Then in 1830 they built a brick house, the first brick house in that neighborhood.

A History of the Neshannock Church has an incident or two that throws some light on William. It says of the pews in the first church:

the most noted pew was that occupied by Squire William McMillan and his wife Sally. It was noted not only because it was different from all the others, but also because of those who occupied it. The seat was simply a loose slab placed on five wooden pins inserted in augur holes in the wall.[41]

Luke Irwin once joked with McMillan about his having taken a noisy nap during the sermon time. Luke said: "Billy, I'll have you churched for sleeping." Billy was quick with his answer: "When I was a boy, I was taught not to fight, but today after fighting sleep for awhile, I remembered that it was very wicked to fight on Sunday, so I quit."[42]

William and Sarah had no children. The will designated that at Sarah's death the 235 acres of land be divided for the most part in sixths among three sisters, a brother, and a nephew. Jefferson College was given $1200 to provide a scholarship fund for poor young men.[43] William was buried in the Neshannock Church cemetery one mile west of New Wilmington, Pennsylvania. He died in May, 1850; his wife, in 1860.

The third of the seven McMillan children was Margaret. She was born in North Strabane Township, Washington County, in the McMillan manse, on June 28, 1781. She grew up in the surroundings of the manse and in the company of theological students. She was in her nineteenth year when John Watson, who had just had a Call from the church at Washington, Pennsylvania, and one from the Miller's Run church, asked for her hand. She and her sister Jean were married in a double wedding in 1800, and on November 30, 1802, John Watson died.[44] Only a few months before, he had been elected principal of the newly organized Jefferson College. He was looked upon as a young genius. He left two children, John Watson II and William Morehead Watson (who was born the day his father died). About eight years later Margaret married John Neill, an elder in her father's church. He lived in Peters Township near where the Center Presbyterian Church now stands. He had had eight children by his first wife, who had died in 1808. Five children were born to his marriage with Margaret McMillan Watson. She died in 1853 at the age of seventy-two and was buried in the Center Church cemetery.

Mary, the third daughter, was born September 11, 1783. In 1810 she married John Weaver, a stone mason in Chartiers Township. There were nine children in their family. Mary McMillan Weaver spent her entire life near Canonsburg where she died on April 28, 1839, at the age of fifty-six.[45] She was buried in Chartiers Cemetery.

The youngest daughter, Catherine, was born May 28, 1785. She married, on October 30, 1805, Moses Allen, who had graduated that summer from Jefferson College and had begun his theological studies under her father.[46] It was Moses Allen who transcribed McMillan's theological lectures in 1806.[47] Later he was an active trustee of Jefferson College. His life work was his ministry at the Raccoon Church in Washington County. There were ten children born to Catherine and Moses Allen. Moses Allen died January 16, 1846. Catherine died April 30, 1857. She is buried at Crab Apple, Ohio.

John McMillan II, the sixth child, was born on the McMillan farm, October 9, 1787. He remained at home until 1811, when he married Rebecca Anderson. They began housekeeping on another part of the farm. Rebecca died in 1812, less than two weeks after she had given birth to John McMillan III. Two years later, on February 1, 1814, John II married Sarah Weaver, a sister of John Weaver, his brother-in-law. They had five children. Sarah Weaver McMillan died in 1824. After her death, John II married in 1825 Mary Johnston. They had six children.[48] His mother died in 1819 and Samuel, John's youngest brother, had been living in the McMillan manse caring for his father, now grown old. Samuel died in 1826. After Samuel's death John and his wife went to live at the manse, and Samuel's widow took John's home. Boyd Crumrine in his *History of Washington County* writes that the military draft of 1812 took four regiments of men from Washington County.[49] John II was in military service for nine months. He was described at that time as twenty-five years old, five feet and eleven inches tall, stout, dark of complexion, and a farmer. His death occurred suddenly on October 12, 1854, from a heart attack. He is buried in Chartiers Cemetery. His wife lived until early November, 1866.[50]

The youngest of the children was Samuel, born in the manse at Chartiers, December 5, 1789. In 1813, when he was twenty-four, he married Isabelle Harper. After their marriage they lived on with Samuel's parents at the manse, where four children were born to them. Samuel died on November 9, 1826, only thirty-seven years old. He was buried at Chartiers, too. When his wife died in 1876 she was eighty-one years old, the last among McMillan's sons and daughters-in-law.

Catherine Brown McMillan, the wife of John McMillan and the mother of the seven children, died on November 24, 1819, after forty-three years of marriage. She was, so it seems, a humble woman. After she left Brandywine in October or early November of 1778 (she had married in 1776), she never again, so far as is known, went back to her old home. Here and there letters and records show dim glimpses of the many matters that filled her days—her training of her seven sons and daughters, her care of students who lived at the manse, her going about other daily household work, her summer gardening, and her weaving in the winter months. Besides these, she had her part in the life of her community and her church. To be remembered, too, is the struggle of the earlier, pioneer years, when she and her husband first came to Chartiers.

In a letter to Matthew Brown dated October 1, 1846, Robert Patterson, remembering what Mrs. McMillan and Mrs. Joseph Smith did for the students writes: "I knew them well and they were both eminently mothers in Israel."[51]

Soon after the death of Catherine—a peaceful and triumphant death—McMillan wrote the Reverend Doctor Johnston of Newburgh, New York, a touching letter. He tells of his wife's difficulty in obtaining access to God during her illness and of her finding God again a little before she died. "She exhorted all around her to secure an interest in Christ, and to make that the main business of their lives."[52] The glory of God seemed to fill her bedroom. The way McMillan speaks of her in this letter and in others shows she was a loving wife, an admirable mother, and a consecrated servant of her God.

MINISTERS, LAYMEN, AND STUDENTS

McMillan was, of course, associated with many persons not of his family. With some his association was close. Near him on the frontier had settled three Presbyterian ministers, James Power, Thaddeus Dod, and Joseph Smith. McMillan and they ("The Four Presbyterian Horsemen of Western Pennsylvania"[53] they have been called) were united by a common purpose. Then, too, James Dunlap, Matthew Brown, and Matthew Henderson, of the Associate Presbytery were part of McMillan's life. Most of his friends were laymen, but few records survive of his friendship with them. More than a hundred students had sat under McMillan's theological teaching, many of whom came back later for counsel.

James Power, one of the three ministers mentioned as friends of McMillan's, had crossed the Allegheny Mountains in 1774, a year before McMillan's first crossing, and as a missionary, spent that summer on the frontier in what are now Washington, Allegheny, Westmoreland, and Fayette counties. In the fall of 1776, James Power and his wife and four daughters came over the Alleghenies by way of Laurel Hill on the "Braddock's Trail." They rode horseback—his wife on one horse, he on another with his oldest daughter behind him and his youngest, almost a baby, on a pillow before him. The two other children sat, each in a sort of hamper basket hung on either side of a led horse.[54] Power settled at Dunlap's Creek, near Brownsville, and preached at the church scocieties in that region. McMillan was the first "called" Presbyterian minister west of the Alleghenies, but Power was the first Presbyterian minister to bring his family over the mountains.[55] Power ministered at Dunlap's Creek, Laurel Hill, Tyrone, Unity, Vance's Fort, and other places. In 1779 he became resident pastor of the Sewickley and Mount Pleasant congregations in Westmoreland County.[56] In August 22, 1787, he was released by the Sewickley church because he wished to give all his time to his growing Mount Pleasant congregation. From that church he was to receive a yearly salary of 120 pounds.[57] Evidently, for many years, the relation between the Mount Pleasant congregation and James Power was a happy one. He was particularly interested in children and young people and they liked him. In the book, *Centennial of the Mount Pleasant Church,* he is described as:

a man of medium height, slender and erect. Unlike his co-laborer, Dr. McMillan, he was extremely neat in his dress and had acquired an easy and gracious manner. Though his voice was not loud, he could be heard at a great distance because of his remarkably clear and distinct enunciation. His sermons were expressed in well chosen words. With a memory for faces and names that was remarkable, he called every person by name throughout his entire district.[58]

Though he retired August 15, 1817, he lived among his people until he died on August 5, 1830 in his eighty-fifth year of age.

Tradition and written evidence show that McMillan and Power were friends. Tradition has it that the McMillans lodged with the Powers for one night, in 1778, on their way to Chartiers, and that the families had a pleasant evening together. The *Journal* gives a preaching appointment on the Thursday following the last Sabbath of June 1779 "at Mr. Powers."[59] At that time Power had been settled in his pastorate only a short while. Other entries show that they often assisted each other and that their friendship continued. Their ministries in parishes not far separated ran parallel for more than fifty years.

A second friendship of McMillan was Thaddeus Dod. He came in the fall of 1777 to Fort Lindley on Ten Mile Creek. It seems he knew Jacob Cook and Demas Lindley, two respected elders in the church who had come from New Jersey out to the frontier. These two men were happy to have him at Fort Lindley. The next year he brought his family from Patterson Creek, Virginia, where they had been taken when Indian outbreaks were reported on the settlements nearby. Dod was pastor of the churches at Lower Ten Mile and Upper Ten Mile, which were organized into one congregation with one bench of elders. They were ten miles from the county seat and ten miles apart. Dod had had much training earlier as a teacher of mathematics and Latin, and so it is not surprising that he opened a log cabin school in a building near his home. His son, Cephas Dodd,[60] (who added an extra *d* to the family name) wrote of his father:

He (The Rev. Thaddeus Dod) felt the importance of a better common school education, and, in order to promote it, visited the schools and counseled the teachers as to the best manner of performing their duties. For the special purpose of educating young men for the gospel ministry, he had a building erected within a few steps of his own dwelling, in which he opened a classical and mathematical school, in the spring of 1782.[61]

Thaddeus Dod had rare and fine abilities. He probably was a better teacher of Latin, Greek, Hebrew, and mathematics than any of his brethren.[62] He was an admirable preacher; and his people remembered his sermons as earnest, persuasive, and attractive. "He is said to have been more calm and less impassioned in his manner of preaching than most of the early ministers in this part of the country."[63] He was slender and sallow in complexion; but his eyes, it is recorded, were keen and lively. On April 1, 1789, he and John McMillan and Joseph Smith opened an academy at Washington, Pennsylvania, in the old Court House. This academy had been incorporated by the legislature of Pennsylvania, September 24, 1787. It had scarcely opened its doors when a fire destroyed the old Court House building. Dod went back to Ten Mile and his ministry there. His death on May 20, 1793 brought to an end his great work at Ten Mile.

He and McMillan never were intimate in their friendship. They were, though, friends, and they co-operated with one another in Presbytery and church and teaching. McMillan was one of the warm supporters of Washington Academy, which Dod headed, and it is thought that Dod and McMillan exchanged students in the early days of their log cabin schools. The *Journal* repeatedly refers to their joint ministry at the Lord's Supper. They were two of the four ministers who founded Redstone Presbytery. The others were James Power and Joseph Smith.

In the spring of 1779, the Reverend Joseph Smith came to the Western Country. He preached in several of the churches and then after a short visit returned to the East. A Call, dated June 21, 1779, followed him. It asked that he return to the frontier as a resident pastor, and it began: "A call from the United Congregations at Buffalo and Cross Creek, to the Rev. Joseph Smith, a member of the Presbytery of New Castle."[64] He was to receive seventy-five pounds from each congregation. To the Call were signed 204 names, a number which proves that many Presbyterians lived in the two communities.

Smith's great power was his preaching. Some thought him a "revival preacher." "He would often rise to an almost supernatural and unearthly grandeur, completely extinguishing in his hearers all consciousness of time and place."[65] Two who had heard both McMillan and Smith agree that Smith preached with an unusual eloquence. One of the two is quoted as saying, "It was altogether different from Dr. McMillan's manner. He was sometimes awfully solemn and impressive. But Mr. Smith's manner had a strange kind of power about it, totally indescribable."[66] To an unusual degree he gave himself to prayer. He would, at times, rise in the night and engage in intercessory prayer for any who had a special need.

Not later than 1785 he opened a school to train young men for the ministry. This school, called "The Study," was started in the kitchen of his home at Upper Buffalo. It was a Latin School; some believe it was "the first school that was opened with a special view to the training of young men for the sacred office."[67] Later, by mutual arrangement, this school for languages and sciences was moved to Chartiers, near Canonsburg, and placed under the care of McMillan. It became, in 1791, part of Canonsburg Academy.

The strain of Smith's ministry and his other labors was so constant and so severe that he died on April 19, 1792, when only fifty-six.

McMillan in the *Journal* often writes of his and Smith's exchanging pulpits. These references suggest strong friendship between the two. Some later writers suggested there may have been rivalry among the three schools—the Smith School, the Dod School, and the McMillan School. There is no evidence of unfriendliness among the four men of God who came to western Pennsylvania almost at the same time. "The Rev. Messrs. McMillan, Dod, and Smith were not rivals nor antagonists; they co-operated harmoniously in the cause of education and religion."[68]

James Dunlap, a graduate of the College of New Jersey and former member of New Castle Presbytery, might well be called the "fifth horseman." He came within the bounds of Redstone Presbytery soon after it was organized and was the first minister to apply to it for admission.[69] Dunlap's Creek had extended a Call to him, and in October, 1782, he was ready to begin his pastorate there. He had already been teaching a few young men who wished to be ministers. He was, the *History of Jefferson College* tells, exceptionally qualified to teach languages. One biographer has written of him: "He was especially distinguished for his accurate attainments in classical literature."[70] The *History* quotes Joseph Smith as saying of him: his "person was small, his features pleasing, and his manners popular. His health was not very robust; but his conscientious diligence in the discharge of his duties secured him the respect and affection of the Trustees and students."[71] That he was held in high esteem seems proved by his being selected as a member of the first board of trustees of Jefferson College and later, in April of 1803, as second president of the College.

McMillan seems to have liked and respected him: in 1807 when Dunlap wished to resign, "several of the Trustees," says the *History*, "including Dr. McMillan, were anxious that he would not withdraw from their service."[72] He did not leave the College until 1811, when the infirmities of age made it expedient he resign. As friends and associates Dunlap and McMillan saw many things eye to eye.

Among those who were part of McMillan's life, though in the background of it, is Matthew Henderson. Henderson was born in Scotland in 1735 and came to America after he had finished his theological training.[73] He served the churches at Oxford and Muddy Creek in Chester County and lived within six miles of the McMillan homestead. They were unquestionably friends before they came to the West. He became pastor, in 1782, of the Associate congregations of Chartiers and Buffalo, and about a year later he and his family settled at Chartiers. He worked earnestly and ably with McMillan. He and McMillan are listed as trustees of the Academy organized at Washington, Pennsylvania, in 1787. After the burning in 1789 or 1790 of the Court House, the two went together to see J. Hoge, Esq. and others in an attempt—unsuccessful —to get contributions for the school.[74] In July of 1791, just before Canonsburg Academy was organized, he with McMillan and others spent the greater part of a day in prayer for the Academy. At the opening of the Canonsburg Academy in 1791 he was called upon for the dedicatory, or consecration, prayer. Since he was seventeen years older than McMillan and McMillan liked and valued him, no doubt McMillan went to him as a counselor and fatherly friend. Matthew Henderson was killed in 1785 by a falling tree. It is written, "All who knew him were exceedingly grieved at his passing."

Another minister, a contemporary of McMillan in the Western Country though twenty-four years younger than he, was Matthew Brown. He was born in 1776, studied at Dickinson College, Carlisle, Pennsylvania, and after a short pastorate in Huntingdon Presbytery, Maryland, came in 1805 to Washington, Pennsylvania. "There he labored in the double capacity of pastor and principal of the Academy, having an assistant to aid him in the business of giving instruction."[75] When Washington College was chartered in 1806 he was elected its president. Ten years later, because of dissatisfaction, he resigned as president of Washington College but continued pastor of the church. In 1822 he was elected president of Jefferson College. McMillan seems to have enjoyed his friendship with Matthew Brown. Brown, for eight years after he went to Canonsburg in 1822, preached a part of each Sabbath at Chartiers. McMillan then was in his seventieth year. Long after the death of McMillan, Matthew Brown became one of his most kindly biographers.[76]

The life of John McMillan was touched by the lives of many laymen. When he first came to Chartiers and Pigeon Creek, Patrick McCullough, Arthur Forbus, Patrick Scott, John McDowell, and others had been most helpful. James Ross was one of his first teachers and the friendship continued down through the years. In the days when the Canonsburg Academy idea was developing some of the same men, namely Colonel John Canon, James Allison, Alexander Cook, Esq., James Foster, Thomas Brecker, and Robert Ralston, and others whose names are not recorded worked with him in this educational project. At Chartiers, on the session, McMillan planned and served over the years with John McDowell, James Allison, Moses Coe, George Craighead, James Foster, Samuel Logan, Thomas Briceland, Richard Johnston, Samuel Miller, John Neill, and John Phillips. At Pigeon Creek the elders were James Wherry, Patrick McCullough, Hugh Scott, William McCombs, and Patrick Scott.[77] During the Whiskey Insurrection, in 1794, and the political activities of that year McMillan went among the people and talked among them earnestly about such matters as submission to decrees of the newly organized federal government, the need of keeping even judgment in the difficult times, and the importance of voting for a congressman who would give right leadership. In the activities of his churches and of the College he was associated with hundreds of laymen. Each of these and many others contributed to McMillan's rich experience.

The students who sat under McMillan in his log cabin school or in the divinity courses at Jefferson College were immeasurably benefited by having him as a teacher. A great number of them he boarded without charge in his home.[78] Three of the McMillan daughters, Jean, Margaret, and Catherine, married young ministers who had studied under their father. Of the estimated one hundred who had some training with him a good number shared part of his later experiences. John Watson and William Moorehead were the two sons-in-law whose promising careers were cut short the same day. Moses Allen, another of his sons-in-law, served a church in the Canonsburg region and later was trustee of Jefferson College. William McMillan, his nephew, was, in 1802, graduated in Jefferson's first class and later became president of the College. James McGready studied under McMillan and lived at his home in the early days of the log cabin school. Near the beginning of the nineteenth century McGready started a mighty revival in Kentucky which spread far through the West. Andrew Wylie, one of the most distinguished graduates of Jefferson, was elected to the presidency of that College two years after his graduation. Later, he was president of Washington College and of Indiana University.

Chartiers, his wife and sons and daughters, his brothers and sisters, those ministers who were his friends and with whom he worked, laymen, and students—these all made up much of McMillan's living. His home became the western settlements; its center, Chartiers. And always the church, which meant so much to him and which he served so faithfully, was dominant in his long life.

III. NOTES

1. The *Journal*, Part I. See Appendix A.
2. Records of Donegal Presbytery. III. 336. See also the *Journal*, Part I.
3. Records of Yogohania County. March 24, 1778. Cf. *Centenary Memorial*. 407, 408.
4. See Appendix A, Part II.
5. McMillan's Letter to Carnahan. See Appendix C.
6. George Chambers. *A Tribute to the Principles, Virtues, Habits and Public Usefulness of the Irish and Scotch Early Settlers of Pennsylvania*. 138.
7. Boyd Crumrine. "Chartiers Presbyterian Church," an article in D. M. Bennett's *Life and Work of Rev. John McMillan, D.D.* 280, 281. See also Boyd Crumrine's *History of Washington County*. 877.
8. David X. Junkin. "Life and Labors of the Rev. John McMillan, D.D.," *Centenary Memorial*. 27.
9. Bennett. 329, 330. This description was written by Mr. Bennett after a trip to the old manse in March, 1932. It was then intact but has since been dismantled.

10. Samuel J. M. Eaton. *Lakeside.* 18. Also Joseph Doddridge. *Notes on the Settlement and Indian Wars.* 88.
11. McMillan's Expense Account. See Appendix B.
12. *Ibid.*
13. A letter from John Watson to John McMillan, May 13, 1796.
14. William B. Sprague. *Annals of the American Pulpit.* III. 355.
15. James Veech. "The Secular History," *Centenary Memorial.* 30. See A. B. Hulbert. *Pioneer Roads and Experiences of Travelers.* II. 64-93. This volume is No. 12 in the series, *Historic Highways of America.*
16. *Centenary Memorial.* 22.
17. Charles A. Hanna. *Ohio Valley Genealogies.* xxiv.
18. William W. McKinney. *Early Pittsburgh Presbyterianism.* 32-37.
19. *Records of the Presbyterian Church, 1706-1788.* Minutes, May, 1776. See W. F. Dunaway. *A History of Pennsylvania.* 350.
20. *Ibid.* 376.
21. Joseph Smith. *Old Redstone.* 240-244.
22. Doddridge. 94-96.
23. Solon J. and Elizabeth H. Buck. *The Planting of Civilization in Western Pennsylvania.* 131.
24. *Ibid.* 133.
25. *Ibid.*
26. Joseph Smith. *History of Jefferson College.* 413, 414.
27. *Allegheny County Will Book.* I. 61. (typed copy)
28. The *Journal,* Part II. See Appendix A.
29. *Ibid.* Part I.
30. *Ibid.*
31. *Allegheny County Will Book.* I. 61.
32. *Ibid.* III. 93.
33. *Ibid.*
34. See Appendix A, Part II.
35. *Allegheny County Will Book.* I. 61.
36. See Appendix A, Part II.
37. David Elliott. *The Life of the Rev. Elisha Macurdy.* 283.
38. Bennett. 342.
39. Recorded in Washington County Court House. *Will Book.* V. 108.
40. *Pennsylvania Archives.* Sixth Series. II. 105.
41. Hubert Rex Johnston. *A History of the Neshannock Presbyterian Church, New Wilmington, Pa.* 166.
42. *Ibid.*
43. *Will Book.* III. 292. Mercer County Court House.
44. Elliott. Appendix, 261.
45. Bennett. 336, 381ff.
46. "Moses Allen," a paper prepared by his grandson, M. R. Allen, of Washington, Pennsylvania.
47. Mrs. Helen Wragg has a transcribed copy of these lectures.
48. Bennett. 419.
49. Crumrine. *History of Washington County.* 306f.
50. Bennett. 419-421.
51. *Old Redstone.* 81.
52. *Ibid.* 202.
53. McKinney. 45.
54. *Old Redstone.* 225.

55. Elliott. 277.
56. James I. Brownson. *Centennial Celebration of the Presbyterian Church of Mount Pleasant.* 9.
57. *Old Redstone.* 231.
58. McKinney. 51.
59. See Appendix A, Part II.
60. Thaddeus Dod spelled his surname Dod, but his son Cephas spelled his name Dodd.
61. *Presbyterian Magazine.* September, 1854. Also *History of Jefferson College.* 9.
62. *Old Redstone.* 144.
63. Elliott. 303.
64. *Old Redstone.* 61, 62.
65. *Ibid.* 67.
66. *Ibid.*
67. *Ibid.* 76.
68. Francis J. Collier. Address, "Chartiers Church and Its Ministers," *Centennial Celebration of Chartiers Church.* 13. McKinney. 214.
69. *Old Redstone.* 318. Smith has recorded in detail the forty-one meetings of Redstone Presbytery from September 19, 1781 to October 15, 1793.
70. Elliott. 260.
71. *History of Jefferson College.* 67.
72. *Ibid.* 87, footnote.
73. *Ibid.* 234, 235.
74. *Ibid.* 12.
75. *Ibid.* 184.
76. *Old Redstone.* 166-215. Smith's sketch of John McMillan is taken in part from an unfinished biography of McMillan by Matthew Brown.
77. Crumrine. "Chartiers Presbyterian Church," Bennett. 277-284.
78. *History of Jefferson College.* 417.

IV. CHURCH

WITHOUT question, John McMillan is the father of the Presbyterian churches in the West. This title he deserved from the time he settled at Chartiers. He deserved it for many reasons. He was the first settled pastor of the Presbyterian Church in the West: itinerant ministers had preached there but McMillan was the first to accept a Call to serve in any of the parishes. McMillan realized there was great need for Christ and His church and gave his whole heart, unselfishly, with immense ability and great good sense and unending work to carry out the mission which had brought him to Pennsylvania. He did succeed, so far as success is ever possible, in his work for his Master. James Allison has said:

Dr. John McMillan is admitted to have been at the head of those noble ministers of the gospel who laid the foundations of the Church and education in western Pennsylvania, in enterprise, breadth of view, boldness of design and force of character. These qualities by common consent gave him his high and honored position of leader.[1]

So for fifty-five years after he had settled at Chartiers, McMillan served the church through his charges at Chartiers and Pigeon Creek, through his ministry to other churches, through his preaching and revival services, and through his teaching.

CHARTIERS AND PIGEON CREEK

McMillan was the first pastor of the Chartiers and Pigeon Creek congregations. It is possible, though unlikely, that these churches had been organized before he preached at the settlements late in the summer of 1775. By that time, many substantial Scotch-Irish had settled along Chartiers and Pigeon Creeks. They were intensely eager to have religious services in their settlements. Occasionally Presbyterian clergymen on tour, among them Charles Beatty, George Duffield, and Levi Frisbee, preached at Fort Pitt, and one or all the three may have come to Chartiers or Pigeon Creek. Certainly, John Power, in the summer of 1774, for three months did missionary work in what are now Allegheny, Fayette, Washington, and Westmoreland Counties[2] and preached both at Chartiers and Pigeon Creek. As Boyd Crumrine writes, "There can be no doubt that the settlers had previously met many times for divine worship."[3] In both settlements, the desire for religious services was so strong that pious laymen often met at some home for "social worship." At such a meeting there were singing, praying, Bible reading, and, though not often, the reading of a sermon. "The guiding spirits in the early Presbyterian meetings were often made ruling elders when a congregation was formally organized, McDowell and James Allison of Chartiers, James Wherry and Patrick Scott of Pigeon Creek, and other ruling elders led in meetings; at best, poor substitutes for the formal church service.

When McMillan on his first missionary trip came to Chartiers Creek, he preached at the house of John McDowell. The *Journal* entry reads: "Saturday travelled about 16 miles to John McDowell's on Shirtee Creek where I tarried till Monday morning. The 4th Sabbath of August preached at said John McDowell's."[5] As there was no church building, the service probably was held out of doors, perhaps near McDowell's house or under a spreading tree. The next Tuesday McMillan preached at Arthur Forbus' on Pigeon Creek and then went ahead in his tour among the churches until he recrossed the Alleghenies.

Only a few months after his first visit, McMillan came again to Chartiers and Pigeon Creek, and on most of the Sabbaths from January until the end of March, 1776, he preached at one of these settlements or the other. This seems to indicate that by the time he made his second visit he had decided that when a Call was given him by the two churches he would accept it. If the congregations had not been organized before McMillan's visit, the visit brought them together.[6]

An obituary notice of a clergyman, Reid Bracken, in the *Presbyterian Advocate,* August 1849, has in it a reference to McMillan and the Chartiers Church. Bracken, it seems, had been brought from York County to Washington County in September 1778, when he was six weeks old. This obituary says he was the first child McMillan baptized at Chartiers Church. What McMillan writes in a letter to James Carnahan seems to contradict this: "I however visited them as often as I could, ordained elders, baptized their children, and took as much care of them as circumstances would permit."[7] Yet if the word "church" in the obituary is taken as meaning the sacred building, and not the congregation of people, the statements agree and Bracken was the first infant baptized in the newly built church.

At first the buildings used by the congregations at Chartiers and Pigeon Creek were called meeting-houses.[8] In the *Journal* many entries tell of McMillan's preaching on his first visit at a meeting-house. One is the "Forks meeting-house," another, "a meeting-house on Long Run."[9] McMillan preached, in August, 1779, in a meeting-house at Laurel Hill. Johnson gives this description of it:

> The Laurel Hill Presbyterian Church in Fayette County, erected in 1772, was built entirely with the ax. No nails were used—the clapboard roof was secured by logs and the doors by wooden pins. Small openings in the logs, glazed with paper or white linen oiled with lard or bear grease, served as windows. The seats were of cleft logs set in blocks. The raising of a log church was a gala occasion; the entire community assembled, bringing ox teams and tools to cut and notch the logs. Through the forethought and generosity of some individual, a jug of whiskey was often provided to cheer the workers. The smaller churches were four-sided and each side was a single log's length.[10]

In summer open air services were possible and common. Other seasons brought need of shelter.

Since McMillan's visits to Chartiers and Pigeon Creek were infrequent for the first two years of his pastorate, it is thought that no meeting-houses were built in the two places until after he came permanently to Chartiers. Probably they were built soon after 1778. A record dated 1782 shows John Robinson, being duly sworn, attested "that sometime in May last, at the Meeting House of Revd. Mr. McMillan, a large number of people being convened. . . ."[11] This reference to "The Meeting House of Revd. Mr. McMillan" directly contradicts Joseph Smith's opinion "that no churches or houses of worship were erected in the country until about 1790."[12] But Smith may be in error because he takes too literally some phrasing in a series of papers written by Judge Wilkeson:[13] it cannot be established that the buildings called "meeting houses," though they were used at times for general purposes, were not churches.

The first Presbyterian church at Chartiers probably was built in 1778. It was made of logs. It was unheated. It had in it no organ. Its congregation did not sing hymns, but psalms, nor was the church a place for vain displays. Indeed by 1778 there were few luxuries in the West. Even clothing was scarce. Smith says: "Among the men who attended public worship in the winter, ten were obliged to substitute a blanket or a coverlet for a great coat, where one enjoyed the luxury of that article."[14] This early log church was used until 1800. Then a church was built of stone—of stone, it is told, got from an Indian mound that topped the nearby hill.[15] The new stone church had stoves to heat it. And—to look forward a generation—the second structure was enlarged and bettered in 1832, at about the time Lemuel F. Leake succeeded McMillan as

JOHN McMILLAN

pastor at Chartiers. These are the major early dates for the church at Chartiers.

But back in the 1790's McMillan and his congregation had their young church to build up. It prospered so much that after the General Assembly of the Commonwealth passed its Act of 1791 the Church applied to the State for a charter. This application stated the purpose of the association was to worship God. On the application the signatures of thirty-four members follow McMillan's. Nine men from the congregation are listed as the first trustees. The Act of 1791 had made clear that the issuance of a charter to any church had no religious implications. A charter was issued solely to establish the church as a corporation and a body politic in the law. The Chartiers Church was granted its charter as of March 28, 1798.[16]

Two documents, both in McMillan's writing, deal with the members of Chartiers Church. One is in the possession of Mrs. John A. Wragg, a great-great-great granddaughter of McMillan. It is a record of reception of communicants. On the outside cover McMillan has written:

A Memorandum Book of such as have been admitted to the Sacrament of the Supper in the congregation of Chartiers from June, 1815, to February, 1830. Total admitted to the Church on examination from May, 1797, to February, 1830, was 450. Of these 30 became Ministers of the Gospel.

Each entry opens with such phrases as "to the sacrament of the Supper, administered in June, 1815, were admitted on examination," [names listed] . . . "on certificate" [names listed]. The list of June, 1816 includes "Alice Kopkins (a black woman)." Another "black woman" was received in February, 1819, a third in September, 1823 and a "black man" in September, 1824. These negroes may have been slaves in such families as the Canons, the Morgans, the McDowells, the Allisons, or even in McMillan's own household. The entries show that brotherhood was alive in pastor and people.

The second document is the "Records of Chartiers Church." It was owned by Francis J. Collier before 1875 but is now lost. These records, Collier tells, cover the eighteen or nineteen years from 1807 to 1825. They were written in very fine script on thirty-two pages of rough unglazed paper, a size smaller than "commercial note." Twenty-one cases of discipline were recorded, and in each instance the charge, the testimony, the verdict, and the sentence were given. Collier sums up a number of the cases:

A civil magistrate was severely censured for marrying a couple in jest. A postmaster wno had been accused of breaking the Sabbath by opening and distributing the mail, and was dismissed from the church at Washington, made application for admission to Chartiers, and was received and restored to his church privileges. The decision in this case written by Dr. McMillan, covers a page and a half, and is clear and forcible. It shows that the accused was a conscientious man; that he had protested against the requirements of the Post Office Department, and had tendered his resignation, which was not accepted.[17]

The "Records," written by McMillan are preces of session cases and actions, not full records of the session, which have been kept by the clerk. McMillan has left a great deal of his writing, all in longhand. The two records, 135 or more sermons of a dozen pages each, the *Journal* and *Diary,* the *Expense Account,* 250 pages of theological lectures, and other writings reveal something of McMillan's constant industry with the pen.[18] The "Records of Chartiers Church" might have had in it a reference to George Washington if Washington had not followed the advice of John Canon. The "Diaries" of George Washington say that he visited "Col. John Canon" in Washington County during September, 1784, and almost fell into grievous error. Washington owned much land in that region. He had appointed Canon "to collect the rents from his western tenantry."[19] Since he wished to shorten his stay, Washington thought of taking care of some business on the Sabbath. What the following entry shows he did, undoubtedly was done because of the Colonel's advice:

19th, Being Sunday, and the People living on my land apparently very religious, it was thought best to postpone going among them till tomorrow —but rode to Doctr. Johnsons (John Johnson) who had the keeping of Colo. Crawfords (surveying) records—but not finding him at home was disappointed in the business which carried me there.[20]

Washington's tenants lived in McMillan's parish, probably were members of his church. Had the Sabbath been violated as the General had first thought of doing, probably McMillan would not have kept a silent tongue. It seems reasonable to believe that McMillan met Washington on this tour of the West.

The parish of Pigeon Creek, which McMillan held from 1776 till he resigned it in 1793, covered a wide territory. Here were "from the first, some eminently pious people who had emigrated from Nottingham, Chester County; and the Spirit of God was remarkably poured out several times during Dr. McMillan's ministry among them."[21] In many ways its history parallels Chartiers. Its first church was of logs with clapboard roof and a clapboard door, and it was not heated. It, too, was replaced in a few years by a stone church, and in 1829 by the present brick building. Once

JOHN McMILLAN

in the early days of the church history, the floor gave way during the service and carried the congregation with it to the ground.[22] No one was injured. The families of Pigeon Creek were asked to supply their own pews and "the variety of styles was almost as bytery met at Pigeon Creek more often than anywhere else; "and here by the remarkable orderings of Divine Providence, they held great as the number of pews."[23] Smith reports that Redstone Prestheir first meeting."[24] For a little over seventeen years McMillan carried on the pastorates of both this Church and the Church of Chartiers. Then in 1793 he asked the Church and the Presbytery to permit him to give his pastoral labors wholly to Chartiers. Boyd Mercer was formally called in 1794; he had, however, been a supply at Pigeon Creek before that. McMillan also continued to preach as a supply. McMillan did not stop his occasional visits to the other churches. Indeed, his missionary work had become so much a part of his life that he went on with it until the end of his ministry.

OTHER CHURCHES

To McMillan, a part of his mission and high privilege was to organize and to help as many churches as he could. On his earliest journey in the West he preached, first, at Mt. Moriah, August, 1775. Because of rain not many were present, but, the *Journal* says, "a few tears were shed."[25] On that first journey he preached at many places: John Armstrong's on Muddy Creek, John McKibben's on Dunlap Creek, James Pickett's, Pentecost's, Forks Meeting House, Shirtee Creek (Chartiers), Pigeon Creek, Thomas Cook's, a meeting-house on the Monongahela, David Andrew's, Josiah Richard's on Robinson Run, Fort Pitt, Long Run, Hannastown, William Perry's on Loyal Hanna, Conemaugh, Proctor's tent, James McMillan's, and Ligonier.[26] Because few of the settlements McMillan went to had meeting-houses, he preached often in the open, near the farm house. Word of time and place had to be sent ahead to the next settlement at which services would be held. Several times notice did not reach the community, or the day and hour of preaching were not understood. Usually the time and the place were of necessity fixed by the schedule of the itinerant preacher. The settlers could almost always fit their plans to his.[27]

On his second tour, in January, February, and March of 1776, McMillan revisited many of the places where he had already preached and went to several new ones. On that tour he first preached at David Allen's. At Henry Newkirk's he preached on Luke 13:5, and at Thomas Edgerton's on Matthew 16:26. Later he was at Jacob Long's, at John Munn's on Mingo Creek, at John Canon's, at John Allen's, at a Baptist meeting-house on Pike Run, and at another Baptist center near Monongahela.

McMillan, when he came on his third journey, was the pastor-elect of the Chartiers and Pigeon Creek Churches. He, however, had the right to preach in other places; during the few weeks of this visit he held services at Long Run, Peter's Creek, and James Breadon's on Ten Mile,[28] and on his third visit, in 1777, he held services at Mount Pleasant and Hannastown. After he had settled at Chartiers (November, 1778) he was for many years away from his charge about one Sabbath and the following Monday of each month. In this way he helped organize many churches and preached to many congregations which had no pastor.

McMillan helped especially the Peter's Creek Church which later divided into Bethel and Lebanon. He is recognized as having organized the Peter's Creek Church on November 5, 1776. On his third missionary journey McMillan writes in his *Journal* of one incident: "Monday (November 4, 1776), I went down to my brother's house. Tuesday, preached at Peter's Creek, baptized 5 children."[29] Both Bethel and Lebanon accept this as the date of their foundings, though the two had services together until sometime after 1785.[30] McMillan preached about twice a year at Peter's Creek until John Clark became pastor there in 1783. But it was McMillan's zeal which organized the Peter's Creek congregation before they divided and took the names Bethel and Lebanon. William C. Degelman says: "Rev. John Clark possibly suggested these names to his congregations as he had previously been pastor of two Bethel churches and travelled the Lebanon valley during his early ministry."[31] A pulpit chair preserved at Bethel Church and dating back it seems to 1780 was used by McMillan. "This chair," says Degelman, "is probably the oldest and rarest piece of original church furniture west of the Allegheny mountains."

The *Journal* entries usually record, side by side with the place and the date and the text, the stipend McMillan received for each of his services away from Chartiers. Here are typical entries, from the *Journal* of May and June, 1781.

The 1st Sab. of May at Shirtee from Phil. 3.8
The 2d. Sab. at Pidgeon Creek from—Rom. 5.20
The 3d. Sab. at lower Cross Creek and the monday following at upper. Thursday at Shirtee being the fast from—Hos. 2.19
The 4th Sab. at Shirtee from—Song. 5.1 and administered the Sacrament of the Supper being assisted by revd. Joseph Smith who preached Saturday, Sab. evening and Monday.

The 1st Sab. of June at Shirtee from—Hos. 2.19
The 2d. Sab. at Pidgeon Creek from—Act. 16.33. Josh. 24.15
The 3d. Sab. at Peter's Creek received 142L 3s 10d
The 4th Sab. at Shirtee from—Rom. 8.6
    Thursday ye 28th of June 1781, Margaret McMillan was born between eleven and twelve o'clock at night.[32]

The amount of these stipends is rather startling. On the third Sabbath of June, 1781 he received L142, 3s, and 10d. The total gifts for five services exceeded $800 in Pennsylvania currency of the time, and at least five other Sabbaths are mentioned on which money may have been received and not recorded.

On the first Sabbath of December, 1781, McMillan preached at the Raccoon Church near Midway in Washington County and received L7, 10s, and 6d. He was there in June of 1779 when he received L13, 17s, and 3d, and again in June of 1780 when he received L46, 11s, and 6d. It is thought that other ministers had preached earlier at Raccoon Church, but that church points to McMillan's first visit as the date of its beginning.[33] Thirty-nine years later the son-in-law of McMillan, Moses Allen, who married Catherine McMillan, became the second pastor of the Raccoon congregation.

Another church with which McMillan was familiar was Long Run Church. He preached there first on Wednesday, September 13, 1775; in October of 1776 he held services there and baptized fourteen children; in 1781 he preached there again. The Long Run Church, for want of a more certain date, has taken the year 1781, the year of the erection of Redstone Presbytery by the Synod of New York and Philadelphia, as the date of its organization.[34]

The Montour Church, first called Manture's Run, was another mission church which McMillan aided. Until 1789 it depended upon Redstone Presbytery for supply preaching. The congregation built in 1789 its first church and called Joseph Patterson to serve them in conjunction with his Raccoon charge. As early as 1785 McMillan preached to the Montour people. He was the first minister assigned by the Presbytery to preach among them. The Redstone minutes read: "at Mantures, ye 5th Sab. of July."[35] McMillan has an honored part in the story of Old Montour Church.[36]

Other congregations—Cross Roads (King's Creek), Cross Creek, Jefferson, New Providence, and Neshannock of Mercer County—were helped by John McMillan in their early days.[37] The *Journal* states that Conemaugh had agreed to build a meeting-house. Such a statement shows that McMillan had given the congregation counsel and direction. There were many other churches he helped.

Whether he stood in the pulpit or moved among his people as their pastor, McMillan's character and special power made him a wise and strong leader; and his missionary spirit and energy and foresight immensely advanced Presbyterianism in all the western settlements.

THE PULPIT

A typical church service by McMillan began with his solemnly and reverently ascending his pulpit and calling out in stentorian tones: "Let us worship God." The people then rose and sang *Old Hundredth,* "All people that on earth do dwell;" or perhaps they sang Psalm 84, "How lovely is thy dwelling place."[38]

In his pulpit he was somber and austere. E. H. Gilbert has written: "He was almost a Knox in boldness, energy and decision."[39] Like John the Baptist he had a unique power that made him seem "The voice of one crying in the wilderness."

McMillan wrote out his sermons in full and memorized them. He wrote them on pages of such a size that he could put them in a pocket Bible, hold the pages with his thumb, and by careful manipulation keep his audience from realizing that he had even so much as short notes. It is remarkable, indeed, that he was able to hide the mechanics of mind and hand while he was preaching with vehemence and profound conviction. James Carnahan says: "He had, I think, no great talent at extemporaneous preaching,— at least in early life."[40]

All McMillan's ministry was centered in Christ. After the fashion of his day he dwelt long on the awful danger of the sinner exposed to the wrath of God, who was both holy and just. William Neill testifies that as he sat under that thundering voice with its clear expositions of Biblical truth and solemn warnings, he was "often roused, terrified and melted to tears." He adds that McMillan's preaching made him "to feel that he was a sinner and that it was a fearful thing to be in a state of condemnation, with the wrath of God abiding on him."[41] He later renunciated his sinful ways and became a minister of the Gospel.

There were times when the seriousness of what he preached so moved McMillan that his voice was raised and his words poured forth in a torrent that offended the more delicate ears.[42] Dr. Clarence E. McCartney says a statement is recorded that one declared he had heard clearly at the distance of a mile McMillan's voice as he said in his sermon—"The Sovereign Grace of Almighty God."[43] When asked how Dr. McMillan preached a very old lady replied, "Oh! but did he riddle the sinners over hell."[44]

Occasionally he was truly eloquent. Moses Allen wrote:

> He could, however, move and melt in the sweet strains of gospel grace. Dr. McMillan was sometimes truly eloquent, When absorbed by his subject, he could, unconsciously to himself, throw into particular words and phrases a deep-toned tenderness of pathos that was quite peculiar, that has more than once reminded us, at least, of Garrick's remark, that he would give a hundred guineas to be able to pronounce the interjection O! after Whitefield's manner.[45]

God's sovereignty and God's grace were the pillars that upheld the homilitic structure of McMillan's times, and they were body and soul of his message. Yet when divine law and the need of salvation had been made known, the emphasis or application was to the hearts and feelings of his hearers. McMillan's appeal was for an entire change of heart.

REVIVALS

The revivals of the early eighteenth century in the middle colonies did much to bring revivals under McMillan at Chartiers and Pigeon Creek. Colonial revivals began with those of Theodorus J. Frelinghuysen, a pietistic pastor of four Dutch Reformed Churches in the Raritan Valley, New Jersey.[46] These prepared the way for later Presbyterian revivals under the Tennents and other Log College enthusiasts. Gilbert Tennent, the eldest son of his illustrious father, became the moving force in awakening the Scotch-Irish people to their spiritual need. His revival movement in New Jersey " 'was essentially an original movement' and not merely an expansion of the revival among the Dutch Reformed."[47]

Among those trained at the Log College in the revival method of evangelism were Samuel and John Blair. Samuel Blair led a revival at Nottingham in the spring of 1740, and John Blair preached as a revival leader in Hanover County, Virginia, in 1743.[48] During their pastorates at Fagg's Manor they did not diminish in their evangelistic fervor. Thomas Murphy has written of Samuel Blair at Fagg's Manor: "Almost immediately after his settlement there began one of the most wonderful revivals of that age of extraordinary religious interest."[49] Robert Smith, the founder of Pequea Academy, had the same intensity and purpose. With John Blair at Fagg's Manor and Smith at Pequea, McMillan came deeply to believe that Christianity was a matter of the heart, as it was of the head. This belief was strengthened in McMillan by the insistence of the "New Side" that a conversion experience was "a prerequisite to entrance into the ministry."[50] In a letter to Carnahan in March, 1832, he refers to his having received at the revival under Smith at Pequea his first deeply religious experience. If McMillan had had no conversion experience of his own until that time, the new experience would fit him to join the Log College-Princeton group of ministers. A revival which took place under John Witherspoon in McMillan's first year at Princeton had, too, left with him an indelible impression.

The revivals throughout the colonies and his own religious experience did much to make McMillan "eminently, 'a revival preacher.' "[51] From the first his ministry was an endeavor not only to edify Christians but also to bring to Jesus Christ those unsaved. The first revival under him began on a Thursday morning in December of 1781, a day which had been set by Congress as a day of thanksgiving for the surrender of Cornwallis at Yorktown. Many of McMillan's people at Chartiers were touched when he suggested that they mingle their thanksgiving for national blessings with calling upon God for the presence of His Holy Spirit among men. In his sermon McMillan reminded his congregation of the many irresponsible and irreligious people who had come into their midst during the years of the Revolution. The congregation were visibly touched and were moved to action.

They were encouraged to appoint other meetings for the same purpose; and the favorable appearances still increasing they continued to hold "Sabbath night societies" (or prayer meetings) for nearly two years. It was then usual to spend the whole night in religious exercises. "Nor did the time seem tedious," says McMillan, in his letter to Dr. Carnahan, "for the Lord was there and His work went pleasantly on."[52]

There were forty-five accessions to the church at the first communion service during this revival. "This time of refreshing continued in a greater or less degree till 1794."[53] After each sacramental occasion in those twelve years a number entered into the church through the revival efforts.

During the time of the first revival McMillan appointed a day for all the children within a reasonable distance to come to his home. After talking solemnly to them in words they could understand he asked each to come to him, where he was standing. He then suggested that each give him his hand and make a solemn promise to remember his creator and to pray daily for a new heart. "Dr. McMillan, shortly before his death, said he believed a great

The second revival under McMillan was in 1795. He says of it number of those children became members of the church."[54] in a letter to Carnahan:

This, however, was not very extensive nor of long continuance; yet during this year about fifty were added to the church, most of them continued by their walk and conversation to manifest that they had experienced a real change of heart; and some of them became successful preachers of the gospel though there were some lamentable instances of apostacy.[55]

In the spring of 1799 came a third revival within his church. He said that the Lord again revived his congregation at Chartiers. Many of the people of the community and several of the students were awakened to a serious concern about their immortal souls and made to enquire about salvation. About sixty united with his church. "This revival," said McMillan, "as well as that of 1795, was carried on without much external appearance, except a solemn attention and silent weeping under the preaching of the word."[56] His way of preaching the Word was sometimes fearful and wonderful. He so denounced vice that no one could mistake his meaning and few of the guilty could do other than feel the barbs of conscience pricking them. "His descriptions of the wrath of God and the danger and doom of the impenitent were awful."[57] Yet at times his preaching was so mellowed by Divine Grace that he won his listeners to Christ by setting forth His love.

The great revival in McMillan's church was the fourth. This was really part of the "Great Revival in the West," 1797-1805. The "Great Revival" began in southwestern Kentucky and from there spread southeastward into North Carolina and northeastward into the Upper Ohio Valley.[58] James McGready, who had been a pupil under McMillan, started this revival. Of its effects he wrote to McMillan in a letter dated November 18, 1802:

We have but few instances of apostacy since our beloved revival began. It is true there are many instances of persons being alarmed, and sometimes struck down under deep convictions, who have grown careless again, but the instances are very rare of persons who have professed to have obtained real religion, going back again.[59]

During the spring and summer of 1802 there were signs of the revival fervor in the Cross Roads and Upper Buffalo Churches. Then on the last Sabbath of September Elisha Macurdy at Three Springs saw the revival begin at his communion service. The heightened spirit was so strong that, at the end of the service held the next Monday evening, those assembled were unwilling to leave the grounds. They remained together all that night and until noon the next day, in great concern and anguish of spirit.

This was a very solemn season; the people were almost universally bowed, some deeply affected and lying prostrate, their cries for mercy enough to pierce the Heavens, while they appeared to be on the brink of despair.[60]

McMillan's churches were not without a part in this Great Revival. He says that from 1799 to 1802 there was gross indifference about religion except in the few who had been brought under serious impressions in 1799; that sinners had grown bold in their sinning; that even the efforts of the pious had become weak; that few were prepared to meet the Lord and bid Him welcome; that the coming of the revival in 1802 so astonished even the pious that its coming seemed like a dream; and that this fourth revival differed from his others in that generally the body was strangely affected. He wrote to James Carnahan:

It was no unusual thing to see persons so entirely deprived of bodily strength that they would fall from their seats, or off their feet, and be as unable to help themselves as a new-born child. I have seen some lying in this condition for hours who yet said they could hear everything that was spoken; and yet their minds were composed and more capable of attending to divine things, than when their bodies were not thus effected.[61]

No doubt McMillan remembered accounts of George Whitefield's preaching at Fagg's Manor, where stories of his revivals were yet fresh in memory when he was a baby. Whitefield had said of those who listened, "some were struck as pale as death, others lying on the ground, others wringing their hands, others sinking into the arms of friends."[62] The Revival in Kentucky began in 1797, and the reports of "jerking," "jumping," "barking," "yelling," and the like had come to McMillan long before. He probably never expected to see at a revival in his church what he did see; yet he did not doubt the religious nature of these actions once he had seen them. If he had known more of the laws of psychology, he would have realized that the strange reports from the West and South did affect the emotion of his own people.

This "Falling Work" or "Bodily Exercises" was thought of, at the time, as issuing from the Holy Spirit. Yet in 1839 Dr. Charles Hodge prints: "that such bodily affection owe their origin, not to any divine influence, but to natural causes, may be inferred from the fact that these latter are adequate to their production."[63] He also adds that such acts propagate themselves by a kind of infection.[64] However this may be, McMillan accepted the actions of the people as a means to a worthy end. He knew that many opposed revivals and called them "an evil work," "a work of enthusiasm," "a work of delusion."[65] The Associate Presbytery or Seceders had come out against the revivals and had denounced them "as fanatical and of Satanic origin";[66] yet knowing this did not prevent McMillan from showing respect for what was happening. If questioned about such physical actions, he would no doubt have said the Holy Spirit instigated them that many should be saved from their sins. He writes that between fifty and sixty joined the church as the fruits of this revival and that for some time after on each sacramental occasion others joined his church. Among those converted were many students in Jefferson College who later became ministers of the Gospel. "Since that time," McMillan writes to Carnahan, "religion has been on the decline, though still we are not left without some tokens of the Divine Presence."[67]

The fifth and last revival under McMillan came in 1823. "Nothing very remarkable," he writes, "took place until the year 1823, when God again visited this dry and parched congregation with a shower of divine influences."[68] The doctor was then in his seventy-first year, but he yet preached with such power that his people were convicted of their sins and turned to God. "The preaching of Dr. McMillan had the signature of divine approbation. By means of it hundreds, and probably thousands, were converted and trained for heaven."[69]

Through all these revivals McMillan was not stampeded into such fanaticism as was attributed to others, for example to James McGready. And McMillan and his session examined with care those who sought entrance to the Kingdom. If after the excitation subsided, these who had been moved still believed and deserved to be instructed "in the Word of God which is contained in the Scriptures of the Old and New Testaments,"[70] they were welcomed in the fellowship of Christian believers.

While all this was happening at Chartiers and Pigeon Creek, in pulpit and in pew, and while the revivals were coming as periodic gusts of Heavenly Wind, McMillan kept steadily preparing young men for the ministry. His theology had not the originality that might have made him famous. He taught simply but with fervor the standard Presbyterianism or Calvinism of his time.

MCMILLAN'S "MEDULLA"

For thirty years after 1802 McMillan was professor of divinity at Jefferson College. To theological students there he gave a series of lectures on "Theology: Natural and Revealed." The Reverend Matthew Brown, first president of Washington College (1806) and later the president of Jefferson College (1822), who was a friend of McMillan's though twenty-four years younger than he, says that these lectures "might well be called McMillan's Medulla."[71] Indeed they contain the pith or marrow of his spiritual life and teaching.

In the library of the Western Theological Seminary is the manuscript of these lectures. It is in McMillan's handwriting on 251 pages, each six inches by eight inches. In March 1806 this manuscript was copied out in full by Moses Allen, McMillan's son-in-law: the copy is now owned by Mrs. John Wragg of Pittsburgh. McMillan's manuscript is in only fair condition; the copy of it is well preserved. No doubt McMillan took full notes during his class under Smith at Pequea and used them when he wrote his *Lectures*.

On the first page of the Allen copy is:

> THEOLOGY, NATURAL AND REVEALED
> Compiled by the Rev. John McMillan, D.D.
> Transcribed by Moses Allen; March 1806
> *in systemate hoc, summae contineunto Religionis profitemer; et aptae omnibus, studenter juvenilus*
> Cannonsburg, 1806[72]

After he has defined the subject—theology—McMillan gives his proof that the scriptures are divinely inspired. This is the basic discussion. All later arguments and instances assume as their major premise the divine authority in the text of the Bible.

I. What is theology?
   1. Theology is a science respecting God and Divine things.
II. What is natural theology?
   1. Natural theology is that knowledge of God and Divine things which we may attain by the light of nature; or by the exercise of our natural powers, unassisted by revelation.
III. What is revealed theology?
   1. Revealed theology is that knowledge of God and Divine things he has revealed in the word, or in the scriptures of the old and new testaments.

Another question, which opens a wide field of thought is, "What is a miracle?" McMillan defines and discusses miracles, and he concludes that a miracle is the accomplishment of a work in an unusual manner. Its purpose is to attest a message from heaven and so to prove the truth of the doctrines revealed in the message. Starting with his definition McMillan made considerable effort to show that the miracles in the Scriptures are real, not fabulous. The miracles of the Pentateuch are considered first of all. Proof that those unusual happenings did occur is deduced from a belief that the Jews did accept a record of them shortly after they happened. The Jews could not, he reasons, have permitted fabulous stories to take the place of the commonplace unless such things were true.

Of the miracles in the New Testament there could be no rational doubt unless the apostles and other reporters purposely perpetrated a fraud, or had their senses so imposed upon that they merely thought they saw, heard, and felt. "To admit these absurdities, would be to admit greater miracles than any recorded in these scriptures," McMillan says. The writings of Tertullian, Irenius, Cyprian, and others are cited as containing passages quoted from scriptures in the same words the Bible contains today. Since the first witnesses of the miracles were not deceived, and since they had no intention of deceiving, and since their testimony has come down to us in such an infallible way, "there remains no doubt concerning its authenticity . . . the miracles recorded in the scriptures are real and not false."

Consideration is given to the being and attributes of God. McMillan asks these questions: How do you prove the being of a God, a priori and a posteriore? How are the attributes of God distinguished? What are the three degrees of God's love? In answer to this third question McMillan writes that there is a love of benevolence whereby "God wills or designs good to his creatures from eternity"; there is a love of beneficence, whereby "the creature receives benefits in time according to God's good pleasure"; there is a love of complacency, whereby "he is pleased with, or delights in the creature on account of the rays of his own image, which he beholds in it."

The chapter on the Trinity is of interest in part because, in 1808, Joseph Kerr, a member of the Ohio Presbytery, charged McMillan with Socinianism. Among the several Christian doctrines denied by the followers of Laelius Socinus was the Doctrine of the Trinity. "How do you prove a trinity of persons in the God-head?" McMillan asks. His answer is that this doctrine is expressly asserted in the scriptures; that Father, Son, and Holy Spirit are one God in essence; that the Son is equal with the Father; and that the Holy Spirit is equal with the Father. He ends his discussion of the Trinity by asserting:

The existence of three persons in one essence is a mystery, which to all eternity we should not be able to fully comprehend. Yet we are bound nevertheless to believe it, because God has revealed it to us in his word.

In his chapter "Of Creation," he asks, "What is creation?" "What is to be understood by all things being created very good?" "What was the image of God after which man was created?"

The chapter "Of Sin, Original and Actual" deals with a favorite subject of his. McMillan explains sin as a want of conformity to the law or a transgression of the law. Original sin consists in a guilt that resulted from Adam's first sin; it is want of that righteousness which man at first possessed. One proof for this doctrine is cited in the story of the flood. Many infants perished who had never been guilty of actual transgression yet who surely were not punished without a cause, unjustly. Therefore they must have been guilty of original sin. A second proof given is the text of Genesis 5.3, which says Adam "begat a son in his own likeness and after his own image." Knowing that Adam became sinful and depraved, it is to be expected that his son would be sinful, also. A clean thing does not proceed out of an unclean. Original sin thus infected the race of man and made him "odious to God and deserving of Hell."

An interesting question he raises is, "Will Christ continue to be God and man forever, are the union between the two natures indissoluble?" Without any hesitation he answers that the eternity of God's divine nature is not to be denied by anyone. About His human nature McMillan says, in substance, this: that at the tomb Christ was given opportunity to lay the body aside but that He ascended visibly into heaven: that He will come again in a visible manner to judge the world at the last day. The eternity of Christ's human nature becomes an eternal expression of His love to mankind, and an eternal means of drawing forth their love to Him.

Another question that called for subtle analysis is "As Baptism, and the Lord's Supper are both seals of the covenant of grace, in what respects do they differ from each other?" McMillan explains that Baptism is to be considered chiefly as the seal whereby God authenticates and ratifies the covenant He has made. The Lord's Supper, on the other hand, is the seal of the believer, whereby he not only confirms the acceptance of the Supper but also places himself under its obligations.

Two words commonly used but which McMillan held involved errors of interpretation and understanding were: "Transubstantiation" and "Consubstantiation." McMillan defines transubstantiation as the changing of the material elements, bread and wine, into the real body and blood of Christ. A belief in this change is, he says, contrary to reason and finds no support in the scriptures or the early Christian Church. Consubstantiation was the word Luther used instead of transubstantiation. Luther's word and his discussion of it are, McMillan says, unintelligible. "If the words have any meaning," wrote McMillan, "they involve one of the principal absurdities that embraces the other doctrine—which is that the same body should be present in different places at the same time."

McMillan thought of the Lord's Supper primarily as a memorial feast—a means of remembering the Christ.

McMillan in his lectures discusses most of the fundamental tenets of his Church: "Of Providence," "Of the Covenant of Works," "Recovery by Grace," "Union of the Human and Divine Nature," "Incarnation," "Of Christ's Teaching," "Did Christ Offer His Soul, As Well As His Body?", "Of the Dignity of Christ's Sufferings," "Steps of Christ's Humiliation and Their Necessity," and "Steps in Christ's Exaltation and Their Necessity."

After the lectures are a series of problems and "Practical Questions." In this series first comes: "Prove that in the application of redemption the Holy Spirit is efficient; or that no moral means whatever will avail, to the conversion and sanctification of a soul, without the invincible influence of the Holy Spirit." A definition of regeneration is asked for, and of conversion, sanctification, conviction, repentance, saving faith, assurance. McMillan required from his students ability to discuss: "Prove the perserverance of the saints," "Where do departed spirits go immediately after death?" "Prove the general resurrection," "Prove the general judgment," "Define the moral law," "What are the external seals of the covenant of Grace?", "As baptism and the Lord's Supper are both seals of the covenant of Grace, in what respects do they differ from each other?", "Who are the proper subjects of baptism?", "What is the nature and end of the sacrament of the Lord's Supper?"

Matthew Brown has said of the teaching in what he calls "McMillan's school of the prophets":

> The mode of instruction was by written lectures, containing a complete system of theology. The system the students transcribed, and were expected to recite literally. The system itself was excellent, containing a concise discussion of all the principal doctrines, with copious notes and quotations from scripture. It was concise, condensed, *multum in parvo,* lucid, and forcible.[73]

Such teaching and such study laid a solid foundation for the full theological training which followed, at the theological seminary.

THEOLOGICAL SEMINARY IN THE WEST

In 1825 the General Assembly of the Church approved the plan "to establish a Theological Seminary in the West."[74] This decision made a reality of what had begun as a hope about forty-three years earlier. Each of the four pioneering ministers, Thaddeus Dod, James Power, Joseph Smith, and John McMillan—the "Four Presbyterian Horsemen of the West"—had determined to keep up the Log College tradition of training young men who wished to enter the ministry. By some their schools were called "grammar schools,"[75] but their schools were the beginning of advanced general and theological education in the West.

McMillan did more than any of his colleagues in the establishing of a theological seminary in the West. He worked for this longer than they, and aimed more definitely at theological education. The log cabin school near his home was an embryo theological seminary, where he prepared many for the ministry. Matthew Brown, a president of Jefferson College, writes in his unfinished life of McMillan, whom he knew well, that "perhaps about one hundred ministers were trained, more or less, in his school of the prophets; many of whom were eminently useful."[76] The historian of the Presbytery of Erie says much the same: "Of the first twenty-eight on the roll, embracing a period of twenty years of its history . . . twenty-two pursued their theological studies in the West and no less than eighteen at Dr. McMillan's log cabin."[77]

When Canonsburg Academy became Jefferson College McMillan had preferred for himself the title and position "Professor of Divinity" rather than "President of the Board of Trustees."[78] Jefferson College so valued him as a leader that it, in 1814, "appointed a committee to prepare and present a petition to the Synod of Pittsburgh, at their next meeting, praying that measures might be taken for erecting and maintaining a Divinity Hall, to be connected with the College."[79] Smith adds in a footnote that though this petition does not appear in Synod's Records, its absence from the Records does not lessen the value the College placed on the teaching. Later, in 1821, the need for a theological seminary in the West came again, in another way, to the Synod's attention. Realizing that Princeton Theological Seminary was too far removed from western Pennsylvania, even as Scotland or New England were in Tennent's Log College days, it took first steps to provide a theological institution beyond the Alleghenies. The presbyteries had long been accepting into the ministry the young men whom McMillan had trained. The Synod wished now to build upon the foundation of McMillan's training a more advanced training. The Synod of Pittsburgh, therefore, in 1821, passed this resolution:

Whereas, it appears to this Synod that a number of promising young men, who are setting their faces toward the Gospel ministry, are not in circumstances to attend the Theological Seminary at Princeton; therefore, Resolved That this Synod take measures for procuring a library for the benefit of such, to be under the control and direction of this Synod. That it be recommended to every member to solicit books or moneys for this important purpose, and that this library be located at present, in the edifice of Jefferson College, at Canonsburg, and placed under the care of Reverend John McMillan, D.D., Professor of Theology in that Seminary.[80]

This resolution and succeeding actions of the Synod and the General Assembly show they recognized clearly the eminence of McMillan's theological teaching. In 1822 the Synod appointed a committee to proceed in establishing a seminary in the West. The committee's first resolution was "Resolved That a Theological School, for the above purposes, be established by the Synod, the present site of which to be at Jefferson College."[81] The facts at hand make clear that the Synod of Pittsburgh at that time purposed to continue McMillan's work by establishing the "Theological Institution" at Jefferson College, Canonsburg.

In the next four years they changed part of their plan. After the General Assembly had approved the plan of 1825,[82] the newly elected Board of Directors of the Western Theological Seminary of the Presbyterian Church in the United States made known that they would entertain a bid from any town which wished the institution built in it. Alleghenytown's promise of $21,000 and eighteen acres of land worth $20,000 was considered the best of the thirteen bids.[83]

Though the Presbyterian Church's Theological Seminary in the West was not at Canonsburg, yet the Church knew that McMillan had a great part in its being founded.

In his unfinished life of McMillan Matthew Brown praises McMillan's log cabin seminary for the efficient, practical, and useful preachers trained in it. He praises, too, the service of these men in all parts of the world. At the end of Brown's paragraph Joseph Smith adds a footnote: "This last statement is, perhaps, not correct, unless made in reference to the school, considered and continued by, and merged into, the Allegheny Theological Seminary."[84] Such judgments show that the men who knew McMillan's school saw in this new seminary of the West, a continuation and advancement of his work. The relation of McMillan's log cabin seminary to the Western Theological Seminary was in many ways like the relation of William Tennent's Log College to the College of New Jersey at Princeton. Each began well the kind of teaching the larger institution continued.[85]

Through sixty years McMillan served his Church. The same qualities of mind and soul which made him a great Christian pastor made him, too, a great teacher and a great leader in education.

IV. NOTES

1. *Addresses and Historical Sketches Delivered at the Centennial Anniversary of the Presbyterian Churches of Upper and Lower Ten Mile.* 21.

2. William W. McKinney. *Early Pittsburgh Presbyterianism, 1758-1839.* 50.

3. Boyd Crumrine. "Chartiers Presbyterian Church" in D. M. Bennett's *Life and Work of Rev. John McMillan, D.D.* 277.

4. Roy H. Johnson. "Frontier Religion in Western Pennsylvania," *The Western Pennsylvania Historical Magazine.* XVI, No. 1. 28.

5. See Appendix A, Part I.

6. Francis J. Collier. Address, "Chartiers Church and Its Ministers," *Centennial Celebration of Chartiers Church.* 9.

7. McMillan's Letter to Carnahan. See Appendix C.

8. James Veech. "The Secular History," *Centenary Memorial.* 324, 325.

9. Bennett. 162, 163.

10. Johnson. 28.

11. Samuel Hazard. *Pennsylvania Archives.* IX. 572.

12. Joseph Smith. *Old Redstone.* 44.

13. *Centenary Memorial.* 324.

14. *Old Redstone.* 44.

15. Boyd Crumrine. *History of Washington County.* 283.

16. *Ibid.* 876.

17. Collier. 23, 24. These minutes were most valuable as historical records, and it is unfortunate that Collier did not place them where they would have been preserved.

18. Most of these writings are in the possession of Mrs. Wragg.

19. John C. Fitzpatrick (ed.). *The Diaries of George Washington.* II. 293.

20. *Ibid.*

21. *Old Redstone.* 313.

22. Bennett. 288.

23. *Ibid.*

24. *Old Redstone.* 313.

25. See Appendix A, Part I.

26. *Ibid.*

27. Johnson. 30.

28. See Appendix A, Part I.

29. *Ibid.*

30. See *Bethel's 175 Years of Christian Service, 1776-1951.* William T. Martin, editor.

31. W. C. Degelman. *Historical Narrative of Bethel Presbyterian Church.* 21, 22.

32. See Appendix A, Part II. The figures in this paragraph and the following one are from this source.

33. Margaret S. Sturgeon. "History of Raccoon Church," an article in Bennett's book.

34. Charles W. Maus. *History of the Long Run Presbyterian Church.* 21.

35. Minutes of the Presbytery of Redstone, 1781-1831. 15.

36. "Montour Presbyterian Church," Bennett. 298-303. See "Old Montour."

37. Bennett. 122. See Crumrine's *History of Washington County.* 876, 877.

38. Clarence E. Macartney. *Not Far From Pittsburgh.* 26.

39. *History of the Presbyterian Church in the United States of America.* I. 268.

40. W. B. Sprague. *Annals of the American Pulpit.* III. 354.

41. *The Centennial Memorial of the Presbytery of Carlisle.* II. 170.

42. *Annals of the American Pulpit.* III. 354.

43. Macartney. 125.

44. Mrs. J. L. Dawson. "Early History and Contrasts," *Presbyterian Banner*. October 15, 1925.
45. Moses Allen. Centennial Address, "Rev. John McMillan, D.D." See *Old Redstone*. 208.
46. William W. Sweet. *Religion in Colonial America*. 274.
47. Guy S. Klett. *Presbyterians in Colonial Pennsylvania*. 149.
48. Sweet. 289, 294, 295.
49. Thomas Murphy. *The Presbytery of the Log College*. 88.
50. Charles H. Maxon. *The Great Awakening in the Middle Colonies*. 27.
51. Allen. Centennial Address.
52. Aaron Williams. "Religious History," *Centenary Memorial*. 42.
53. *Ibid*.
54. Robert Patterson. "Dr. John McMillan," *The Presbyterian Advocate*. VII, No. 38.
55. See Appendix C and *Old Redstone*. 188.
56. *Ibid*.
57. Allen. Centennial Address.
58. Catherine C. Cleveland. *The Great Revival in the West*. 83, 84.
59. "Account of the Great Revival in Kentucky, 1802," from the original copy of the article in the library of the Western Theological Seminary, Pittsburgh. This account is based on a lengthy letter from McGready to McMillan dated November 18, 1802, in the same library. In this letter McGready gives his impressions of the revival.
60. *Western Missionary Magazine*. 1802. 329. Cf. Gillett. *History of the Presbyterian Church*. I. 541. See Elliott. *The Life of Rev. Elisha Macurdy*. 46.
61. Cf. *Old Redstone*. 189.
62. Cf. *Centenary Memorial*. 52.
63. Charles Hodge. *Constitutional History of the Presbyterian Church*. Part II. 87, 88.
64. Dr. George A. Baxter. "The Bodily Exercise," *Presbyterian Advocate and Herald of the West*. March 11, 1840.
65. Collier. 23.
66. Joseph Smith. *History of Jefferson College*. 202.
67. See Appendix C.
68. *Ibid*.
69. Allen. Centennial Address.
70. *The Constitution of the Presbyterian Church*. 291.
71. *Old Redstone*. 209. Quoted from Matthew Brown's unfinished life of John McMillan.
72. The original copy of the lectures is in the library of the Western Theological Seminary, Pittsburgh. The transcribed copy is in the possession of Mrs. Helen Wragg. Since the original and the transcription are identical, the latter copy has been used because it is in better condition. The material in the following pages of this section is taken from it.
73. Quoted from Brown's unfinished life of McMillan in Smith's *Old Redstone*. 209.
74. *Minutes of the General Assembly*. 267.
75. Joseph Doddridge. *Notes on the Settlement and Indian Wars*. 151.
76. *Old Redstone*. 209. Also James I. Brownson. "Educational History," *Centenary Memorial*. 113.
77. S. J. M. Eaton. *History of the Presbytery of Erie*. 7, 8.
78. *History of Jefferson College*. 58-60.
79. *Ibid*. 90.
80. *Records of the Synod of Pittsburgh*. October, 1821. 178.
81. *Ibid*. October, 1822. 197ff.

82. *Minutes of the General Assembly.* 1825. 267.
83. Allen D. Campbell. "The Founding and Early History of the Western Theological Seminary," *Western Theological Seminary Bulletin.* XX, No. 1. Mr. Campbell was one of the original directors of the Seminary.
84. *Old Redstone.* 210.
85. W. W. McKinney. *The Challenge of a Heroic Past.* 3-8. Murphy. 121-131.

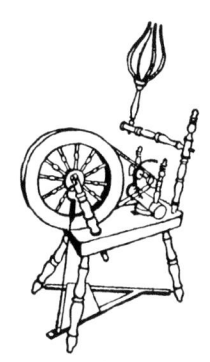

SPINNING WHEEL

V. EDUCATION

THROUGH all the years McMillan went on steadily emphasizing the need to deepen and advance the teaching given students preparing for the ministry.

At least as early as 1780 McMillan began a Latin school in a one room log house on his farm. This school was the Tennent-Blair-Smith type of school known as the "log college." There were others of these log schools set up wherever there was a church and a minister who could gather students in his home. Some were "English schools" and some were "Latin" or "Classical schools"; some lived for a period of years and some disappeared in a short time. The length of their lives depended on the energy of the minister and upon the need in his parish.

So energetic was McMillan in his teaching and encouragement of schools that contemporaries called him "father of education in western Pennsylvania."[1] His steady and unflagging purpose was to give young men, as many of them as he could, a sound knowledge of Latin, some familiarity with jurisprudence, and an intelligent outlook on life. Most of all he hoped to carry some of them along until they were ready for ministry in the church.

This chapter discusses the beginnings and early development in Pennsylvania of the "log college," the school of Scottish tradition; its continuance under John McMillan; the assistance he gave to many schools: to Washington Academy and to Jefferson College in their early days; and especially his help to Jefferson College during both its prosperous and its difficult days.

LOG CABIN SCHOOL

It was the way of the Scotch-Irish in America to set up school as soon as they had made a settlement. It was, too, the hope of the Church that its clergy should "look out for some pious young men and educate them for the ministry,"[2] this to be done by giving them advanced schooling and a training in the highest principles of the Church. After eastern Pennsylvania had its farms and towns and churches and lower schools, the Reverend Mr. William Tennent, pastor at Neshaminy, some miles north of Philadelphia, in 1726, began such a school.[3] He held it in a log cabin only about twenty feet square.

As frontier settlements moved westward other schools of advanced learning were set up. At Fagg's Manor, east of the Alleghenies but beyond the Schuylkill River and Brandywine Creek, Samuel Blair, a student of William Tennent's, established the Fagg's Manor school in 1739. At Pequea, a few miles north and west of Fagg's Manor, Robert Smith, a graduate of Fagg's Manor, established in 1750 the Pequea school. Both were patterned on Tennent's log cabin school. Then in 1776 John McMillan became pastor at Chartiers, beyond the Alleghenies, and he, who had studied both at Fagg's Manor and Pequea, followed the advice of his teacher, Robert Smith, and in 1780 began his log cabin school. Out of these beginnings west of the Alleghenies later came Canonsburg Academy, Washington Academy, and finally Jefferson College and the Western Theological Seminary.

In his eightieth year McMillan wrote in a manuscript which he left along with his *Journal* and which is reprinted in Joseph Smith's *History of Jefferson College:*

When I determined to come to this country, Dr. Smith enjoined it upon me to look out for some pious young men, and educate them for the ministry; for, said he, though some men of piety and talents may go to a new country at first, yet if they are not careful to raise up others, the country will not be well supplied. Accordingly I collected a few who gave evidence of piety, and instructed them in the knowledge of the Latin and Greek languages, some of whom became useful, and others eminent ministers of the gospel, viz., James Hughs, John Brice, James McGready, William Swan, Samuel Porter, and Thomas Marquis. All these I boarded and taught without any compensation, except about forty dollars, which Mr. Swan gave to my wife after he had settled in the ministry.[4]

This statement which was repeated with a few changes in the letter to Carnahan gives McMillan's aims. And, by what it suggests rather than by what it clearly says, it lines in his clear good sense, his unending work, his devotion, and his steady holding to what he believed worth doing.

Some understanding of the earlier schools which were McMillan's inspiration and models may help the reader realize what education in Pennsylvania owes the Presbyterian log colleges. Some of them, we know, grew into academies which were the liberal arts colleges of the eighteenth century. And later these have grown into larger colleges and great universities, a few of which, to be sure, have in later years become nonsectarian in character.

William Tennent, the father of the log college schools, was born around 1673, in Ireland.[5] It was long supposed that he attended Trinity College, Dublin, but an entry of his being granted a degree July 11, 1695, has been found in the records of the University of

JOHN McMILLAN

Edinburgh.[6] He was ordained a deacon July 1, 1704, and on September 22, 1706 he became a priest of the Episcopal Church. In May of 1702 he married Catharine Kennedy, a daughter of the Reverend Mr. Kennedy of County Down in the North of Ireland. His wife is spoken of as a woman of unusual talent. Their four sons, born in Ireland, were distinguished preachers in America. Tennent came to America in 1718. Soon after he came, he decided to enter the ministry of the Presbyterian Church. He made application for admittance to the Synod of Philadelphia on September 17, 1718. Tennent's reasons for leaving the Established Church of Ireland are given in the records of the Synod: "Their government by Bishops, Arch-Bishops, Deacons, Arch-Deacons, Canons, Chapters, Chancellors, Vicars, wholly anti-scriptural . . . besides I could not be satisfied with their ceremonial way of worship."[7] The Synod was well satisfied with his credentials, witnesses, and testimony, and it enrolled him as a Presbyterian minister. He moved to East Chester, New York, and remained there until 1720 when he removed to Bedford, New York.[8] There are signed manuscript sermons which show that he preached at Bedford in 1723 and 1724.[9] In 1726 or 1727 he moved to Bucks County, Pennsylvania. As pastor at Neshaminy he started a school for his four sons and other young men. Since the school's only building was a small log cabin, its students had to be boarded and lodged by neighborhood families or by the William Tennents themselves. "There is no doubt that he benevolently provided for some in this way, and at considerable expense, and probably involved himself in pecuniary difficulties, that he might assist young men in their education."[10]

Tennent may never have thought of his school, which the neighbors in jest nicknamed "The Log College," actually as a college. The only known description of it is in the interesting *Journal* of George Whitefield:

The Place wherein the young men study is in contempt called the College. It is a Log-House, about twenty feet long, and near as many broad; and to me it seemed to resemble the Schools of the Old Prophets.—For that their Habitations were mean, and that they sought not great things for themselves, is plain from those passages of Scripture wherein we are told that each of them took a beam to build them a house, and that passage of Scripture wherein we are told that at the Feast of the Sons of the Prophets, one of them put on the Pot, whilst the others went to fetch some herbs out of the Field. All that can be said of most of our public Universities is, they are all glorious without. From this despised place seven or eight worthy ministers of Jesus have been lately sent forth; more are almost ready to be sent, and a Foundation is now laying for the Instruction of many others.[11]

Tennent met with some difficulties. Criticism often went beyond mere grumbling. In the early 1700's the people around Neshaminy, and especially the Presbytery and the Synod, found the idea revolutionary that young men could be trained for the ministry without going to a well established eastern college or even to a European school. That was one difficulty, Another was the controversy over revivals. Tennent and his sons and their followers believed in revivals and promoted them. The outcome of the controversy was the formation of the New Brunswick Presbytery made up of Log College men, and it was separated from the Philadelphia Synod. Tennent had tried earlier to have Log College taken into the New York Synod, but this the Synod had not regarded favorably.

It was too far from New York; it was within the limits of the home of the other Synod; its plan was too narrow; and besides, the elder Tennent died the very year of the organization of the New York Synod. The work of the Log College was over. Moreover, large-minded leaders like Dickinson and Barr wanted a college organized on a plan far larger than that of the Neshaminy school.[12]

When William Tennent died the original Log Cabin of Neshaminy ended its teaching, but its spirit passed on into many of those other classical and theological schools which were known as log colleges and even into the College of New Jersey which is now Princeton University. One of the log schools which already has been mentioned is Samuel Blair's. Blair had been a pupil of William Tennent, and the school he started at Fagg's Manor or New Londonderry was in the pattern of Tennent's old school at Neshaminy.

One of the most important graduates of the Fagg's Manor School was Robert Smith. "He was led to establish another school similar to that of Fagg's Manor—and both on the model of 'Log College' at Pequea, which became a source of influence and great usefulness in that day."[13]

There were other schools in the spirt of Tennent's, but Fagg's Manor was the one which influenced directly John McMillan. Soon after McMillan became the minister of Chartiers Church in the Western Country, he began a school which was a third generation of log cabin schools: first generation, William Tennent; second generation, Samuel Blair and Robert Smith; third generation, John McMillan, Joseph Smith, Thaddeus Dod, and others.

Within four years after McMillan accepted churches in the West, about 1780,[14] he started his teaching. First he taught students in his home and then in a log house which he built nearby. His first log school burned and with it books and other equipment.[15] Jean McMillan Harper, McMillan's eldest child, has told that the burning was a great handicap because her father had to send over the mountains for new books.[16]. Soon, however, McMillan built a new log school closer to his home than the first had been. Collier has said of it:

> As glass was costly and difficult to obtain, light was admitted to the cabin, in the winter season, as we are informed, through small windows covered with greased paper. The benches were made of slabs, and were rough in appearance and not conducive to comfort.[17]

The ladies of the congregation and especially the ladies of the manse were constant in their help to the school, although their part has usually gone untold. One lady named Irwin wrote in a letter to Joseph Smith that the women of Buffalo, Cross Creek, Chartiers, Bethel, and Ten-Mile furnished the students clothing for winters and summers.[18] The first classes were taught in the manse kitchen; that of course meant extra work for the woman of the house. Most students were boarded by the minister's family without charge (they could not have gone on to school otherwise). McMillan's *Journal* mentions boarding students, and Robert Patterson wrote to Matthew Brown:

> For want of a suitable place elsewhere, the students generally lodged in the minister's family, without profit and sometimes at considerable expense to the household. In this service and toil the wives of those two godly ministers heartily concurred.[19]

The wives he writes of are Mrs. Joseph Smith and Mrs. John McMillan.

There is a curious dispute which began at least a hundred years ago as to which of the third generation schools was the oldest— Smith's at Buffalo, about eight miles west of Washington, Dod's at Amity, about ten miles south of Washington, or McMillan's, about three miles from Canonsburg, and as to what was the curriculum taught in each of these schools. This dispute has seemed important to those who wished to fix the origin of the colleges that were indeed the outgrowth of the early log cabin schools. Some account of this dispute and the arguments advanced are interesting in any life of John McMillan.

There is fairly general agreement that John McMillan started his school before either Dod's or Smith's was started. The greatest point of dispute seems to center around what was taught in John McMillan's school in the earliest days.

Joseph Smith, a grandson of the first Joseph Smith, says that McMillan's school began the earliest but he doubts that it taught the classics. He writes thus in his *History of Jefferson College:*

... though Dr. McMillan's school may have been the first organized, as we believe it was, it did not assume the more distinctive form of a Latin school for training candidates for the ministry until his colleagues [Dod and Smith] had been for some time giving instructions with that in view, and perhaps until they both ceased to teach their schools.[20]

Joseph Smith maintains in his *Old Redstone* as well as in his *History of Jefferson College* that both the McMillan and the Dod school were English schools and that the honor of establishing "the first Latin school" belongs to his grandfather. Others disagree. It is certain that as early as 1785[21] the first Joseph Smith did establish a school, but Jacob Lindley insists that it was not a Latin school.[22] And Cephas Dodd, the son of Thaddeus Dod, asserts that his father's school, which began about 1782, is the oldest Latin school.[23] There is evidence to support the claim that the Dod school was a Latin school; it began in 1782 and lasted until 1785. James I. Brownson thinks that Dr. McMillan's school which opened in 1780 did include Latin and Greek in so far as the demand for them existed, but that probably Dod's school for the three years of its life took over the classical instruction from Dr. McMillan to relieve Dr. McMillan from the pressure of his "abundant labors."[24]

Until *Old Redstone* was published in 1854 it had been the accepted opinion that McMillan's school was the first Latin school in the West[25] and that the date 1780 was the beginning in the Western Country of instruction for young men preparing for the ministry.[26] Smith's school began in 1785 and Dod's in 1782.

This accepted and "common opinion" that McMillan's school was the first Latin school and that 1780 was the time young men preparing for the ministry began to receive instruction has had many supporters.

John McMillan in his manuscript and in the letter to James Carnahan tries to relate events in a definite chronological order. (See Appendix.) A parenthetic comment about the forty-three years of marital happiness interrupts his narrative of settlement at Chartiers in 1778. But the next sentence refers to Robert Smith's injunction bidding him educate young men for the ministry. McMillan says he did that and "instructed them in the knowledge of the Latin and Greek languages." Immediately following, McMillan tells of the first revival in his congregation during December 1781.

We believe this sequence in the telling of events, the carrying out Robert Smith's suggestion without delay, and then the revival of 1781, show that the school began before 1781. As a point to clinch the argument for McMillan's case, presenting facts in a definite chronological order, is a statement near the close of the letter to Carnahan which reads: "I forgot to tell you in the *proper* place that..."

Robert Patterson is one of those sure that McMillan's was the oldest Latin school. He tells that he and John Weaver called on an aged lady named Sarah Park, the daughter of Judge McDowell, on Saturday, June 15, 1854. They found her, as they said, in perfect possession of her faculties and in full remembrance of the time when the McMillans first came west and lived temporarily in her father's home. She remembered that when she was twelve years old (1781) several young men were studying at the McMillan home from books she could not read. She was perfectly sure they were Latin books.[27] The students were David Smith, John Brice, James McGready, Francis and Thomas Reno. Her testimony is taken as proof that the school was a Latin school and not an English school, for she stated firmly that the school was known throughout the country as "the Latin School" and that James Ross was the first teacher.[28]

Joseph Smith (the grandson), on the other hand, puts forward a statement by Jacob Lindley as evidence that Thaddeus Dod had the oldest school. He quotes an elderly lady named Irwin who says there was no school at Chartiers in 1785, that James McGready labored on McMillan's farm, and that Cephas Dodd claimed John Brice, James McGready, and David Smith had never studied under John McMillan.

Now, of course, Jacob Lindley's statement does not discount the evidence of Sarah Park, for the same students may have attended first the McMillan school in 1780 and then the Dod school in 1782. It was not unusual in those days for the students to transfer from school to school. Sarah Park was five years older than Jacob Lindley and her memory went back further than his. It would be very difficult for anyone to explain how James McGready, if he had been only a laborer on the McMillan farm, could have passed the examinations of Redstone Presbytery in logic, moral philosophy, Latin, and Greek. This he did after less than eighteen months training in Joseph Smith's school,[29] which he attended after leaving John McMillan's. Again it is very unlikely indeed that John McMillan would keep a young man who had come to his home from North Carolina for the definite purpose of preparing for the

EDUCATION

ministry as a laborer on his farm, and without instruction.[80] He must have studied under John McMillan from 1782 until 1785, before he attended Joseph Smith's school.

Robert Patterson offers another bit of evidence for John McMillan's school. On the twenty-fourth of April, 1854, he went with the Reverend William Ewing to visit John McMillan, Jr., who was living on the old McMillan homestead. John told them his father had often said that Mr. Ross had taught Latin in the McMillan school, the "first Latin school in the country."[31] Jean McMillan Harper, John McMillan's oldest child, on August 3, 1854, added further testimony: she said that Mr. Ross and Mr. McGready studied languages with her father while they were teaching for him—Mr. Ross taught the Latin scholars and Mr. McGready, the English scholars.[32]

In recent years a book was found in the attic of the old McMillan farm which adds another link in the evidence. The book is Ovid's *Metamorphoses* and there are notes on several of the pages. On page 153 is written: "James McGready finished Ovid's *Metamorphoses,* Feb. 4, A. D. 1784." On page 314 is written: "James McGready Legit hunc Librum sub directione Johanii McMillan Theologne Chartiers." On page 443 is written: "James McGready Legit hunc Librum in Decembro 1783 & nunc legit Dialogos Liciani, June 1785."

A conclusive bit of evidence is that found in a letter from H. M. Brackenridge. It reads in part:

I have always understood that the first Latin School ever established in the Western part of Pennsylvania, was set on foot by the Rev. John McMillan at Canonsburg, or near that place, in a log cabin by the roadside. I have heard my father say that once, on his way from Pittsburgh to Washington court, he was induced according to a practice almost invariable with him, to stop at the School in the log-cabin referred to, and there he found James Ross teaching a Latin class. . . . This must have been prior to the year 1785, for this reason: my father established himself as a lawyer in Pittsburgh in 1781, and Mr. Ross must have been at least seven years at the bar before 1794, when he was a senator of the United States. My father, on inquiring into his future prospects, advised him to study law, and gave him letters to his friends in Philadelphia, especially Mr. Coxe, with whom Mr. Ross completed his studies. From this we may form an idea of the time which must have elapsed before he came to the bar, and of the time necessary to acquire such distinction as to be elected to the Senate before the year of 1794. It would seem to me that this would surely carry the period at which my father saw him teaching in the log-cabin, beyond the year 1785. . . . This is the first time I ever heard the fact of Mr. McMillan's being the first to establish a Latin School in the West, called in question.[33]

This letter to Robert Patterson bears the date of June 12, 1854.

JOHN McMILLAN

As another bit of evidence supporting the priority of the McMillan school, Francis J. Collier writes:

Professor Robert Patterson . . . showed very conclusively that the author of *Old Redstone* was mistaken when he said that although Mr. McMillan's School was started before Mr. Dodd's or Mr. Smith's and survived theirs, yet it was at first only an English and afterwards a classical school. Prof. Patterson proves that McMillan's Log-Cabin School was begun, continued and ended, as a classical and theological school.[34]

And so the evidence has piled up by those who have thought it important to establish the claim that the McMillan school was a Latin school which preceded the schools of Thaddeus Dod and Joseph Smith, and that McMillan's school was the first to provide the fundamentals needed to prepare young men for the ministry.

ACADEMIES AND COLLEGES

The academies of the eighteenth century were the liberal arts colleges, set up to train young men in more than just the mere rudiments of learning. It was natural that people living together in communities who knew the traditions of the Scottish university and the opportunities for learning already long established east of the mountains should want this kind of education for their sons. There were two academies chartered by the legislature in western Pennsylvania in 1787: the Academy at Pittsburgh, February 29, 1787 and the Academy at Washington, September 24, 1787. John McMillan was named as a trustee for both academies, the earliest chartered institutions of higher learning in the Western Country. There is no evidence that he continued as trustee at Pittsburgh Academy long after its incorporation.

Washington Academy Chartered, 1787

The Washington Academy, with which he was more closely associated, received with its incorporation by the legislature a grant of five thousand acres north of the Ohio River[35] in what is now Beaver County. This land was unproductive then but potentially rich. It is said that John McMillan and the judges, Allison and McDowell of the legislature, were the main influences through whom the charter and the land grant were obtained. Along with John McMillan the trustees were Joseph Smith, Thaddeus Dod, John Clark, and Matthew Henderson, Presbyterian ministers; John Corbly, a Baptist; Judges Allison and McDowell; and several elders from nearby churches. It has been said, too, that Benjamin Franklin recommended a teacher for the school and contributed fifty pounds for books.[36]

After several unsuccessful attempts were made to find a principal, Thaddeus Dod accepted the principalship on condition that he keep the appointment for one year only.[37] He took the position with the approval and good will of all the trustees, including John McMillan.

Classes began in the upper rooms of the Court House in Washington on April 1, 1789, and there were about twenty or thirty students attending. Thaddeus Dod continued three months longer than the year and then David Johnston, his associate and a teacher of English, succeeded him. In the following winter the Court House burned and the Academy suspended its teaching.

John McMillan and Matthew Henderson, representing the two branches of Presbyterianism, tried to persuade J. Hoge, Esquire, a wealthy trustee, to give the Academy a building lot within the town of Washington. He refused. Then they went to Colonel Canon of Canonsburg; he gave a plot of ground and advanced money for a building.[38] It seems that Colonel Canon, Judges Allison and McDowell, Alexander Cool, Esquire, James Foster, Thomas Brecker, Robert Ralston, and others had wanted to found an academy either by enlarging the McMillan school or by starting a new one. When the Washington Academy seemed to be succeeding they held back, but now they saw a chance to carry out their ideas.

John McMillan in a report that was incorporated into the Minutes of the trustees of Jefferson College, dated December 29, 1817, and in his own hand, has written, "So indifferent were the inhabitants of that town to the interests of literature in general and to the demand of the church in particular that notwithstanding the state's donation an academy could not be supported."[39] Jacob Lindley's account is similar: "The inhabitants of Washington at that time, had but little piety, science, or liberality to build a house or sustain a literary institution, and none to sustain a preacher."[40] There is evidence, too, that Thaddeus Dod and David Johnston tried in vain to interest the townspeople.

Canonsburg Academy Founded, 1791

The next development for Canonsburg is recounted in Robert Patterson's letter to Matthew Brown. He tells of a meeting in July, 1791, following the Sacrament of the Lord's Supper, at which a consultation was held about establishing a Latin school or an academy. His letter reads: "With free expression of opinion and views, it was promptly and unanimously decided that the exigencies of the Western country, including the interests of the church, required the establishment of a Literary Institution somewhere in the West."[41] This meeting was held at Chartiers and indicates that the intention was to start a new academy rather than revive the burned Washington Academy. McMillan suggested building near his log cabin school; Colonel Canon offered the land and money for a building if the new academy was built in Canonsburg. The decision went for Canonsburg, and McMillan, though disappointed, agreed.

Enthusiasm ran so high that opening exercises were set for the following morning at ten o'clock. David Johnston, a graduate of the University of Pennsylvania, the same who was formerly principal at Washington Academy, was elected principal. John McMillan addressed the assembly thus:

This is an important day in our history, affecting deeply the interests of the church and the country of the West; affecting our own interests and welfare in time and eternity, and the interest, it may be, of thousands and thousands yet unborn.[42]

Matthew Henderson invoked the blessing of God upon the institution. A short lesson in Latin was recited by Robert Patterson and William Riddle, his fellow student, in a fence corner "under the shade of some sassafras bushes."[43] In attendance were the judges, McDowell and Allison, Craig Ritchie, a perspective student, Abraham Scott, and others. The exercises concluded with a prayer by Joseph Smith. And in a few weeks the academy roll included: Abraham Scott, Robert Patterson, William Wylie, Thomas Swearengen, James Snodgrass, Ebenezer Henderson, James Duncan, James Allison, Joseph Doddridge, Dorsey Pentecost, James Dunlavy, Daniel McLean, William Kerr, Philip Doddridge, and Alexander Campbell.[44] Until Colonel Canon's fine large stone building was ready for occupancy the following autumn, an English school nearby was used.

It had now become apparent that it would be very difficult to interest people further in reviving Washington Academy. All energy and enthusiasm centered in Canonsburg.

The lay members of the Washington board, however, continued some efforts to revive the older academy, and the success of the people of Canonsburg only made them more determined to succeed at Washington.

The greater part of their energy was expended along legal and political lines—striving to get their lands located and titles perfected, and seeking gifts of ground from the county authorities, and gifts of money from the legislature. In these efforts they were successful in part, getting a location for the academy from the proprietors of the town, Messrs. John and William Hoge, viz: the southeast corner of the present campus but getting nothing from the county. But they found themselves shut out largely from all the Presbyterian churches of the county when they tried to raise money for the building and the work of erecting it dragged along through four years.[45]

John Hoge, Esquire, the trustee who had refused John McMillan and Matthew Henderson at first, now came forward and donated to Washington Academy a substantial plot of land in what is now a part of the Washington and Jefferson College campus.[46] Stung by the interest shown at Canonsburg the townspeople of Washington were aroused and subscribed enough money to build in 1793 a central building. McMillan continued as a trustee of Washington Academy for a few years, attending meetings occasionally. But his interest in Canonsburg Academy grew to a point where he felt that he could not serve both places. On September 20, 1795 he resigned from the board of trustees of Washington Academy, and his place was filled by William Hoge.[47]

The legislature granted the Washington Academy, in 1796, three thousand dollars for building, and the money was used to complete the building begun in 1793.[48]

Washington College Chartered, 1806

In the spring of 1806 the legislature issued a charter making Washington Academy, Washington College. Matthew W. Brown assumed the presidency of Washington College on December 13, 1806, and the real growth of the College dates from the beginning of his presidency.

Another dispute that has held the interest of many people is the part John McMillan and his log cabin school had in the founding of Canonsburg Academy. Joseph Smith in *Old Redstone* tried to disprove that McMillan took any active part in founding the Academy at Canonsburg.[49] He somewhat modified his position in his *History of Jefferson College:*

But we think that in the strict history of the case, there was here, soon after, a coalescence between the Institution already begun at Canonsburgh and now further enlarged, and the "Log cabin" school—rather than as has often been asserted that "the Canonsburg Academy grew out of the "Log Cabin" and was simply an enlargement of it.[50]

Thus in the face of evidence to the contrary, Joseph Smith denies the continuity of the two schools with the word "coalescence."

Indeed it seems to be so much the common belief these schools had a connection that it is interesting to show the logical arguments that have been advanced to support this point of view.

First of all, when Colonel Canon and others of the Chartiers group offered to establish an academy in Canonsburg, they accepted the leadership of John McMillan.[51] McMillan although he had hoped the new academy would be centered in his own log school at his own home, accepted the new site. The generous offer of Colonel Canon was a strong deciding factor. He said at some later time, "I had still a few with me when the academy was opened at Canonsburg, and finding that I could not teach and do justice to my congregation, I immediately gave them up and sent them there."[52] This leads to the conclusion that the people of Canonsburg were willing and anxious that the new and large institution should continue the good work started by John McMillan.

There is, however, more conclusive proof. In 1817 James Ramsey and John McMillan presented to the trustees of Jefferson College a report in the handwriting of John McMillan which was forwarded to the trustees of Washington College and given wide circulation. The report included this statement:

A house was built and a Latin and a Greek school which he (John McMillan) kept at his own house, for the purpose of supplying the Church, as far as was practicable, was transferred to this infant Academy (Canonsburg Academy), the original fountain of science and literature in these western counties.[53]

Now McMillan and all present knew well that Pittsburgh Academy and Washington Academy had been chartered before Canonsburg Academy was chartered. And so, when he refers to Canonsburg Academy as "the original fountain of science and literature in these western counties," he can mean only that Canonsburg Academy was the continuation of his own school founded in 1780. When the trustees received this report in the words of John McMillan, they were pleased and they did not challenge it—nor was there a challenge from Washington Academy or from the public.

Further proof that Jefferson College recognized the unity of McMillan's log school and Canonsburg Academy is in the catalogue of July, 1833.

Jefferson College was chartered by the State, and regularly organized in 1802. Prior to that time there existed an academy, called Canonsburg Academy, which commenced soon after the first settlement of this country. This was the first literary institution west of the mountains. It originated in a small log cabin, where the first Latin school was taught by the Hon. James Ross, of Pittsburgh, under the patronage and direction of Rev. Dr. McMillan.[54]

At the same time that this catalogue was printed John McMillan, though eighty years of age, was physically and mentally active and he was vice-president of Jefferson College. There were many living who had been his scholars, and no denial was made of the truth of the catalogue statement by them or by McMillan. It appears that until Joseph Smith's *Old Redstone* was published in 1854 followed by his *History of Jefferson College* in 1857 no one had thought otherwise than that McMillan's school was the forerunner of Canonsburg Academy.

To be sure, Joseph Smith claimed "eyewitnesses" who stated that McMillan's school went on after Canonsburg Academy was established.[55] It is possible that theological students continued to live at the McMillan home. But it does not seem at all likely that McMillan actually continued his school, especially when we have his own word that he discontinued it and sent his scholars to Canonsburg.

The records of the Synod and the Presbytery indicate that they accepted John McMillan's leadership, his log school, and his support of Canonsburg Academy as one continuous piece of Christian service.

At its meeting on September 28, 1791, the Synod of Virginia recommended that two institutions of learning be established: one in Rockbridge County, Virginia, and the other in Washington County, Pennsylvania "under the care of the Revd. John McMillan."[56] Thus John McMillan was selected by the Synod of Virginia to manage and take care of the institution entrusted to the superintendence of Redstone Presbytery.[57] Incorporated in the minutes of the meeting on October 18, 1791, is Redstone Presbytery's serious discussion of these matters. They ordered the members to gather contributions for the support of the institution and "put them into the hands of Mr. McMillan, who was appointed treasurer."[58] One year later, October 18, 1792, the minutes read:

The Presbytery unanimously agreed to appoint Canonsburg to be the seat of that institution of learning which they are appointed by Synod to superintend; and that all the young men taken upon the fund for the support of poor and pious youths shall be educated there.[59]

Trouble with the Indians was the reason given for delaying action for a year.

In November of the same year the Presbytery indicated a wish to have Washington Academy share in the Presbytery funds, and a motion was received to reconsider the propriety of selecting Canonsburg as the representative school of Redstone Presbytery. But in April, 1793, the matter was settled: the Presbytery confirmed Canonsburg as the choice, permitting another school to share in the Presbytery funds if the church would benefit. After all, they made clear, the primary interest and intention must be to prepare young men for the Gospel ministry. The donations and supplies gathered from the churches were to be used "for such indigent students" approved by the Presbytery.

Little more than a year after Canonsburg Academy got under way, the following notice appeared in the *Pittsburgh Gazette* September 2, 1792:

The building for the Academy at Canonsburg is now finished and the institution under good relations. The grammar school is taught by Mr. Johnston; and the English, Euclid's Elements of Geometry; Trigonometry, Plane and Spherical, with the later application to Astronomy; Navigation, Surveying Mensuration, Guaging, Dialing Conic Sections, Algebra, and Bookkeeping by Mr. Miller; both well known for their attention and abilities. Boarding in the neighborhood to be had at good houses, at the low price of ten pounds, payable principally in produce. The situation is healthy, near the center of Washington County; the funds raised by the Presbytery are to be applied for the support of a certain number of scholars, annually, is directed by the Synod of the district to be appropriated to this Academy. It is hoped the public will regard, with a favorable eye this institution, and give it all the encouragement that it may deserve.

Later the Synod and the Presbytery, as has been explained, made their endorsement official and the Academy began to prosper.

Canonsburg Academy Chartered, 1794

In 1794 the legislature granted the Academy a charter under the name "The Academy and Library Company of Canonsburg."[60] Contributions for support came from the congregation of Presbyterians and Seceders throughout the Western Country. These contributions were to repay Colonel Canon for the building costs he had advanced, to pay teachers, and to assist young men studying for the ministry. Papers of the Reverend Joseph Patterson show how he collected contributions. The following is copied from a subscription paper he circulated on June 9, 1794; it shows the pledges of the congregation.

James Ewing, 5 bushels of wheat, at 2 shillings
William Flanegan, 1 bushel of wheat, at 2 shillings
Robert Moor, 2 bushels of wheat, at 2 shillings
John Logan, 2 bushels of wheat, at 2 shillings

James Laird, 4 bushels of wheat, at 2 shillings
Samuel Riddle, (in money) 7s.6d
John McMillan, cash $1
Joseph Patterson, cash $6
Mrs. Vallandingham, 6 yards of linen
Mrs. Elenor Thompson, 3 yards of linen
John Gardike (a pious negro), 2 bushels of wheat
John Kelso, 4 bushels of wheat
James McBride, 3 bushels of rye
Hugh McCoy, 4 bushels of rye
Alexander McCandless, 2 bushels of wheat
George Vallandingham, cash, 7s6d
Mrs. Nesbit, 3 yards of linen
Widow Riddle, 3 yards of linen
Her daughter, Mary, 3 yards of linen[61]

Thus were laid the foundations of what was to become Jefferson College, and later Washington and Jefferson College. The people had a will to maintain and support the Academy, and they did. Some of the contributions received by Joseph Patterson and the other pastors were given to McMillan as treasurer and some to Colonel Canon as refund.[62] There are several entries in the Minutes of the Academy that show McMillan lent money to keep the Academy solvent.

In 1798, with universal approval, the Academy elected McMillan honorary president. And when in 1800 a movement was begun to convert the Academy into a college, McMillan, Allison, Cook, and Ritchie were chosen a committee to draft a petition to the legislature. Thus, on January 15, 1802, Canonsburg Academy became Jefferson College.

Jefferson College Chartered, 1802

On April 27, 1802, the Board of Trustees elected McMillan first president of the Board, but since he could not serve on the Board and the faculty simultaneously McMillan resigned the presidency to serve as professor of divinity.[63]

The trustees, the Synod of Virginia, and the Presbyteries of Redstone and Ohio validated this appointment. The trustees required him to have his students write dissertations "on the most striking thing immediately connected with their subjects."[64] This request from the Board to a professor was considered odd even in that day, but it was explained that James Dunlap, the principal, would not make assignments unless directed by the Board. And so to avoid embarrassment the Board included McMillan's department in the order.

JOHN McMILLAN

In 1805 McMillan accepted the position of vice-principal and when James Dunlap resigned as head of the College on April 5, 1811, he assumed the duties of principal, employing professors and attending to administrative affairs until a president could be elected. It was in 1805, too, that Jefferson College conferred both the degrees of Master of Arts and Doctor of Divinity upon McMillan.[65]

Out of the college funds, $266.67 was appropriated to employ teachers for the summer session.[66] At a fall meeting of the Board McMillan was instructed to contract for teachers with the sum of $450.

In April of 1812 Andrew Wylie, a graduate of Washington Academy and of Jefferson College, was elected president of Jefferson College. John McMillan was relieved of his administrative duties, but only until the "college war" of 1815 and 1816.

Washington and Jefferson College Chartered, 1865

The so-called "college war" is an interesting chapter in the histories of Washington College and of Jefferson College. Seldom have the people of the Western Country been so divided in their loyalties. It had become evident that it was increasingly difficult to support two institutions drawing their students from the same area and set up to give the same service to the community. The question of which location, Washington or Canonsburg, should be the home of the united college was not easily decided.

At the Jefferson College Board meeting, September 26, 1815, a letter was read from the Washington College Board. Washington College said they hoped Jefferson College would appoint a committee to meet with their committee to discuss the union of the two colleges. The Jefferson minutes read: "Accordingly Dr. McMillan, and Messrs. Kerr, McDonald, and Murdoch were appointed a committee on that business to meet at Emory's Tavern on the ensuing Friday."[67] No decision was reached.

A second meeting of a committee of six, three from each institution, met at Graham's Tavern, which was half way between the two institutions, a month later. It was not easy for either college to yield. The Washington committee made a financial offer and a proposal that the college be located in Washington.[68] The Jefferson committee refused to accept any proposition "until the hand of Providence was revealed more clearly." They did say that they would accept five thousand dollars from Washington if they could have half the trustees and carry the whole thing back for discussion with their teachers. But the plan for union was not approved: there was a tie vote for it and against it.

The students of Jefferson College framed a resolution to keep the College in Canonsburg. Rumors flew and hot words were exchanged by the townsfolk of both communities. To make matters worse President Wylie of Jefferson accepted an appointment as president of Washington College. The trustees of Jefferson College refused to discuss the matter of union any further and expressed themselves in this way in a communication: "This Board, therefore, cannot . . . open a correspondence with the Board of Washington College until they explain their conduct respecting the agreement they made with Mr. Wylie, the late principal of Jefferson College, while in our employ."[69]

The "college war" was on in earnest. The *Washington Reporter* published Washington College's reply. Jefferson College responded in a document reported by James Ramsey and John McMillan. McMillan accused Wylie of secret communications with Washington College officials.[70] Wylie published an article with the title "Hint of What May Be Said in Opposition to the Report of the Committee of the Board of Jefferson College So Far As the Author Is Implicated by That Report, and Its Sister, The Protest." This article involved McMillan with the others in these caustic words:

And how will they who have endeavored to blast my reputation and ruin the usefulness and comfort of my whole life,—I say, how will they answer for it to a generous public, a republican public who have the same sympathy for a poor man as for a rich man; above all, how will they answer for it to their God, if it can be substantiated that they! yes! they! Rev. McMillan and Matthew Brown, and the whole of them of the opinion that the union of the College was formed and actually binding! All of the Jefferson Board were of this opinion except Mr. Ramsey.[71]

Thus we see that McMillan took sides in the "college war." Joseph Smith in *Old Redstone* says "After the battle was over, and the smoke dispersed from the field, we never heard that he was much hurt anyway . . . though it was, for a while, one of Dr. McMillan's very serious annoyances."[72]

In 1820 the Synod tried to unite the colleges at Washington, but nothing came of their efforts either. There was, in the early 1860's, an attempt to unite the schools but have the teaching divided between two campuses. As might have been expected that plan did not work because it was neither economically practical nor unifying.

In the meantime, in 1817, John McMillan's nephew, his brother William's son whom he had educated, was made president of Jefferson College. Dr. McMillan's pleasure at this appointment was not long lasting, for in 1821 William's presidency came to an embarrassing close. President William McMillan refused to accept the Board's leadership in settling a student "rebellion."

It was during McMillan's lifetime that Jefferson College built a new building which Moses Allen named Providence Hall.[73] There was a meeting hall in the building sixty by ninety feet, there were classrooms and laboratories and meeting rooms for the two literary clubs, and there was a refectory in the basement.

Another important incident in the growth of Jefferson College happened in McMillan's lifetime. In 1824 the Jefferson College Board was asked to permit a medical college in Philadelphia to operate under their charter but remain independent in the power to grant its own medical degrees. This, the second medical school in Pennsylvania, added greatly to the prestige of Jefferson College. On April 19, 1838, however, Jefferson Medical College became an institution in its own right with no further dependence upon Jefferson College.[74]

It was not until after John McMillan died that the union of the two colleges was really consummated. In 1865, not without bitterness of feeling from many people, the state legislature issued a charter uniting the colleges of Washington and Jefferson into one institution to be located in Washington, Pennsylvania.

It must have been a hard decision to make, to ask the people of Canonsburg to give up their local college to which they had contributed so much in energy and hope. But some decision had to be made, or the work of all the people back to the log schools of the frontier might have been in vain. How John McMillan and those other pioneers, Joseph Smith and Thaddeus Dod, would have felt about the consolidation, of course we shall never exactly know. There is good reason to believe, however, that any immediate disappointment would have dissolved, as the years that have passed have shown their pioneer efforts and their good works united firmly in the strength of the fine old western Pennsylvania college of liberal arts, Washington and Jefferson College.

V. NOTES

1. *National Cyclopedia of American Biography.* 251.
2. See the McMillan Manuscript printed in Joseph Smith's *History of Jefferson College.* Appendix, 413-417.
3. Thomas Murphy. *The Presbytery of the Log College.* 73-75.
4. *History of Jefferson College.* 416, 417.
5. Murphy. 68.

6. Charles A. Briggs. *American Presbyterianism.* 186.
7. Murphy. 9, 10.
8. Thomas C. Pears, Jr. and Guy S. Klett. "Documentary History of William Tennent and the Log College," *Journal of the Presbyterian Historical Society.* March, June, and September, 1950.
9. These manuscript sermons are in the Department of History of the Presbyterian Church of the U. S. A., Witherspoon Building, Philadelphia.
10. D. K. Turner. *History of the Neshaminy Presbyterian Church.* 18.
11. George Whitefield. *Journal of George Whitefield.* 44, 45.
12. John Dewitt. "Historical Sketch," *Princeton Sesquicentennial Celebration.* 332.
13. Murphy. 89.
14. Francis J. Collier. "Chartiers Church and Its Ministers," *Centennial Celebration of Chartiers Church.* 11. James I. Brownson. "Educational History," *Centenary Memorial.* 74. James D. Moffatt. "Scotch-Irish in America," *Proceedings and Addresses of the Eighth Congress at Harrisburg, Pa.* 181.
15. *History of Jefferson College.* 6.
16. Gaius J. Slosser. "Concerning the Life and Work of the Rev. John McMillan, D.D.," *Journal of the Department of History of the Presbyterian Church, U. S. A.* XV. 135.
17. Collier. 12.
18. *History of Jefferson College.* 15.
19. Joseph Smith. *Old Redstone.* 81.
20. *History of Jefferson College.* 14.
21. *Old Redstone.* 81.
22. *History of Jefferson College.* 374.
23. Cephas Dodd. "Memoir of Dr. T. Dodd," *Presbyterian Magazine.* IV. September, 1854.
24. *Centenary Memorial.* 74.
25. *History of Jefferson College.* 384.
26. *Old Redstone.* 81.
27. *History of Jefferson College.* 386, 387.
28. *Ibid.* 388.
29. *Old Redstone.* 350.
30. *History of Jefferson College.* 381, 382.
31. *Ibid.* 386.
32. *Ibid.*
33. *Ibid.* 390.
34. Collier. 13. See *History of Jefferson College.* 373-397.
35. Brownson. 75.
36. Eliakim A. Jeffers. "Historical Sketch of the Period of the Schools and Academies, 1780-1802." *Centennial Address.*
37. *History of Jefferson College.* 11.
38. *Ibid.* 12.
39. *Ibid.* 18, 19. See the Minutes of Jefferson College. The original minutes have been found and are a recent acquisition to the Library of Washington and Jefferson College.
40. James D. Moffat. "Presbyterianism in Washington, Pennsylvania," *The Proceedings at the Centennial Celebration of the First Presbyterian Church of Washington, Pa.* 64.
41. Robert Patterson. "Letter to Matthew Brown," *The Presbyterian Advocate.* September 1, 1849.
42. *Ibid.*
43. Brownson. 76. Boyd Crumrine (ed.). *A History of Washington County.* 438.
44. *History of Jefferson College.* 29.

45. Moffat. "Presbyterianism in Washington, Pennsylvania." 65.
46. *Ibid.*
47. Minutes of the Board of Trustees of Washington Academy, 1787 to 1806.
48. Moffat. "Presbyterianism in Washington, Pennsylvania." 65.
49. *Old Redstone.* 80.
50. *Ibid.* 20.
51. *History of Jefferson College.* Appendix, 395.
52. See Appendix C.
53. *History of Jefferson College.* 385.
54. *Ibid.*
55. *Old Redstone.* 193.
56. Minutes of the Synod of Virginia. I. 79.
57. James R. Allbach. *Annals of the West.* 758.
58. *Ibid.* 425. Alfred Creigh. *History of Washington County.* 221.
59. *History of Jefferson College.* 439.
60. Creigh. 221.
61. *History of Jefferson College.* 32. See also *History of the Presbytery of Washington.* 31.
62. *History of Jefferson College.* 31.
63. Matthew Brown Riddle. "Historical Sketch of Jefferson College," *Centennial Celebration of the Chartering of Jefferson College.* 7, 12.
64. *History of Jefferson College.* 74.
65. *Ibid.* 72. See "Class of 1805" on an unnumbered page near the close of the book.
66. *Ibid.* 88.
67. *Ibid.* 92.
68. Minutes of Washington College, October 26, 1815.
69. *History of Jefferson College.* 99.
70. Minutes of the Presbytery of Ohio. IV. 54.
71. *Washington Reporter.* September, 1818.
72. *Old Redstone.* 201.
73. Creigh. 224.
74. George M. Gould (ed.). *The Jefferson Medical College of Philadelphia.* I. 87.

VI. PRESBYTERY

McMILLAN was a presbytery man for more than fifty-nine years. He was a licentiate of New Castle one and a half years (October 26, 1774-April 22, 1776), a member of Donegal for five (May 25, 1776-May 16, 1781), of Redstone for almost twelve and a half (May 16, 1781-October 15, 1793), and of Ohio for forty years and one month (October 15, 1793-November 16, 1833). During his lifetime McMillan was under the jurisdiction of three different synods—New York and Philadelphia, Virginia, and Pittsburgh.

By temperament and training McMillan was a pioneer, a missionary, a "revival man," a preacher with first-rate theological training, hard-headed practical good sense, immense energy, deep and sometimes rigid faith in the form and spirit of his Church; and certain the Church should push on into the West. Through most of his life, he was dedicated to building up Redstone and Ohio, each at its beginning the western presbytery of the synod, and he was suited for his work.

To know a little of the history of the presbyteries and synods to which McMillan belonged, something of the ministers he worked with rather closely, and some of the matters in which he was busy may help to make clear how zealous he was in his church and may show, too, how lasting was the urgency which at twenty-four turned him to the western parishes of Chartiers and Pigeon Creek rather than to any in the East.

HISTORY

On October 26, 1774, "within a few days of twenty-two years of age," McMillan was licensed to preach by the Presbytery of New Castle.[1] This Presbytery was within the Synod of New York and Philadelphia. The first synod in America, the Synod of Philadelphia, established in 1717, the authority for three presbyteries—Philadelphia, Long Island, and New Castle[2]—had divided in 1745 into the Synod of Philadelphia and the side Synod of New York and New Jersey because "of the different views entertained about the closeness and searching stringency to which candidates for the ministry should be subjected, in inquiries about their *experimental acquaintance* with religion."[3] In 1758, a "happy reunion" of the

Synods of Philadelphia and New York had taken place. Within the Synod were lands west of the mountains, though its limit in the West and, later, the boundary between it and the Synod of Virginia were as unsettled as was the boundary between Pennsylvania and Virginia.

In 1788, the Synod of New York and Philadelphia *"Resolved unanimously,* That the Synod be divided" into four synods, one of which "shall consist of the Presbyteries of Redstone, Hanover, Lexington, and Transylvania; to be known by the name of the Synod of Virginia."[4] Since the organization of the first presbytery in America, the Presbytery of Philadelphia, by seven ministers in 1706,[5] the western land had been a region for missionary endeavor; when McMillan was licensed there was alive a remarkable missionary spirit in the New Castle Presbytery. McMillan having decided after his trip over the Alleghenies to accept Calls from Chartiers and Pigeon Creek was at his request "dismissed [April 22, 1776] to join the Presbytery of Donegal."[6] The Presbytery of Donegal, though named for a town east of the Alleghenies, stretched undefined beyond the mountains and so included Chartiers and Pigeon Creek. It was the Presbytery reaching farthest into the West.

In 1781, five years later, four ministers with charges in this region beyond the mountains—Joseph Smith, John McMillan, James Power, Thaddeus Dod—requested the Synod of Philadelphia and New York "to be erected into a separate Presbytery to be known by the name of the Presbytery of Redstone."[7] The Synod allowed this request (May 16), and appointed its meeting for "Laurel Hill the third Wednesday of September next, at 11 o'clock, A.M." However, the meeting was not held at Laurel Hill "by reason of the incursions of the savages, rendered it impracticable."[8] On September 19, 1781, the time appointed, it was held at Pigeon Creek, one month before Yorktown. Three ministers—Dod, Power, and McMillan—and three elders attended. Dod preached; McMillan was chosen moderator.

HISTORY OF THE PRESBYTERY

Redstone is the name of a creek which flows into the Monongahela not far below Brownsville in Fayette County, a place then often called Redstone Old Fort. Redstone Presbytery included "most of the country, whether claimed by Pennsylvania or Virginia which lay west of the mountains."[9] It had "ecclesiastical jurisdiction over Presbyterians scattered throughout the entire western frontier."[10] Redstone, then, became the presbytery farthest west. In 1788 it was attached to the Synod of Virginia. McMillan regularly attended the meetings of the Synod "though it cost him long and fatiguing journeys across the mountains."

The four who organized Redstone were a notable group. All were relatively young—Smith, forty-five; McMillan, twenty-nine; Power, thirty-five; and Dod, forty-one. Each was sharp-cut in appearance and actions. Each had come to the West because he chose to work in a pioneer parish. All worked with great and constant vigor. All were effective ministers, though their ways of preaching differed. McMillan was brusque, direct, speaking with "his voice like the rumbling of thunder;" Dod was "gentle," "earnest," a "moving" preacher, "persuasive," "particularly attractive to the young," a scholar in the classics and in "the exact sciences," "with the happy faculty of infusing into those who were capable of it, an intense love of science and literature;" to describe Power, those who knew him repeat the words "graceful in manner," "neat," powerfully evangelical," "a polished gentlemanly man," easy and gracious in manner, and a good judge of a horse; Joseph Smith was "tall and slender," of fine countenance, eyes brilliant, a great educator, a kind and vehement man, "a happy man" with "peculiar charm about his cheerfulness," often a preacher whose sermons were fully logical yet "of unearthly grandeur," who could set hell flames flickering before the sight of his listeners, who did the "kind of preaching that drives a man into a corner of his pew, and makes him think the devil is after him."[11] All were scholars; three set up schools in which were trained the second generation of ministers for the West. All reached high position in their community and their church; and all deeply affected many people who later settled western New York, Ohio, Indiana, Illinois, and the lands beyond.

MEN OF THE OHIO PRESBYTERY

Then, in 1793, twelve years after the beginning of Redstone, McMillan and four other ministers on the frontier requested they be formed into the Presbytery of Ohio. The Synod of Virginia established this new Presbytery, in which McMillan continued until his death. Since the division the Presbytery of Redstone (1781-1793) has often been called Old (undivided) Redstone. The four other ministers who with McMillan organized the new western-facing Presbytery were John Clark (1718-1797) of Lebanon and Bethel; John Brice (1760-1811) of Three Ridges (West Alexander) and "at the forks of Wheeling;" James Hughes (1766-1821) of Short Creek and Lower Buffalo; and Joseph Patterson (1752-1832), pastor at Raccoon for twenty-seven and a half years. When the Presbytery was organized McMillan was forty-one; Clark, seventy-five; Brice, thirty-three; Hughes, twenty-seven; and Patterson, forty-one.

Finally, the Presbytery of Ohio, still looking to the West, became part of the Synod of Pittsburgh. This, the first Synod centered in the West, was "erected by the General Assembly, in May, 1802."[12] "The act recites 'that the Presbyteries of Redstone, Ohio, and Erie be constituted a Synod, to be known by the name of the Synod of Pittsburgh, and that they hold their first meeting in the Presbyterian Church, in Pittsburgh, on the last Wednesday of September next.'" The Synod met on September 29, 1802. McMillan, he being then in his fiftieth year, opened it with a sermon from Romans, the sixth verse in the eighth chapter: "For to be carnally minded is death; but to be spiritually minded is life and peace." Thirty-one years later in October, 1833, McMillan, when he was eighty-one, preached twice at the meeting of the Synod in Pittsburgh, scarcely a month before his death.

John Clark (1718-1797)

John Clark came to live in western Pennsylvania when he was sixty-three. He may have visited it the year before. Probably he was born in New Jersey. He was graduated from Princeton in 1759, licensed to preach in May a year later, and the next April ordained as an evangelist by the Presbytery of New Brunswick. For twenty years he was in New Jersey, Maryland, Eastern Pennsylvania, and New York, either as an evangelist or as a minister in a series of congregations.[13]

It is supposed that during 1781, his first year within the limits of Redstone Presbytery, he "labored as the stated supply" of two congregations, Lebanon and Bethel (eastern and western divisions of Peter's Creek), which probably he named from pastorates he had held in the East. These congregations McMillan had a close interest in, for he had helped build them up. In his *Journal*, 1776, he writes: "Tuesday after the first Sabbath of November preached at Peter's Creek, baptized five children" and again in 1779 he preached there "at Oliver Miller's," and once again in 1779 and twice in 1780. While Clark was the supply, McMillan visited the church—twice in 1781, three times in 1782—and after Clark had become a member of Redstone Presbytery and had been installed as pastor (March, 1783) fairly often the *Journal* has such entries as the one of May, 1783: Administered the Sacrament of the Lord's Supper, being assisted by Mr. Clark who preached on Saturday," and that of August: "Assisted Mr. Clark in the administration of the Lord's Supper." McMillan and Clark, it seems, often were working together.

The minutes of Redstone Presbytery for March, 1783 record:

The Reverend John Clark formerly a minister of the New Castle Presbytery now makes application to be admitted as a member of this. Upon his producing sufficient testimonials and his dismission from the Presbytery, he is accordingly received and takes his place as a member of this.

He was at once installed as pastor of the two churches he had been supplying. He gave up Lebanon in 1788 partly because of ill health and partly because the number in the two congregations had increased; at Bethel he was minister until April, 1794, three years before his death. He is buried in the churchyard there, beside his wife Margaret, who died in 1807 and who, if the epitaph has been read correctly, was born in 1729.

John and Margaret Clark, so it seems, had no children.[14] In 1779, however, while they were still in Maryland, they took into their family a Welsh boy of four and a half, William Jones, whose father had been killed that year in the battle of Stony Point and whose mother had died.[15] Clark was then sixty-one. When they came to Bethel the boy was about seven; he was twenty-three when Clark died sixteen years later. Clark left him all or part of his library and money for his education. William Jones studied at Canonsburg Academy, taught school in Pittsburgh in 1804, came back to Canonsburg for his theology, was licensed in 1808 and ordained by the Presbytery of Lancaster on the day after his twenty-sixth birthday on December 26, 1809. He served in the ministry about fifty-nine years after he was licensed. Into his eighties, he was active in the Presbytery of Columbus, Ohio. He lived a long life of more than ninety years; and it was written of him sixty-five years ago, he lived "in favor with God and man—a laborious worker, a faithful and acceptable preacher." Like Clark, "He had considerable skill in sacred music and was fond of teaching it to his young people, and was revered and loved by them accordingly." Six of his twenty children became doctors; one became a minister. His life and Clark's cover almost one hundred and fifty years, from the time the thin crescent of Penn's Settlements edged the lower Delaware until the time when three million people made up the commonwealth of Pennsylvania, and the Pacific Ocean bounded the United States three thousand miles west of the Delaware.

Clark was active in the Presbyteries of Redstone and Ohio, though for fewer years and less intensely than McMillan. He regularly attended meetings. He served as supply; for instance, in April, 1792, the supply preaching for one fast day was, as the minutes record, to be done "by most of the members two Sabbaths each, and by Mr. Clark, four Sabbaths." He was then seventy-four. He was agent for inquiries made for the Presbytery when a minister or a congregation or a layman brought a question to it, and often, for the Presbytery, he gave counsel or rebuke, or he worked to bring agreement between those at odds. He was one of the Presbytery when it decided in the Barr case. He was an original trustee of Washington Academy in 1787[16] along with McMillan, Dod, and Joseph Smith. Early in its history Jefferson College had a fund of more than six thousand dollars left by Clark.[17] He, like other members of the Presbytery, took a few young men into his home and taught them theology, though, as the *History of Jefferson College* says, "We cannot learn that . . . the *Rev. John Clark* . . . had any personal charge of a school." We do know, however, that John McPherrin, "a scholarly and saintly minister" of the next generation, after studying with Smith at Pequea Academy and being graduated from Princeton, did "prosecute" his theological studies "under the direction of the Rev. John Clark, pastor of Bethel, Allegheny County, Pennsylvania."[18] We know, too, that Joseph Patterson, when he was twenty-two or twenty-three, was in Clark's congregation in Saratoga County, New York, apparently "influenced in this choice of a residence, by a desire to enjoy the instructions of this estimable man."[19]

Those who tell of him in the West, tell he was "of very feeble health" (he lived to be seventy-nine); "spare almost to leanness"; "grave" and "sedate"; at times preaching with a deeply moving power of emotion; under whom "there was an extensive revival of religion"; a man "revered and beloved by his parishioners"; esteemed and venerated." Joseph Patterson "often spoke with great respect and commendation" of Clark's "sincere godliness and useful labors."

Clark wore eighteenth century smallclothes with buckles and a stock, and it is said he was the only minister in the region who affected a white peruke tied into a queue. Like many of the time he held slaves, probably two. It is a legend that at his church the singing of the Psalms was good, "owing partly to the uncommon vocal powers of a pious colored woman belonging to Mr. Clark. Her voice, which was very sweet and melodious, could be heard above all the voices of the congregation." Her name was Dido. "He had also a colored man, Dave, whose bass alone was sufficient for a large congregation."[20] In his will he provided Dave should be free after the death of Mrs. Clark if "he behaved himself."[21]

In 1794 the Whiskey Rebellion was on in western Pennsylvania. The morning of June 17, five hundred men were gathered "at the site of an old refuge from Indian attack, known as Couch's Fort," only a little way from Clark's church, Bethel Church. They planned to march on Bower Hill, General Neville's estate four miles away, "the only fine mansion in the country," "a princely estate" with a "manorial mansion" worth, it is said, ten thousand dollars "and richly furnished and surrounded by quarters for fifteen or twenty negro servants." They intended to demand General Neville's resignation as inspector of the fourth survey. Clark, strongly on the side of the government, went to them and "besought and counselled the people not to proceed in such an unholy and unlawful business." "They heard him patiently," told him he was departing from his profession by meddling in politics and marched on to Bower Hill. At Bower Hill there was a battle; the insurgents burned all the buildings except one smoke house. Some say that Clark's was the only "considerable opposition"[22] the insurgents met on their way.

John Brice (1760-1811)

John Brice was born in Harford County, Maryland, a county bordering on the Susquehanna River and Chesapeake Bay. He came with his father and mother to western Pennsylvania, probably to Washington County, before 1781, when he was a student, for a short time, under McMillan. And by 1783 or 1784, it seems, he was studying with Thaddeus Dod at Upper Ten Mile. Upper and Lower Ten Mile—two country communities—were about ten miles from Washington and about ten miles apart, and they were, then, "by far the most perilous posts of our western Zion."[23] The two made up Dod's parish. For protection Lindley's Fort had been built about 1774 near Upper Ten Mile, close to what is now the village of Prosperity. The Fort "was one of the strongest forts in the western country . . . it was the most exposed to the hostile incursions of the savage inhabitants."[24]

When Brice, in August, 1786, offered himself before the Presbytery "to be taken on trial,"[25] he had studied under McMillan

JOHN McMILLAN

as one of his first students according to the McMillan manuscript, had been a student in Dod's school, and had studied with Joseph Smith in his Kitchen School at Upper Buffalo. After the Presbytery had satisfied itself at this meeting of Brice's fitness to be a candidate, it then examined him in Latin, Greek, metaphysics, logic, and moral philosophy, and assigned him an exegesis to be given in the spring before the Presbytery. His subject was *An mortuorum resurrectio erit?* In April 1787 Brice discussed his thesis and, as the minutes record, it was sustained. He preached at least four sermons before the Presbytery and passed further examinations in philosophy and systematic theology. He was dicensed April 15, 1788 and at thirty was ordained, April 22, 1790, and installed as minister for the congregation of Three Ridges (near what is now West Alexander, fifteen miles southwest of Washington close to the West Virginia border) and of the Forks of Wheeling. Thaddeus Dod preached the ordination sermon, and McMillan presided and gave the charge. Brice was one of the first two ministers who were wholly trained and ordained west of the Alleghenies; the other, James Hughes, was ordained the day before Brice.

For eighteen years (until June, 1808) he was minister of the same two congregations, "constant in his care," until he resigned because of ill health. In 1810 he was dismissed to the new Presbytery of Lancaster, "but returned his certificate without using it."[26] Until the year before his death, as his health allowed, he did missionary preaching in Greene County, often "in what is now the Unity Church,"[27] and in northwestern Virginia. On August 26, 1811, he died. He is buried in the old graveyard of Unity Church. He was married twice, first to Rebecca Kerr, sister of James Kerr, an elder of Pigeon Creek Church who was a member of the state legislature for ten terms. She died in 1792, "on a Sabbath-day, whilst he was two or three miles away administering the Sacrament";[28] the second time to Jean Stockton, sister of the Reverend Joseph Stockton, a student of McMillan's, principal for ten years of Pittsburgh Academy, and a teacher in the Western Theological Seminary. Brice lived fewer years than any other of the five who organized the Presbytery of Ohio, and the number of his preaching years was less.

Brice has been written of as a man of "deep piety," "an admired and successful preacher," one who had a lasting effect for good upon the growth of the churches he served and upon his people. "Many rich fruits of his ministry appeared . . . in his . . . charges and in the country adjacent." He was "of nervous temperament, subject occasionally, to great despondency of mind." He seems never to have been robust. "He was once, perhaps twice, suspended from his ministerial functions on account of mental derangement."[29]

Brice is a shadowy figure only here and there given outline by scattered points of fact. He seldom becomes more than a general statement pinned down now and then with a date. Though he is mentioned often in the church writings of his time what is said of him is a repetition and emphasis of one or two of the qualities he had; there is little variation on the human theme, little taking him from a wide angle. Yet he was one of the men and women in southwestern Washington County who lived on the edge of danger. For more than twenty years after about 1770, the Indians kept up attacks there. Lindley's Fort and the other ones had to be strong. A ruling elder in the church was a benefactor—Demas Lindley was —when he gave land for the first fort as well as land for the first church. In 1792 "an old lady, Mrs. Nancy Ross, near where West Alexander now stands . . . went out to look for her cow, when she was . . . tomahawked and scalped."[30] Others were killed, about this time and later, in West Finley County and on Wheeling Creek, country first settled about 1785. Again and again in the records of the Executive Council of Pennsylvania is a minute like: "twenty-five pounds specie to be paid . . . for two Indian scalps taken in the county of Washington"; or "twelve pounds, ten shillings specie, to be paid to Adam Poe for taking an Indian scalp in the county of Washington agreeably to the proclamation of the Board."[31] An entry of this sort comes fairly often in the records, especially just before the Revolutionary War and during it. Until after the 1790's southern and western Washington County clearly was a frontier.

While Brice was studying for the ministry he was in the midst of this. It is told in one of the few accounts that make Brice seem real that as Thaddeus Dod was preaching at Caleb Lindley's house news was brought that Indians had massacred a family on Wheeling Creek, eighteen miles away. This was in 1783 or 1784. Dod ended the service at once, and some young men in the congregation, among them one or two of Dod's students, set out with their guns for Wheeling Creek, "to bury the dead, or to follow the Indians if practicable." The young men "started on the run in Indian style." "I think," writes Dr. Lindley, who saw all this, "John Brice started in this company."[32]

A little about Adam Poe seems justified. Even up to 1785 most land north of the Ohio River was wilderness. South of the river, for thirty or forty miles west from Pittsburgh "a bold and hardy race" had come in the 1760's, most of them from eastern Virginia, migrants, shifting from place to place. They hunted the woods and prairies. They fought in Indian ways. When in 1769 western Pennsylvania was opened for settlement they were by training and temper "well suited . . . to act as a life-guard, as a protecting *cordon*"[33] to the settlements. Even with this protection to the north of them, the settlers found "every hour . . . full of peril . . . they worked in the field with weapons by their sides, and on the Sabbath met in a grove or rude log church, to hear the word of God, with their rifles in their hands." Yet it was possible for northern congregations—McMillan's at Chartiers and Smith's at Cross Creek—to be set up fairly early and to count on being fairly safe. Most of the congregations south and west in Washington County—Brice's and Hughes' for instance—were set up later; or if like Thaddeus Dod's at Ten Mile they began before 1780, they did not have any certain margin of partial protection. Adam Poe was a hunter and trapper along the Ohio. He and men of his sort—the Poes, the Wetzells, the Bradys, John and Isaac Williams—were great figures in early stories of western adventure. And they gave great service to the western lands. Adam Poe was paid in 1782 his twelve pounds and ten shillings specie for an Indian scalp; three years before, he signed the call for Joseph Smith to come as minister to Cross Creek and pledged he would pay one pound annually toward Smith's salary—two acts rather typical in the early history of Western Pennsylvania.

James Hughes (1766-1821)

James Hughes, the youngest of the five who formed the Presbytery of Ohio, was born February 22, 1766, in York County, Pennsylvania, to which his parents—"esteemed for their consistent religious character"[34]—had come from England. About a year after the death of his father, Rowland Hughes, his mother, Elizabeth Smiley Hughes, in 1780 took the family to Washington County, then very much the Indian frontier. She was a woman "eminently pious," three of whose sons became ministers. One of them, Smiley Hughes, died soon after he was licensed.[35] Another, Thomas Edgar Hughes, after being graduated from Princeton, studied theology with McMillan and founded an academy at Greensburg (Darlington), Beaver County, Pennsylvania.[36]

The *Letter* to Carnahan and the *Manuscript*, both written in 1832 by McMillan, make clear that Hughes studied in McMillan's school as early as 1781. As was said in Chapter V, the two papers give the events one after another, chronologically, as they happened. The *Letter* and the *Manuscript* show McMillan was careful to set events in a sequence of time. He made this clear when, toward the end of the *Letter,* he explained "I forgot to tell you, in the proper place, that I was born on the 11th of November, 1752." Just before he mentioned the revival of December, 1781, he wrote that he undertook to educate "pious young men for the ministry," and he put Hughes among the students who studied classics with him. The revival of 1781, then, came after Hughes entered his school.

Hughes is next named as a student with Dod between 1782 and 1785, and as studying later with Smith when Smith opened his school at Upper Buffalo. This shifting from one school to another is understood when it is realized that the different schools taught different subjects at different times. One school might be emphasizing classics, and another science, and another theology; Smith in *Old Redstone* says that while Hughes was with Dod he "developed a taste for the accuracies and intracacies of science." McMillan and Dod and Smith were friends, working together for a common end; it was not at all unusual for students to move or to be moved from one of them to another. Hughes studied with all three, and it is not unlikely that having begun with McMillan he returned to him after he had finished his study with Smith.

It has been argued that Hughes, who in 1780 was fourteen years old, was then hardly of an age to be classed "a pious young man" preparing for the ministry. Yet Ross taught in McMillan's school when he was eighteen and was a member of the Bar at twenty-two. McMillan himself had been graduated from Princeton at twenty and had married and accepted the Chartiers call at twenty-four. Thaddeus Dod though he "suffered interruptions in his studies from sickness" had his A.B. from Princeton at twenty. Joseph Hughes was a graduate of Jefferson College at nineteen and a licentiate at twenty. John Watson, though "almost unaided by a teacher's instruction", and though he learned his first Latin from a broken-backed dictionary and the tags of Latin heading *Spectator Papers,* and though he was kept busy tending the store and the tavern, was at nineteen teaching in Canonsburg Academy as an honor student; and at twenty-six his wide "scholarship embraced ... Spanish, French, Italian, Hebrew, Arabic as well as Latin and Greek."[87] It is to be remembered that the voters who in western Pennsylvania settled the Whiskey Rebellion were "male citizens of eighteen years of age or over." And it is, too, to be remembered that some parents did dedicate their very young child to the service of the church and educated him steadily to meet that dedication.

In August, 1786, Hughes and John Brice

> appeared before Presbytery, and offered themselves to be taken on trials in order to their being licensed to preach the gospel. The Presbytery proceeded to converse with them on their experimental acquaintance with religion, and proposed to them several cases of conscience, and having obtained satisfaction on these points, agreed to take them on trials.[38]

Hughes, they examined that day in logic and moral philosophy and mathematics and natural philosophy and Latin and Greek and metaphysics, and being satisfied they assigned to him, for the spring meeting, an exegesis on original sin. In the next two years he preached at least four sermons before the Presbytery, one of them a "popular sermon" on Psalms 89:16. Again he "satisfied" the Presbytery, and on April 15, 1788, at the age of twenty-two, he was licensed to preach; "the first minister licensed west of the Alleghenies." Two years later, November, 1790, the Presbytery, after hearing his assigned sermon, appointed his ordination at Short Creek the next April. There, the twenty-first of April, 1790, they, to use the customary phrasing of the minutes, "did, by fasting and prayer, and with the imposition of hands, set apart to the holy office of the gospel ministry." Smith, his father-in-law, preached a sermon on John 4:36: "And he that reapeth receiveth wages, and gathereth fruit unto life eternal: that both he that soweth and he that reapeth may rejoice together." McMillan presided and gave the charge. Hughes was the first minister at Short Creek and Lower Buffalo.

Hughes labored at Buffalo "with great usefulness" for twenty-four years, not only in the congregation but in supplying weaker churches and in "Missionary work among the Indians and settlers in Ohio,"[39] and in other activities of the Presbytery. He was, too, on the first board of trustees of Canonsburg Academy and a trustee of Jefferson College, 1804-1814, and later of Miami University, 1815-1819.[40] "He became the first teacher of the institution."[41] It is told he was a "faithful and unpretending preacher," "a prominent presbyter and greatly respected," "zealous," a pastor under whose ministry "a number of revivals occurred," a man who had "escaped all contentions about worldly affairs," and always was greatly anxious for the prosperity of the Church.

After twenty-four years, he resigned from his congregation "in order to evangelize the Indians and settlers in these western wilds" and went to Urbana, Ohio. There, in the Presbytery of Miami, from 1815 to 1818, "he acted as stated supply and missionary." The rest of his life he was pastor of the Presbyterian church at Oxford, which "it seems clear" he organized,[42] and was principal of the Grammar School connected with Miami University.[43] He died May 22, 1821.[44]

His interest in missions was constant. Constantly, he went farther and farther West with the tides of immigration. He made many missionary tours among "destitute settlements" and at least twice (probably more) went among the Indian tribes on the Sandusky River. The journal of his mission among the Wyandots is a piece of interesting writing.[45]

In 1838 someone, who, fifty years before, heard Hughes preach to a congregation on the far edge of the frontier, tells what he remembers of the preaching. To read what he has written may half-suggest the enthusiasm and force with which some ministers were pushing ahead into what McMillan, though he lived on the frontier, has called the "backwoods":

Arrangement was completed for organizing a religious congregation many miles in advance of any existing congregation. Preparations were made in the depth of the forest. A rough wooden erection was constructed as a pulpit, and felled timber . . . as seats. Thursday was the day . . . for the first meeting; and the sun never shone on a more genial day . . . of June. For miles around the whole population was collected together. The minister came to make his trial sermon, a young licentiate, with his wife in company.[46]

The young man was James Hughes, at twenty-two; the young wife was the daughter of Joseph Smith.

Joseph Patterson (1752-1832)

Joseph Patterson's religion, it seemed to many who knew him, made him happy and secure. A friend wrote: "He went among us as the happiest person in society,"[47] and later he added: "His course was early taken—and his onward march was steady to the last."

Patterson was born in County Down, Ireland, March 10, 1752, the same year McMillan was born in Chester County, Pennsylvania. They died one year apart.

When Patterson was a boy plowing his father's land "the affectionate explanation of his pious father" led him to accept the faith he held the rest of his life. At twenty he married Jane Moak.[48] In the next fifteen years he had many changes of occupation and many adventures. The year he was married he immigrated to Eastern Pennsylvania; next he went to Saratoga County, New York, where his son, Robert, was born in 1773; a year later he went again to Pennsylvania when his parents settled there; and having by then somehow got academic training he taught a school near Germantown. At Philadelphia he heard the first public reading of the Declaration of Independence, and since "his mind . . . had those exalted sentiments of patriotism which then . . . consecrated the intelligence, and piety, and reason of our country"[49] he volunteered for the war. In 1778, after at least two years of service, he was out of the army and among the settlers gathered because of Indian raids at Vance's Fort, now Cross Creek, fifteen miles northwest of Washington in Pennsylvania. He was twenty-seven years old, "an intelligent and pious man," and had been active as a lay preacher while at the Fort. Soon, however, he left the Fort and with his family he was at work in Washington County.

This was frontier country, a long way from the safe eastern slopes of the mountains. It had few settlers, thin-scattered farms, almost impassable roads, uncertainty of government (Did the land belong to Virginia or Pennsylvania?), and it was "subject to the most appalling scenes of massacre."

Few congregations in this country had a resident minister though the people there were eager in their religion, and so, when in the early 1780's new settlers began to flood over the Alleghenies, there was "great destitution among the people of the means of grace." Even in 1784 Redstone had only six ministers for the established congregations and the constant supplies. The Presbyterian Church of America had been, since its founding (1706), a missionary church and on the lookout for young men fit to enter its ministry. Patterson had been active in his church; indeed he had wished to become a minister but had had his family and his parents to support. To the churchmen who knew Patterson's devotion and ability he seemed "as one on whom the hopes of Zion could be fixed." What came about Patterson wrote years later for a friend:

> In the fall of 1785, being thirty-three years old, it was thought best, with the advice of the Presbytery of Redstone, that I should endeavor to prepare myself for the gospel ministry. There being no places of public education in this western country, I with a few others, engaged in preparatory studies with the Rev. Joseph Smith of Buffalo congregation.[50]

A good many days each week he had to be away from his family. With Smith he studied three years or so. During this time, in

April, 1787, he "offered himself to the Presbytery to be taken on trial for licensing"; was examined on "experimental acquaintance with religion, cases of conscience, logic and moral philosophy," natural philosophy, and presumably Greek and Latin; read before the Presbytery an exegesis on the divinity of the miracles; several times preached before it, the last time a "popular sermon"; was licensed to preach in August, 1788 and served often as a supply; and on the tenth of November, 1789, was ordained.[51] The next day he became pastor at Montour Run, and at Raccoon where he was minister for twenty-seven years.

So when he was thirty-seven Patterson began his active ministry. After thirteen years he gave up his charge at Montour Run because each of his congregations by that time could support its own minister; at Raccoon he stayed until he was sixty-four years old—until "bodily infirmities rendered it impossible." The rest of his life—fifteen years—he lived in Pittsburgh, "this ungodly city."[52]

In Pittsburgh, Patterson "when in tolerable health and the weather favorable" divided his day among three occupations: "reading and meditation and prayer"; meeting friends, visiting those sick or in trouble, talking with whoever came for his advice or his prayers; and distributing Bibles and Testaments for Bible societies. He is said to have given away almost seven thousand Bibles.

At some seasons of the year, almost every day of the week would find him passing along the shores of our rivers, entering hundreds of boats . . . of emigrants . . . kindly inquiring after the welfare of these . . . giving . . . advice as to their secular concerns . . . and making sure that they were supplied with a copy of the Bible . . . and it is believed that there are hundreds of families scattered through the vast regions of the West, who will long remember the kindness and counsels of this apostolic man, whom they never saw or knew, but when they touched for a few hours at the wharves of this city.

Sometimes they would follow him from boat to boat . . . at others, they would betray a strong curiosity to know what could be his motive, in taking so much pains, at his advanced age, to ascertain whether they . . . wanted anything which he could supply . . . they treated him with great respect . . . in the most grateful manner.[53]

The last half of his life, the time after he came to Raccoon was fairly level, different from his earlier adventure and change, yet it showed what kind of man he was. And it may be right to name here part of what he was most busy over in these years. He carried on his heavy work in the congregation: "He was still remembered at Raccoon (1870) as a good and great man—prompt to his word and conscientious in the discharge of his every duty."[54] All the time, too, he often went as supply among "new and destitute settlements" and "young and feeble churches," and in 1802 he was among the Shawnee Indians. Before he came to Pittsburgh, he preached—so it is recorded—2,572 "morning sermons," not counting "afternoon discourses" and discussions and talks and the sermons he gave with less formality in the homes of his parishioners. He was on the first Board of Trustees of Jefferson College and was indefatigable in working for missionary societies and Sunday schools. He still preached fairly often after he came to Pittsburgh. His last sermon was in the Second Presbyterian Church of Pittsburgh a month before his death. He preached then on "the path of the just is as a shining light."

Some of those who knew him have told what qualities they found in him. They write of his "moral fervor", his fire of belief, his humbleness (in his letter of resignation from Raccoon he said: "I resign my charge . . . after being pastor of Raccoon twenty-seven years and six months, for every day of which I need pardon through the Blood of Christ"[55]); his continuing happiness, his tranquillity; his love for his family—his parents, his wife and children and grandchildren—and his care for them; his great capacity for cheerful and long friendship with persons as different as those in the Presbytery (of whom McMillan was one) and the tough riverboat men; his firm faith in his religion and the tenets of his church; his practical ability (Even when he was a boy, he was a good ploughman); his charming manner—easy and "polished"; his thinking no evil about any man yet seeing clearly that one act was right and another was evil; his giving to young ministers help not tainted by patronage or the superiority of his longer experience; his "accurate practical judgment" and his unworldliness; his humble closeness to God, Whom he held in awe but with Whom he could talk over little or big matters; his "power of extended exhortation," and, equally, of short striking proverbial speech; his gift of interesting children, "who loved to hear him speak and to greet him . . . in the streets . . . to do him some act of kindness"[56]; his secure scholarship; his touch of mysticism.

Perhaps the differences among these qualities and their variety and contrast may keep Patterson from seeming too much a paragon, or a figure for an allegory, or an uncomfortable and impossible and unlikable perfection.

Many incidents have been told which line in Patterson's character. Patterson—so one story goes—had subscribed six dollars toward building a meetinghouse for the congregation. This must have been before the days of his ministry. When the morning came to pay the money he did not have it but with his gun on his shoulder he started out for the schoolhouse where he would need to tell he did not have the money. He came to a grove where "God and nature seemed to invite him . . . to prayer." While he was praying he heard a rustling among the trees. He opened his eyes and saw a panther stalking him. He raised his gun, shot the panther, skinned it, brought the scalp and the pelt with him to the schoolhouse "as a trophy of his victory," and sold them for six dollars, and paid what he had promised. This "is a tradition in the northern part of this county (Washington, 1870) in regard to the Rev. Mr. Patterson, verified by the most substantial aged men of our county."[57] This legend has variations in detail, as legends which stay alive do have: the panther is a wolf[58]; Patterson needs four dollars not six; he is an elder of the church; he is praying in an open meadow. But the core of the meaning stays.

Once while he was "a poor student of divinity" he was to go to a meeting of the Presbytery. In a letter to his wife he told her that as he looked at it he

regarded with mortification the napless, worn-out hat. In retirement for special prayer yesterday, the Lord let me talk familiarly with him about many things; particularly about a hat; and he made me willing to go to Presbytery with my old one. I came away . . . well pleased with all his government; and this day was one bought for a guinea and is sent to me, a present from A. S.[59]

After he came back from the first missionary journey to the "Indians beyond Pittsburgh," McMillan asked him how he had got on. "Well we started with no provisions but corn meal and bear's grease. My stomach revolted . . . as I believe in special prayer, we knelt down. I told the Lord I was willing to serve Him, but He must give me something I could eat or I would die." McMillan asked if the prayer had been answered. "Yes! . . . I laid down in the forest . . . and when I awoke he gave me an appetite so voracious that corn meal and bear's grease tasted *good*, which was as much an answer to prayer as though He had sent me beef and pudding."[60]

For many years a legend persisted that after Patterson had gone away from Rancoon sometimes he still might be heard praying alone in the church there.

Many other stories are told of him.

PRESBYTERY MATTERS

The records of each Presbytery to which McMillan belonged show how earnestly he was part of it. After he was ordained, his

JOHN McMILLAN

name almost always follows the *Ubi post preces siderunt* — the opening formula before the list of members who "sat" in the meeting. No one else in Redstone Presbytery worked more at church business. When the Presbytery of Ohio was established he might well have ended his work in Redstone but he went on with it and attended the meetings as a corresponding member. Joseph Smith writes, "McMillan attended to this duty . . . and . . . attended the meetings of Redstone Presbytery for eleven years after Ohio Presbytery was formed." "This duty" was his being supervisor and treasurer of the school at Canonsburg, which the Synod of Virginia had commissioned Redstone and Ohio to carry on together.

He gave many kinds of services. He preached at the opening of a session. He examined candidates who presented themselves. For the Presbytery, he went to meetings of other Presbyteries, to the Synod, and to the General Assembly. He presided and gave charges at ordinations. He preached when ministers were installed. He made inquiries for his Presbytery. He served on committees, unendingly. For sixty years McMillan worked. The center of his life was his constant search to know God's will so he might try to fulfill it. And for him the way of his Church was the way through which to find out God's will on earth and to establish it.

McMillan's presbytery years had in them matters—some much like others, and in general pleasant to him, and recurring fairly often; some unusual, and at times unpleasant. To tell a few may give realization of what McMillan was very often busy about or may show what come only once; and the telling of the recurring or the special matter a hundred and fifty years after it happened, may make his long years in the Presbytery better understood and, so, more alive.

BARR CASE

When the Redstone Presbytery met in December 20, 1785, "Samuel Barr of the Presbytery of New Castle, being present"[61] (as was McMillan), asked that the Presbytery approve his accepting a call from Pittsburgh and Pitt Township. Redstone approved, "provided Mr. Barr became a member of this Presbytery." At once Barr accepted the call; but Redstone did not receive him from New Castle until a year and four months later, during which time he was the minister at Pittsburgh without being installed. On April 17, 1787, he was received into Redstone Presbytery from the Presbytery of New Castle. Almost exactly two years after this, at the meeting which began April 21, 1789, Barr formally asked "for

118

dismission from the united congregations of Pittsburgh and Pitt's Township"; and the Presbytery ordered that "the congregations be notified thereof and to attend at our next meeting, to show reason, if any they have, why Mr. Barr's request should not be granted." Then for a year and a half followed discussion and rediscussion by the Presbytery, by a committee of the Synod, by the Synod, and by the General Assembly. In the end, on the last day of September, 1790, Redstone did dismiss Barr, as he had asked. Behind the spacing of these dates is a fairly tangled story which cannot be understood without some knowledge of the facts of Barr's life, the kind of town Pittsburgh was about 1790, the acts of the Presbytery and the Synod, and the part McMillan had in the case.

* * * * *

Samuel Barr, when he was thirty-three, came from County Londonderry, Ireland into the Presbytery of New Castle in Delaware.

He was born, his daughter Jane writes, February 4, 1751, near the town of Londonderry:[62] He was the oldest son. His father, who died young, was "a respectable farmer," and his mother was "of Scotch parentage . . . distinguished for her devoted piety and great decision of character," who instructed her children "in the great principles of the Christian religion, praying with them, and for them, and dedicating them." From 1775 to 1783 he studied arts and theology at the University of Glasgow, from which he was graduated and from which in April, 1780 he had been certified to preach. Then he went back to County Derry, where in 1784 the Presbytery of Londonderry certified him.[63] That was in May. We know he was in America by the middle of the year, for records show that when he presented his credentials to the Presbytery of New Castle in October he had been preaching for some months.[64] The Presbytery, after examining the soundness "of his character, ability, and religion" and after testing him for nine months by having him "preach to the congregations within our borders, which he did with great acceptance," "certified him, *sine titulo,* in June 1785, to travel to various churches in the Southern states."

Almost as soon as he was ordained he started West—in June. He stopped at New London, twenty miles from New Castle, where he presented a letter of introduction from a friend in Ireland to James MacDowel, whose daughter Mary he married the next year. He preached at New London and was "immediately invited to fill their pulpit, as stated supply, which he did for several months, so much to their acceptance, that they gave him a unanimous call."[65]

At the time he did not make definite answer, though the congregation was a rich and well-established one, but went on over the mountains to Pittsburgh.

His daughter conjectures that his going to Pittsburgh and later staying there as minister came about in this way:

Mc. MacDowel, my grandfather ... extensively engaged in the manufacture of flour ... and had a train of wagons ... employed in carrying it to Fort Pitt, then the very far West. ... Hotels were scarce ... and all genteel travelers ... coming east ... were all entertained at his hospitable mansion. ... My father meeting these responsible gentlemen from Pittsburgh there, *as I suppose,* was so impressed with the importance of the field and its entire destitution that he decided in favor of Pittsburgh.[66]

At Pittsburgh he was invited to preach the Sunday "after he had shown to the leaders of the congregation his credentials from New Castle." He was the first Presbyterian minister to preach there in nine years. Pittsburgh, it is to be remembered, had no well organized congregation. After this first service, Barr was "entertained at dinner at the home of Robert Galbraith, Hugh Henry Brackenridge being among the guests."[67] Barr's sermon and his whole manner seem to have pleased those he met and Barr seems to have been pleased with them—with Robert Galbraith and Judge Wilkins and Judge Wallace and Colonel Gibson and Colonel Bayard and General Butler and the others. After Barr had preached both at Pittsburgh and at Pitt Township and other nearby congregations, Galbraith one morning offered him a subscription paper which he had taken around before "Barr was out of bed," and told him "the people wanted to try their abilities, whether or not they could support a minister"[68] and wished him to be their minister. Barr encouraged the idea but did not give his decision. The congregation went ahead: it got subscriptions for church support, had the Reverend John Finley write the necessary formal Call, saw to other matters, and then Pittsburgh together with Pitt Township forwarded their Call to the Presbytery of New Castle.[69] The Presbytery approved the Call and the same day "put it into Mr. Barr's hands for consideration" (October 28, 1785). Barr was then back in New London. On October 29 he declined the Call from New London, accepted the one from Pittsburgh and Pitt Township, and was married to Mary McDowel. "A few days later," writes his daughter, "they set out for Pittsburgh, performing the whole journey on horseback, and taking with them as a servant, a colored girl, who also rode a horse to which she was strapped to prevent her falling off in case she went to sleep." December 20, as has been said, Barr asked Redstone to approve him as minister for Pittsburgh.

At first Barr had great success. The membership of his church grew, and they and many besides agreed with Brackenridge that he was "a gentleman of reputation, and a good preacher."[70] In the East he got money for his church, as the Presbyterians of New York and Philadelphia, eighty years or so before, had got help from England or Scotland. He had a part in the General Assembly's incorporating, September 29, 1787, "the Presbyterian Congregation of the town of Pittsburgh and the vicinity thereof" instead of the "religious Christian society, under the care of the Rev. Samuel Barr" which Brackenridge had advocated in his bill to the General Assembly. He had part, too, in getting John Penn, Junior, and John Penn to deed two and a half lots of land on Sixth Street and Virgin Alley (one of three such church grants) to the Presbyterian congregation "in Consideration of the laudable Inclination which they have for encouraging and promoting Morality, Piety and Religion in general, and more especially in the town Pittsburg as of the sum of Five Shillings."[71] (September 24, 1787). On this land, where the First Presbyterian Church now stands, the log church begun in Barr's first year in Pittsburgh, he dedicated in 1787, probably in May. He and Brackenridge were the most active in organizing the Pittsburgh Academy in 1787, and he was one of the three "to report a plan for building a market house and establishing market days."[72]

Yet, from the first he met difficulties. The trustees of his church were largely officers who had served in the Revolution, practical politicians, keen and successful business men—not especially sensitive or especially scrupulous about details. Nor did they care much for Redstone Presbytery's strict standards, which they thought "narrow and intolerant." Barr held his office in honor. Clearly, he wished to carry out what he judged were his responsibilities, but he found he often was hindered by the leaders of his congregation. The incorporation of "the Presbyterian congregation" roused "warm argument," especially between him and Hugh Henry Brackenridge, which broke into rather untempered letters to the *Gazette* (March 17, June 16, 30, 1787). His salary was not fully met. More serious were the differences between him and some of his parishioners over what beliefs and speech and conduct were right for a member of the congregation; differences, that is, over card playing, swearing, immoderate drinking, and "worldliness and loose living." These differences grew more sharp until, after he had been four years in Pittsburgh, Barr at a meeting of the Presbytery said that he wished to resign (April 23, 1789). Then followed the long dispute.

In the dispute the trustees made many charges against him, but in the end their own testimony showed some of them had said Barr had embezzled when they knew he had not embezzled; some had made false statements against him and had locked him from the church to keep from paying him his salary; and some had intentionally been boorish to him—for instance at a supper party when he had spoken of the church's attitude toward card playing. In the end every witness against Barr when questioned changed or did not wish to repeat his earlier testimony. So the Synod, after a year and a half, dismissed Barr to the Presbytery of New Castle, where his new charge was.

For most of the next ten years only supplies preached at Pittsburgh; one of these, Francis Herron, preached before only eighteen persons; and as he puts it preached "to the . . . annoyance of the swallows,"[73] which seemed to claim the neglected log church. The congregation did give two Calls to candidates who had preached as supplies but neither was acceptible to the Presbytery.

Barr, his wife, and their two boys went to this pastorate at New Castle, Delaware, "within twenty miles of my mother's home," writes his daughter. The church was one of the three oldest in America, probably founded before 1700, well established and well supported. He did not come to Pittsburgh again but he was at Pitt Township in 1795. His daughter makes no reference to any difficulty within the Pittsburgh church. She clearly implies her father left because her mother, "a timid woman," never was happy in Pittsburgh and, besides, wished to live in the well established community where her own father was living. His daughter regrets "exceedingly that in the frequent removals of my father's family after his death most of his valuable papers were scattered and lost."[74] Barr lived at New Castle until his death, May 3, 1818. His pastorate there was a success. He and his wife, who died four years before him, are buried in the cemetery of the old church, and around them are the graves of many of their twelve children.

His daughter writes that her father was "prudent and sensible," "devoted as a husband and a father," "consecrated to the good of the Church in America." He is said to have liked people and to have been a cultured man, with undiminishing interest in books and in the affairs of his town and his country.

His daughter's recollections are by far the best personal record of Barr, and yet even the formal evidence from records of the trial shows much about him. Barr was an emotional man but he had excellent intelligence. He was courteous, well bred, more of a reader than most ministers about him; never personally vindictive even when he was fighting for what he thought was right; ready to overlook much so long as he did not need to overlook a principle; tenacious and energetic yet hardly tough-skinned enough for the company he was in; surprisingly practical in the affairs of the town; possibly thinking Redstone not the absolute in all church doctrines and manners, possibly even thinking it "contracted," but never wishing to get partisans by criticising Redstone, since he and the Presbytery were both trying to know and to carry out the will of God.

* * * * *

Pittsburgh in 1875, when Barr came to it, was a frontier trading post; that is, it was a town of contrasts and contradictions. Those who wrote then about Pittsburgh often differed violently. All agree it was a "metropolis," alive with trade into the immensity of country west and north and south; but they have little agreement about the size of the place and the kind of people who lived in it.

The enthusiasm of H. H. Brackenridge in the first number of the Pittsburgh *Gazette* of July 26, 1786 shows one side. He gives the town:

A hundred dwelling houses with buildings appurtenant. More are daily added and for some times past it has improved with an equal but continual pace.... It must appear like enchantment to a stranger... to see all at once, and almost on the verge of the inhabited globe, a town with smoking chimneys, halls lighted up with splendor, ladies and gentlemen assembled, various music and the mazes of the dance.

He writes that the inhabitants are sturdy, hardworking, religious and number "about fifteen hundred." He writes much of the beauty of the islands and hills and fields and rivers; "there is not a more delightful spot under heaven to spend any of the summer months than at this place." "When I first saw the town in 1781," so he wrote in the first article in *Gazette Publications,* "it was in fact a few old buildings, under the walls of a Garrison, which stood at the junction of two rivers. Nevertheless it appeared to me as what would one day be a town of note." (Years later he explained that he "intended to give some reputation to the town with a view to induce emigration to this particular spot.")

A German traveler, a surgeon for German troops used by the British in the Revolution, however, in the fall of 1783 sees "perhaps sixty wooden houses in which live something more than a hundred families" who are "poor, lazy, ravenously greedy, and unwilling to work for reasonable wages." "Of public houses for worship . . . there are none."[75] Arthur Lee, from Virginia, in 1784 found in Pittsburgh Irish and Scots "who live in paltry log-houses, and are as dirty as in the North of Ireland or even Scotland."[76] Even John Wilkins, who lived in Pittsburgh for forty years, when he first came in 1783 could see "no appearance of morality or regular order . . . no signs of religion."[77] In other accounts the people, almost all of them, are the shifting men and women of the river traffic, the residue of the army, those who bought and sold in the Indian trade, and those who offered lodgings without comfort. Probably at the time there were about thirty-six log houses, one stone house, one clapboard-finished house, and six or seven stores. Probably less than four hundred people were in Pittsburgh then.

Yet we know that in the town and in the country about, lived men of culture and wealth and high intelligence, educated at the best universities of the East and of Scotland and England, highly able in law and medicine and the church and the army, accustomed to discuss national affairs and philosophy and history, and knowing the classics and English literature and especially the French Encyclopedists and Shakespeare and the Bible. We know that in 1784 a town plan—Woods' Plan—was drawn up for the Proprietors, the Penn's, which plotted a good design of streets and spaces for churches and an academy and gardens and the building of homes. We know that by 1787 many lots had been sold and some houses built. The map for this plan exists and so does proof that the plan was carried out fairly soon and rather fully. The first church building came in 1786; the Academy in 1787; the *Pittsburgh Gazette* in 1786; the public market a year or so later. We know that in the country about, mansions began to be built with true taste and to be furnished with elegance which came from memories of eastern and southern houses. "Bower Hill," built by General Neville before 1790, was a "mansion," and so was General Morgan's, whose "fashionable family" once drove to McMillan's church in their fine carriage. The O'Hara's, by 1790, had "brought elegance to Pittsburgh" when James O'Hara and his bride came to their new house on the edge of the King's Orchard, by the Allegheny River. In their house was oak paneling, books, Georgian silver, gold-framed mirrors, and carpets—a floor covering quite new to Pittsburgh and, as it seemed to many, "coverlids" hardly to be walked upon.

These violent differences were unified by Pittsburgh's being a pioneer town. Since the frontier often required action close to the earth, a simplification of the differences among many kinds of people came from their having to act together. They might have been used, some of them, in other times and places, to thoughtful talk and quiet and conventional manners, to wax candles and Georgian silver and walnut paneling, and may have read classic English and Latin and Greek, but the first church was a church of squared logs, at the building of which even a gentleman of the town, as one of them tells it, "took off his coat and worked with his hands" and with assistance "chunked and daubed"[78] the new building. A merchant and a lawyer and the others did truly put their hands to getting the church built and to many other necessary and simple frontier acts. From a settled and cultured community, Barr and his wife came to Pittsburgh over trails hard to follow and thick with mud and dust; they and others were used to the amenities of Philadelphia and the established East. It is true that there were no sidewalks until 1802 and that the sidewalks then were gravel or cinder paths held in by planks, but weeping willows and poplars were already planted along the new streets. There were no churches or school buildings or markets when Barr came; but these soon were built. Brackenridge lived at John Marie's rather free and easy tavern—some called it a "tough tavern"—but the tavern was often the meeting place for discussing the building of the Academy and the church, and the good of the town, and the intensely interesting shift and play of politics, and the establishment of trade, and the war against the Indians and insurgents. The truth is, these men allowed the demands which pioneer ways put upon them, and, it seems, they enjoyed—most of them—the lusty, full-blooded, down-to-earth opportunities and necessities of the place and time. Into these conditions Barr came in 1785.

* * * * *

Samuel Barr is named first in the minutes of Redstone Presbytery for October 18, 1785, when John Hopkins and McAllister "represented to the Presbytery . . . that Mr. Barr . . . during his preaching in these parts, appeared to neglect" some usual requirements for baptism. The Presbytery agreed that inquiries ought to be made "into the supposed irregular conduct of Mr. Barr." This inquiry is not again mentioned in the minutes. However, at this meeting, McMillan, Clark, and Smith were made a committee to examine "all ministers and candidates as may come into our bounds before the next meeting." They were "to stand, as it were, at the gates of the city";[79] a phrase which in part at least sums up what these early ministers held their first duty.

Next, December 20, 1785, Barr is "approved" as minister for Pittsburgh and Pitt Township but not admitted to membership in the Presbytery. Then (April 17, 1787) sixteen months afterward, he is received from New Castle as a member. The minutes give no cause of this delay—or probation.

Almost two years later (April 21, 1789) Barr, sitting with the others of the Presbytery, asked to be dismissed from his parishes and gave his reasons. The Presbytery, the same day, "referred Barr's request to his congregation." At the next meeting, in May, a "number of commissioners . . . appeared from Pittsburgh," and the Presbytery, after hearing the tangle of contradiction, decided "there were some difficulties which could not be settled without meeting on the spot," and adjourned to meet at Pittsburgh in June for inquiries.

June 9, the Presbytery met at Pittsburgh. Finley, Clark, Smith, McMillan, Barr, and a number of elders were present. McMillan opened the session with a prayer. Next, Barr gave reasons for wishing to leave his two congregations. He said—to put it briefly —"too few" supported him in church discipline; the trustees did not "comply with their agreement" (they had as much as told him "he might hunt after his salary from door to door"); some of the elders often "indulged themselves in drinking and card-playing," were "covetous," "circulated false reports," and had kept "the congregation and himself from worshipping God in a peaceable manner in the house of worship." (Later, an elder testified that he and three other elders "one Sabbath last spring"[80] had locked Barr out of his church.)

Speakers for the session and the trustees answered: Mr. Barr "had not done his duty," "abstaining himself at sundry times"; Mr. Barr had failed by "not visiting the families" and had not baptized and examined "as he ought to do"; Mr. Barr had not given account of "a considerable sum of money" collected in the East "for the use of Pittsburgh congregation." The charges filled the two meetings on Tuesday. The testimony of Barr and his witnesses filled the next two days. On Friday the Presbytery gave its judgment: "The reasons offered by Mr. Barr why he desired a dismission . . . are groundless"; "his own misconduct principally . . . occasioned the people's non-attendance on his ministry." In short, "he ought not to exercise any part of his ministerial office until the mind of our Synod is known thereon." The Presbytery gave many reasons for their judgment. "The Rev. Messrs. Finley, Smith, and McMillan are appointed to transact the affairs relative to Mr. Barr's suspension."

On October 21, 1789 the Synod of Virginia met in Lexington. It listened to a transcript of the testimony given before the Presbytery, heard the new evidence Barr brought (it seems agreed that Barr acted with great skill as his own lawyer), and at the end of the third day, October 24, Saturday, decided that justice required a complete retrial. "The Synod therefore agrees to refer the consideration of the whole affair *de nova*"[81] to a committee which should meet in Pittsburgh and report at the Synod's next session.

Three members—a quorum—of the committee, Dodd, and Edward Crawford and James Montgomery, both of Lexington Presbytery, met in Pittsburgh on November 25, 1789. About "twenty pages, quarto, of charges, evidence, doings, &, &, read to the Synod, was put on the record." Barr again presented his case and called his witnesses. "Wallace, Wilkinson, Wilkins, Robert Galbraith, all being called upon collectively and severally (being present) intirely declined and do decline to have any hand now to support these charges against Mr. Barr."

The same gentlemen declared that they would never have exhibited any charges against Mr. Barr had they not been afraid, that if Mr. Barr left them without blame, that some arrearages due to Mr. Barr would still continue a burden upon the congregation; or in their own words, be saddled upon the congregation.

All who earlier had made accusations withdrew them or quite changed their testimony; no one of Barr's accusers repeated his charges. In Barr's favor new testimony in writing and by word of mouth was given. Pitt Township laid before the committee "a remonstrance signed by all its one hundred and sixty members witnessing that Mr. Barr had in all respect acquitted himself to their satisfaction." So at the end, the committee found "matters to stand in a different view, and theretofore determined that the charges . . . against Mr. Barr were wholly unsupported and that he be considered in full and regular standing in the church." This was, as has been said, in November, 1789.

At Winchester, September 30, 1790, the committee reported the evidence given before it and its verdict to the Synod. The Synod accepted the report and "consider Mr. Barr in the regular standing in the church." That same day Redstone Presbytery met at Winchester—Dod, Smith, McMillan, Finley, Patterson, McPherrin, Porter, and Barr being present—and "does dismiss Mr. Barr to New Castle since Mr. Barr is restored to the full exercise of his ministry."

Perhaps it should have been said earlier that just after the committee had cleared him but before the Synod had met, Barr again had come to the Presbytery and asked dismissal from Redstone. Redstone did not "see then the way clear for giving him a dismissal" because "they were not satisfied . . . all charges had been disproved" or "examined into, and because he was supposed to have preached while under suspension."

* * * * *

The Barr case grew out of the "chronic irritation"[82] between the Presbytery and the Pittsburgh church. Some causes of this irritation seem fairly clear.

For one thing, the town's absorption in trade and the value it set on quick prosperity, its laxness and its elegance, its tolerant carelessness about some doctrines and ways of living, its rather condescending superiority, brought it sharply up against other congregations and against the Presbytery. In other congregations most of the people lived far from one another, on land lately settled and often just cut from the forest. They built their own houses, made most of their furnishings and implements, spun most of what they wore, and raised what they ate. The man in Fayette County who built in 1783 a "two-story house of hewn logs, immortalized himself"; "the place was known for fifty years afterwards as 'the high house.'"[83] When people went on a journey they rode horseback or walked: no "gig, nor barouche." They lived close to earth in quite different ways from the ways of townsmen in the "metropolis." "The grand peculiarity of Western Pennsylvania . . . was the existence of a . . . free Christian yeomanry, without any towns whatever."[84] It was the country churches which sent ministers into the towns as supplies. In 1818 Wheeling had a thousand people in it, yet, as one man wrote,

This town was considered within the bounds of the Forks of Wheeling Presbyterian Church, six or seven miles distant and was visited by the pastor of that church . . . once in two weeks. . . . There were several respectable families in the town, called Presbyterians; but on inquiry I could find but one man and five or six old ladies who were communing members of that church.[85]

In 1802 many towns were classed by the presbyteries which made up the Synod of Virginia as "unable to support a minister." Most members of churches had "aversion, at first, to go into towns to attend upon public worship." They did not favor "building places of worship . . . in villages."[86]

And as a whole, Presbyterian congregations in the Western Country took their sermons and revivals and baptisms and sacraments with serious intensity. A sermon might last an hour and a half or longer, and more than one sermon might be given in one day, and services might go on for days. They were "accustomed to religious conversation, especially on the Sabbath." McMillan was a farmer, a revival preacher, an austere and dedicated man, "a guardian at the gate." He did not, at thirty-five, find some practices of the town easy to understand or allow. He and the other ministers of the Presbytery (in 1788 there were only seven permanent ministers besides Barr) might well be anxious over those who seemed to them absorbed in business and card playing and dancing and wine drinking, who used a "worldly tone of conversation," who seemed "triflers, or buffoons or merry-andrews."[87] He found the trends of town life (Pittsburgh was even then the town) contradicting much he believed.

Then, too, most Redstone congregations lived isolated, on the edge of danger. Pittsburgh they thought was safe, made so by an army and the United States fort. In country places many still took their guns when they went to church. "The Rev. Porter of Congruity used to examine his rifle before he announced his text."[88] They saw or had seen their neighbors scalped or carried off. In their isolation they had to build their own block houses. They thought they were burdened with responsibilities and dangers the town did not have. No wonder that "the ministers of these churches" were generally men of great gravity of manners and their dress and demeanor secured for them uniformly much respect, and, with younger people, even a kind of dread." Yet "all of them [the ministers] indulged in a hearty, joyous spirit. More cheerful men never lived."[89]

The Barr inquiry was only one of many such inquiries. From the first the Presbytery had felt a strong duty to examine intently —more intently than the town saw any need of—the doctrines and practices of "any candidate who came into our bounds." Two men whom it had allowed to preach had turned out "no acquisitions, but, on the contrary, sources of much vexation and trouble." The credentials of another "wandering star," given him he said by churches in South Carolina and England, were "judged ... forged."[90] Another who later asked to be installed at Pittsburgh withdrew his request when closely examined "upon experimental religion and cases of conscience." Of course good men were accepted—Clark and Finley, for example—and some good men were rejected. The point is the Presbytery felt profoundly responsible for those it sent among its churches. It found within its limits "an immense amount of ignorance, ungodliness and profanity," toward any form of which it could not be lenient. And so toward what it thought the sophisticated callousness of the town and a preoccupation, as it seemed, with things of this world, it could not, for any charm or vigor the town might have, be less than severe.

Barr was the minister of a congregation "not remarkable for its exemplary piety," one in which many members did not hold to the strict tenets of the church. Their training and occupation and interests were not those of most people in the bounds of the Presbytery. Dr. Herron later spoke of "the mournful absence of . . . vital godliness" in his early Pittsburgh congregation, and others said much the same. Joseph Smith in 1854 wrote that a large part of Barr's people were "gay, fashionable, worldly . . . living in conformity to the manners of the times." Most of the trustees of Barr's church did not come off well at the questioning of the later inquiry. Brackenridge—at first a close friend of Barr's —had wanted a "Religious Christian society,"[91] not a "Presbyterian congregation," and he had argued that to establish a church was "a high political good" and that being at services "teaches the lower class to attend to dress and to cleanliness" and "kindles in their minds a love of what is elegant."[92] He gives higher reasons than these but he puts upon utility an emphasis the Presbytery would have strongly denied.

Yet Barr, though McMillan did not at first see it, was standing pretty much for what McMillan stood for. In his sermon dedicating the log church he said the town had been "the very spot of the Western Country which was most noted for vice and immorality," and had been "a wide field of folly and dissipation," and had "squandered away" "29 years . . . in carelessness and ingratitude." But Barr was sure, as he said then, that "dark clouds of folly seem now to be passing by."[93] All of which some of his people counted as close to foolishness and to platitude, and as being what the eighteenth century might have named, with distaste, "enthusiasm." Indeed Barr's difficulty probably came less from lax standards than from not explaining clearly to his trustees and congregation what his standards were. And his difficulties may have come, too, from his not having the gift either of leading his people by persuasion into the ways he thought right or not having the firmness needed to drive his congregation, so diverse and so newly organized, on a tight rein. Barr, it is to be recalled, did succeed in his Eastern charge.

McMillan was never prominent in the Barr inquiry. He never comes as a partisan or prosecutor. Because he belonged to the Presbytery he carried out duties, usually minor ones: after the first complaint against Barr in 1785 he was one of a committee to examine *all* candidates; he was appointed to notify witnesses they should appear at the Pittsburgh inquiry; he gave the opening sermon when the Presbytery met at Pittsburgh for its inquiry; he was delegate from Redstone to report to the Synod the findings of his Presbytery; presumably he voted in the final judgment given by the Synod.

Yet in the testimony are many implied and some direct references to him. The verdict which ended the inquiry is based on beliefs he held. He probably more than anyone else embodied for the people of the Western Country the principles on which the Synod gave its verdict. Some of the questions put to witnesses before the committee which cleared Barr seem to show this. So do the questions Barr in his own defense put to Judge David Duncan:

Question:—"Did not the Committee of Pittsburgh express their desire that I would not connect myself with the Presbytery on this side of the Mountains."
Answer:—"Mr. Duncan answered, it appears to me that it was the wish of the Committee at that time."
Question:—"Did you hear any reasons from the Committee for expressing such a desire?"
Answer:—"Mr. Duncan replied, the reason he could not well remember, but they looked upon the Presbytery as rather rigid."
Question:—"Did Mr. Duncan hear me say at that time the Presbytery of Redstone were people of contracted minds?"
Answer:—"Not that I can remember."
Question:—"Did you previous to my coming to Pittsburgh hear the people belonging to the congregation of the Rev'd. Mr. McMillan called McMillanites?"
Answer:—"Yes."
Question—"Did you ever hear me call them by that name?"
Answer:—"No."[94]

Five trustees, one a judge and the others high Army officers, agreed with the substance of these answers and with others which cleared Barr.

McMillan is not often named in the inquiry. Yet his energy in the affairs of the Church, his straight-out if "severe" ways, his integrity and ability and devotion which all recognized, indeed just the force of his personality and even his big body and great voice, made him to many the symbol of their frontier church. In the end, almost all upon which the verdict is based, McMillan could have signed with his approval.

The Taylor Case

In April, 1784, in the early years of Redstone Presbytery, Henry Taylor of the Chartiers congregation, a man important in Western Pennsylvania, came before the Presbytery to appeal the judgment passed upon him by his church. It found him guilty of "encouraging a *promiscuous dance* at his house."[95] He denied the charge, denied it had been proved against him, and denied he had ever told McMillan, his pastor, "he had done what he was charged with." What he was charged with was, more exactly, that he had "directed and assisted the company in going through a reel in dancing." After hearing both sides, the Presbytery put off any decision until their next meeting because of "the smallness of the number present and the importance of the case."

Taylor was "necessarily absent" from their next meeting, nor do the minutes of Redstone show he was present before June, 1785. Then he again denied "that the charge against him was proved, or that he had ever confessed that he had done what he was charged with." The Presbytery heard witnesses. One testified that Taylor allowed the dancing at the request of the company only for an hour, and as recreation. Some members of the Presbytery testified they had heard him say he had allowed the dancing. In the end the Presbytery decided against Taylor. It did not consider the judgment of the Chartiers session too severe. "Mr. Taylor, in order to admission to church privileges, ought to acknowledge his fault before the Presbytery, or before the session . . . and be admonished." McMillan was to tell the congregation Taylor had acknowledged his fault. Taylor answered that he reserved the "liberty of appealing to Synod, if, upon deliberation, he should think proper."

A year later Taylor did come before the Presbytery, and he told them "that, upon deliberation, he was earnestly desirous that the jar between him and the Presbytery, respecting a judgment concerning his conduct on a certain occasion, be removed," for he wished "to live in love and concord with that branch of the church where he resides." He was sorry he had given offense; he would "guard against like conduct in the future"; he was "willing to submit to an admonition before the Presbytery." All this surely means Taylor had made "a relation" to McMillan. The Presbytery accepted his submission to its judgment, and it directed he be admonished by its Moderator and its judgment read before the congregation at Chartiers. Taylor was admonished then and there and the case ended after two years.

* * * * * *

Henry Taylor when he first came before the Presbytery was forty-six and already had taken large part in the affairs of Washington County. Even by 1784 it had a history dramatic, varied, and acted in by men strongly individual and full of energy. Taylor certainly held to his opinions and acted on them. He deserves to be seen as more than a figure in a church trial, though the trial does show much about him and about the Presbytery. To know more of him may help place him; and his being more real may help make more real the people of McMillan's congregation and the country and the customs behind them.

He had come West from Cecil County, Maryland, probably in later 1769,[96] the year the Land Office in Philadelphia was opened. There, for the first time, settlers could take title to land in the new country. Before this all the land had been Indian land. In 1770 Taylor settled in what was known as the Rich Hills, near Washington, to the northeast; that year he was "blazing out upon the trees the lines of his land" and building a cabin "about a mile northeast of Washington on the old Pittsburg clay road." Later, to make his rights secure, Taylor got a warrant signed by John Penn in February, 1771, for one hundred and fifty "Acres of Land on the Middle Fork of Chartiers Creek," near where McMillan came, "on the Path leading from Catfish Camp to Pittsburg."[97]

His holding was threatened when in 1782 someone made claim to it. To secure his title "suits of ejectment were brought by Henry Taylor . . . claiming under his Pennsylvania rights."[98] The case turned on who had first settled the land and marked its boundaries by blazing a line of trees. Alexander Bowling swore that in 1770 he saw Taylor with another man "surveying and Marking a Line" of his claim; "said Taylor was marking this White Oak Tree which stands about north-west of where Mr. Yates now lives." And Bowling saw there "a plain marked line toward the south east" and "his Cabban was a little way from where they then stood." Frederick Lamb, so he swore, "had seen on a Tree a small distance from them, with H T on it." This was "Land where Richard Yates now dwells on," and he thought it was Taylor's claim. Lamb swore, too, that Polser Shilling had said to him, "Yes, it is his Claim, and that he (Polser) was working there on purpose to affront said Taylor; . . . to quarrel with him, and give Taylor a Thrashing and would Black his eyes well." Taylor, Lamb went on, was a civil man and would not fight. John Williams swore that in 1770

he seen Henry Taylor Living in a new Cabban on the Rich Hills . . . . that when he was hunting there he saw New Marked lines which was Called Taylor's Lines" and "that Cabban on the Rich Hill where Taylor was living in was the first he knew or ever seen on the forks of Chartiers Creek.

John's brother, Isaac Williams, one of the "roving pioneers and hunters," not themselves settlers but of great protection to the settlers in the Indian wars, swore

That in the year 1770, that he saw Henry Taylor living in the forks of Chartiers Creek, that he understood he was Improving that Land that is now in Dispute, and to make a settlement thereon . . . . that he knew the work to be Done, as he hunted to get provision for the men while they were doing the work.

Taylor asked Isaac if Baltzer Shilling "did not make a practice of Running about Through the woods and Marking and Hazing trees and calling that his Improvements" (the settlers called this Tomahawk Improvement). Isaac Williams answered "he knew it well to be his constant practice." In the end Taylor kept his land. Definitely, Henry Taylor was a vigorous actor on the frontier scene. From his first coming into this country, Taylor was active at many things. In 1777 he was one of a "Council of War at Catfish-Camp in the District of West Augusta on Tueasday the 28th day of January, Anno Dom., 1777," against the British and Indians. He was a major then, and later "Brigadier General of the Brigade of militia"[99] drawn from Washington County. In 1781, the year Washington County was organized, he became the first president judge of its court, and later associate judge, although he was not a lawyer and never had been admitted to the Washington County Bar.

When McMillan came to his Chartiers congregation, Taylor was a member of it, an earnest if a most individual member.

The Birch Case

For eight years Thomas Ledlie Birch caused McMillan annoyances and troubles. The history of the Birch case is long and complicated and difficult to keep clear. Chiefly two men were involved, McMillan and Birch, and two groups, the Presbytery of Ohio and the congregation at Washington.

McMillan, in 1800, was forty-eight years old, distinguished in the Church, in education, and in public affairs.

Birch in his book, *Seemingly,* published at Washington, Pennsylvania, in 1806, wrote that for twenty years before he came to America he had been pastor of a Presbyterian church in Ireland, and that he had been persecuted (a word which may explain much he did later) and driven from Ireland. In 1798 he came to the United States and in Philadelphia preached to the congregation. At Washington were "a number of his old hearers and neighbors from Ireland," who Birch implies, suggested he come into the Western Country. So in 1800 he did come to Washington. He was a foreign minister, entitled to preach though he was not joined to the Presbyterian Church in the United States.

The Presbytery of Ohio, which in 1800, 1801, and 1802 heard Birch's charges and passed judgment on them, began in 1793. In early 1800 sixteen ministers are named as belonging to it. In 1802 it "consisted of sixteen ordained ministers"—not exactly the sixteen of 1800—and the elected elders.

The congregation at Washington had been from 1778 until 1793 part of McMillan's pastorate at Chartiers, but a local organization was effected in 1793 by the consent of the Presbytery of Ohio and four elders were ordained. It seems clear, though, that some sort of organization had been formed as early as 1785, for Alexander Addison, then a licentiate from Scotland and later president judge of four western counties of Pennsylvania, was then its supply, and the minutes of Redstone seem to imply there was a congregation at Washington which wished to call him as its regular minister.[100] However, from 1781 to 1793 supplies did generally preach there, in the courthouse, though for about a year after April, 1794, James Welsh, a licentiate from Transylvania, served until he resigned to go back to Kentucky; then until October, 1800, other ministers, among them Thaddeus Dod and Boyd Mercer, preached occasionally. The congregation seems to have been eager for a resident pastor.

The action of the Birch case may perhaps be said to begin when, October 23, 1800, Birch came before the third session of the Presbytery of Ohio at Raccoon and asked "to be taken under their care."[101] The Presbytery, which then had in it seventeen ordained ministers, examined his credentials and questioned him. In *Seemingly,* Birch reports some questions asked:

Question:—Wherein consisted the difference between regeneration and conversion?

Answer:—Regeneration, the work of salvation begun, Conversion, the work completed, ending in progressive Sanctification.
Question:—From whence Christ became the object of my worship and love?
Answer:—Christ being possessed of all those glorious attributes, uncreated perfections and excellencies which constitutes Deity, etc.

The Presbytery in the end decided they "did not receive such satisfaction as would enduce them to take him on any further trial." Birch said he would appeal to the next General Assembly. Though he did not belong to the Presbyterian Church in America, he could appeal to the Synod or to the General Assembly; the Assembly, however, could not give him membership in any presbytery. Birch, unsatisfied, asked McMillan, who had been the clerk, for an explanation. The explanation as Birch gave it was:

that the Presbytery charged me, with not receiving Christ as an all-sufficient Saviour. With bearing to Christ the love of an harlot, in alleging Christ the peculiar object of my love in bearing to me the relation of Creator and Redeemer . . . that I was held in error for asserting the terrors of hell were a motive . . . and that I also maintained that an unregenerate person could have saving faith.[102]

Birch had another talk with McMillan but about all he learned was that McMillan had no special love for him or his preaching.

On Christmas Day of 1800 part of the Washington congregation asked the Presbytery that Birch be named their pastor; and the next day Birch came a second time, and said he had withdrawn his appeal to the General Assembly. He asked that he be appointed at Washington. The Presbytery, after talking with him for a second time about his experimental acquaintance with religion, found that he was not "to consider himself as having any authority or permission from them to preach the Gospel." From this decision Birch said he would appeal.

The next April—April 21, 1801—part of the Washington congregation again supplicated that Birch be taken into the Presbytery and assigned to their church; again, the next day, the Presbytery heard Mr. Birch; again, the third time, it decided it could not receive him; and again Birch said he would appeal. The day after the Presbytery's decision part of the Washington congregation, April 23, "requested the P.b.y. to communicate to them their reasons for rejecting Mr. Birch." The Presbytery answered—as the minutes phrase it—"that after repeated conversations with him . . . they have not obtained that satisfaction which they conceived necessary to his reception." They added that Birch never had their authority or approbation to preach the Gospel, and that his ordination of elders and attempt to organize a congregation within the bounds of an old established congregation is deemed highly irregular, and directly contrary to the order of the Presbyterian Church."

All this time Birch was acting as the minister at Washington.

This would seem to settle the question definitely, but the first of July the Washington congregation repeated its request to the Presbytery. Birch himself asked a fourth time to be taken under the care of the Presbytery.

Whereupon after considering the matter the P.b.y. did resolve that they would have nothing further to do with Mr. Birch, as to his trials for the Gospel ministry. In doing that they conceive themselves fully justifiable from the frequent and full conversations which they had formerly with him, and from the general report which prevails with respect to his imprudent and irregular conduct.

Immediately, the same day the Presbytery had given its decision, the Washington congregation presented both its own complaints against the decision and the complaints Birch had ready for the General Assembly at its next meeting (May, 1802).

Before the General Assembly met Birch handed to the Presbytery (October 22, 1801) an enlarged list of charges—five this time—he would bring to the Assembly. Part of the complaint reads:

I complain of the P.b.y.'s being led to this unbrotherly act, by hearing reports from the Rev'd. John McMillan and William McComb, elder (behind my back) .... The Rev'd. John McMillan having informed me in my own house ... that he made conscience of telling the P.b.y. that on his road from the last general Assembly in Strasburg, a Thomas McConnell, Blacksmith, and James Mahon, his Journeyman, told him unasked, that I was in the shop a few days before, upon my way from the general Assembly, and that I was fond of Whiskey as a Dutchman; upon which Mr. McMillan asked them, what evidence I gave of being so! When McConnell and Mahon replied, I was staggering thro' the street, and talking fool talk.

This seems to be the first time Birch turned his accusations upon McMillan. Birch added that the Presbytery alone was responsible for any scandal and criticism that might come; "I complain of the decision of the Revd. P.b.y. of Ohio as void of Mercy"; he himself was ready for reconciliation. He further charged that McMillan had told Alexander Littel and Andrew McMahon he (McMillan) had spread a report of Birch's drunkenness, that McMillan had called him a "preacher of the Devil," and that McMillan had said he would use "every endeavor to drive him out of the country." After Birch had made his complaints, the Presbytery put into its minutes its reasons for not receiving Birch; it had some discussion of the charges against McMillan; and, to give Birch time to bring witnesses and affidavits, it adjourned the inquiry until its next meeting, January, 1802.

When it met on January 19, 1802, Birch came a fifth time before it and added another charge against McMillan: McMillan had been "asserting a corrupt, deliberate falsehood" on the floor of the Presbytery to avoid being censured for defaming him. He then handed in a second draft of complaint for the General Assembly with another charge against McMillan for "falsehood and defamation," and against the Presbytery for failing to discipline him. Strangely enough, on this same day, Birch offered to withdraw his complaints. This the Presbytery would not allow because "sd. complaint contained very high and groundless charges against P.b.y. which had been publicly read." It told him to carry the matter to the Assembly.

The Presbytery met for five days on April 20-24, 1802. In that time it considered what Birch had charged against McMillan; it passed over what he had charged against the Presbytery itself. In substance, Birch had accused McMillan of slandering him by saying he was a drunkard, a preacher of the devil, and a liar. In answer, McMillan said he had told the Presbytery in October that Thomas McConnell of Strasbourg had said "he thought Mr. Birch was the worse of spirituous liquor" when he stopped to have his horse shod as he was on his way home from General Assembly in June. McMillan also told the Presbytery he had said "he believed Mr. Birch to be a minister of the Devil." He explained the basis for his believing this: "the Presbytery had three times conversed with Mr. Birch" and found no evidence that he was "a subject of special grace."

Birch denied the three charges. To prove he was no drunkard, he gave a sworn statement of Thomas McConnell, a blacksmith, in which McConnell denied he had said to McMillan Birch had been drunk in Strasbourg. Then James Mahon, McConnell's journeyman, testified McConnell was one who "frequently spoke falsehood" because his mental powers had been impaired through the use of "spirituous liquors"; other witnesses testified Birch drank excessively and spoke deliberate falsehoods; and McMillan presented to the Presbytery a letter in proof that prominent men in the Washington congregation had written Birch while he was in Philadelphia "in order to prevent his coming among them."

This letter said that a "reversion of sentiment . . . has arisen from a degree of intemperance exercised by you at the houses of several of those men, who would have gone all together to support you."

Then McMillan gave two instances of Birch's lying. The first was Birch's statement in the *Western Telegraphe and Washington Advertiser* (January 11, 1802) that Andrew Swearingen, an elder in the Washington Church, had told Birch he had seen McMillan "take very hearty groggs"; that McMillan was losing his "usefulness and piety" and "getting all wrong of late"; and that McMillan had used rough language about a clergyman of another denomination.

Swearingen, under oath, had sworn the whole story in the newspaper was false; he had not said a word of all he was quoted as having said against McMillan. Swearingen added to his denial serious charges against Birch's character and actions as a minister.

The second instance was another statement of Birch's in the *Western Telegraphe* of January 18. He had written that McMillan "was the Father and ordainer of the Revd. P.b.y. of Ohio and of all the Elders of the Washington congregation; and that only Messers. Stockton and Wherry waited upon him from sd. congregation, with an invitation to settle among them." Robert Stockton and Joseph Wherry, elders of the Church, swore all this was untrue.

After hearing the testimony the Presbytery considered another of Birch's charges: "McMillan had asserted a corrupt, deliberate falsehood before P.b.y. in October last." James Patterson and Thomas Marquis, both ministers in the Presbytery, Alexander Little of Washington, Robert Anderson, leading partisan of Birch's in 1800 and 1801, Judge James Allison, and others told what they had heard McMillan say. After listening to all of this testimony the Presbytery asked Birch "whether he had any more testimony to offer?" He said he had not and "wished the P.b.y. to come to a decision."

Saturday, April 24, the Presbytery gave its decision. It found none of the charges against McMillan was supported by the evidence; yet because "the phrase Minister of the Devil is very harsh and ungaurded," they directed that Mr. McMillan be admonished by the Moderator "to be gaurded with respect to such expressions for the future." To this judgment McMillan submitted and was "admonished according." Before the Presbytery adjourned that day Birch handed in a paper, as the Minutes call it, a rambling letter for the General Assembly almost a thousand words long.

Again Birch did not accept the decision. As he had said he

would, he carried his case to the May meeting of the General Assembly. On June 29, the Reverend Thomas Marquis, one of the commissioners appointed to the General Assembly, reported to the Presbytery what had happened at the Assembly's May meeting. Birch had complained there that the Presbytery: (1) had "rejected him in opposition to decision and intention of general Assembly"; (2) had "passed an unjust and defamatory sentence"; (3) had "rejected all offers of Gospel accomodation with said Birch"; and (4) had "passed a corrupt judgment." The Assembly after deliberating found each charge was unsupported.

Birch did not accept the decision of the Assembly though he had written earlier "I . . . repose my honor and character in your hands." In the minutes of the Presbytery for June 29, 1802, is a letter from Birch saying that because the Presbytery had withheld papers from the General Assembly, he now had the "most disagreeable necessity" of entering civil suit against McMillan "in vindication of his character, and reparation of great injuries sustained." He asked the Presbytery for a copy of its records; and he ended his letter "Your injured but willing to be reconciled friend, upon Gospel terms." After his signature he added:

N. B. Though much injured as Birch wants not Mr. McMillan's money, nor to hurt his person, character or usefulness, if he will acknowledge he has wronged him, and promise to be a good neighbor—and this to be inserted in the minutes of your P.b.y. and of the very Revd. General Assembly, he shall be forgiven. T. L. B.

The Presbytery decided that the papers had not been withheld; that Birch could have a copy of the testimony given during the inquiry; that it was "improper that he should have either the names of the members at each session or the original depositions." And the Presbytery called upon him to go on with his appeal from the judgment of the session of the Washington congregation: he had made an appeal at the April meeting. Birch answered "he never would prosecute that charge or anything else before this P.b.y." The congregation had come, late in 1801, to an open division between the friends of Birch and those who, like the elders, followed the decision of the Presbytery. The four elders had "procured Washington Academy, in January, 1802, for religious worship, while it was closed against the adherents of Mr. Birch." The church was not reunited until the spring of 1805, when Matthew Brown, "an able and eloquent minister . . . received a unanimous call." [103]

Birch filed suit against McMillan in the Court of Common Pleas, Washington County. It was brought first at No. 41, November term, 1802; was transferred to Circuit Court at No. 8, September term, 1803; and was tried October 24, 1804, before Justices Jasper Yeates and Thomas Smith of the Supreme Court sitting on circuit in Washington.[104] For Birch, the lawyers were James Mountain of Pittsburgh (earlier a teacher in Canonsburg Academy and Pittsburgh Academy, a "most perfect classical scholar," "distinguished for his . . . humor and eloquence, a typical Irishman"), Joseph Pentecost and Cunningham Semple of Washington. McMillan's lawyers at the trial were James Ross (a teacher in McMillan's log cabin school and a student of theology with him, and at thirty-two a United States senator, 1794-1803), and Alexander Addison (a licentiate in Scotland, a stated supply at Washington, "President of the Courts of Common Pleas of the Fifth Circuit of the State of Pennsylvania"[105] until 1803, a distinguished and urbane and kind and learned man) both of Pittsburgh, and Parker Campbell ("the chief leader for many years of this [Washington] bar") and James Allison (a trustee of Washington and Jefferson and an associate judge of the Circuit Court) both of Washington.

The jury found "for the plaintiff in the sum of three hundred dollars damages and six cents costs."

At the first meeting after the decision of the Circuit Court in October, the Presbytery (December, 1804) put in their minutes that:

They seriously feared that if the law be as this decision makes it, that reasonable and necessary freedom of speech in Church Courts which is so essential to self defense, and a faithful and conscientious discharge of duty will be restrained and destroyed, and ecclesiastical discipline so useful to the morals of professing Christians, will be relaxed and subverted.

They decided to petition the legislature for a law which should give in church courts the rights of speech customary in civil courts. And, third, they "looked upon it as a duty they owed to themselves, to the churches under their care, and to their Fellow Christians" to state why in spite of the court's decision, the Presbytery stood firm in its earlier judgments: Birch drank to excess; he had "in several instances deliberately violated truth"; and McMillan had deserved only to be censured for calling Birch a minister of the devil. They added: "It is expected that this statement of the case will vindicate this conduct in retaining Mr. McMillan as a minister in their communion without any present judicial process or examination."

After the trial in the Circuit Court an appeal was taken to the Supreme Court "on a writ of error" by McMillan's counsel, Ross and Addison. The Supreme Court, sitting at Pittsburgh, handed down a decision, dated Saturday, September 13, 1806.[106] Chief Justice William Tilghman wrote the opinion, Justice H. H. Brackenridge concurred. The decision reversed the judgment of the lower court on error: the case was opened for retrial in the lower court.

The alleged slanderous words when spoken in a duly authorized hearing before the presbytery, were privileged and not actionable, unless spoken with actual malice toward the plaintiff.

The Chief Justice's decision—to give it in more detail—first defined the action:

It was an action for slander brought by *Birch* against *McMillan*, for calling him "a liar, a drunkard, and a preacher of the devil." The declaration stated that the plaintiff was "a man of learning, integrity, and piety, and that for twenty-eight years past he had been and then was a minister of the gospel in the Presbyterian church."

He then gave the principle upon which the court based its reversal of the case:

I consider malice an essential ingredient in slander.

He developed this by asking a question which he did not answer:

May not the occasion of the defendant's speaking be fairly and candidly said to warrant the conclusion, that he spoke not in malice, but in his own defence . . . ?

It was upon this point—the intent of malice—that he sent the case back to the lower court. This point, the Chief Justice wrote, had been

raised suddenly in the course of the trial; it was new; and the judges who tried the case, and who were obliged to declare their opinions in a short time, delivered the impression of their minds, not without doubt.

It seems, then, that to say "Dr. McMillan was acquitted"[107] by the decision is not wholly exact. Toward the end of his opinion the Chief Justice says about the retrial:

Whether the defendant will derive any advantage from it I know *not*.

Boyd Crumrine wrote in 1901 that the case "is a leading authority upon the principle of privileged communications in actions for libel and slander." *Bouvier's Law Dictionary,* page 3080, today a leading reference, cites it under *Slander,* and the A. L. R., the Pa. L. R., and other current law reports cite it. One case in the Pennsylvania Superior Court, 1945, quotes for a page from the decision.

After the decision of the Supreme Court, "the Circuit Court, on motion of Mr. Mountain, awarded a venire de novo": that is, the Court granted Birch permission to bring the case before it as a new case. However, on September 27, 1808, a short time before the trial, it was, as the docket of the Circuit Court says, "discontinued by the Plff."[108] McMillan agreed to pay the docket and three hundred dollars to Birch as damages. Birch accepted payment and withdrew the suit.

McMillan, it seems, never gave fully his reasons for dropping the case; he may have thought that explanation was not needed. Perhaps he decided that by another court trial, the church would gain nothing. Then, too, Alexander Addison, a friend and one of his two counsel before the Supreme Court, had been impeached in 1803—most unjustly many believed—and had died in 1807. James Ross, his other counsel, had become a Federalist candidate for governor in the election of 1808, at the time Birch's suit was about to come before the Circuit Court. In that campaign McMillan was attacked viciously and the Birch case brought again to the front because McMillan had written a letter commending Ross's "religious convictions." One opposition paper printed that McMillan "had signed a false certificate in favor of Mr. Ross's religious character";[109] and other abusiveness was printed. Besides, the suit was about where it had been when it began in the courts back in 1802. All these and the wearing ordeal of the eight years of controversy probably had part in McMillan's decision.

As a summary of the whole case it may be fair to say this: (1) McMillan deserved the rebuke the Presbytery gave him for his "harsh and ungaurded phrase, 'a minister of the devil,' " but since the Presbytery and the General Assembly had upheld him for two years, his having to go through six years of civil litigation was unjust. (2) The Presbytery was patient with Birch, and was wise in disregarding his charges against the Presbytery itself and in seeing the implications of the Circuit Court's decision; but the Presbytery was scarcely wise in letting Birch, to whom they had denied acceptance, stampede them into an immediate and rather unconsidered trial of McMillan. (3) Birch, it seems, brought charges before the Presbytery and the General Assembly and the civil courts mainly because the Presbytery was not willing to "take him under its care" or to accept him as a minister for a congregation within its limits. This last is the central point of all the controversy; it has hardly ever been spoken of. No doubt Birch blamed McMillan for the Presbytery's not accepting him.

Birch wrote in 1806 that he was "persecuted" years before in Ireland, and later was unfairly used by the General Assembly. The Chief Justice, however, wrote: It was proved in the trial . . . that the plaintiff . . . apprehensive [because he had] committed some irregularities in *Washington* county, by administering the sacrament and ordaining elders, in violation of the rules of the church, withdrew from the jurisdiction of the General Assembly."[110] Birch's difficulties came from his following ways the Presbytery judged not right for any one to follow.

This whole experience might well have embittered McMillan and have ruined his career. There is no evidence that it harmed him at all. Indeed the Birch case seems to have left him stronger than he had been eight years before. It has been said he was more bitter after 1808; of this there is no evidence. During the case and afterwards even those who did not accept much of what he stood for, seem almost never to have questioned his ability and integrity and strength, though they resented, many times, his ways of speaking and acting. The opponents of Ross did write loudly against him but this was an accepted part of an election campaign. McMillan had been, and remained, a power in the land.

The Kerr Accusation

While the last rumblings of the Birch case were continuing in 1808, Joseph Kerr, a minister of the Ohio Presbytery, charged that some ministers of that Presbytery held Socinian and Arminian beliefs. A part of his accusation was that "he understood by some persons that Dr. McMillan was a Socinian."[111] To the Church of this time, a Socinian, a follower of the teachings of two Italian writers of the sixteenth century, Laelius Socinius and his nephew, was one who denied the Trinity, the divinity of Christ, or other of the Church's fundamental teachings. Socinians held that the whole of Christianity was included in the practice of morality and the belief in a future state. Arminians differed from the Church about predestination, redemption, and grace.

Kerr does not seem to have had any malice in accusing McMillan; but all Presbyterians and especially all ministers were so sensitive about heresy that no one was above suspicion. So Kerr, who could not have known McMillan well and who seemingly felt that his information was reliable, was not hesitant in making the charge. To name any person in the Presbytery as holding such error showed rash judgment; to name McMillan was utter foolishness. The Presbytery had heard him preach many times on the fundamentals of its faith—on the Trinity, for instance, and the divinity of Jesus. Some who sat in the Presbytery had been trained in his theological school. Little was left for the Presbytery to do but to institute a process of scandal against Kerr.

The Ohio Presbytery constituted a committee from its members —James Hughes, Thomas Marquis, and William McMillan— to prosecute Kerr before the Presbytery for slandering his brethren in the ministry. This committee failed to make progress. The Presbytery, then, empowered John McMillan, Samuel Ralston, and Andrew Gwinn to obtain certified statements from the witnesses Kerr had named. Just at this point, the inquiry was complicated because Kerr said that Ralston was the authority for his statement. Ralston denied he had made the statement. The inquiry was more difficult because Kerr would not tell or could not remember the one to whom he had said McMillan was a Socinian.

Ralston took steps to clear himself by securing signatures to this statement:

We whose names are hereunto annexed do certify that we never heard Mr. Ralston say that Dr. McMillan was a Socinian, nor did he ever tell the Rev. Joseph Kerr any such thing. Given under our hand this 15th day of March, 1809.

At length, at the April meeting of the Presbytery in 1810, the committee reported to the Presbytery. They said that Kerr had been called before the committee to justify his conduct in publicly denouncing McMillan as a Socinian, and that he had cited a private conversation between McMillan and a man named Wilson in which McMillan had made a statement of heresy. This statement is not given in the record of the committee's report. The committee after hearing Kerr had advised him that the interpretation he had given McMillan's words would "not only be very difficult but perhaps impossible fairly to support." The committee added that they had conferred with a committee like their own of the Associated Reformed Presbytery, and that McMillan had come before them and had "avowed his firmest belief in the perfect equality of the Persons of the adorable Trinity...." The committee added "and who does not know that he has taught and still teaches this fundamental doctrine of our holy religion both from the pulpit and in the Theological School over which he presides."

After the committee had reported, the Presbytery dropped the Kerr accusation. McMillan, it seems, was little disturbed by the whole inquiry. There is no suggestion he pushed charges against Kerr. He was certain that the others in the Presbytery knew what was his theology, and he realized that such a difficulty might come at almost any time to a member of the Presbytery.

McMillan had heavier difficulties yet to face. The next one he met did trouble him, and he faced it with sorrow.

THE GWINN CASE

Andrew Gwinn, after he had finished his theological study with McMillan at Canonsburg, was ordained and installed at Pigeon Creek and Pike Run, in June, 1800, McMillan presiding and giving the charge. McMillan had held the pastorate at Pigeon Creek until 1794. Boyd Mercer, the second pastor, was installed in 1795 and stayed there until 1800. He had supplied there earlier than 1795. For seventeen years Gwinn served his congregations well and sustained his friendship with McMillan and the others. Then, in March, 1817, the Ohio Presbytery was rocked by a charge of immorality brought gainst Gwinn.

The Presbytery met on March 18 at a special meeting called by the moderator to consider the charge; McMillan opened the first session with a sermon from John 6:44. On the second day of the meeting at the end of the testimony "Mr. Gwinn not being prepared to enter his defense against the above charge ... the farther consideration thereof was postponed to the first Tuesday of May next."[112]

Less than a month later, Gwinn by letter asked "for a dismission from the congregation of Pigeon Creek. The Commissioners from the congregation concurring, Mr. Gwinn's request was granted and the congregation declared vacant." This was done at a meeting held April 15 at which McMillan was present. In early May after two more days of testimony the Presbytery "resolved that he be and do hereby declare him to be deposed from the work and office of the gospel ministry."

Gwinn "entered his appeal to the Synod" of Pittsburgh before the Presbytery, and asked leave to bring more testimony. The

Presbytery appointed McMillan, Elisha Macurdy, Samuel Ralston, Judge Allison, and others as a committee to hear the testimony. This committeee, meeting at Pigeon Creek, heard the testimony, reported back to the Presbytery, and the Presbytery decided they could not "reverse their former decision." Gwinn at once went to the Synod.

The Synod after hearing Gwinn asked the Presbytery to reconsider its decision because there seemed some "obscurity" in the case and "some evidences of a conspiracy against the character of the appellant."

During the next year the Presbytery reviewed the case. It heard more evidence and in August, 1818 it changed its verdict: it did "remove the sentence of deposition . . . and he is hereby suspended from the exercise of the office of the Gospel ministry, sine die." Presbytery appointed McMillan, Marquis, and Allen "to defend their judgment before the Synod, in case Mr. Gwinn should prosecute his appeal." Gwinn appealed; the Synod reversed the judgment of the Presbytery; the Presbytery did not change its decision and appealed to the General Assembly in 1819. The General Assembly on May 31, 1819, "after a long discussion of the subject . . . determined . . . that the appeal of the Presbytery of Ohio be sustained, and the decision of the Synod of Pittsburgh in the case of Andrew Gwinn be reversed." The minutes of the Presbytery tell that "The Commissioners of Presb'y who attended the General Assembly reported that among a variety of other interesting business the Assembly took up Mr. Gwinn's case, reversed the judgment of the Synod, & affirmed that of the Presb'y." It seems that "their report was received & their fidelity approved." After the judgment of the Assembly, Gwinn again asked that the evidence be re-examined and after the Presbytery had examined and re-examined the evidence, the Presbytery having "not received such new light as to induce them to alter their former decision" refused to change their judgment (June, 1821). Though the case comes up in the later minutes of the Presbytery, this judgment holds, in general, the final verdict.

McMillan at first did not believe Gwinn guilty. Smith writes, "At first Dr. McMillan warmly engaged in the defense of Gwinn, believing him innocent."[113] Fairly early in the case, however, McMillan was convinced Gwinn was guilty though not certain of the degree of his guilt, and took his stand against Gwinn. Gwinn had been a student of his, a member with him of the Ohio Presbytery, an accustomed friend, the pastor in a church McMillan had helped to found and had been minister there a long time. To stand against Gwinn "cost him no little trouble and sorrow."

In the whole case, for more than five years McMillan was "a guardian at the gate"; he was active in the interests of the Presbytery but so far as the records show not sharply aggressive against Gwinn. He was on committees, a commissioner to the Synod, a witness, and he was the supply at his old parish of Pigeon Creek a good many times, probably more than anyone else. He did all these because he wished to carry out his duties to the church.

SALARIES

For the Church on the frontier there were matters equally troublesome, and even more personally annoying for the individual minister, than accusations of wrongs and defaults. The failure of a congregation to pay its minister's salary is again and again reported in the Redstone minutes. Frontier congregations were poor. They found it hard to make payments. This was an old difficulty. It had been brought before the Synod of New York and Philadelphia in 1765, not by the ministers but by "elders and gentlemen" of the congregations. The next year the Synod formally stated that it did "look upon such affairs to be of much importance," and it recommended that "in each congregation a committee be appointed who shall, twice in every year, collect the minister's stipend and lay his receipts before the Presbytery at the meeting preceding the Synod." At that meeting the ministers were to "give account of their diligence in visiting and catechising their people."[114] Later in the history of the Church each minister reported what his church owed him. For more than a century this was the practice of the Church.

Most congregations of Redstone at some time lagged in their payments. The minutes record for instance that Cross Creek, on the exposed West, owed Joseph Smith, in 1783, L113 5s 3d, and that other "congregations were satisfied with the care and diligence of their respective pastors." In 1784 Lebanon still owed Clark more than forty pounds and Bethel more than eighteen pounds. The next year "Unity Congregation is in considerable arrearages to Mr. Power," as were Mt. Pleasant and Sewickley.

To McMillan by the first of February, 1784, Chartiers owed "the just and full sum of L42 7s.6d.," and Pigeon Creek more than L40 17s. 3d. of the last year's stipend." In April of 1785 (April was the usual time for the report) each of his congregations owed him over twice what it had the year before. Only in a few years did the two congregations pay him fully and promptly. In the Ohio

Presbytery it was much the same. The minutes of April 15, 1823, read: "Dr. McMillan reported the congregation of Chartiers indebted to him $652.52."

Brice and Hughes and others report failures in payment. What happened in the Buffalo congregation may stand as an instance of the understanding and good sense the Presbytery used in such difficult situations. The day after Hughes was installed at Buffalo as permanent minister, "the Presbytery finding that the congregation of Buffalo have paid but small part of their salary to Mr. Hughes, for the last year" (when he was serving as supply), told the congregation "unless they pay up this salary before next meeting, Mr. H. will be under the necessity of removing from them." The congregation did not pay, and in September the Presbytery ordered Hughes to tell it that "settlement, will be expected by the next meeting." This it could not make. Then at this next meeting came a wise decision: "the congregation of Lower Buffalo not having complied with the requisition of Presbytery, respecting salary—the Presbytery recommends to the congregation of Short Creek and Lower Buffalo to alter their first plans, and enjoy Mr. Hughes' labors according to their strength."[115]

When Barr brought charges, one was that the trustees had "appointed him to collect his own salary . . .; which was as much as to say he might hunt after his salary from door to door—it was none of their business."[116] And the trial showed that four of Barr's trustees locked him from his church on a Sabbath in spring[117] because Barr's year was up and they did not want him to begin another; as they said later, they wanted to save money. Nothing like this is told of any other Redstone congregation.

When in early 1784 McMillan had reported what was owing him, he had added, "The three preceding years remain unsettled in both congregations."

There was just cause for early frontier congregations to delay their payments. These had been three years "of great trial and hardship . . . on account of the inroads of the Indians." "Frightful murders were committed all around the frontier." "The blood of many a family had sprinkled their own fields." Men of Washington County were among those massacred with Colonel Crawford by the Wyandots in June, 1781. "The outskirts of every congregation in the Presbytery, unless it might be Chartiers and Dunlap's Creek, were in immediate danger during all this time." The Presbytery's first meeting could not be held at the time set by the Synod; and "the incursions of the savages"—(1781 and 1782)—

kept the Presbytery from holding two of the three meetings it had planned. In the early days on the frontier the ministers were patient even in expecting that their salaries would be paid. When Joseph Smith came to Cross Creek and Upper Buffalo in 1780, he found "a willing and united people"; but since they were "unable to pay him a salary which would support his family," he accepted that he, like "all the early ministers, must cultivate a farm."[118]

The story of what follows is well-told in *Old Redstone*.

Smith bought his farm on credit. The congregations had said in their call to him, "we promise to pay yearly and every year . . . the sum of one hundred and fifty pounds, Pennsylvania currency," (money of the value of 1774). When the time came to pay for the farm, his salary for his first three years was still due him. Unless he kept the farm he would have to leave his "beloved people." And so "the people were called together, and the case was laid before them; they were greatly moved . . .; the congregations were unable to pay a tithe of their debts." Then a way was found. Wheat, of which there was much in the community, was ground at Mr. Moore's mill and the flour put aboard a small flatboat, which William Smiley, "an elder in the church, sixty-four years of age," said he would, by Providence, take down the Ohio and the Mississippi to New Orleans—a good market. There he would sell the flour. "Two young men were induced, by hope of a large reward, to go as his assistants."

The trip—from four to six months long—would be "perilous in the extreme," for the way downstream was through "wilderness, and gloomy tales had been told of the treacherous Indian" along the banks. The return by land was again "through the wilderness, a distance of about 2000 miles," "over roads infested by Indians and outlaws and fugitives from the States."

When the day of starting came the congregation "gathered together, and, with their *pastor at their head,* came down from the church, fifteen miles away, to the banks of the river, to bid the old man farewell." They offered a prayer and sang a hymn. Nine months later Father Smiley was back with money enough from the wheat to pay "what was due Mr. Smith, to advance his salary for the year to come," and to reward Father Smiley with three hundred dollars," "which he refused to receive till the pastor was paid," and to pay all the others of the congregation who had part in the enterprise. It was difficulties like these McMillan had in mind when in 1784 he had spoken of the unsettled years.

PRESBYTERY

THE DUTY OF ZION'S WATCHMEN

It is not hard to understand, maybe easier today than it has been, the deep and rigid sense of duty which John McMillan and the men of the Presbytery felt to be their obligation. Life on the frontier was a practical struggle; death was sudden and often violent. There was always danger that people would find it easy to live like savages—to wander away from doctrines and standards so hard won and sometimes seemingly so unimportant when held against the need just to provide and stay alive. The men of God felt an unrelenting responsibility to *watch* and to *guard* themselves, each other, and their people. Being good was a stern responsibility; to yield in little things was to open the way to more serious default. John McMillan, his colleagues, and their congregations were to be guardians of the right.

In the spring of 1833, at Chartiers, where he had been minister for almost fifty-six years, McMillan preached before the Presbytery for the last time. Forty years earlier, he had been one of the five who founded the Presbytery. None of the others was living, and McMillan was in his eighty-first year. His text was Isaiah 62:6, 7—I have set watchmen upon thy walls, O Jerusalem, which shall never hold their peace day nor night: ye that make mention of the Lord keep not silence, And give him no rest, till he establish, and till he make Jerusalem a praise in the earth.

Zion was the Church, the congregation of the righteous, the City of God; it had its "useful and beautiful regulations and order." It had its enemies, and so it was "emcompassed with walls for its defense." Its watchmen were the "ministers of the Gospel . . . set upon her walls . . . that they may watch . . . night and day, to give warning of her dangers." The chief business of each faithful servant of the Church was, like Isaiah, to use "unremitting endeavors to promote the weal of Zion, until her righteousness go forth as brightness."[119]

After these definitions he gave the outline for the rest of his sermon: Thus McMillan began.

I shall endeavor
   1. to describe the duty and character of a faithful watchman.
   2. Speak a little of the blessings for which we should pray, as mentioned in our text.
   3. Illustrate the nature of intercessory prayer, and its power as a mean, to obtain promised blessings for the church, and then conclude with some practical improvement.

JOHN McMILLAN

About his first point—the duty and character of the minister, the watchman—he said in part:

> As he performs many services for Christ in the church, he is called a Minister—As he feeds the flock with spiritual knowledge, he is termed Pastor—As he is to rule well . . . and be wise and prudent for an example . . . he is denominated an Elder or Presbyter— But as he is appointed to give warning of danger . . . he is called a Watchman.

Next he told what qualities the leader needs in the battle, what he must do, whom he is at war against. One enemy from without is Satan—Satan, the "grand foe," who is fighting him and the Church, who ceaselessly will "frighten or surprise into sin," who when "storms and open violence will not avail transforms himself into an angel of light." Satan comes in many forms—"infidel and dark enthusiast, would-be religious philosophers, the sour bigot and the wild latitudinarian." A minister must watch. He must be "filled with the fervor of all the graces" and with "sound truth believed in the heart and practiced in the life." Danger from without, McMillan talked of with much fullness.

But the greatest danger to the church came from "enemies within her walls." Some of these "would appear as friends," yet "content themselves with mere orthodoxy, and external form." Some "treat religion as if it consisted in mere scientific knowledge or dull formality, without interesting the conscience or taking hold of the heart." Some rest upon "a passing meteor, a transient swell in the affections, without the solid change and turn of the soul to God . . . Others are so crafty . . . they may preach and yet not faithfully because they conceal the great truths of the Gospel." McMillan talked much about evil men in the church and Satan's ways of using them, and of the qualities vigilant watchmen should use against them—knowledge, ability, faithfulness, constant work in season and out of season, purity of heart.

Here, half way through his sermon, McMillan took up the second point: what the flock and its guardians should pray for and what intercessory prayer is. The faithful are to pray that Jerusalem shall be "established," that she be "firm and unbroken" not "bone disjointed from bone and sinew from sinew." They are to pray "that the church should become a praise and a glory in the earth," and that the power and presence of God be in it and manifest through it.

McMillan went on by defining intercessory prayer. It is "pleas, importunity, and perseverance" until the blessings asked for are obtained. Such prayer is earnest "argument," a continued pleading for a special or a general blessing; it is wrestling with the angel; "I will not let thee go," Jacob had said, "except thou bless me." The power of such prayer, McMillan continued, is testified by the answers granted to Elijah, Joshua, Hannah, the Apostles, and unnumbered others of the glorious company. And answers to such prayers have come to those listening to him, within the times their lives now have lasted.

When McMillan had ended the discussion of intercessory prayer, he was nearing the end of his sermon. What else he said, he said directly to his "brethren in the ministry . . . and candidates for that office," many of whom he had taught or helped ordain. He was applying the earlier matters of his sermon to the action and belief of each one listening to him. It was a personal appeal from him to those his brethren in the church. The whole sermon is pretty much an emotional exposition of his long-held beliefs and deep convictions.

* * * * *

The sermon is at rough calculation ten thousand words long. It has unity, but unity mainly from the fervor which glows all through it and brings it back again and again to the central idea— the church, the duty laid upon its members, and the bliss which may come to those who have fought for Zion. The outline of the thought is blurred, at least to some readers today, by the involved plan and what seem disgressions. Its unity is from the sound of the trumpet more than from the listing of points.

The meaning is always clear. The words usually are short and exact, and constantly carry suggestions of Biblical phrasing. Indeed McMillan's long reading of the Bible shows everywhere in the sermon: in its rhythms, its phrasings, its illustrations, its method. The Bible is the only book McMillan mentions in the sermon.

McMillan does not spend many of his ten thousand words on abstract theological discussion. Though of course the sermon is exposition and application of the Church's creed, it is a plea, a personal pleading, an "importunity." This is helped by his sometimes bringing in his own experiences. He tells them without egotism or display. His intense wish to make real to his listeners what he has to say keeps the sermon above self-display.

* * * * *

To understand the sermon even partly, it is necessary to remember two facts. It is a fact that McMillan was and had been for many years both a revival preacher and a teacher of systematic theology: his Medulla does underlie all this sermon. And it seems a fact, too, that in the sermon he does not emphasize the terrors of hell and the inherent evil of men so much as the bliss into which his hearers may enter. Yes, men must fight the enemy. Within the City and outside are much sin and many evil men—yet a man may win if he is diligent. That Zion shall win, the watchmen on the walls must be alert and the people constant. As he ends the sermon McMillan says to the ministers and to all of the congregation:

> Let us be faithful . . . to transmit the Gospel uncorrupted down to the children . . . We hope the priests of the Lord will keep his charge. But should they neglect it, let our honest elders attend to theirs. Should they neglect their duty, let honest church members in common awaken up to theirs. But should they neglect . . . let our pious matrons engage . . . .

The church is to be kept strong; it is her people—the minister and all the congregation—who must strengthen it.

Though he has spoken much of the dangers and temptations and horrors of evil, he ends on the power and grace that may come to any who is righteous. In the end he shows, as he has shown earlier, his belief that men though profoundly full of sin may attain to the great gift. He fights for good because men have through grace the possibility of attaining goodness. In the last sentence he says again that all must "wrestle and give the Lord no rest until he establish and make his church a praise and glory in the earth." So almost in the words he began the sermon with, he ends it.

Joseph Smith wrote only twenty years later that there was at the time "rising conflict between the Old and the New schools," and that "Dr. McMillan was not only of the Old School in his views of both doctrines and measures, but he disliked and dreaded the compromising spirit of many of our ministers."[120] No doubt what he says is true. McMillan's personality and training made it natural for him to believe the tenets he had followed for sixty years. And yet through more than two-thirds of his sermon McMillan affirms not what separated the Old and the New but what was the foundation of all his hearers' faith.

VI. NOTES

1. Joseph Smith. *Old Redstone.* 179.
2. Thomas C. Pears, Jr. "The Foundations of Our Western Zion: The Pre-Redstone Period."
3. *Old Redstone.* 121, 122.
4. *A Digest Compiled from the Records of the General Assembly of the Presbyterian Church in the United States of America.* 38.
5. Pears' Manuscript.
6. *Old Redstone.* 185.

7. *Ibid.* 311.
8. Minutes of the Presbytery of Redstone, September 19, 1781.
9. *Old Redstone.* 311.
10. William Wilson McKinney. *Early Pittsburgh Presbyterianism.* 45.
11. *Old Redstone.* 69. *Centenary Memorial,* 210, 211 and *Old Redstone* are the sources for most of these descriptive phrases.
12. *Centenary Memorial.* 228.
13. Old Redstone, 297-301 and David Elliott's *The Life of the Rev. Elisha Macurdy,* 298, 299 are the most important sources for Clark's biography.
14. E. B. Welsh. A letter to Percival Hunt, May 1, 1952.
15. *History of the Presbytery of Washington.* 428. Much of the material in this paragraph is from pages 428, 429 of this book.
16. Joseph Smith. *History of Jefferson College.* 11.
17. C. M. Ewing. A letter to Percival Hunt, July 16, 1952.
18. *Old Redstone.* 367.
19. *Ibid.* 387.
20. *Ibid.* 301.
21. *History of the Presbytery of Washington.* 397.
22. Leland D. Baldwin. *Whiskey Rebels.* 118. Other sources for this story are *Centenary Memorial,* 370, 371 and 388, 389; Creigh's *History of Washington County,* Appendix, 68; and *Old Redstone,* 258.
23. *Old Redstone.* 143.
24. Creigh. Appendix, 55.
25. Minutes of Redstone Presbytery, August, 1786 to April, 1790, is the source for this paragraph.
26. *Presbytery of Washington.* 399.
27. "One Hundred Fifty Years, The Presbyterian Church, West Alexander, Pennsylvania." 11.
28. *Old Redstone.* 344.
29. Welsh's Letter. The preceding phrases are from different sources.
30. Creigh. Appendix, 57.
31. *Ibid.* 62.
32. *Old Redstone.* 143.
33. *Ibid.* 64.
34. *Old Redstone.* 344.
35. Elliott. 247. This and the two preceding books are sources for much of the quoted material not footnoted in Hughes' biography.
36. *Centenary Memorial.* 100.
37. *History of the Presbytery of Washington.* 407.
38. Minutes of Redstone Presbytery, August 15, 1786. The Minutes are, of course, the source for this entire paragraph.
39. Edgar W. King in a letter to Percival Hunt, April 18, 1952, enclosed a sketch of James Hughes taken from the *Miami University Alumni Catalog,* 1809-1909. It contains this phrase.
40. *Ibid.*
41. Edgar W. King in his letter also quoted from History of the Presbyterian Church of Oxford (Ohio) 1818-1900 by Thomas Jackson Porter. The excerpt contains this information.
42. *Ibid.*
43. W. C. Smyser. A letter to Percival Hunt, March 18, 1952.
44. Authorities differ on this date; some give May 2.
45. *Old Redstone.* 346.
46. *Ibid.* 345. Smith quotes this story from Charles Hammond's "Fragment of Recollections" published in the *Cincinnati Gazette* in 1838.

47. *Old Redstone*. 405. The sketch of Patterson in *Old Redstone* was written by E. P. Swift, D.D.
48. *History of the Presbytery of Washington*. 400.
49. *Old Redstone*. 387.
50. *Ibid*. 389.
51. Minutes of the Redstone Presbytery, April, 1787 to November, 1789.
52. *Old Redstone*. 398.
53. *Ibid*. 394, 395.
54. Creigh. 112.
55. *Old Redstone*. 391.
56. *Ibid*. 396.
57. Creigh. 112, 113. The story of the panther is from the same source.
58. *History of the Presbytery of Washington*. 270.
59. *Old Redstone*. 408.
60. *Centennial Volume of the First Presbyterian Church of Pittsburgh*. 193.
61. *Minutes of the Presbytery of Redstone* from December 20, 1785 until September, 1790 is the source for much of this section.
62. *Centennial Volume of the First Presbyterian Church*. 237. Miss Jane A. Barr's "Brief History of the First Pastorate" printed in the Appendix, 237-241 has been a valuable source for this section.
63. Thomas C. Pears, Jr. A manuscript on Barr and the Barr Chronology.
64. *Ibid*.
65. Jane Barr's "Brief History" in *Centennial Volume*, 238.
66. *Ibid*.
67. Pears' manuscript on Barr.
68. *Ibid*.
69. *Ibid*.
70. *Centenary Memorial*. 273.
71. *Centennial Volume of the First Presbyterian Church*. This quotation is from a copy of the original grant of property by the heirs of William Penn printed in the Appendix, 253.
72. *Pittsburgh Gazette*. March 10, 1787.
73. *Centennial Volume of the First Presbyterian Church*. 30.
74. *Ibid. Appendix*, 240.
75. McKinney. 68. See also an article from the *Pittsburgh Evening Telegraph* of December 11, 1875 printed in *Centenary Memorial*, 280-283.
76. *Centennial Volume of the First Presbyterian Church*. 18
77. *Ibid*. 17.
78. *Ibid*. This is quoted from John Wilkins' account.
79. *Old Redstone*. 338.
80. Minutes of the Synod of Virginia. I. 39.
81. *Ibid*. 13. Much of the material in the following pages is from this source and from the Minutes of Redstone Presbytery.
82. *Centennial Volume of the First Presbyterian Church*. 29.
83. *Old Redstone*. 152.
84. *Ibid*. 220.
85. *Centennial Volume of the First Presbyterian Church*. Appendix, 242. This story is from a letter written by Redick McKee in 1884.
86. *Old Redstone*. 221.
87. *Ibid*. 136.
88. *Centennial Volume of the First Presbyterian Church*. 190.
89. *Old Redstone*. 136, 137.
90. *Ibid*. 130.

91. *Centenary Memorial.* 275.
92. *Pittsburgh Gazette.* August 26, 1786.
93. *Centennial Volume of the First Presbyterian Church.* 22, 23.
94. Minutes of the Synod of Virginia. I. 28-30.
95. Minutes of the Presbytery of Redstone. April 13, 1784. Other entries during the next two years are sources for the following two paragraphs.
96. Boyd Crumrine. *The Courts of Justice, Bench, and Bar of Washington County, Pennsylvania.* 35.
97. Boyd Crumrine. *History of Washington County.* 147.
98. *Ibid.* 146, 147. All of the material in the paragraph is from this source.
99. Crumrine. *Courts of Justice.* 35.
100. Minutes of the Presbytery of Redstone. December 20, 1785.
101. Most of the material on Birch is from the Minutes of the Ohio Presbytery, I, 66-156 (October, 1800—December, 1804).
102. Thomas Ledlie Birch. *Seemingly.* 42.
103. Creigh. 174, 175.
104. Crumrine. *The Courts of Justice.* 47.
105. Alexander Addison. *Reports of Cases.* I. Title page.
106. Horace Binney. *Reports of Cases Adjudged in the Supreme Court of Pennsylvania.* I. 178. The quotations from this case are from this source, 178-188.
107. *Old Redstone.* 196.
108. Crumrine. *The Courts of Justice.* 48.
109. *The Commonwealth.* IV, No. 12. See IV, No. 10.
110. Binney. 178, 179.
111. Minutes of the Presbytery of Ohio. II. June 28, 1808. The material on Kerr is taken entirely from this source, 36-114 (June, 1808—April, 1810).
112. Minutes of the Presbytery of Ohio. III. 124 (March 19, 1817). The Minutes from March, 1817 (III, 119) to April, 1822 (IV, 269) are the source for this section. The Minutes contain a surprising number of pages of testimony and the record of the actions of the Presbytery, the Synod of Virginia, and the General Assembly on the Gwinn case during these years.
113. *Old Redstone.* 201.
114. *Ibid.* 322, 323. Smith quotes from the Minutes of the Synod of New York and Philadelphia, 1766.
115. Minutes of the Presbytery of Redstone. April 20, 1790, September 21, 1790, and October 19, 1790.
116. *Ibid.* June 9, 1789.
117. Minutes of the Synod of Virginia. I. 40.
118. *Old Redstone.* 71. Most of the material in the story that follows is from pages 71 and 72.
119. All except one of the quotations in this division are from "The Duty of Zion's Watchmen."
120. *Old Redstone.* 205.

VII. POLITICS

JOHN McMILLAN was never a "politician" as the name is generally applied. He always, however, had a strong sense of responsibility for the public good. And he did not believe it was possible to realize public goodness, complete and whole, without having laws and the men who made and enforced them responsible in big and little public interests.

His personal influence was great, his energies tremendous, and his sincerity deep and genuine. It would have been impossible for him or for any man in the eighteenth century of his strength and conscience to keep out of public affairs.

The frontier, by 1790, was losing some of its simplicity. The numbers of people who poured into the Western Country after the Revolution, from across the sea, from the east, and from the tidewater were large. And they were people who were determined to keep and hold a freedom won by hard fighting and much sacrifice. McMillan twice had taken part in the division of the Presbytery to provide closer government of church affairs and he had seen Western Pennsylvania break up into new counties for which the people sought new offices. The cost of government was a matter for great concern. People with European backgrounds of intolerable government taxation and with the more recent experience of the Revolution were rugged individualists or, at best, interested more in their immediate and local social problems than they were in national problems.

The federal excise law taxing whiskey, a commodity that was the core of social life and economic prosperity in the area, was considered by many frontiersmen an overt act of government and an abridgement of personal rights. The farmer whose wheat could be transported over mountain trails and rough roads at far less cost as whiskey than as grain resented what he termed "oppression." Other factors, of course, centered the objections—heredity, for one, and the psychology of the farmers for another. It seemed to many that the Revolution had been fought to win independence of government excise. And farmers whose whiskey was used as barter felt the tax as a drain on their limited cash resources. The story is familiar to oldtimers and their descendants in western Pennsylvania. They and others not so familiar with the facts can read the whole and authentic story in Leland Baldwin's *Whiskey Rebels*.

POLITICS

The Whiskey Insurrection called every man in western Pennsylvania to action, on one side or the other, and perhaps more than any other single occurrence brought John McMillan into politics. McMillan, recognizing in the rebellion a threat to the orderly life the Church stood for on the frontier, took the side of law and used the pulpit and every persuasive power of his leadership in the community in the defense of that side. To be sure, he was not entirely sympathetic with the excise law, and like his neighbors he accepted whiskey as a commodity for trade and, in moderation, drank it, too. He felt, however, that he had come west of the mountains to preserve the more settled and orderly interests.

After the home of General Neville, federal inspector of revenue, was burned by the insurgents and men like David Bradford had aroused the countryside, McMillan stirred to action. The Federalists of the Western Country stood with the government. They were men of substance and character whose homes were mostly in Pittsburgh and in Washington, Pennsylvania: the Nevilles; the Kirkpatricks; Isaac Craig, who had been stationed at Fort Pitt in 1780; John Woods, whose father had been a land agent for the Penns; James Ross of Washington and Pittsburgh, lawyer of skill and scholar with social prestige; Alexander Addison, a president judge, violently partisan; James O'Hara, prominent merchant and industrialist; John Wilkins; and others of their wealth, ability, and social prestige. Those against the Whiskey Rebellion had, too, on their side the *Pittsburgh Gazette.* John McMillan stood with them and won to their side, if not to their political party, many strong leaders.

THE WHISKEY REBELLION

A bare outline of the Whiskey Rebellion seems needed. Armed opposition to the excise laws began in midsummer of 1794, when a United States marshal came to Washington County to put federal laws into effect. It ended with the ending of summer.

On July 17[1] insurgents burned Bower Hill; July 23[2] they held a large meeting at Mingo Creek, with radicals dominating; in the first days of August about five thousand of them[3] (some estimates are much lower) marched into Pittsburgh to punish the people of "Sodom," burned a barn (one of the "unsuccesful attempts" on the mansion of Major Kirkpatrick), were fed, "drank four barrels of Brackenridge's whiskey," and then marched out of the town, leaving the people much alarmed. Among the marchers, it seems clear, were many who held no land, who were merely part of the rootless, shifting population along the frontier.

On August 14, at Parkinson's Ferry (Monongahela City) 226 delegates, all but eight from the four counties—Washington, Westmoreland, Allegheny, Fayette—held a meeting to settle what answer should be given to the five commissioners then in the region: the three United States commissioners—Judge Jasper Yeates of Pennsylvania Supreme Court, Senator James Ross of Pennsylvania, and Attorney General William Bradford—and two appointed by Governor Mifflin of Pennsylvania.[4] At the meeting David Bradford held out for resistance; Brackenridge with much skill and almost too much finesse, and Gallatin in a long and able speech counseled accepting the federal laws. At length, out of the large committee a standing committee of sixty was appointed, and out of it was appointed a conference committee of twelve (plus three from Ohio County, Virginia, who never took part) to meet with the commissioners.[5] This committee and the commissioners met at Pittsburgh on August 20, 21, 22, 23, and after conference, voted by secret ballot to recommend to the standing committee submission to the laws and acceptance from the federal government of amnesty "with the conditions attached." August 28-29 in a final meeting of the standing committee at Brownsville Gallatin and Brackenridge from the conference committee, "at great danger," presented their report. After many stormy words and some stormy actions the meeting accepted the report by a secret vote thirty-four to twenty-three. Later six said they had voted *nay* through misunderstanding.[6]

This decision to be valid needed an agreeing vote in the four counties of the regular "taxable inhabitants" plus that of all other male citizens of eighteen or upward. This the committee had decided. The balloting, which was not secret, was done September 11. When it was over the *ayes* had it, though there was left the dregs of much opposition and much resentment. Less than one-fourth of the 13,800 inhabitants of the four counties and probably less than one-sixth of all who were eligible to vote voted for submission.[7] For about two weeks in October President Washington himself visited the troops. He had sent into the West, in late September, more than thirteen thousand militia levied east of the mountains.[8]

After the voting in September an end came, though at first a most uneasy one, to organized opposition; by the close of the year the troops had been withdrawn and almost all who had been arrested had been freed. As a whole, the opponents in the four counties did not change their opinion of the excise laws, however much they subdued their opposition into lawful methods. The only two who were convicted were pardoned by the President.

In 1794 McMillan was forty-two years old and had been eighteen years in the Western Country. He had great influence there. He himself never held a political office, but he did have strong beliefs which he put into political actions. "Upon occasions he closed his regular religious services and before his congregation could disperse, plunged immediately into a discussion of politics."[9] Indeed, to him politics was one way of carrying out his religion.

In the West, through the 1790's, differences over federal law steadily had grown more sharp and dangers greater. After the excise on whiskey had been suggested in Congress, then imposed, and finally resisted with violence, McMillan used his influence vigorously with his people. When Bower Hill had been burned and David Bradford and Tom the Tinker and the rest were heading open rebellion, McMillan and most of the clergy—Presbyterians, Episcopalians, Methodists, and men of other denominations—worked to bring the flaming resistance under control. At Bethel, close to General Neville's home, John Clark tried—and failed—to hold back the mob storming after the tax collector. Gallatin and Brackenridge and Judge Addison and Judge James Edgar and General Wilkins and many other leaders were pressing the people to meet with the five commissioners of the federal government and find a way out. McMillan was much in the center of the pressure for settlement.

After the commissioners had met with the conference committee of twelve (the members from Ohio County, Virginia, did not take part) and had come to an agreement on August 28-29 but before the voting on ratification on September 11, McMillan and John Clark and Samuel Porter at Congruity Church and James Finley at Rehoboth and most of the ministers went ahead to get their people to vote *aye*. So did Brackenridge and others.

The vote itself was a vote on submission to the federal laws and acceptance of amnesty; but besides this each voter was required to sign a promise (1) to submit to the laws of the United States, (2) not to oppose carrying out of the excise laws, and (3) to "support, as far as the law requires, the civil authorities in affording the protection due to all officers and other citizens."[10]

The two weeks before the voting were weeks of tension and uproar and diplomacy in the four counties, especially in Washington County. During this time McMillan used all his energy and prestige. Many in his Pigeon Creek congregation were in special need of the amnesty,[11] since many had done violent acts. McMillan set about to see they did vote for acceptance. Part of the Pigeon

Creek congregation lived in the Mingo Creek district, a main center of rebellion, less than ten miles from Chartiers. On Mingo Creek, two miles south of Finleyville, a log meeting-house had been built. There, supplies had preached before the rebellion got under way, and there in the early months of 1794 was formed the Mingo Creek Society (the Mingo Creek Association, it sometimes is called) made up of "those subject to military duty of eighteen years of age and upwards." It had been formed with these admirable purposes: "to hear and determine all matters in . . . dispute between parties, encourage teachers of schools, introduce the Bible and other religious books in the school, encourage the industrious and men of merit."[12] It was an "anomalous association," a blending of politics and military, often called the Mingo Boys and very openly charged with using "tar and feathers, fire and ruin"[13] against opponents. For a year at least it took over civil and police powers: "in fact it seems . . . to have governed [the entire community] during 1794."[14] At any rate, whether or not some of McMillan's people had part in this violence, and probably some of them had, they were in danger from the law. Mingo Creek was, no question, a center of violence and treason. Brackenridge on the day of voting met someone just come from Mingo who had seen about two hundred men present at a meeting, "all to a man pledged . . . not to sign and to shoot any man who will."[15]

McMillan went ahead to correct the judgment of his people and assure their right vote. First, a meeting was called at the Mingo Creek Meeting House. McMillan is said to have called it. What happened at the meeting seems not clearly recorded, but it is recorded that McMillan did go to it and that with him went Judge James Edgar, who had been one of the committee meeting with the commissioners. Even Brackenridge, not given to straightout approval, tells that Edgar was "a man of sense, and not destitute of eloquence." He wrote, too, that "Judge Edgar . . . was a kind of Rabbi in the Presbyterian churches in the western country," and that the Judge seemed "like the figures of the old republicans in the time of the long parliament in England."[16] Others have given Judge Edgar more direct praise. He spoke at the meeting but, says James Veech in *Centenary Memorial,*

to no good purpose. He was hissed and pelted with mud and stones. The table upon which the papers to be signed were laid was carried away, and the meeting broken up in an uproar. Some of the members of the Doctor's church were implicated. . . . He was alarmed but not disheartened.[17]

Then, too, McMillan postponed the communion service of his

congregation until after September 11, purposing to refuse the Sacrament to those who had not signed the agreement to follow the law. And next, in early September, he called his congregation together. Many came to the meeting. At the meeting he "prayed and exhorted"; Samuel Porter preached on the text whose point stood out in the words "They that resist shall receive to themselves damnation." As he was applying the text "he noticed some frowns and many rising to leave," and so he brought in a story and quite changed the tone of his sermon. "By reason and pleasantry nearly all were brought to agree to submit."[18]

The day for voting came. McMillan was at the polling place, where "he used his immediate influence." At the end of the day, the vote was declared to be in the affirmative. The Whiskey Rebellion was officially over, though the four counties still were in great uneasiness and much difficulty and dissatisfaction. The active rebellion came to an end, but McMillan and the Church knew that the country about them was deeply disturbed. And so the Synod of Virginia at its yearly meeting in September appointed the second day of November—after the election—to

be observed as a day of fasting and prayer to confess our own sins and the sins of the land, to mourn over them before God, and to deprecate the Divine wrath manifested in the many judgments which hang over our land in general and which more especially threaten this country because of the late very sinful and unconstitutional opposition which has taken place to some of the laws of the United States.[19]

McMillan, and the others of his presbytery, heartily "concurred" in holding this day of prayer and fasting.

* * * * *

Some further notes on the Rebellion may not be out of place here.

In the Western Country, the excise laws and the inherited feeling against such laws were the main cause of discontent and disturbance, but even in the West other causes were at work. The French Revolution was reflected in the many Jacobin clubs in America—the one, for example, on Mingo Creek—and in the contagion of rash judgments against a political or economic opponent and, sometimes, in brutal actions. Besides, the West questioned the federal government's power to protect the frontier from Indians and even its wish to protect. On that frontier protection was needed. Indians still were active in parts of Washington County and on its edges; and the Western Country wondered whether or not President Washington realized their dangers and horrors. Then there was the draft. On August 7 the President had called out thirteen thousand militia "to cause the law to be duly executed" in Western Pennsylvania. Through Maryland, New Jersey, Virginia, and Pennsylvania (Pennsylvania sent 5200 militia[20]) the draft caused great resentment. Opposition meetings were held; Liberty Trees were set up; banners, hung out, exclaimed "Liberty and no excise, O Whiskey"; men with blackened faces went about in the dark; there were meetings with much noise and shouting and gusty dangerous oratory. All this was happening in Martinsburg and Winchester, Virginia, and in Carlisle, east of the mountains, and in New Jersey[21]; in the four counties, there may often have been violence, but violence went on in other places. The thirteen thousand militia did come over the Alleghenies—in great discomfort from rain and mud, and from lack of food and tents, and from beef turned bad, and from weak whiskey; part of the army came even to Pittsburgh; but most of them were home again by the end of the year. Wayne's victory over the Indians at Fallen Timber on August 18 showed that the government was strong enough to give protection and that it knew the western danger. Then, too, the Jay Treaty lessened Indian attacks and opened the Mississippi. And the draft became less unbearable as it went on to accomplished act, and the Whiskey Rebellion broke down after September 11.

* * * * *

In many places voting was a confused matter. One cause of this was that two weeks was not time enough for a voter to make his best decision.[22] Two weeks was not time enough for the sound of angry words to die out and for prejudice to be lessened by knowledge and clearer thinking. Indeed, after the procedure was settled by the commissioners the voters had hardly a week. Another cause was that voters went to the polls not certain just what voting *aye* meant and what the questions were or what they meant. If a man voted *aye* need he sign the questions at all? Did accepting "amnesty" carry an acknowledgment of guilt? Did swearing not to oppose the excise laws mean active help in searching for illicit stills? The third cause of confusion was that many voting places did not have ballots on the day of the voting. At some polling places the officials wrote out the questions as they remembered them and understood them. Probably the greatest hindrance to fair voting was the requirement that the voting be public. "Between the hours of twelve and seven, in the afternoon," the proclamation for September 11 said, the proper officials should "openly propose to the people assembled the . . . questions,"[23] and get each man's *aye* or *nay*. To vote with serenity and good judgment would seem to have been difficult.

* * * * *

Some writers call McMillan's putting off administering the Sacrament to rebels a rash and autocratic act. It seems to have been a way of action well accepted through centuries of English history. Religious leaders—John Knox and Cromwell for example—and civil leaders in government had required that religious belief be carried into details of living, large and small. Civil and political matters were seen inextricably part of one another. Religious beliefs had prescribed who should hold political offices and who should be admitted to the university, and what were tests of loyalty to the sovereign and the state. Religious custom—almost as strong as law—had at times prescribed the wearing or not wearing of buttons on a coat and the style of hair or of collar. McMillan's act was backed not only by precedents of history but by the convictions of most of the churches in Europe and America. An illustration of this —small but vivid—is a "Religious Agreement"[24] "entered into on the fourteenth day of February," 1782, by "inhabitants of the western frontier of Washington County" because they saw "the many abounding evils in our own hearts" and in their ways of living. Among the more than fifty evils named are backbiting and racing, cockfighting and dancing and "filthy discourse" or song, "overreaching in bargains," and not "catechising . . . our children and servants or slaves." Another evil they must combat was "suffering sin to remain on our neighbor unreproved." To carry this purpose into practice required, certainly, the conviction that some special act was wrong and some other right. The signers promised they would carry out these beliefs; they would "be careful and watchful to perform by Christian rules" "as Providence shall give us opportunity, and prudence direct."[25] It was a doctrine of special action on a basis of general belief. It was not a doctrine of mere contemplation. McMillan signed the agreement, and so did Judge Edgar and Joseph Patterson and one hundred eleven others. The signing went on over the next five years.

And it is well to remember the independence which a church member felt and which McMillan recognized. A member was not easily dragooned into accepting even a minister's opinion or agreeing to an act. Many church members did not take without opposition the verdict of the session or the Presbytery. Members did walk out on a sermon. After all, members of a congregation "called" their minister, and reported on his "labors among them," and could ask his dismissal.

THE CONGRESSIONAL ELECTION OF 1794

The ballots cast September 11 were hardly counted before McMillan was again active in politics. On October 14, elections were to be held in the four counties for both the state and the national legislatures.

McMillan showed no special interest in the politics of Westmoreland and Fayette Counties or in the state election of Washington and Allegheny Counties. Westmoreland and Fayette Counties did elect Republicans to all state and national offices, among them Gallatin, who went to the state House of Representatives. Washington and Allegheny divided evenly their state delegations. To the national House of Representatives, Westmoreland and Fayette, which were one district, elected as usual James Findley, Republican.

But McMillan was active about the nomination and election of the one congressman from the district made up of Allegheny and Washington. Four men were working for nomination to that office[26]: Thomas Scott of Washington County and John Woods of Pittsburgh, both Federalists, and David Hamilton of Washington County and Brackenridge of Pittsburgh, Republicans. No one of the four wholly satisfied his party as Findley had in his congressional district. Scott, then in Congress, had voted for the excise tax; Woods had stood up for the insurrection but he had a long record of political defeats; Hamilton could not carry the conservatives of his party because he had stood strongly for the insurrection; Brackenridge seemed to many unstable and rash, a "straddler," a "double dealer," a man who had the outlook of the East more than of his own county. Yet Brackenridge, though he lacked the confidence of either party, probably had the best chance of being nominated.

McMillan did not favor any of the four, especially not Brackenridge. He had known Brackenridge almost twenty-five years, since the 1770's, when they had been students at the College of New Jersey. They were not enemies, though McMillan had never approved Brackenridge's giving up his ministry in the New Castle Presbytery; besides Brackenridge had "learned to swear."[27] They were, however, antithetical in almost every quality of outlook and manner. Brackenridge's mind was given to quick shifts of view, to inconsistencies, to sudden enthusiasms, to seeing whimsical contrasts, to watching himself and others with humorous inquiry. He was in many ways a cosmopolitan, a man of literary taste, though at

POLITICS

times not tactful in talking and writing; often changing opinions without weighing results or responsibilities. He was quick, constantly diverting and diverted: witty if somewhat frivolous, overly smart. He was a highly intellectual man, and he had courage. He said of himself that at times in the Whiskey Rebellion he had been afraid, yet he did risk his life and his standing by what he did then. He may not always have been judicious or dependable but he was almost always interesting.

McMillan was sure there was acute need the right man be sent to Philadelphia. He was sure Brackenridge was not the man. Besides, Brackenridge had not come out well in his recent attack on Findley of Westmoreland County,[28] with whom he differed over the national bank, the opening of the Mississippi, the payment for western lands, and a centralized government. Brackenridge was the only representative from the four counties who had voted on these questions with the Eastern congressmen. So, taking it altogether, McMillan was sure Brackenridge should not be nominated for Congress. Equally he was sure Gallatin should.

Accordingly he called together a few confidential friends at Canonsburg, quietly nominated Albert Gallatin who then resided in Fayette County, prepared the tickets and had them distributed. It is said, and is probably true, that this was done without Mr. Gallatin's knowledge.[29]

Some writers doubt that such secrecy could be kept. Preparations had to be made, yet Gallatin was not named a candidate until three days before the election. Possibly all this was done so Gallatin would not have time to refuse nomination.

Gallatin was a strong candidate. He had served in the state legislature since 1790 and had an unusually good record there. He had been United States Senator in 1793. Though during the insurrection he had signed some extreme resolutions, he had kept the voters' approval. They seemed to have valued his sincerity, his idealism, his good sense, his insight, his strength of mind, his will and his power to put up a fight for what he believed, his readiness to admit he had committed at least "one political sin,"[30] his keeping a steady line of action. During the Whiskey Rebellion

He had opposed the excise in principle; he had opposed it actively so long as constitutional measures were employed, and he had urged acquiescence to the government when submission seemed the better policy.[31]

McMillan when he backed Gallatin showed good judgment of men, and he showed, too, a disregard of prejudices he might have been expected to have. For Gallatin was a Republican in politics. He lived outside the congressional district. He had been born in a continental country. He had been in America only fourteen years, and had been settled in Pennsylvania only about five. In Europe he had been touched somewhat by the fire of the French Revolution. He spoke English with a French accent. His election to the Senate in 1793 had been declared invalid, and he had made then an enemy of Alexander Hamilton. In religion he was not wholly orthodox. (Late in his life he said: I never was an infidel, though I have had my doubts. . . . I have always leaned toward Arminianism. . . . I am a bold speculator. Such has been the habit of my life all my life along."[32]). McMillan realized the qualities of mind and of will behind the seeming hindrances.

Gallatin did win a seat in Congress and a seat in the lower house of the state legislature. He won them both on the same day. That Gallatin carried his district by a good margin and that he became one of the most distinguished statesmen of his time shows McMillan had judged him shrewdly and used his own influence well.

After the election, Brackenridge, as was his way, surprised those watching him. He was used to managing the politics of his town and of his district, and yet on October 14 he found that McMillan was giving the political direction. And Brackenridge, then, instead of showing the expected bitterness toward McMillan, showed, for the most part, an astonishing—an almost amused—admiration for him. Perhaps, too, he did not want to antagonize the man whose help he might need later. At any rate his attitude toward McMillan in 1794 was very much the humorous and unwilling appreciation he had felt for many years. Back in 1786 he had published some doggerel in the *Pittsburgh Gazette*, part of which fairly well hit off how he felt then toward McMillan.

McMillan* the ecclesiastic,
Will burn me with religious caustic;
Tell all the people that the devil,
Has bound me hand and foot to evil.
Can I avoid the horrid fury
Of Presbyterian judge and jury?
No. No. 'Tis best t' avoid the sin,
And sleep as usual in my whole skin.
*a clergyman

This is the rhyme as he republished it twenty years afterward in his *Gazette Publications,* 1806.[33] He seemed still to be pleased with it and to have kept much of his old feeling about McMillan. Once in 1796 he wrote Judge Addison that a young man was to come to "study law with me unless the Wand of McMillan shall come over him and transform him into another shape."[34] Here he was not telling his friend—his friend for the time at least—about an election to Congress; but the way he spoke shows again how conscious he was of McMillan's pervasive influence and how fully he recognized McMillan's power.

THE JAY TREATY 1794-1796

McMillan never again directed political affairs as he had in the Gallatin election of 1794. He did, however, take his part in them. When the Jay Treaty came before Congress he worked strongly for its ratification.

The Jay Treaty was negotiated with England in the summer and fall of 1794, by Chief Justice Jay and other commissioners, to settle violations of the Treaty of Paris, 1783, and to regulate some matters of commerce and navigation. As finally written it secured England's evacuation of the northwestern boundary forts (Oswego, Detroit, Niagara, Mackinaw, and others) and an amicable conference over some questions of navigation and boundaries; but it put restrictions on trade, mainly with the West Indies and France, and did not settle the right of England to search American ships and impress American sailors.

Alexander Hamilton and the Federalists were strongly for the Treaty; Democrats were against it. The whole country was racked by the torrent, tempest, and whirl-wind of untempered disputes and personal vilifications. Sixteen days after the Treaty had been presented to the Senate, the Senate ratified it—June 24, 1795. Washington "reluctantly signed it." Next it went before the House at its next meeting, December, 1795, for the voting of appropriations necessary to carry out its terms. The House then had 104 members from the fifteen states, 99 of whom took part in the final vote on the treaty.

The House was deeply divided on the Treaty. Many opposed its terms. The majority called on the President for explanatory papers concerning it. He, with the agreement of his cabinet, refused the papers. Yet however much the House was divided on the advantages of the Treaty, the fundamental division was on the clear-cut question: Did the Constitution require the House to make appropriations to carry out, without considering its merits, any treaty, passed by the Senate and signed by the President? Over this question more than over the merits of the treaty, debate went on for almost five months. On April 30[35] the House resolved—fifty-one to forty-eight, Gallatin being among the nays—"That it is expedient to make the necessary appropriations for carrying the

Treaty with Great Britain into effect." In the House, Tuesday, May 3,[36] without an "aye" and "no" vote, "a bill making appropriations towards defraying the expenses of carrying into effect the Treaty lately concluded between the United States and Great Britain, was read a third time, the blanks filled up, and passed." The appropriation was for $91,920.50.

The people of Western Pennsylvania, too, were divided over the Treaty. Federalists and business men generally favored it and so did many settlers because they thought that most Indian raids would end when British holding of boundary forts ended. Besides, freer trading with Canada and the Northwest was important to frontier prosperity. Against the Treaty stood the Democrats and those who were sure the Senate had no power to direct appropriations or who were in everything strongly anti-British. McMillan, though opposed to Senate dictation, was for the Treaty. On May 5, 1796, he wrote a letter to Gallatin, who had taken his seat in the House after the President had signed the Treaty. He wrote:

Chartiers May ye 5th 1796

Sir

You will no doubt be surprised to receive a letter from me, whom perhaps you cannot recollect ever to have seen; but the extreme anxiety which I have felt respecting the probable result of the debate on the British Treaty compels me to write. Perhaps a little discussion of any public measure may be useful to keep public agents within their proper limits: but the decision ought to be attended to. I have seriously considered the business, and it is my opinion that tho' your House had a right to call for the papers, and that the President ought to have laid them before you, yet you ought not to carry your resentment so far as thereby to do a real and lasting injury to your country, which I think you will do if the British Treaty be not fully and fairly executed. And this, as far as I have had opportunity of observing, is the opinion of every man of reflection here.

I think the present a very important crisis in our national government. I have a perfect confidence in you and I feel myself interested that you should have the confidence of every man in this district. This induces me to speak my mind to you, and inform you of my honest sentiments. If anything more were necessary, it is my purpose to furnish you with it. I have appointed a meeting of my congregation for other purposes on this day week at Canonsburgh. I mean, after the purposes of the appointment are over, to propose this subject to them, and I am sure that every person from whom you would wish an opinion, will express, because I am sure they feel, the sentiment which I have expressed. I shall endeavor to have similar meetings in other congregations.

It is my earnest wish that you will, by your vote, render void all our efforts, and before they appear to you, that you will have established the British Treaty by everything that remains for your House to do.

From your humble servant and sincere friend

(Signed)   John McMillan[37]

The last paragraph in the letter has puzzled today's readers. It means McMillan earnestly wished that Gallatin, before he got the letter, had voted appropriations to carry out the Treaty. If these appropriations had already been voted, the letter and the later petitions would have no point ("will be rendered void"). Evidently, McMillan did not know on Thursday, May 5, that appropriations had been passed on Tuesday, May 3.

McMillan did more than write the letter. The *Pittsburgh Gazette* of Saturday, May 14, reported that on Thursday, May 12, "After the religious service of the day was over, Mr. McMillan intimated that business, of public nature and great importance, required the consideration of the meeting, and he therefore requested that the men would remain. All did." The meeting unanimously voted "that, in the opinion of this meeting, the interests of this country require, that the British treaty should be carried into execution with good faith;" and a petition signed by all at the meeting including "John McMillan, Chairman" was sent to the House asking it to "concur in the execution of the British treaty." In doing all this McMillan seems not to have realized or not to have cared that his letter and his calling the meeting might be taken as acts of a political boss. The acts seemed right; he did them.

How strong McMillan's influence was is shown in a series of letters written by Brackenridge to Judge Addison during April and May of 1796.[38] Brackenridge was all enthusiasm and conviction about the Treaty: "If the Senate stand to it, they will finally prevail; for they are right." So he set about bringing the influence of Addison, who was for the Treaty, upon McMillan.

On April 27, when the House was nearing its final vote, he wrote Addison: "I tell you a plan that will shake Gallatin in all his policies of opposition to the treaty. If One McMillan could be put upon him. What if you were to ride out to converse with father Polycarp . . . and put Him upon Him." Three days later he wrote:

And the point is that unless Cardinal McMillan can be brought over Gallatin will conquer and have the popular side. . . .
I have some trust in the understanding of McMillan, so that if complimented on his Judgment and firmness in Tom the Tinkers day, he may sit right. He will give the tone to all the missioners of his ministry. No pains ought to be spared to enlighten and engage him.

On May 20, knowing of McMillan's letter to Gallatin, Brackenridge wrote rather triumphantly: "The obtaining the Patronage of the Reverend John McMillan whom I denominate the Patriarch of the Western Church was a grand acquisition. . . . It is the alliance of the *Church and State*."

Brackenridge seemed sure that he had manipulated McMillan into writing to Gallatin and calling the meeting. Probably Addison and McMillan did meet and talk of the Treaty, for both wished it to be carried into effect. Possibly Addison did influence McMillan, yet that is not certain. McMillan had been a strong Federalist for years. His decisions were usually his own, and his acts the results of his own decisions. He was forthright and self-reliant. In 1796 he seems still to have been "the watcher at the gate." Brackenridge may have underestimated McMillan or overvalued himself. He believed always in finesse; McMillan ordinarily was not moved by finesse. At any rate the series of letters proves the strength of McMillan's influence. That Gallatin voted against the Treaty did not lessen McMillan's influence nor lessen Brackenridge's belief in it. After he had heard that the House had passed the Treaty he wrote Addison some shrewd comments about the coming election campaign in their district:

For you may be assured that Gallatin . . . will come home Charging you and me with . . . Mischief; and there is no question but that evils & grounds of dissatisfaction will be the natural consequence [of] the Treaty with Brittain, though greater evils would have followed the rejecting it. But it will be said by those in opposition to it, that the evils which have followed the adoption would have been avoided it is therefore of Moment to convince the people that the adoption was unavoidable by the house. . . . there will be great dissatisfaction on the part of France; and by & by there will be partial indian wars, perhaps soon.

So as he tells Addison he does "hope The Patriarch of the west The revd John McMillan has written his pastoral letters, and the clergy have convinced their Congregation." Years later he still spoke of McMillan with the same half-mocking but very real recognition of his power.

McMillan in 1796 was forty-four years old and had been minister of the Chartiers congregation for twenty years.

CAMPAIGN OF 1808

In 1808 James Ross was candidate, a third time, for governor. He was forty-six years old. Earlier, for nine years he had been United States senator; he had married the daughter of George Woods, land agent for the Penns and attorney for the Neville interests; he was fairly wealthy from law practice and land holdings; and politically he was powerful, though the Federalists steadily had been losing. An engraving of Sully's portrait shows him, as someone who knew him wrote, of "imposing presence" and "majestic countenance." The engraving suggests his recognized intelligence and good sense and integrity and kindness.

McMillan had known Ross more than thirty years. He was born, as McMillan had been, east of the mountains. Like McMillan he went to Pequea Academy, and at eighteen he came, as McMillan had, to Washington County. He taught in McMillan's log school, studied with him, and read law from the books Brackenridge lent him.

He went steadily ahead. At twenty-two he was admitted to practice in Westmoreland and Fayette Counties and, it seems, in Washington County. At twenty-five he was one of the incorporators of Pittsburgh Academy. At twenty-six he was a practicing lawyer in Allegheny County. At twenty-seven he was attorney for President Washington's western land holdings; he specialized in land cases. At twenty-seven, too, "the brilliant young Federalist" was elected to the Pennsylvania constitutional convention and was one of nine who wrote the state Constitution of 1790. Then, four years later, he began his nine years as senator. Before 1808 he had twice been the Federalist candidate for governor and had been defeated both times. And he was defeated again in 1808—39,575 to 69,975;[39] he did not carry a county west of the mountains, not even his home county, Allegheny. All his life Ross was a Federalist, unfortunately for his political success. He never again was candidate for a state or federal office, though for seventeen years after 1816 he was president of the Select Council of Pittsburgh, usually the only Federalist member. For more than twenty years, from 1808 until he gave up his practice in 1830, and even afterward, he probably stood first among the lawyers in Pittsburgh.

The campaign against Ross was vindictive and personal and partisan. Simon Snyder, a Democratic Radical, opposed him. John Spayd, the other candidate, scarcely counted.

To read a newspaper of the campaign months brings alive, at least a little, the temper and action before the election. *The Commonwealth,* a Pittsburgh weekly, backed Snyder. Its editor, Ephraim Pentland, was young, and wrote vividly and clearly, and was not unwilling to mix personal abuse with political facts and arguments and innuendos. A copy of *The Commonwealth* looks strange today. The masthead gives the paper's motto (in italics), *"Virtue, Liberty and Independence"* and the price (in small capitals), TWO DOLLARS PER ANNUM. PAYABLE HALF-YEARLY IN ADVANCE." Its page is 10½ inches by 17 and so has about two-fifths the space on the page of a modern newspaper. Each issue has four pages, four columns to a page, is printed tightly but legibly, and carries no large-type headlines. Ordinarily an issue had been 1½ to 2 pages of advertisements —interesting today—and two pages of foreign, national, state, and local news. During the campaign, however, hot political broadsides filled most of the paper, though there still was a column or less of advertisements, a few inches of national news, and fewer of foreign news.

In *The Commonwealth*, "E: Pentland," as he printed his name, kept on week after week accusing Ross of many sins and political heresies. One article headed *Shall JAMES ROSS be our Governor? Fifty thousand Freemen on the 11th day of October will . . . say, NO!!* listed thirteen of these and contrasted with them the serene and homely virtues of Snyder. Ross, Pentland wrote, was an atheist, a deist, a mocker of the Sacrament, "a mean and parsimonious usurer," "an enemy of Liberty and Truth." He had voted for a standing army in time of peace, for direct taxes, for the excise. He was an aristocrat; he had said no poor man should vote. He was a traitor to the American Government. He was a bosom friend of those who had plotted to assassinate the President.

A lurid pamphlet published in Philadelphia told the voters that employees of Ross in evicting a woman had beaten her and left her bleeding in the street, and that Ross himself when he met her and her child had slashed them with a heavy whip.[40]

One means of attack often used was an affidavit, in which a citizen brought some charge against the opposition's candidate or defended his party's. *The Commonwealth* printed many affidavits against Ross and, of course, many for Snyder. One issue just before election had fifteen or sixteen of them. The war of the affidavits went on, back and forth, until after the voting.

The charge that Ross was irreligious seemed to his supporters a most serious charge. They asked McMillan to write to *The Commonwealth*. McMillan wrote:

Certificate

"This is to certify, that I have been intimately acquainted with *James Ross*, Esqr. of Pittsburgh, for more than thirty years; that I have never heard him speak, nor heard of him speaking disrespectfully of religion or religious persons; that the stories which are propagated respecting him, as being a deist, and prostituting the ordinances of the gospel, I believe to be wholly unfounded: in short, I know nothing, nor have I heard anything against his moral character that could in the smallest degree disqualify him for the office of governor, or ought to be objected against him as a candidate for that office, and I am determined to give him all the support in my power, and hope that all the friends of religion and good order will do the same.

John McMillan

Wash. county, Aug. 29, 1808

Pentland printed the letter on September 28, and below it he printed an editorial:

In the first place, no man can scarcely believe that Mr. Ross is so great an infidel as to ridicule religion in the presence of a minister of the gospel. But that he has done so out of Mr. McMillan's presence, can, we understand, be proven by reputable testimony. Secondly, Mr. McMillan is not entitled to implicit credit. He has been convicted in the supreme court of Washington county of slandering a reverend brother and of propagating falsehoods against him. It was proven on the oath of Mr. *Andrew Hunter*, that Mr. McMillan had acknowledged that he told lies against the Rev. T. L. Birch, *for the good of religion, and that he would do so again* Perhaps his certificate in favor of Mr. Ross may be a fulfillment of his promise, to further the good of religion. Lastly, it should be kept in mind, that Mr. Ross is Mr. McMillan's counsel in all cases, and was engaged to defend him in an action of slander at the time he gave the certificate, and which is this week to be tried by the supreme court of Washington county. And it cannot be supposed, but that the man who did tell a lie *for the good of religion* would give an unproved certificate, for the good of himself. . . . from what we have said, we leave the public to judge what degree of creditability ought to be attached to Mr. McMillan's certificate.

McMillan made no reply.

Pentland attacked McMillan only once more, just after McMillan had stopped the retrial of Birch's suit by paying damages, when McMillan must have seemed to Pentland an open and irresistible target. One sentence gives the tone of his editorial: "The praise of a man convicted of lying and slandering ought not to be envied Mr. Ross and his friends."

What *The Commonwealth* printed seems never to have troubled McMillan. Certainly it did not lessen his influence and standing. It left no ripples at all. McMillan thought well of Ross. Pittsburgh —politics aside—thought much the same.

Judge Thomas Mellon wrote of Ross:

My personal knowledge of the Hon. James Ross commenced in 1834, when I entered as a student at the Western University of Pennsylvania. . . .

Mr. Ross' dwelling was but a short distance from the University, and he was a conspicuous figure while on his way to and from the Court House. . . . I should judge that Mr. Ross was some inches over six feet in height, well proportioned and of imposing presence, although the infirmities of age had already begun to manifest themselves when I first knew him.

He was rightly regarded among the students as one of the greatest men of the country, and more especially on account of his high reputation for scholarly attainments. . . .

JOHN McMILLAN

I happened into the District Court one day when he was arguing an important question. . . . He then seldom appeared in Court. I expected quite a formal argument, but was disappointed in that respect. He stood carelessly with one hand resting on the railing in front of the judge, and in a quiet way talked the matter over, as it were. But the close attention with which Judge Grier listened indicated that Mr. Ross was making an able argument, and although he spoke in a conversational way, he presented a chain of strong links logically connected.

His reputation among the lawyers was of the highest order. At the time I speak of . . . the regard and esteem for him approached veneration. . . .

Besides Mr. Ross' professional fame, he possessed other qualities of heart and mind which endeared him to his clients and the general public. He was reputed never to have accepted a retainer in a case unless he was reasonably well satisfied of the honesty of both the case and the client in all matters of importance, personal as well as legal. . . .

Mr. Ross was not only an able and learned and exceedingly industrious lawyer, but a wise and able statesman, and although not of the then dominant political party, frequently had honors thrust upon him. He was one of the honorable class of statesmen who were more numerous in his day than now. [1896][41]

It is worthwhile to match Judge Mellon's opinion against *The Commonwealth's*.

* * * * *

McMillan's letter for Ross and his serenity after he had written it show he was a good judge of men, and stood by those he believed in, and was little disturbed by uproar. Then, too, this short epsiode in McMillan's life does give to some people around him greater clearness of reality. That is, it lights up what they had confidence in, what influenced them, what interested them, what they thought good or bad and why, their 1808 prejudices and common sense and humor, the kind of political attack they accepted because it was customary though they did not find it convincing.

So to know how McMillan and others took the campaign of 1808 may help keep him from seeming only a name plodding down pages of fact.

VII. NOTES

1. *Pennsylvania Archives*. Second Series. IV. 105. The date is in a letter sent by Governor Mifflin to President Washington. Historians give varying dates for these events.

2. Alfred Creigh. *History of Washington County*. Appendix 69. Also Boyd Crumrine. *History of Washington County*. 275.

3. Leland D. Baldwin. *Whiskey Rebels*. 147.

4. *Pennsylvania Archives*. Second Series. IV. 182.

5. *Ibid*. 182, 186. Also Creigh. Appendix 75.

6. *Ibid*. 218.

7. Crumrine. 292.
8. *Pennsylvania Archives.* 123.
9. Russell J. Ferguson. *Early Western Pennsylvania Politics.* 46.
10. Solon J. and Elizabeth H. Buck. *The Planting of Civilization in Western Pennsylvania.* 471.
11. *Centenary Memorial.* 395.
12. Creigh. 243.
13. *Centenary Memorial.* 391.
14. Buck. 469.
15. Hugh Henry Brackenridge. *Incidents of the Insurrection.* 15.
16. *Ibid.* 111.
17. *Centenary Memorial.* 396.
18. *Ibid.* The source of Veech's story is a memoir of the Reverend Samuel Porter.
19. Minutes of the Presbytery of Ohio. I. October 29, 1794.
20. *Pennsylvania Archives.* 132, 133.
21. Baldwin. 206-209.
22. Henry Adams. *The Life of Albert Gallatin.* 138.
23. *Pennsylvania Archives.* 212.
24. Creigh. 48.
25. *Ibid.* 48-50.
26. *Centenary Memorial.* 396, 397.
27. *Ibid.* 397.
28. A record of this quarrel may be found in the *Pittsburgh Gazette,* July 21 to September 22, 1787.
29. James Veech. *The Banner.* February 27, 1867. A similar statement is found in Veech's article in *Centenary Memorial.* 397.
30. Adams. 92.
31. Ferguson. 130.
32. Adams. 678.
33. H. H. Brackenridge. *Gazette Publications.* 20.
34. Brackenridge Letters to Addison.
35. *Annals of the Congress of the United States.* Fourth Congress, First Session. Col. 1291.
36. *Ibid.* Col. 1295.
37. A copy of this letter is in the Library of Washington and Jefferson College.
38. The Brackenridge Letters are in Darlington Memorial Library of the University of Pittsburgh.
39. Creigh. 36.
40. James I. Brownson. *Life and Times of James Ross.* 37ff.
41. Thomas Mellon. "Reminiscences of Hon. James Ross," *Western Pennsylvania Historical Magazine.* III, No. 2. 103ff.

VIII. PERSONALITY

FOR fifty years *The Reverend John McMillan, D. D.* was a power in the Western Country. Even those who did not agree with his aims, who were antagonized by his acts or his speech or his manner, who thought him dogmatic or limited, unwilling to change and unable to change, even those never questioned his having done great things. "Others of the early ministers in Western Pennsylvania had far more learning than McMillan," wrote his grandson, "and were vastly his superior in general culture and greatly excelled him in graceful oratory; but his native force of character gave him a precedence which was acknowledged by all."[1] As records show, he had in him much that drew people to him and much that repelled them.

PREACHING

As McMillan stood before an assembly he was impressive. He was a large man, about six feet tall when he held himself erect, though when he was walking he seemed shorter, for he stooped a little, head bent forward. His body was stout and clumsy; his face rectangular rather than oval; his features coarse, his nose very prominent,[2] his eyebrows thick, his complexion heavily dark; and his expression as he preached stern and forbidding. No art could ever have made his voice musical but it had great volume, clarity, and carrying power. He had preached, it is told, in the open air to as many as two thousand.[3] His voice seemed to sustain, without fatigue, unending effort. He was a commanding presence as a speaker.

His sermons were in structure and in tone somewhat formal. The Reverend Mr. Leake, his successor at Chartiers, writes:

Dr. McMillan's mode of sermonizing was perhaps, rather formal. His regular discourse had, almost invariably, three general divisions, a number of sub-divisions under each, and closed with a practical improvement. They seldom exceeded fifty or sixty minutes in delivery. He had a favorite saying, derived no doubt from his theological teacher, Dr. Smith, which he often repeated: "No conversions are effected beyond the hour."[4]

He wrote out his sermons and slipped the notes for them into his Bible. And "Though he preached from memory, he had," it is said, "the faculty of delivering his discourse in so natural a tone of voice that his hearer would suppose it was perfectly extemporaneous."[5] Though he often repeated word for word part of an earlier sermon, it "always somehow seemed fresh." His language, which showed usually "a studied plainness,"[6] often deepened in exhortation or appeal to a more colored style.

Many who heard him in a religious service have written of the effect he made upon them as he stood before a congregation: they felt his sincerity, his determination, the awful seriousness which the service had for him. "He never used flattery," or "the studied ornaments of speech," or "graces of delivery."[7] "In the pulpit he had ordinarily but little action. He made almost no gestures."[8] Usually his sermons in their substance and the intensity with which he preached them seemed intended to force the listeners toward goodness rather than to draw them by gentler appeals. In his sermons, as in his daily living, he was scornful of whatever seemed to him fanciful and of whatever denied the seriousness of man's responsibility to do his duty here and now, at any cost to immediate happiness. Much in his nature was cast in the stern mold of the frontier, his home for sixty years. Yet many who heard him have left testimony that in his preaching were passages of feeling and touching tenderness.

McMillan was not always formal in his pulpit. He was not speaking formally when he rebuked from the pulpit one family for what he considered vanity of display. Nor was he formal when he called out to two young girls about to leave the service, "Sit down, girls, for we have all seen your combs."[9] Carnahan writes: "I have often seen him when preaching in the open air, under the shade of the native trees, take off his neckcloth or stock, in the midst of his discourse, and proceed without exciting a smile in one of the audience."[10] Such speech or act he seems to have thought not inconsistent with the seriousness and solemnity of preaching.

He aimed to show "the awful danger of the sinner" and "the absolute need of salvation through Christ."[11] Yet he aimed most to bring his hearers into conviction that acceptance gave to them joy, "serenity of mind," "delight"; "I thought that I could see God in everything about me,"[12] he once wrote. To accept the gospel plan McMillan has said was "easy."

He used whatever words he thought would make this alive to those listening, whatever would light up the end and the path. He, most earnestly, told as best he could what he most clearly saw, and he told it in the way he thought would show it sharply to those under his charge. Though by his Catechism classes and his college lectures he taught the tenets of the Church, he was eminently a "revival preacher,"[13] not satisfied with rational argument alone. His sermons seldom presented metaphysical distinctions or theological doctrines separated from a man's immediate acts and intimate beliefs and feeling. To McMillan any manner of talk which helped to the great end was the right one. He had no book for rules nor any set ways for taste. He seemed eccentric because he said what he judged right to say; but all that he said or did had the one center, however he might speak or act.

Of his preaching at Chartiers in the later years, S. C. Jennings wrote:

His preaching on those days had not the variety that it probably once had. Two leading general subjects made the chief discourses, viz.: searching sermons as to evidence of being truly Christians; and second, alarming discourses to the impenitent, especially in the application of his sermons. . . . Sometimes it appeared rather untimely, with a great sameness in public prayers. His days of close observation had then gone past.[14]

McMillan was seventy years old when Jennings wrote this. Read in one way, this comment proves the success of his ministry. After nearly fifty years, the force of his mind and the ring of his voice may have come to be, to his congregation, the normal and expected. At any rate, when away from Chartiers among people less used to hearing him, McMillan until the close of his life did preach with tremendous power. One of his greatest sermons was preached to the Presbytery of Ohio, when he was eighty-one years old.[15]

Against the acts and opinions which show that McMillan seldom moved from what he had once accepted, that he was not pliant and put little value on the virtue of pliancy, against this may be set glimpses which show opposite qualities in him. The glimpses are few. One is the letter to Carnahan in which he writes: "until the fall of 1772 . . . I had great difficulties in my own mind about undertaking the gospel ministry." A second one comes from the letter telling his desolation after the death of his wife. Another is the account of the evening he spent when he was very old at the home of a friend, when his gentle and eager interest drew to him the children of his friend. There must have been other writing and talk like these. We do know his sharp speaking and controversies, his preaching, his theological lectures, his outward and public actions. Of the intimate and most personal—the shifting play of feeling in his home with his wife, his children, his friends, his dependents—little has been told.

No doubt McMillan was dogmatic, often unimaginative, hostile to changes; often a thorny man to those about him; finding it nearly impossible not to be "the Reverend John McMillan" and, in his old age, not to accept himself almost as a legend, for he was, in his later life, "looked upon as an oracle of wisdom and piety."[16] Yet it is well to remember that no one is wholly a type, and that if you type a person, if you merely pigeonhole him, you miss the man himself.

OLD SCHOOL

McMillan did, as the psalmist puts it, "walk in the old ways," and sometimes he assumed that the ways he walked were the only "good ways." No doubt there are moral standards which should be held to, steadily. There are, too, many beliefs and actions which do not involve much of any moral judgment. In these a man does what he does perhaps because of his taste, or his past custom of action, or his wish not to differ without just cause from the people he lives among.

To be sure, with a pioneer's wish for change McMillan went into the frontier, established a new home, new churches, and new schools; but this was a continuation of the migration his people had been doing for centuries and of the missionary spirit in his church. He was not an innovator nor ever a breaker of images merely because they were old. Essentially he was one who carried on what he thought rightly established in theology, in habits of living, and even in lesser matters of dress and speech.

All his mature life he wore the fashion of dress he had worn as a young man—the cocked hat, buckskin or hand-woven cloth breeches with buckles, blue homespun stockings, and a vest of unchanging type.[17] Men of dignity and learning had worn these in the society he knew while he was growing up; he saw no need later to change fashions because others had. East of the mountains, in the middle and later 1700's, dress of this sort drew no comment, but later, west of the mountains, few persons were used to it. McMillan was conspicuous, too, because he wore a clerical collar and stock. It is no surprise that John Dunlap found his ready answer for McMillan. So far as we know McMillan never felt any need to change the old ways of dress for the new and never seriously considered a change.

Nor did he find much patience in him for those who took up the new. There is a story often told—Smith has retold it in *Old Redstone*—of McMillan's seeing for the first time in Chartiers an umbrella. He was talking in a group when a lady came by with the strange new object spreading above her head. McMillan looked, and spoke. He said: "What woman was that with a petticoat wrapped around a stick?"[18] McMillan was among the last in Chartiers to use an umbrella.

He seems to have thought that any ostentation and any concern for things he judged trivial did not fit with the serious duty of living. Certainly he was often impatient and blunt-spoken about them. One Sabbath, he notably offended General George Morgan and his family, relatives of General Neville. The general had moved from Princeton into the bounds of the Chartiers congregation. His land joined McMillan's at the northwest.[19] That Sabbath, "part of his large fashionable family were conveyed to church in a fine carriage." When it drove up to the door of the church, there was the natural high excitement and much staring from the "plain, rural people." "The Doctor," Smith tells, "was annoyed, perhaps more by the diverted attention . . . than by the appearance of the carriage itself, and did not omit in the course of his sermon to intimate that people might travel on the *broad road* in *fine carriages*, as well as on horseback, or on foot."[20] What McMillan said cost him the friendship of General Morgan.

McMillan's congregation at Chartiers was divided several times. At first Washington was part of his parish but when it grew into a small settlement it organized a church of its own. Although McMillan had helped in founding many churches, there is no mention of his helping the one at Washington. It may well be he resented this division. And, too, his refusal to allow Birch to be pastor of this new church and all the conflicts and difficulties that came within the Washington church, though they had other causes, may have been aggravated a little by McMillan's not giving help and counsel. He was opposed to change; any lessening of his Chartiers congregation would not have pleased him. At the first of 1830 or a few months before, Centre church was organized against his will and part of his congregation were dismissed to its communion. Before McMillan's resignation April 21, 1830, it was clear his parish was further to be divided. Canonsburg was to have its church. "Dr. McMillan was opposed to this course, doubted the policy, and resisted it as long as he could,"[21] says Smith. Though all these changes worked for the good of the Church at large, McMillan kept holding to what had been in the past. Chartiers had been so long the child of his affections that he could not adjust himself to inevitable changes. It is thought that he resigned at Chartiers not so much because he was nearly eighty as because of the divisions made and the one about to be made. These divisions had reduced his congregation to less than one hundred members. A little after McMillan resigned at Chartiers the congregation enlarged and improved the church building. Since its membership had been cut from 304 in 1830 to 70 in 1831,[22] the reason of this is hard to find. Perhaps many families had left the congregation because of McMillan's unwillingness to accept changes, and perhaps his successor, Samuel F. Leake, hoped the new improvements would win these many back into the home church.

In the rebuilt church was a new pulpit with two flights of steps instead of the one the old pulpit had had. McMillan disliked this new pulpit. He once caustically said, "The Devil went up one pair while the preacher ascended the other."[23] He would not enter it. When he preached or spoke in the new church, he persisted in standing below the high pulpit. There were those who said they had seen him in the last year of his life leaning against the old pulpit (it had been set up at the side or the back of the room), and that tears were running down his cheeks.[24]

In his theology McMillan changed little as his life went on with the passing years. As has been said already, he could not easily adopt or carefully examine a new way or a new end. He could not —he simply could not—accept new paths, much less follow them in happiness. Nor was he often able to vary details of doctrine to meet the variety among the men and the women in his congregation, each of whom was living in his own world and having his special experiences, and each of whom needed, if he was to see the truth, to have it shown him in a way that would touch his understanding and his heart.

BLUNT SPEECH

McMillan spoke bluntly. His speech was often as rough-hewn as his actions. What he thought true he said, with small regard generally to its opportuneness or to his hearer's sensibility. He did not aim to offend or antagonize. He never spoke from malice, cold unkindness, or cruelty. He simply said what he thought needed saying in what to him was the straightforward way.

In McMillan's first months at Pequea, Robert Smith, his teacher, was troubled by his rough and forbidding manner. He soon found, however, that this was superficial. There was much more to the boy of fifteen than his clumsy body and his often overbearing blunt speech.[25] McMillan when he was young was unpolished, sharp tongued, not sure of himself; and those who knew him in later years spoke of his caustic bluntness. There can be no question that constantly through his life his speech did antagonize. Some felt he had insulted them. Only a man of high worth could have given such an impression and yet been esteemed beyond almost anyone else in his community for his integrity and devotion and humaneness.

One day when McMillan met John Dunlap, the son of the president of Jefferson College, "in gay attire," he said to him: "Joe, can you tell me the difference between the Devil and you?" Dunlap seems not to have been altogether surprised at his question. The students at the College knew that often their professor of divinity was outspoken. His answer was a good-natured "Yes, I can. The Devil wears a cocked hat, a coat of colonial cut, breeches with knee and shoe buckles: but I wear pantaloons and clothing of modern style."[26] McMillan's clothes were in eighteenth-century fashion. Still, the answer did not anger him at all. He had said what he wished to say and it was proper Dunlap should answer as he saw fit.

Once when he was talking to a man recovering from a serious illness, McMillan told him: "It is better that you are here than in Hell."[27] It has been suggested that the sick man knew McMillan well enough to see the twinkle in his eye.

At other times the rebuke was given without the twinkle. One fast day kept by the church, McMillan on his way to the church met young William Neil, "a stout lad from Jefferson College . . . later the Rev. William Neil, D.D.," as Neil was going to shoot pigeons in the woods. "Dr. McMillan . . . inquired what he was doing. Upon young Neil telling him that he was shooting pigeons the doctor remarked: 'What a sad thing to see a poor sinner on his way to hell, killing innocent birds,' and then passed on."[28] Neil had no ready reply as Dunlap had; he was bruised and angered by the rebuke, but later he testified that it "produced in him a proper and increased conviction of sin."[29]

McMillan heard a young man preach what some of the congregation called an "essay," a "moral harangue." Afterward many of the listeners, knowing McMillan's outspokenness, asked his opinion of the sermon. He answered: "That was the most Christless discourse to which I ever listened."[30] Behind such hatchet-strokes of expression were an aim to help and a high moral fervor. But the harshness of expression often cancelled out the good purpose. Such speech roused antagonism. Such forthright bluntness as he used in speaking of Birch and others he felt sure were wrong is, no doubt, an imperfection. Considered abstractly, outside the frontier place and time, it is a fault; yet in the 1700's on the rough edge of the West perhaps it needs little apology. William Darby, Esquire, wrote:

Rough and rude were the manners of that country, at the age under review: yet there was, under this repulsive exterior, much sound moral principle and manly feeling; and I doubt whether there was in the country another man more respected than Dr. McMillan.[31]

HUMOR

McMillan did have a sense of humor, which now and then came out openly into his speech or action. It was more of a slow heavy thrust than a quick flash of wit; sometimes it was good-natured, sometimes a bludgeoning.

After John Dunlap had made his answer to McMillan's question about how the Devil would be dressed, it is said that McMillan joined him in a good laugh,[32] and so it may be that what seemed a rebuke was only a dry jocularity, though pedantic and heavy handed.

An anecdote has come down through the years about McMillan and the Reverend Joseph Patterson, one of the trustees with him on the first Board of Jefferson College. On their way to a meeting of the Presbytery of Pittsburgh they had stopped at an inn "to refresh themselves." Two glasses of whiskey were set in front of them. Dr. Patterson closed his eyes and offered a prayer and a blessing. His grace was long drawn out. When he opened his eyes he saw the two empty glasses. McMillan had drunk not only his whiskey but Dr. Patterson's. No one, it is said could have been more surprised than Dr. Patterson was. McMillan smiled a little sheepishly and added: "My brother, you must watch as well as pray."[33]

About 1823 Matthew Brown brought to McMillan a student who he suggested should be given a grant from a fund McMillan had for helping worthy young men.[34] The student, Brown explained, was married. For a theological student to be married was not unusual but McMillan picked up this chance for humor. "Oh, the fellow's married, is he?" he said, "I don't think my fund will carry double."[35] It has been considered reasonable to suppose that the student did get the aid.

He officiated once, in his own home, at the marriage of a fellow clergyman. Even then it was a long established custom that one minister should not take a marriage fee from another, and so when George J. Junkin, an attendant at this McElroy-Allison wedding, offered the fee McMillan shook his head and declined it with an awkward smile and an offhand, "No! No! Dog won't eat dog."[36]

Sometimes McMillan used his humor to encourage a timid student or to lessen a situation that had become strained. In a letter written about 1854, Samuel Crawford of Greene County says he remembers well the visits McMillan made twice a week to classes at the College. "If a student made a mistake, he was always the first to discover it, and would correct it by some humorous remark which not only corrected the error but palliated it."[37]

His having humor may at first seem strange. His not having humor would have been more strange. Though he was intensely individual, he still was part of the people among whom he lived, bone of their bone. In him the common qualities showed a special definiteness and depth because his mind was so active and penetrating, his purpose so high and clear to him, his will so driving, his devotion and humanity so inexhaustible. He was much of his race and time and surroundings, only it happened that his strength keyed him up to higher effectiveness than most others reached. He was part of his own people. And the Scotch-Irish, however serious they may be, have never lacked down-to-earth straight-hitting humor.

PRACTICALITY

McMillan carried on well the minor and necessary matters of level everyday living, though his early years at Chartiers were interrupted by "great annoyance from the savage foes."[38] At times he and his family and his neighbors had "to seek ... the shelter of the fort." As has been said, he was enrolled in the militia of Washington County which was ordered to rendezvous in May of 1782. These interruptions, however, came only in a few of his early years.

Like the general run of the Scotch-Irish, McMillan, in these minor things, was a practical man. He was a good farmer. The wild country and the cabin of his first years gave way to farmland and a comfortable manse built out of oak, cherry, and black walnut that grew on the land: a "mansion" the neighborhood called it. A great deal of the farming he did himself; he had been brought up to such work on his father's farm. He was expert with the tools of the farm—with the ax ("few of his neighbors could excel him in handling the axe"),[39] the mattock, the grubbing hoe, the maul, log chains, the plow. He knew horses and cattle, planting and reaping in their seasons, and the rest a farmer needed to know. Work with his hands was part of his usual day. James Carnahan says, "He lived almost entirely on the products of his farm,"[40] and his *Expense Account* seems proof of it. Fortunately, all through his life he had great physical strength. To go over the Alleghenies in snow, to ford a river, to chop down trees and get the hay and grain in, to preach twice and walk twenty miles the same day, he seemed to think quite natural activity.

He was thrifty, in small matters and in large. His *Expense Account* as he kept it from 1821 until his death itemizes money spent for himself and the household and the farm.[41] For the most part, they raised or made what they needed or bartered for it. McMillan puts down surprisingly few items each year—fifty-seven in all of 1821, forty-one in 1831, forty-three in 1832. Some typical entries are: shaving soap 25 cents, pound of tobacco 12½, snuff for Dido 25 (an item often repeated), "Dido for past services $10" (Dido was probably his slave whom he had freed), barrel of salt $2.50, snuffbox for Dido 25, repairing watch $1.50. "To Dr. Leatherman [Dr. Jonathan Leatherman had been a trustee of Jefferson College since 1820] $3," overalls $7.50, shoeing horse 37½, repairing axes $1.75, two pounds of lead 25, a pair of shoes 80, a pair of shoes $1.50, stage fare to and from Pittsburgh $3, a book 50, a hat $6, Smith's sermons, watch key, a kettle, a bucket, "Colonization Society $7.50." Contributions to missions were a constant item. "Ye constitution of ye union 31," "To Munroe for advocate $2.50." Cloth, clothing, and periodicals came high. If McMillan has given in full his home expenses, he lived thriftily and, as Carnahan said, "almost entirely on the products of his farm."

Evidently he was a good manager. In his will he disposed of at least 669 acres (his will mentions previous gifts of land and a a manse and many other buildings, and "much goods.") His will mentions one clock, *the* chest, wagons, log chains, sugar kettles, the old cupboard and table; "my case of drawers"; one feather bed and half the bed clothing; another feather bed and the other half of the bed clothes, six silver teaspoons, one looking glass; "my silver watch," books, bound religious magazines, manuscripts, and much else.[42]

Such details may suggest, a little, McMillan's background day after day: the land he walked on, the work he did, the books he used, the household furnishings, some of the tastes and ideas intimately his, the shifting responsibilities he met for those of his household. They may show a little what he was busy about and what he lived among when he was not a public person—not a young minister, or the minister growing old, or at last the "venerable patriarch of the West."

JOHN McMILLAN

READING

McMillan valued books and used them. As a child at his primer and catechism, in the log school, in Fagg's Manor and Pequea academies, in college and theological seminary, and through the years of his teaching and long ministry, he was at his book.

His education, from his lessons at home until he was ordained (1776) by the church he had been dedicated to, required that he master books. He entered the College of New Jersey in 1770 and was graduated from it two and a half years later. For admission the candidate had to turn Virgil and Cicero's orations into English, write "true and grammatical Latin," translate "any part of the Evangelists from Greek into Latin or English," and solve problems in basic arithmetic. It was taken for granted, the trustees stated in 1769, that students read English "with propriety," and spell, and write "without grammatical errors." In the College, freshmen kept at their Latin and Greek and were trained in speaking Latin; sophomores added "the sciences, geography, rhetoric, logic, and mathematics"; juniors had classics (which might include Hebrew) "mathematics, moral philosophy, metaphysics, chronology, and physics"; seniors gave all their time to review and composition, which was to cover "the most improving parts of the Latin and Greek classics, parts of the Hebrew Bible," and "all the arts and sciences."[43]

McMillan must have entered an advanced class, a fairly common custom. An undergraduate in a letter to his brother who hoped to enter as a junior explains: "You will be examined on Virgil, Horace, Cicero, Lucian, Xenophon, Homer, geography, and logic. . . . I would advise you if you come, to study the whole of Xenophon. . . . Try to accustom yourself to read Greek and Latin well as it is much looked to here and be accurate in geography." He makes clear, too, the need of knowing arithmetic, geometry, "vulgar and decimal fractions and square foot."[44] McMillan, then, by the time he left college had given studious attention to many books.

In his early teaching McMillan had the young men he was preparing for the ministry follow as well as might be the course he had followed. Evidently books were essential in this. "Dr. McMillan," wrote someone from Washington, Pennsylvania, "had several books with him when he erected his first log cabin near Canonsburg."[45] Jean McMillan said that after the burning of this log cabin in 1780 her father sent over the mountains for new books. Evidently, too, books were hard to come by and were handed on from one student to another. In the library of Washington and

Jefferson College is an Ovid's *Metamorphoses* used first in Princeton by a student about 1758. McMillan owned this book. That other young men studied it year after year is shown by the scribblings in it. James McGready while with McMillan wrote in it: "Legit hunc librum in Decembro, 1783." Another in the summer of 1788 wrote, appropriately for Ovid if not for his own scholarship, "I'm so in love that I cannot read."

* * *

McMillan seems not to have read widely, not much beyond what would give him direct help. His lectures in theology[46] are an instance of this. In the first 128 pages of the lectures—half the manuscript—he names only the Bible, to which he makes constant, almost countless references. In the lectures he speaks with assurance of ancient history and old philosophies but he cites only six authors. He quotes Socrates once, he paraphrases Cicero once (both on page 4 of the manuscript); and on page 11 he names four church fathers. After the eleventh page, there are no more such references. Each lecture is closely reasoned, a logical progression of thought starting with a major premise McMillan thinks proved by nature or the Scriptures or reason. Usually a later lecture rests upon a truth demonstrated in an earlier one; it is only after he had shown the divine inspiration of the Scriptures that he uses a biblical verse as a proof. McMillan did know his logic-books and his Bible. He does, though, recognize limits to what logic can prove and reason explain. He writes that the doctrine of the Trinity remains "a mystery: which to all eternity we shall not be able fully to comprehend."[47]

* * *

As has been said, the aesthetics of writing did not interest him. Even when in a lecture on theology he does state the Old and New Testaments are written with "sublimity," he is using sublimity of style as one of five proofs that the Bible is inspired Gospel. Here is his discussion:

Fifth, from their sublimity. There is a majesty, and dignity in the very plainness and simplicity of the scriptures. They do not labour to please men's ears and on the matter (sic) with the curious ornaments of speech, but represent the very matter itself to the soul, as that which is in itself worthy of all acceptation, and needs no human eloquence to command it. Yet the sentiments conveyed in this humble stye (style), are more sublime than any to be found in human compositions. An (and) as one observes "no Book in the world do we find written in a more simple style," no where does there appear the least affectation of ornament, yet nowhere else, is the Almighty represented, as either acting, or speaking, in a manner so becoming the Eternal Ruler of the world.[48]

For style in a book as style, as a kind of alchemy, as the stimulus of emotion below a statement of fact, as raising fact into experience and so giving it life, he does not care. He hardly recognizes it. That is, at times he speaks of style and seems to value it, but for him it has value only because it is one direct proof of a doctrine which he and his church believe. The point is, he read books for a purpose. They brought grist to his mill. And it is interesting that he names only two qualities of style in the Bible—the "sublime" and the "clear." These two are the chief styles his sermons and his lectures strongly show.

As far as we know, he bought only books which helped him understand the Bible or which concerned the Church or his teaching or the affairs of his people. The more than twelve years we have of the *Expense Account*[49] show money paid for religious periodicals and newspapers ("The Pittsburgh Record" $2.) Typical of books he bought are: "a bible for John," bibles for Hannah, for Thomas, for Catherine (to whom a year earlier he had given a primer), "ye constitution of ye union," in 1830 "to pedlar—pilgrims progress—50," and in 1831 "to Munroe [who sold books and bound them] for ye holy war—50" [probably Bunyan's *The Holy War*], "a book," "a book," "a book." Possibly some obscure pamphlets and sermons are listed in the *Account,* unrecognizable today because what may be titles are not capitalized.

There is other record of books he owned. In his will he bequeaths to his oldest son "my large bible, Hennings Commentary [Henry's Commentary] in six vol. [now in the library at Washington and Jefferson College], Witherspoons works in 4 vol, the assembley's Missionary Magazines, *the* book case." To his "beloved daughter Catherine Allen" go "all my manuscripts, Knox Life, and all the volumes of the Christian Advocate, and the Western Mission magazines 2 vol." And "whatever books ... may remain"[50] were to be divided among his heirs.

* * *

Nowhere does one come upon a book of English poetry old or new, of science, of the classics of eighteenth century prose. Yet during McMillan's lifetime, great experiences and great ideas were stirring into great expressions in poetry and prose. A great wind was blowing in Europe and in his own country. McMillan's books give little record of that.

He may have read other books. It may be he had a literary interest in them, not merely a doctrinal or teaching interest, a service interest. Fuller study of his sermons and his manuscripts and of other writing of his time may show his wider general reading. But as records stand it seems fair to say that there is little to suggest it.

For him a book never was an easy, pleasant, constant, friendly companion, from whom day after day he got recurring happiness and the lift which happy companionship gives. He seldom if at all merely enjoyed books or did *pure reading,* which is not after any direct statement of an ethical point.

McMillan probably never read merely because he liked to read.

FEELING

When McMillan believed an idea or an action right, he upheld it not with cool detachment but with blazing zeal. He was often, as it was phrased, "strongly moved"; and since many others could not accept his views and were not moved as he was, he ran into controversy and opposition, into struggles which were sometimes bitter. He met stiff opposition to his plans of education, to his ways of preaching, to his customs in his church. He could not easily compromise. He was too much the Old Testament prophet. And he did not have much of the imagination which gets two sides of a question even while it stands for one. Fixed beliefs, and deep feeling about them, were characteristic of McMillan from his log college days to his last years. In him, as long as he lived, tides of intensity flowed.

But in what did not concern abstractions of belief or general rules for action, that is, in his relation with persons, he could show a deep and sensitive and surprising concern for others. There seems no doubt that McMillan felt lasting bonds with his family—his wife and children, his father and mother, his brothers and sisters and less close relatives. His first journey into the Western Country might not have been made if a sister and at least one of his brothers had not been living there. In his *Journal* he speaks of the "distressing tidings of my brother William's death." He took William's son into his household and saw to his education. His father and his sister Mary, he encouraged to settle near him in Western Pennsylvaniy. He visited a relative's home whenever he passed that way. He notes in the *Journal* illness of the family. Indeed, he seems constantly to have felt responsibility and solicitude for those of his blood.

* * *

The *Journal,* it should be said, almost never records emotion; it records the fact. Generally for any month McMillan lists under the date of each Sabbath his place of preaching, his text, the offering at the service, the weather. He does add, though not often, a statement in bare form of what is happening in his family, his parish, and his new country. Personal feeling goes unexpressed. Yet what he selects shows below the statement a little of what he was thinking about and feeling about. Here is a typical early entry:

Friday, Sab. & monday. Preached at Middle Spring and on Wednesday arrived again at Brandiwine.
Thursday, Saturday, & Sab. Preached at Brandiwine. And on Monday after hearing Mr. Smith, I rode to fag's mannor.
Tuesday. Took my young mair to Pequea.
Wednesday. Returned again to Brandiwine.
The 3rd. Sab. of May. Preached at Brandiwine.
The 4th Sab. Had the pleasure of hearing Mr. Cooper at Brandiwine.
This week went twice to Fag's manor, my mother being sick.
Saturday the 31st of May at half past Seven O'clock post meredian Jean McMillan was born. 1777. [51]

* * *

His sermons often did appeal directly to the feelings of his hearers. He spoke many warnings of impending doom; but he could speak in a moving way, a way that touched his people deeply, of God's love for fallen mankind. Such sermons were most often given on a fast day or when he administered the Sacrament. A hearer who sat at one of McMillan's communion services about 1830 has given his impression: "So tenderly did the Doctor portray the scenes of Calvary, that every eye ran over, every heart was full. My dear friend Cloud was convulsed with emotion and the entire audience was moved."[52] Though many times McMillan's listeners heard the mutterings of Sinai's thunder and saw the sharp strokes of its lightning, yet when McMillan told of the love of Jesus "his voice would mellow to the tenderest tones." "He was all benevolence."[53] To a communion sermon dated June, 1821 and February, 1829, this is his ending: "O put in for a share of his love: it is free love. . . . O be not so cruel to yourself as to slight this love . . . but haste, haste to embrace a Saviour, and come and seal the marriage contract at his own table."[54]

On the frontier there were, recurringly, food shortages. In those times McMillan opened his granaries to those who had need. Carnahan writes of one such active benevolence. Between 1780 and 1790 there were shortages of bread stuffs all through the western frontier. During the months of April and May this scarcity was most critical. Many persons who could not buy the grain in the market would come to McMillan to buy from him. In his usual harsh voice he would ask if they had money to pay for grain. If any of them said "yes" his answer was, "I have no wheat or corn for you. Buy elsewhere."[55] To those who had no money he gave several hundred bushels of his wheat and corn. They could return it, he told them, after harvest. McMillan kept no record of these loans. He was generous to missions, to Canonsburg Academy and Jefferson College, to churches newly established, to the old and the needy and the dependent.

* * *

Those "pious young men" whom he began taking into his house soon after he was pastor at Chartiers and whom he educated for the ministry, he boarded and lodged and taught without charge. He kept on supporting young theological students until a fund was set up for that purpose after Canonsburg Academy and Jefferson College were founded. In this way, Carnahan says, "Patterson, Porter, Marquis, Hughes, and several eminently useful ministers were trained."[56] Joseph Smith tells that since Samuel Porter "was without means of support, Dr. McMillan kindly gave him board and instruction, free of expense."[57]

* * *

One young man McMillan helped was John Watson.[58] Watson's father, "a poor but respectable man," died when Watson was nine. A friend, the keeper of a tavern and a retail store, took the boy into his family and taught him writing and arithmetic so he could help in the store and at the bar, "as circumstances required." By the time Watson was nine or ten he was "passionately fond of . . . the best works of fiction, owned by the wife of his employer." At eleven or twelve he came upon Addison's *Spectator*. He liked it and because he did not understand the Latin quotations heading each paper, he got hold of a *Horace* and an old broken-backed Latin dictionary. He had no Latin grammar, but he did learn to read the Latin.

Judge Addison, holding a session of the Court of Common Pleas, lodged at the tavern where Watson worked. When one night very late he came in "he found the young barkeeper stretched on the floor before the fire reading *Horace* by the firelight." He talked with the boy and promised to bring him some books when he came at the next session of Court. The day he rode there again he did bring in his portmanteau the books: a Latin grammar, Aesop's Fables, *Selectae Veteri Testamento,* and a good Latin dictionary; and he told the boy how best to use the grammar. "Never," Watson said, "did I experience a more joyful moment." Judge Addison

JOHN McMILLAN

kept on lending him Latin and Greek classics, histories, belles lettres, books on natural and moral philosophy, metaphysics, and the like: and the judge got a man who taught in the grammar school of the village to help Watson.

When Watson was about nineteen Dr. McMillan heard of the boy's ability and worth (by this time he was studying Latin, Greek, literature, and science), and had him appointed usher at Canonsburg Academy. He stayed there eighteen months, and then McMillan "believing him worthy the best advantage our country afforded, procured him a place on the Latin Fund in the College of New Jersey."[59] Income from the fund was not enough to pay board and college fees, and so Father McMillan (it seemed he was often called that in western Pennsylvania) paid the rest of his expenses. As soon as he was graduated, he was chosen principal of Canonsburg Academy, and was chosen president of Jefferson College in 1802, when he was thirty. He could "translate with facility French, Spanish, and Italian . . . was good in Hebrew and Aramaic" and shorthand. He had, too, deep interests in literature and science.

All this shows McMillan's readiness to help and his good judgment. And it puts a cutting light on some men and women who lived in the New Country.

* * *

McMillan was not the scholar Watson was. His mind was clear and strong and honest; essentially a stable mind, though he had his ripples of irritation, his times of exhaltation, his "searchings" and deep despondency. He seems not to have been quickly imaginative, adaptable, original, nor usually to have had the patience and long-suffering which come from understanding that variations of thought and feeling pull different men into different purposes and actions. Yet he did have the virtues of strength, clear purpose, devotion, integrity, and unending labor.

There is small evidence that McMillan had a conscious aesthetic interest in nature or cared for any forms of art. His ways of writing, however, do fit his meanings; he varies his style—it seems unknowingly—for differing thoughts and feelings.

His lectures on theology and much of his sermons show exact thinking, go ahead in straightforward order, and have direct, easy, clear expression. He never uses trite wording, worn down by dull repetition, and he does not phrase his sermons in foolish, if unconscious, parody of Bible language. He talks honestly, one man to another. That he did respond to the strength and beauty of Bible prose his sermons and his lectures seem to prove. At times his style has something of the Authorized Version's steady nobility, and rises into highly accented prose as his emotion rises. Yet fortunately he always rings true; always it is McMillan himself speaking.

His letter to Carnahan is admirable. It expresses without self-consciousness or pretence what is moving in his mind as he looks back on the flow of his long life. He tells facts—dates, places, actions—because they have had their place in his life, and he tells more than facts. He tells that he has "outlived all the *first* set of ministers who settled on this side of the mountains . . .; and all the *second* set who were raised in this country. . . . Several of the *third* set are already gone to rest." He tells of his religious experience as naturally as he tells of the night he and his family first came to Chartiers. He tells of the death of his wife: "my wife and I lived together comfortably for forty-three years." He tells that he is somewhat troubled with rheumatic pains, yet he enjoys "pretty good health" and is "still able to preach, though my memory has much failed"; and he adds "my lungs are still good as ever."[60] Evidently he knew what was often said of his strength of voice.

* * *

Catherine Brown McMillan died, after forty-three years of marriage, when McMillan was sixty-seven years old. He wrote to a favorite pupil of his, Dr. Johnston of Newburg, New York, this touching letter:

I am a poor lone creature and have none to sympathize with me in the ills inseparable from old age. My children treat me with all the tenderness that can be expected; but the young are no company for the old; they are entirely unacquainted with their feelings. The principal comfort which I now have is in preaching the gospel and attending to a divinity class.[61]

No doubt he was austere; his appearance, his speech, his whole manner seemed to many unsympathetic and forbidding and stern. This letter shows what he kept from sight—a tenderness, and an intensity of desolation which may come to those left in loneliness.

* * *

One incident in the last of his life expresses what McMillan often left unexpressed. Only a few weeks before he died he stopped overnight in Washington on his way back to Chartiers and passed the night at the home of a friend. The Reverend Dr. Elliott, pastor of the Washington church, writes that he spent part of the evening with McMillan and "engaged him for breakfast the next morning." Dr. Elliott's wife and children had heard much of McMillan but had never seen him. They had heard of his gruffness, his blunt manner, his uncompromising speech, his patriarchal dignity in old age. They expected strain, and some discomfort. But the meeting was a delight. McMillan drew all of them to him. "Upon receiving an introduction to Mrs. Elliott and the children, he took each of them by the hand, saluting them in the most kind and affectionate manner." He was gentle, benign, forgetting himself in them. He showed so clearly his interest in the smaller children that soon he had them close around him. Dr. Elliott adds: "The patriarchal simplicity of his manner and his humble, affectionate, and condescending spirit captivated us all."[62]

Such feelings did move in McMillan. Their strength and the expression of them were often obscured by his compelling sense of ever-present sin, by the austerity of his surroundings, by his conviction of the brevity and seriousness of living and of his own constant responsibility. He often tore, unconsciously—it may seem carelessly—the heart of a friend or an opponent. Yet certainly he never doubted men were brothers, though he may have forgotten at times that a brother must bear with his brother's infirmity and that, since men are brothers, a rebuke commonly should be given in the gentle spirit of brotherhood.

RETIREMENT

After McMillan had requested his release from Chartiers Church on April 20, 1830, because of "the labours of his pastoral office," and his request had been granted by the Ohio Presbytery, he did not give up what for more than fifty years had been his greatest interests. He merely got release from the exacting routine of active ministry. His *Journal* shows fairly well what he went on doing, and so a few entries in it may suggest what to him were important—his preaching (during his ministry it is said he preached more than six thousand times), his assistance at the Sacrament and the baptisms, his visits to other churches, the death of a kinsman or of someone he had known a long while. For 1830 the *Journal* is kept almost fully; in 1831, 1832, and 1833 the entries become few and broken. However, in these years he kept his *Expense Account* almost as fully as ever and wrote it as legibly as he had ten years earlier.

Here is a little from the *Journal:*

The 2d. Sab. at Bethany in the forenoon (June, 1833)
This week attended P.b.y. and returned to Canonsburg on Thursday.
Mr. Craig Ritchie died on ye 13th of June 1833

The 1st Sab. of Sept. assisted to administer the Sacrament at Chartiers, and preached on friday the fast day from Joh. 15.2
The 2d. Sab. assisted Mr. Allen to administer the Sacrament at Racoon, and preached on friday, saturday, Sab. morning and monday.
The 3d. Sab. assisted McCurdy to administer the Sacrament at ye Cross Roads and preached on friday, Sab. morning and Monday at Frankfort Wednesday.
The 4th Sab. assisted Mr. Scott to administer ye Sacrament at Mill Creek, and preached on friday, Saturday, Sab. morning and evening and Monday.
The 5th Sab. at Chartiers from—Joh. 15.2 [63]

And with this his *Journal* ends.

In 1832 he wrote to Carnahan, then president of Princeton College, "If my life and health continue I design this spring and summer to visit some of the old congregations I helped to collect and see how they do and blow the Gospel trumpet among them."[64] He made the journey. In April, May, and June of 1832 he visited many churches he had helped at their beginnings or had supplied with pastors. At Cross Creek and Cross Roads in May, and at Raccoon in June, he administered the Lord's Supper to the people; at Raccoon he stayed six weeks. During the three months he preached seventeen sermons "with more than usual fervency,"[65] and though his dependence on his notes was greater than it had used to be, yet, as he wrote Carnahan, he still could "bawl almost as loud as ever." McMillan was proud of his voice. A little before he died he said that he "wished he could leave his lungs as a legacy to the church, for they would serve some poor-voiced fellow of another generation."[66] Carnahan wrote: "During the year 1832 he assisted in administering the Lord's Supper eleven times and preached about fifty times; on occasions leaning on his crutch and in the eightieth year of his age."[67] McMillan's "crutch" was probably a cane with a crossbar handle.

The year 1833 until his illness, which began November 5, was a busy time for McMillan. He administered the Sacrament at seventeen services and preached about seventy-five sermons, on some Sabbaths more than one. "He was honored with the strength and the opportunity to labor to the last and die with his harness on."[68]

Early in October, 1833, McMillan, feeling in excellent health and spirits, attended the Synod of Pittsburgh at Pittsburgh. He went to each meeting of the six day session, and he walked the half mile to and from the meetings, leaning on his cane. Twice he preached to the Synod: and evidently he took an active part in its business, for its record shows that "The following committees were reported to examine the records of the Presbyteries, viz.—

JOHN McMILLAN

the Records of the Presbytery of Redstone, Dr. McMillan and Mr. Coulter."[69] S. C. Jennings in "Recollections of Useful Persons" writes of McMillan as he saw him at the Pittsburgh Synod in 1829 (on this visit McMillan preached at the Second Presbyterian Church in Pittsburgh): "There sits near the Moderator Dr. John McMillan robust with rather a swarthy face . . . his hair not entirely white, he holds his hickory staff . . . His aid is sought in religious service, and he is treated as a father, for at this time he is 76 years old."[70] At the Synod of 1833 some members asked him where he thought the next one should meet. He answered "he would be home before that time and was not interested in the place of meeting."[71] The session being over, he went with "several clerical brethern" by steamboat to Wheeling. There he stayed twelve or fourteen days, preaching sometimes both morning and evening "with much acceptance."[72] Altogether in the four weeks of this last journey, he traveled by stage and steamboat more than two hundred miles and preached at least twenty sermons.

Tuesday, November 3, he came by stage to Canonsburg. "He took a hearty meal." He seemed tired but cheerful and "in his ordinary health." That night he was violently ill; and "he suffered much bodily pain." At daybreak he went to Dr. Jonathan Leatherman, his physician and a trustee of Jefferson College. He said to the doctor: "Doctor, I had a messenger sent for me last night and I must go."

His disease was paralysis of the prostate gland, induced as was supposed, by too great exertion—preaching too frequently—for his strength. Of this he was himself aware, but he did not regret it. He seemed to regard it as a high privilege to fall a martyr in a cause he so much loved.[73]

His mind was clear and strong, and though he knew he was close to death he was tranquil. Eleven days later, Saturday, November 16, in his eighty-second year he died. He is buried with a raised stone slab covering his grave in the Chartiers burial ground beside his wife.

On the third Sabbath of June that year he had preached from II Corinthians 5.8. This verse is: "We are confident, I say, and willing rather to be absent from the body and to be present with the Lord."

* * * * *

That he was a man of power has not been questioned. He was possibly the most eminent citizen in the Western Country. Certainly he was the most eminent man of his Church. At the time of his death the *Daily Pittsburgh Gazette* printed: "The deceased was the apostle of the Presbyterian Church in the West, the founder

PERSONALITY

and father of her institutions in this section of the country."[74] Nearly one hundred years ago, in 1854, Joseph Smith gave this estimate: "the records . . .will save from oblivion the usefulness and worth of Dr. McMillan." In 1888, Matthew Allen wrote: "he impressed all with whom he met, and even those who only saw him, with a sense of great personal power. And the broad and solid views which he took on all great questions, civil as well as religious, confirmed the idea given by his personal presence."[75]

Today these judgments seem to stand.

VIII. NOTES

1. Moses R. Allen. "Rev. John McMillan, D.D." Centennial Address, 1888.
2. James Carnahan. Letter to Sprague in W. B. Sprague's *Annals of the American Pulpit.* III. 354.
3. *Ibid.*
4. Joseph Smith. *Old Redstone.* 208, 209.
5. *Ibid.* 206.
6. *Ibid.* 207.
7. E. H. Gillett. *History of the Presbyterian Church in the United States of America.* I. 41.
8. Allen. Centennial Address. Allen quotes this from Rev. Lemuel Leake.
9. Francis J. Collier. "Chartiers Church and Its Ministers," *Centennial Celebration of Chartiers Church.* 15.
10. *Annals of the American Pulpit.* III. 354.
11. Allen. Centennial Address.
12. McMillan's Letter to Carnahan. See Appendix C.
13. Allen. Centennial Address.
14. S. C. Jennings. *Recollections of Seventy Years.* 121.
15. See the closing section of Chapter VI.
16. Samuel Colver. Excerpts from a letter in Daniel M. Bennett's *Rev. John McMillan, D.D.* 243.
17. Collier. 15.
18. Smith. 204.
19. Bennett. 331.
20. *Old Redstone.* 204.
21. *Ibid.* 203.
22. Records of the Synod of Pittsburgh. 318, 338.
23. *Old Redstone.* 204.
24. *Ibid.*
25. Lemuel F. Leake. "Notes on the Early Life of Dr. J. McMillan," *The Presbyterian Advocate.* VII, No. 52.
26. Clarence F. Macartney. *Not Far From Pittsburgh.* 129.
27. Collier. 15.
28. Allen. Centennial Address.
29. Ebenezer Erskine. *Centennial Memorial,* Carlisle Presbytery. 171.
30. Allen. Centennial Address.
31. *Old Redstone.* 207.
32. D. X. Junkin. "Life and Labors of the Rev. John McMillan, D.D.," *Centenary Memorial.* 32-33.

33. Macartney. 129.
34. McMillan's Treasure Book for the Support of Poor Scholars from 1805 to 1826 has been found only recently and is in the Library of the Western Theological Seminary. This book shows the persons or groups making contributions to the Fund and the students who received grants, along with the amounts granted.
35. *Centenary Memorial.* 33.
36. *Ibid.*
37. Bennett. 244.
38. *Ibid.* 258.
39. *Ibid.* 257.
40. *Annals of the American Pulpit.* III. 355.
41. See Appendix B.
42. These details are taken from Mrs. Wragg's copy of McMillan's will.
43. Thomas Jefferson Wertenbaker. *Princeton 1746-1896.* 91-93. All of the material in this paragraph is from this book.
44. *Ibid.* 94. This is quoted from a letter written by Edward Crawford to James Crawford, August 29, 1774. It is in the files of the Presbyterian Historical Society.
45. Bennett. 107.
46. Mrs. Wragg permitted me to use her copy of these lectures.
47. This is from the lecture, "Of the Trinity."
48. This is quoted from the first lecture under the division entitled "How are the Scriptures of the old and new testaments proved to be a divine revelation?"
49. See Appendix B.
50. Quoted from Mrs. Wragg's copy of McMillan's will.
51. See Appendix A, Part I.
52. *Centenary Memorial.* 28, 29.
53. *Ibid.*
54. The text of this sermon was Song of Solomon 1:2. A copy of this sermon was presented to the Library of Washington and Jefferson College by Mrs. Esther Caldwell Humphreys.
55. *Annals of the American Pulpit.* III. 355.
56. *Ibid.*
57. *Old Redstone.* 369.
58. Bennett. 356-359. A biography of Rev. John Watson by Rev. J. S. Fisher is reprinted from the *Presbyterian Banner* (June 30, 1910) by Bennett. Most of the material in Fisher's article on Watson was taken from a letter written by President Carnahan of Princeton College.
59. *Ibid.* 358.
60. See Appendix C.
61. *Old Redstone.* 202, 203.
62. *Ibid.* 212. Bennett also tells Dr. Elliott's story on pages 232, 233.
63. See Appendix A, Part III.
64. See Appendix C.
65. Bennett. 237.
66. W. W. McKinney. "Eighteenth Century Presbyterianism in Western Pennsylvania," Part I, *Journal of the Presbyterian Historical Society.* X. 65.
67. *Annals of the American Pulpit.* 353.
68. *Old Redstone.* 211.
69. Records of the Synod of Pittsburgh. IV. 6.
70. Bennett. 241. Bennett quotes this from Dr. Jennings' book.
71. *Pittsburgh Christian Herald and Missionary Reporter.* November 23, 1833.

72. *Old Redstone.* 211. This is quoted from Dr. Elliott.
73. All of the account of McMillan's illness and death is taken from *Old Redstone,* 213, 214.
74. *The Daily Pittsburgh Gazette.* November 21, 1833.
75. Allen. Centennial Address.

FIREPLACE

APPENDIX A
THE JOURNAL

Appendix A contains Parts I, II, III of the *Journal* of John McMillan. The holograph of Part I has not been seen for many years. The copy of Part I printed here is in the Library at Washington and Jefferson College.

Part II and Part III (holographs) are in the home of Mrs. John A. Wragg, 1133 Lancaster Street, Pittsburgh. Mrs. Wragg is a great-great-great-granddaughter of John McMillan. A note in the handwriting of another person has been added to her manuscript of Part III. It reads: "Memorandum at the times and places in which Dr. McMillan preached during the whole of his ministry, from which appears that he had preached about six thousand sermons." This note suggests that a complete *Journal* or *Diary*, from 1774 to 1833, existed at one time. There are no entries, however, from 1791 to 1820 and there is no record of anyone's having ever seen them.

JOURNAL—PART I

This is Part One of McMillan's *Journal* as copied in November, 1909 by L. M. Allen, attorney at law, 426 Diamond Street, Pittsburgh, Pennsylvania. Mr. Allen's copy is now in the Library of Washington and Jefferson College, Washington, Pennsylvania.

October ye 26th, 1774, East Nottingham.

Being licensed to preach the everlasting Gospel of Christ Jesus, accordingly attempted it at the following places, viz: at Fag's Manor ye 4th Sunday of Oct. at Middle Octorara ye 1st Sabbath of Nov. at Little Brittain ye 2nd S. of Nov. at Pequea ye 3rd S. at West Nottingham ye 4th S. at Fag's Manor ye 1st Sabbath of December. at West Nottingham, 2nd ch. ye 2nd S. at Pencader, ye 3rd S. at Little Brittain ye 4th S. and 1st S. of January. At Soldiers Delight ye 2nd and 3rd S. at Slate Ridge, ye 4th S. at Chaunceford. ye 5th S. at Carlilse. Ye 1st S. of Feb. at Monaughany, ye 2nd. S. at Carlilse ye 3rd. S. at Big Spring ye 4th S. & 1st S. of March, at Hanover ye 2nd and 3rd S. at Conowaga ye 4th S. at Georgetown ye 1st S. of April, at Middle Octorara ye 2nd. at Little Brittain ye 3rd. at Soldiers Delight ye 4th. Deer Creek ye 5th, at Fag's Manor ye 1st S. of May at Pequea ye 2nd. at East Nottingham ye 3rd at Leacocks ye 4th at Hanover ye 1st S. of June, at North Mountain Metting House ye 2nd at Tinhting Spring ye 3rd and 4th at D (not sure of this letter) S. ye 1st S. of July at Mr. Cummings ye 2nd. In Bottlecourt Court House, ye 3rd. On Monday returned up the forks of James River in company with Mr. Newsberry. In the afternoon we turned out of our way to take a view of that Strupendous piece of Nature's workmanship, Cedar Bridge. Missing the right path, we tied our horses in the woods and went on foot about half a mile down the creek where we found the object we desired to see, and indeed it was a most amazing sight. The whole bridge consists of solid limestone rock, pillars, arch and all. The creek runs in a narrow valley between two lofty hills, which nigh the bridge terminate in perpendicular rocks of perhaps two hundred feet heigh. At the place where the rocks approach highest to each other, stands the bridge; the arch whereof is but part of these same rocks which stand on each side the water, and is perhaps thirty ft. in depth. The height of the bridge from the water to the upper surface of the arch is computed to be about two hundred ft.

In the concavity of the arch there are multitudes of swallows, but the height is so great we could not observe their nests. After we had crawled up to the top and viewed it all around, we returned up the creek to the place whence we set out. When we came there I found my horse at some distance from the place where I had left him, with the saddle hanging under his belly, a part of the bridle on his head and the remaining part hanging on the brough whereunto he had been fastened. I went unto him and with great patience and composure of mind, returned the saddle to its proper place, knotted up my bridle, mounted and rode through a pathless, rugged way to the great road and lodged that night at Hugh Berklys.

Tuesday morning I travelled about two miles to the James Gilmer where I got a shoemaker to mend my bridle. The remainder of the day together with Wednesday I spent chiefly in writing. Thursday being ye day appointed by ye Congress to be observed as a fast throughout ye colonies, I rode about seven miles and preached to a large congregation in the woods nigh to Buflers Creek. Lodged that night with John McKee. Friday I went to Wm. McKee's and tarried there till Sabbath. He being an old acquaintance, I got little done. The 4th Sabbath of July I preached at Halls meeting House to a crowded audiance and went that evening to Mr. Browns in company with Mr. Graham. Monday traveled 20 miles to John Trimbles. Tuesday, this morning wrote a letter to Pequea. About 9 o'clock set off on my journey toward Fort Pitt. Mr. Trimble accompanied me 10 miles. He then returned home and I proceeded on my way and was overtaken by John Henderson, who rode with me to Tyger's Valley. This day we travelled 35 miles, crossed the North Mountain and lodged at John McClurge in the Cow Pasture. Wednesday, this morning we buckled on our leggins took horses and set to the Mountains again and passed over three of them, viz. the Warm Spring Mountian, Back Creek Mountain, and Naps Spur, the day being wet made travelling very disagreeable, however, made out 30 miles and lodged at Moses Moore's on Green Briar. Thursday, the rain that fell last night, and yesterday made the mountains very slippery, however we got over five of them, viz. Thorny Branch Mt. Green Briar Mt. Allegheny, Elk and Cheat Mts. This day we travelled 35 miles, passes but one house, and about dark arrived at Darley Conley's in Tyger's Valley. Here we tarried all night but got very little rest. My bed was very hard and the flies very plenty. Friday, went about 5 miles to Richard Ellits' where I tarried and sent word that I intended (to preach)* on the sabbath at a place where it was supposed to be most convenient for the inhabitants. The 5th sabbath of July preached at Charles Wilsons in Tygers Valley to a small but very attentive and seemingly affected audience. Returning again in the evening to Richard Ellis' and continued there till Tuesday. Tuesday ye 1st of August, started again, rode about 15 miles and preached to pretty large number of people at Jacob Westfall and there accidentally met with some who were travelling my way. After sermon we

---
*These words were not in the original copy.

rode about ten miles, and lodged at Wm. Clever's. Wednesday, this morning we crossed the Laurel Hill, travelled about 17 miles, and about 12 o'clock came to Wm. Barker's. Here my company left me and Mr. Barker, who had promised to accompany me to ye next house, which was about 30 miles distant, not having his horse at home, I was forced to tarry there till 5 o'clock when the horse coming home we set off. Nothing remarkable happened by the way, save that Mr. Barker shot a doe, part of which we carried with us, night coming on and being far from my house, we were forced to think of taking up our lodging in the woods. We sought for a place where there was water unsaddled our horses, hobbled them with hickory bark and turned them to the hills. We then kindled a fire, roasted a part of our venison and took our supper, about 10 o'clock we composed ourselves to rest, I wrapped myself in my great coat and laid me on the ground, my saddle bags served me for a pillow, Thursday, This morning we rose very early eat our breakfast, got our horses and set to the road again, about noon we arrived at Ezekil York's. Here my company left me, and I had to take the woods alone. Crossing two hills, which if they were in some parts of the world would be called lofty mountains, and after travelling what they called 12 miles through an almost pathless way, I came to the glades. My lodging this night was not much better than the night before. I had a deer skin and a sheet spread under me, some clothing above me, and a pillow was laid for my head; this however I put under my hench to keep my bones from the floor, and placed my coat under my head. Friday, I left the glades and travelled 12 miles to one Coburn. Here I got some grain for my horse, which was the first he had since Wednesday morning. They told me I was then about 10 miles from Col. Wilsons, where I intended to tarry the remainder of this week, but the day being very wet, the road difficult and the houses scarce, I lost my way very often. Some places I could get no directions, and what directions I got I could not follow because of the multitude of paths that are everywhere through ye woods. About sunset I came to a plantation where I intended to tarry all night, but when I came to the cabin it was waste. I searched all about but could find no inhabitants. I then took another path which led me to a cabin, but there was nobody at home and the door was barred, I then took my horse and went further along the path to see if there was any other cabin nigh, but could find none. The night being very dark and rainy I therefore resolved to return to the forenamed cabin. When I came there I found the door still barred and nobody home. I, however, unsaddled my horse and turned him into a field, which lay convenient. Finding it impossible to open the door, I climbed up the wall and went in at a hole in the roof, which served instead of a chimney. I then opened the door, brought in my saddle, kindled a fire, and after I had ordered affairs as well as possible, I laid myself down on a sort of bed and slept very comfortable to morning. Saturday, this morning I buckled on my wet clothing, got my horse, barred the door, and left my lonely lodging not knowing which way to steer, but before I got many rods I met the owner of ye cabin returning home. I told me the story, got directions of the road, and came to Mr. Wilsons in time for breakfast. The 1st sabbath of August, preached at Mt. Moriah, but the day being rainy there was only a small congregation, however, they seemed pretty attentive, and a few tears were shed by some. In the evening I returned to Col. Wilsons and tarried there till Wednesday morning part of which I spent in writing, Wednesday, I rode about 14 miles and preached at John Armstrong's on Muddy Creek to a small congregation. Here I remained till Sabbath morning but the weather rain and the house small, I got but little done. The 2nd Sabbath of August rode about 4 miles down the river and preached at John McKibbens on Dunlaps Creek, and lodged with him that night. Monday finished my first sermon and began a second on Luke 14,23. (Aug. 1775) Tuesday, spent the forenoon in writing and then rode about 4 miles to Mr. Adams, where I spent the remainder of the day. Wednesday preached at James Pickets to a pretty large congregation, and then rode about 5 miles to David Allens. Thursday, spent the forenoon in conversation with my old acquaintance and in the afternoon preached to a number of the neighbors. Friday traveled about 12 miles to Edward Cook's where I tarried till Sabbath. The 3rd Sabbath of August, preached at Mr. Pentecost's to a very small congregation. The people had been dilatory and had not given proper warning. I tarried there till Wednesday when I rode about 6 miles and preached at the Fork Meeting House. In the afternoon I traveled about 6 miles further and lodged that night with my brotherinlaw. Thursday and Friday I spent visiting friends and acquaintances. Saturday traveled about 16 miles to John McDowell's on Shirtee Creek where I tarried till Monday morning. The 4th sabbath of August preached at said John McDowell's. Monday rode about 8 miles to Patrick McCullough's on Pigion Creek. Tuesday preached at Arthur Forbuses' and lodged with Patrick Scot. Wednesday traveled about 8 miles and preached at Thos. Cook's. Thursday returned to my brotherinlaw's, being about 12 miles where I remained till Sabbath. The 1st sabbath of Sept. preached at a meeting house on the banks of the Monongahela, but the day being very wet I had a few hearers. In the evening returned again to my brotherinlaw's where I continued till Wednesday. Wednesday I preached at the above named place to more hearers than on Sabbath. Thursday I left my brotherinlaw's and traveled about 21 miles to David Anderson's on Miller's Run where I remained that night. Friday preached at David Andrew's and in the evening rode about 7 miles to John Barnett's. Saturday preached at Josiah Richards on Robinson and rode about 13 miles to Ft. Pitt. and lodged at Mr. Armobey's. The 2nd sabbath preached at Ft. Pitt and rode about 7 miles to Thos Ross where I tarried till Tuesday. Tuesday I rode about 14 miles to Eli Cluter's in company with Janet (or Samuel) Ross. Wednesday preached at a meeting house on Long Run. Thursday rode about 20 miles to Hannahstown and lodged at Mr. Hannahs till sabbath, most of which I spent in writing. The 3rd Sabbath preached to a pretty numerous congregation. I remained at Mr. Robert Hannahs until Wednesday a great part of which time I spent in writing. Wednesday I rode in company with Mr. and Mrs. Hannah and Robert Sample about 10 miles to Wm. Perry's on Loyal Hannah, where I had appointed to preach, but the people some how mistaken the day, notice was given to meet on Thursday. I therefore waited and those who had accompanied me out of town returned. Thursday the people met and after sermon I returned to town again in order to meet with Mr. Slemons who was to preach there next day. Friday the people met me for sermon, but Mr. Slemons not coming in time. I was forced to preach myself. He came in the meantime and we spent the evening in conversation. Saturday parted with Mr. Slemons, left Hannastown and rode about 18 miles to Samuel Irwin on Conamaugh. The 4th sabbath of Sept. preached at Conemaugh at a place in the woods nigh Wm. Dunlaps where they agreed to build a meeting house. Returned in the evening to Mr. Irwins. Monday rode about 7 miles to Mr. Sloans where I continued till Wednesday. Wednesday preached at Proctor's tent and lodged with Mr. Lochry. Thursday rode about 24 miles across the Laurel Hill, and in the evening came to James McMiallas in Brothers Valley, where I found my brother. Here I left in company with my brother to go to his house,—on, and the path scarcely discoverable in daylight, we lost the way, and after wandering till we were tired, we lay down by the root of a tree and wished for day. The night was very cold and somewhat wet, we slept little I broke my old shin going over some of the logs which lay everywhere, plenty in the woods. Friday we left our cold lodging as soon as daylight appeared and after a little we found the path and came where we desired to be the night before. Here I spent the rest of the day and in the evening went down again to James McMillan's where I preached to a few of the neighbors, and tarried there all night. Saturday, went again over the Laurel Hills and lodged with Robert Laughlin. The 1st Sabbath of October 1775 preached at Ligonier and in the evening returned to Mr. Laughlin. Monday set out on my journey homewards, crossed the Laurel Hill and between Quebshone and Stony Creek overtook a young woman who was travelling to York. After riding 24 miles we come to John Miller's at the foot of Allegheny where we lodged that night. Tuesday we crossed the Allegheny Mts. and in the evening came to Bedford where I met Wm. McCombs with whom I tarried that night. This day we rode about 30 miles. Wednesday, this proved a wet day, however we set to ye road. I parted with my female companion at the foot of Siding Hill but not was not left alone. At night we came to Lyttleton and lodged at Mr. Burd's. This day we traveled about 30 miles. This day we crossed the Tuscarora Path valley and Blue Mts. and after having traveled about 25 miles came to Mr. Coopers' in Shipensburg, where I continued until Saturday. Saturday we rode about 10 miles to James Irwins on the Big Spring and lodged with Allen Loper. Monday traveled about 15 miles, passed through Carlilse and lodged at Samuel McCalls. Tuesday after having rode about 22 miles I came to Samuel Fergusons in Hanover, where my leg being very sore, I continued that week. Ye 3rd sabbath preached at Hanover. Ye 4th at Pequea. This week attended the prsbytery and received fresh orders to Augusta and Westmoreland. The 5th at Pequea. The 1st sabbath of Nov. 1775 at Brandywine, then returned to Fagg's Manor, where I preached on Wednesday. Friday left my father's and lodged with my old friend John Love, where Andrew Gibson had appointed to meet me. Saturday, Mr. Gibson coming. we left Mr. Love's crossed the river at McCall's Ferry and lodged at Jacob Gibsons'. The 2nd sabbath of Nov. preached at Slate Ridge, and lodged with Patrick Scott. Here Mr. Thompson came to me, 20s. Monday preached at Chamford and lodged with Hugh Ross. 10. Tuesday got my horse shod; set out on my way for Augusta. Passed through York, and after travelling about 26 miles we came to the buck, where we tarried that night, spent 9 shillings Wednesday got free lodging last night, this day passed through McAllister's town, Lyttleton and Tarrytown, and in the evening, after having traveled 43 miles, came to Bentley's Tavern where we tarried that night, 1,4, Thursday, passed through Fredericktown, crossed Monockesay and

Potomac and lodged at Mr. Harpers. This day traveled about 31 miles, spent 4 shil. Friday after Travelled 34 miles and passed through Winchester, we came to John Gilcover's, but he had a husking frolic, we thought it improper to tarry all night, however we left our horses there and walked over to Robert Wilsons. I thought to have taken off my boots as they were inconvenient to walk in, but upon examining my saddlebags, I found I had no shoes, spent 4,4 Saturday, the sabbath drawing near, I found I could not reach my other congregation in time to give the people warning, therefore concluded to remain here till Monday. The 3rd Sabbath of Nov. 1775, preached at Opechan meeting house, and lodged with John Gileason, 15 S. Monday, passed through Stephensburd, Stoverstown and Millerstown, crossed Shanadra and after traveling 48 miles we come to a dutchmans where we tarried all night. Tuesday, this day we rode 35 miles crossed North River and lodged at widow Watsons'. Wednesday about noon came to Stanton, where it being court time, I met with a number of my old acquaintances who professed great joy to see me. I stayed in town till towards evening and then rode to John Trimbles. This day I rode 22 miles and spent 8 S. 10P. Thursday continued at Mr. Trimbles, Friday went to John Moffatts'. Saturday returned to Mr. Trimbles, and in the evening Benjamin Brown brought me a pair of shoes for which I paid him 8 S. The 4th sabbath of—preached at the North Mt. and lodged with Mathew Thompson. Monday, this day I rode in company with John Thompson about 16 miles to see my Uncle on Back Creek. Found them all well. Tuesday this morning proved very stormy we thought it most convient to return again to the settlement accordingly I took leave of my relatives, and though it snowed exceedingly we set to the road and in the evening came to Mathew Thompsons. Wednesday went to Hugh Torbots, from there to Alex Mitchel where I tarried all night. Thursday came to Joe Blairs, Friday ye 1st of Dec. 1775 rode to John Moffatts'. In the evening got a tooth pulled by Wendle Bright. Tarried here till sabbath and began to write a sermon on Mathew 16, 26. The 1st of Dec. preached at the Stone Meeting House and in the evening rode into Stanton in company with Mr. Reed, lodged at Mr. Moffatt's. This evening began a sermon on Luke 13,3. Tuesday this day spent chiefly in study. Wednesday, this day I moved my campt to Wm. McFeeter's. Thursday and Friday continued at the same place, spending my time chiefly in study and finishing my sermon on Luke 13,3. Saturday met with Mr. Fithian at John Moffatts, we both went to John Trimbles where we tarried that night. The 2nd sabbath of Dec. preached at the N. M. and returned again to Mr. Trimbles. Wednesday went to John Berrys'. Thursday and Friday continued at Mr. Berrys, finished my first and began a second sermon on Mathew 16, 26. Saturday returned to Mr. Trimbles. The 3rd sabbath of Dec. 1775, preached at the stone Meeting House, and lodged with John Finley, where I remained till Tuesday morning. Tuesday called at James Phillips and Robert Phillips and in the evening came again to Mr. Trimbles where I tarried until Thursday morning. Thursday went over to John Moffatts'. Friday the weather very cold and snow upon the mountains. The 4th sabbath of Dec. (December 24th, 1775) snow fell very fast last night and this morning insomuch that I almost gave up hopes of going to meeting, but it cleared up about 11 o'clock, I set out and preached at N.M. to a very thin assembly, lodged with Jos. Blair. Monday continued in the same place. Tuesday hearing last night that Mr. Graham was at Geo. Berrys, I set out this morning expecting to find him there but was disapointed. I then set off for Mr. Browns where I arrived a little after dark, after riding about 21 miles. Mr. Graham got there about an hour before me and Mr. McKnight came about an hour after. Wednesday (12/27/1775) spent the day with my old friends. Went to the school house and heard the scholars speak their orations. Thursday at the request of Mr. Graham preached at the school house and spent the evening in study. Friday, this evening I left Mr. Browns in company with Mr. McKnight and came to Joseph Blairs after riding 16 miles. Here I continued until sabbath, I forgot my penknife at Mr. Brown's. The 5th sabbath of Dec. preached at Stone Meeting House and lodged at John Trimble's.

1776

Monday ye January 1st at Peter Hanger's preached to a large assembly and lodged at Elijah McLaughlin's received between 8 and 9 pounds. Tuesday, this day I set out on my journey for Shirtee and on Thursday evening came to John Gilkeson's near Winchester. The roads were very muddy which rendered travelling very disagreeable. In this journey I spent 5 S. 8p. Friday rode about 8 miles through Winchester to Hugh Gilkeson's where I tarried that night. Saturday returned again through Winchester, dined with Wm. Holliday and lodged with John Gilkeson. Spent 1 S. The 1st sabbath of January preached at Opechan and lodged with Wm. Holliday 18 S. Monday being disapointed in getting company, I continued to Mr. Holliday's. Tuesday about 12 o'clock Mr. Gray who was to be my company a part of the way, being ready to start, we left Winchester, dined with Mr. Hog. passed through Petticoat Gap, crossed Hog creek, and came to Robert White's where, the evening being excessively cold, we determined to tarry all night, thos we had traveled no more than 10 miles. Spent 8 S. Wednesday passed through the North Mountain, crossed Back Creek and Big Kepkeper and in the evening came to Samuel Prichard's. This day we traveled 22 miles, the roads were covered with ice and so exceedingly slippery we were forced to walk ye most of the way. Thursday crossed the North River, Little Kepher, passed over the Chestnut Ridge and about 3 o'clock came to Samuel Turk's in Runnag after having travelled about 20 miles. The weather being very cold, the water very high and travelling very difficult, I determined to tarry till sabbath in hope that by that time I might go on my way without endangering my life. Friday continued at the same place reading some old books and writing a little. Saturday spent the chief part of the day in an out house amusing myself in reading and preparing for the sabbath. The 2nd sabbath of January, this morning Mr. Manning the parson of the parish, came contrary to the expectations of the people, and would preach, though requested by the people not to do it. After he had gone through his service as he calls it, and preached a short sermon, I also preached in my turn. This morning I left Runnag in company with Mr. Johnston and after riding 12 miles I preached at his house to a mixt multitude of Baptists and presbyterians. Lodged at his house, spent 1S. Tuesday left Patterson's creek at Mr. Gregg's overtook one John Keith who also was going over the mountains. We rode together to Potter Tittle's where we remained that night. This day I went 20 miles, Wednesday ye 17th (Jan. 17th, 1776). This morning proved very cold and snowy, however, we made out to travel 28 miles and lodged at Mr. Rices' spent 4 S. Thursday ye 18th though the snow fell very fast yet we started to the road. On the Laurel Hill my company left me. While alone my feet got very cold, and getting down to walk a while, I left my horse walk before me as usual. We had not walked far until he taking some mad notion or other started off the road, broke past me at full gallop, my saddle bag broke and fell off. I followed him near a mile but could not come in sight of him it now being after sundown and not knowing how far it was to a house, I gave over the pursuit, took my saddle bags in my arms, and after walking between 2 and 3 miles I came to a poor cabin where one Wm. Decas dwelt. It being now after dark I determined to tarry until morning, my bed was a parcel of husks on the floor. Travelled 28 miles. Spent 2S. Friday ye 19th 1776, early this morning my landlord set off in search of my horse. I, in the meantime mended my saddlebags, went over to Thomas Gest, where I tarried all day. In the evening Philips Bachus came back with my horse for which I gave him 7 S. 6p. Saturday ye 20th. This morning after riding 3 miles I came to David Allen's where I continued until Monday, spent 3S. The 3rd sabbath of Jan. 1776 preached at David Allen's to a pretty numerous assembly. This evening it snowed very fast, 14S 6p. Monday ye 22nd. This morning set out in company with John Carmichael to go over to Shirtee, but hearing that the river could not be crossed, we stopped at Hugh Laughlin's after travelling 6 miles. Tuesday ye 23rd of Dec. [Jan.] 1776 crossed the river upon the ice, and after riding 18 miles I came to James Wherry's. Wednesday ye 24th. I travelled about 4 miles, called at Partick McCullough's and lodged the remainder of the week with Patrick Scot, spending my time chiefly in study. The weather very cold with some snow. The 4th sabbath of Jan. preached at Arthur Forbush on Pigeon Creek from Tim. 4-8. Returned again to Mr. Scot's where I continued till Thursday, when I finished my second sermon on Mathew 18, 26. The weather moderated, inclining to thaw. Thursday 1st snowed very fast in the forenoon in the afternoon I went about 3 miles to James Scott where I tarried till Saturday, the Weather very cold. Saturday some snow fell in the morning, rode to John McDowell's where I continued till monday. The 1st sabbath of Feb'y preached at Mr. McDowell's from Romans 3 and 31 Monday set out to see my sister where I arrived in the evening. Found them all well and continued with them till Friday. The weather warm for the season which affords no small joy to the inhabitants, many of whom were out of bread, ye mills being frozen up. Friday returned again to my congregation, stopped at Thos. Cooks on Mingo Creek, where I continued till Sabbath and began a sermon on Isaih 32-2. The 2nd sabbath of Feb'y preached at Arthur Forbush from Rev. 19-18. and lodged with him that night, Monday went over to Patrick Scot's where I continued until Wednesday, spending my time chiefly in writing. Wednesday I rode about 7 miles and preached at Henry Newkirk's from Luke 13-5. Returned again to Mr. Scott's where I continued till Sabbath. This week I finished my sermon on Isaiah 32-2. The 3rd sabbath of Feb'y preached at Thod. Edgerton to a pretty numerous assembly again to Pigeon Creek and lodged with Patrick Scott until the sabbath. The 4th sabbath of Feb. preached at Arthur

Forbuse's from Rev. 19 and 16 to a pretty large very attentive and much affected assembly. Return again to Patrick Scott's where I continued till Tuesday. Tuesday rode about 8 miles to Josia Crawford's. Wednesday preached at Jacob Long's and returned again to Mr. Crawford's. Thursday preached at John Munn's on Mingo Creek and lodged at John McDowell's the weather very cold and some snow. Friday ye 1st March continued at Mr. McDowell's till sabbath. The 1st sabbath of March preached at John Cannon's to a large attentive and pretty much affected assembly from Math. 16 and 16, and in the evening rode 8 miles to Patrick Scott's. Monday rode about 23 miles to John McKibbon's on Dunlop Creek, spent 10p. Tuesday preached at Mr. McKibbon's rode about 8 miles to John Allen's received 7S 3p. Wednesday preached at David Allen's and tarried there all night. 12S. Thursday returned again over the Monongahela, and after riding about 13 miles, I came to James Rodger's. 6p. Friday preached at a Baptist meeting house on Pike Run from Rom. 8 and 6, and in the evening rode about 8 miles to Patrick Scott's where I continued till sabbath. The 2nd sabbath of March preached to Arthur Forbus's to a large, solemn and attentive assembly, from Malch 6 and 8, and returned again to Mr. Scott's. This day I heard the distressing tidings of my brother's death, who departed this life the 24th of January 1776, after 2 weeks and 3 days illness. Tuesday rode to James Allison's. Wednesday preached at Thos. Edgerton's from Amos 4 and 12. Lodged with Mr. McDowell till Sabbath. The 3rd sabbath of March preached at the woods at the forks of Shirtee to a large and attentive assembly from Isa. 32 and 2. Lodged at Thomas Cook's. Monday rode to my brotherinlaw's and preached at a Baptist meeting house near Monongahela Rev. 18 Se. Tuesday rode about 18 miles to Thomas Ross's S. 1. S. Wednesday about 20 miles lodged at Mr. Taggart's. Thursday rode 10 miles to Hannahstown where I tarried until Sabbath and began a sermon on Eccles. 12 and 1. S. 3d. The 4th Sabbath of March [four lines obliterated here] Tuesday crossed Quenishone and Stony Creek, passed over Allegheny, and after riding 20 miles came to Mr. Anderson's. Wednesday rode 3 miles, lodged at the foot of Sidling Hill. Spent 4S 8p. Thursday rode 34 miles and lodged with Mr. Cooper in Shippensburg 1s. 5d. Friday rode 15 miles and came to David Ralston's where I continued till Sabbath. The 5th sabbath of March preached at Big Spring and lodged at George Browns. My horse being sick I tarried till Tuesday. Tuesday ye 2nd of April, attended sermon by Mr. Craighead, and afterwards rode 12 miles to Carlilse, 2S. 5d. Wednesday rode about 24 miles and lodged with George McMillan 7S. 3d. Thursday came to Samuel Ferguson's where I tarried till Monday. The 1st sabbath of April preached at Hanover R 1 pound, Monday rode 45 miles to John Torbot's S1 2d. Tuesday rode about 10 miles to Thomas Slemons. Wednesday, the day being very wet, I was forced to tarry there. Thursday rode about 18 miles to my father's where I tarried till sabbath. The 2nd sabbath of April preached at Fagg's Manor and tarried the rest of the week at my fathers and finished my sermon on Eccles. 12 and 1. The 3rd sabbath of April preached at Fagg's Manor. This week attended the presbytery, on Tuesday ye 22nd accepted a call. Saturday went to Upper Octorara, lodged with James Boyd. The 4th sabbath of April preached in Mr. Foster's meeting House and lodged with James Boyd. Monday went to Brandywine, and lodged at Mr. Brown's (father of my wife). Wednesday went to Pequea lodged at Thomas Slemons. The 1st sabbath of May preached at Pequea. Monday returned home.

This week was fought ye noted battle between the Rosebuck, and the Ragallies. The 2nd sabbath of May preached at German Bridges in Q An's, Friday at the same place, Saturday at Middletown. The 3rd sabbath and Monday at the same place. This week I attended the synod. The 1st of June preached at Brandywine. The 2nd West Nottingham 1st Church. The 3rd at Big Spring, on Tuesday at Chamberstown. Wednesday ye 19th of June was ordained and lodged at John Jack's. My horse taking sick I was forced to tarry till Tuesday. Friday preached at Mr. Long's meeting house. Saturday bought a new horse at 24 pounds, and rode over to Marsh Creek where I tarried till Tuesday. The 4th sabbath of June preached at Marsh Creek. The 5th at Fagg's Manor. The 1st sabbath of July at Fagg's Manor. The 2nd at Little Britan, the 3rd at Fagg's Manor. The 4th at St. George.

The 1st sabbath of August at Slate Ridge.

Tuesday ye 6th of August 1776 I was married to Miss Catherine Brown, in troublous times, by Mr. Charmickel.

(This transcript completed March 30th—1899)

JOURNAL—PART II

A continuation of the JOURNAL of Dr. John McMillan, being a memorandum of the places where he preached from August 1776 to July 1791.

1776

Thursday of August fast appointed by ye Synod—preached in the afternoon at brandiwine.

The 2d. Sab. of August at Brandiwine.

Wednesday. My wife and I rode to Pequea.

Thursday. Left her at Pequea and went to fulfill my various appointments.

The 3d. Sab. at Hanover.

Friday, Saturday, Sab. & Monday, at Big Springs

Wednesday at John Jack's.

The 1st Sab. of September at Marsh Creek.

Wednesday. arrived again at brandiwine.

The 2d. Sab. Preached at brandiwine in ye afternoon.

The 3d. Sab. at fag's manor.

The 4th Sab. at John Brown's near Chester.

The 5th Sab. at Brandiwine.

Tuesday set off on my journey to the back woods.

The 1st Sab. of October at Hanover. this week I attended the presbittery at Shipensburg.

The 2d. Sab. at Bedford. wednesday at John Reed's.

The 3d. Sab. at Long run baptized 14 children.

Last Saturday night my horse broke out of the pasture and went back to Hannah'stown which detained me till Wednesday after-noon when I set to the road crossed the Monongahale and came to my brother's.

Thursday. Came to John McDowell's on Shirtee.

The 4th Sab. I preached at John Cannon's from—Eccles. 12.1 & baptized 4 children.
 Monday came to Patrick Scott's on pidgeon Creek where I continued till Sab.

The 1st Sab. of November I preached at Pidgeon Creek from—Luk. 14.23 & baptized 6 children and lodged with Thos. Cook.
 Monday. went down to my brother's house.
 Tuesday. Preached at Peter's Creek baptized 5 children.
 Wednesday. Returned to John McDowell's.
 Thursday. went to James Bradford's where I continued till Sabbath.
The 2d. Sab. of November. Preached at Shirtee from—Cant. 5.16. lodged with Mr. Cannon baptized 6 children.
 Monday went to James Allison's.
 Wednesday. Preached at Thos. Cook's from—Jer. 25.4 & baptized 3 children, lodged at Patrick Scott's.
 Thursday. Lectured at James Breadon's on ten Mile from—Joh. 3.1-9 & baptized 5 children.
The 4th Sab. Preached at Shirtee from—Mal. 7.21. baptized 2 children. Received from the congregation, S. 12.
 This week I set out in my journey homeward and on Saturday arrived at Mr. Vance's in virginia, where I continued till tuesday morning.

The 1st Sab. of December. Preached at Back creek, Virginia. this week I attended the Presbittery at Elk-Branch.
The 2d. Sab. Preached at Marsh-Creek.
 Wednesday arrived at Brandiwine, some snow fell this night and last night, the weather cold and cloudy.
The 3d. Sab. Preached at Brandiwine. the weather clear and partly cold till friday.
 Friday. Went to Fagg's Manor. Some snow fell last night, this day was cold and rainy. more snow fell in ye night.
The 4th Sab. went to the meeting-house expecting to preach but was agreeably disappointed, and had the pleasure of hearing Mr. Spencer.
 Tuesday. Returned again to Brandiwine.
 Wednesday. Being Christmas, my wife and I went to Mr. Carmichel's. the weather clear pinching cold. some snow still on the ground.
 Thursday. Last night and today abundance of snow fell, until it was nearly knee deep over ye face of we earth.
The 5th Sab. Preached at William Brown's, the weather clear and moderate.

A.D. 1777

 Wednesday, this day was warm and the snow melted away exceedingly, some rain also fell.

The 1st Sab. of January. Preached at Brandywine. Some snow fell in the fore-noon, but it presently cleared up again. The weather for ye most part clear and cold.
The 2d. Sab. Preached at Little Brittain, and lodged with Mr. Armstrong: the weather very cold and clear.
 Tuesday crossed the Susquehanna, and came to James Edgers, where I continued the remainder of the week.

The 3d. Sab. Preached at Chaunchford, lodged with Mr. Ross. the weather still cold and clear.
> Tuesday. attended the Session at Chaunchford. Wed. Moderate.
> Thursday & friday. the weather rainy inclining to a thaw.
> Saturday. came to Patrick Scott's.

The 4th Sab. Preached at Slate Ridge.
> Monday went to Joseph Ross's.
> tuesday. to James Edger's.
> Wednesday to Mr. Samples.
> Thursday. went to hear Mr. Culbertson. Lodged with Hugh Ross till (after) Sab. weather wet and cloudy.

The 1st Sab. of February. Preached at Chaunchford. continued still at Hugh Ross's.
> Tuesday. went to Rolin Hugh's, clear & moderate.
> Wednesday. Preached at William Caldwell's and lodged with James Edger, some rain fell last night.
> Thursday, married William Thompson to Orsla moor. lodged with Patrick Scott till Sabbath; moderate.

The 2d. Sab. Preached at Slate Ridge lodged with Mr. Sample. some rain yesterday.
> monday. In company with Mr. Sample and Mrs. Work I set out on my way homeward, lodged at Mr. Work's in middle Octorara. ye weather moderate and clear.
> Tuesday. Last night it began and continued to snow ye greater part of this day; in the evening I arrived at Brandiwine.
> Thursday. attended an examination at William Denny's. It snowed this day and night and a great part of the next day, until it was about 8 inches deep.

The 3d. Sab. Preached at Brandywine.
> Thursday & friday excessive cold.
> Saturday more moderate, this day I went to fag's mannor.

The 4th Sab. Preached at Fag's Manor this night & monday. a great deal of snow fell, about a foot deep, which detained me in fag's manor till Thursday, when I went to Pequea; but—I expected, I returned again on Friday.
> Saturday, more snow fell.

The 1st Sab. of March. Preached at Fag's Mannor.
> Monday. Returned to brandywine by ye way of Pequea where I continued till Friday.

The 2d. Sab. Preached at W. Notingham.
> Monday. Came to Pequea. And Tuesday to Brandywine.

The 3d. Sab. Preached at Fag's Manor; and on monday returned to brandywine; fine spring weather.
> Wednesday. Attended the funeral of John Henderson a child, and rode in company with my wife, to Pequea.

The 4th Sab. Preached at Uper Octorara.
> Monday rode thro Brandywine, and lodged at widow Cowan's.
> Tuesday, went to Fagg's manor, attended my Father Tuesday and on Wednesday returned to Pequea. Weather this week cold for this season.

Thursday went to Lancaster lodged at John Torbit's and on friday came again to Pequea.
Saturday. Went to Fag's manor—cold weather.
The 5th Sab. Preached at Fag's Manor, and in the evening returned to Pequea. the weather moderate.
Monday. Went with my wife to Brandywine.
Tuesday, 1st of April. Returned to Pequea.
Wednesday. Rode 35 miles, lodged 3 miles from York.
Thursday. Came to my Aunt's at Marsh-Creek where I continued till Sab.

The 1st Sab. of April Preached at Marsh-Creek in ye forenoon, and on monday at my Aunt's. this time I attended the p'b'y..
The 2d. Sab. Preached again at Marsh-Creek .... 30s.
Monday. came to Mr. Anderson's at ye ferry.
Tuesday. Came to James Henderson in Brandywine.
The 3d. Sab. Preached at Brandywine in ye afternoon.
Monday. Went to Fag's Manor.
Tuesday. attended the p'b'y. at New London. and on Wednesday returned again to Brandywine, where I continued till Sab.
The 4th Sab. Preached at Pequea in ye after-noon.
Monday. I set out on my journey towards Shipensburg; and on Tuesday evening came to George Brown's in Big Springs congregation, where I continued till Friday.

Friday, Sab. & monday. Preached at Middle Spring and on Wednesday arrived again at Brandywine.
Thursday, Saturday & Sab. Preached at Brandiwine. And on Monday after hearing Mr. Smith, I rode to fag's mannor.
Tuesday. Took my young mair to Pequea.
Wednesday. Returned again to Brandiwine.
The 3d. Sab. of May. Preached at Brandiwine.
The 4th Sab. Had the pleasure of hearing Mr. Cooper at Brandiwine.
This week went twice to Fag's manor, my mother being sick.
Saturday the 31st of May at half past Seven O'clock post meridian Jean McMillan was born. 1777.

The 1st and 2d. Sabs. of June at Brandiwine.
Thursday. Being ye fast appointed by ye Synod, preached at fag's mannor.
The 3d. Sab. at Brandiwine.
Thursday at Leacock.
The 4th Sab. at Brandiwine.
The 5th Sab. at Pequea, over the hill.

The 1st Sab. of July. Preached at Slateridge and on Wednesday returned again to brandywine.
The 2d. Sab. at Pequea. went to fag's manor on monday. and on wednesday returned again to Brandiwine.
The 3d. Sab. at Brandiwine in the afternoon.
The 4th Sab. at Fag's mannor. and on monday returned again to Brandywine.

The 1st Sab. of August. At Brandywine in ye afternoon.
Wednesday set out for Shirtee, lodged at John Torbit's.

214

Thursday. Last night my horse broke out of ye field and detained me till friday.
Friday. My father and I set out on our journey and lodged about 6 miles above York.
Saturday. Came to my Aunt's at Marsh-Creek.
The 2d. Sab. at Lower Marsh-Creek. lodged with James Slemons . . . . 38s.
monday. went to John Jack's. where we got our horses shod.
Tuesday. crossed the cove mountain, lodged at McConnald's tavern. we would have gone farther but bad news stopt us.
Wednesday. Crosses Sidling hill, lodged at Ellots near Bedford.
Thursday. Crossed the Allegheny mountain, and lodged at Stony creek.
Friday. We arrived at my brother's where we continued till Saturday.
Saturday. Crossed the Laurel hill, lodged with William Lochry.
The 3d. Sab. at Proctor's tent, lodged with William Waddel . . . 20s.
Monday. Continued at the same place.
Tuesday. Preached at Mount Pleasant near Jacob's creek; lodged with Robert Thompson at Swickly creek . . . . 23s.
Wednesday. crossed the Yough and Monongahale. lodged at John McElheny's.
Thursday. Came to James Allison's at Shirtee.
The 4th Sab. Preached at Shirtee from—Luk. 4.2 and received 3 L.
Thursday. Preached again at the same place from—Phil. 2.12 lodged at Patrick Mccullough. 2L. 12s 6d.
The 5th Sab. Preached again at the same place from—Isa. 1.18 & Song. 5.16. lodged with James Allison. 3L.
Monday, ye 1st of September came to John McElheny's where I continued till Thursday.
Thursday. crossed the Monongahale and came to Hannah's town.
Friday. After preaching at hannah's town we rode to the 4 mile run.
Saturday. We came to my Brother's.
The 1st Sab. of Sept. Preached at my brothers. 15s.
Monday. This morning we set out in our journey, and on friday came to Samuel Ferguson's in Hanover.
The 2d. Sab. Preached at Hanover. 20s.
Monday. Returned again to Brandywine.
Thursday. The English army drawing nigh to brandywine my wife & I removed to Pequea.
The 3d. Sab. had the pleasure of hearing Mr. Smith.
The 4th Sab. Preached at Pequea in ye afternoon.
The 1st Sab. of October at Brandywine in ye afternoon.
The 2d. Sab. together with ye Saturday preceeding at Pequea.
Saturday, Sab. and Monday at Quen Anns.
The 4th Sat. at Middle Octorara, where I was detained till Wednesday, when I went to Pequea and on thursday returned again to Brandywine.
The 1st Sab. of November. Heard Mr. Carmichel.
Monday went to Pequea, got some clothes made, and in latter end of week went to Hanover.
The 2d. Sab. Preached at Derry, lodged with Mr. Roan and on Wednesday

arrived again at Brandywine, and on Saturday my wife and I went to Pequea.

The 3d. Sab. Preached at Pequea.

Tuesday. Set off in our journey for Hanover lodged at John Torbit's in Leacock.

Wednesday. Proced on our journey and at night Lodged at Mr. Peden's tavern at big chickes.

Thursday. Arrived at Samuel Ferguson's.

The 4th Sab. Was detained at home by reason of a very sore leg.

The 5th Sab. Preached at Hanover.

The 1st Sab. of December. Went to Derry, but did not Preach. Mr. William Linn being there.

The 2d. Sab. Heard Mr. Beard at Hanover.

The 4th Sab. together with the Saturday preceeding at David Hay's in Derry . . . 35s.

1778

The 1st Sab. of January. Preached at Paxton. 30s.

The 2d. Sab. at Hanover, and the thursday following at John Barret's for —week day. 35s.

The 3d. Sab. at Hanover.

The 4th Sab. at Paxton and the thursday following at middletown. 1L. 10s.

	L	s	d
The 1st Sab. of february at Derry	4L	7s	6d.
The 2d. Sab. at Hanover	1	10	0
The 3d. Sab. at Hanover			
The 4th Sab. at Derry	1	10	0
The 1st Sab. of March at Hanover			
The 2d. Sab. at Paxton	1	10	0
The 3d. Sab. at Derry	1	10	0
The 4th Sab. at Hanover Thursday at the same place			
The 5th Sab. at Hanover			
The 1st Sab. of April at Derry	1	10	0
The 2d. Sab. at Hanover			
The 3d. Sab. at Carlisle	2	8	0
Wednesday at Carlisle	2	0	0
The 4th Sab. at Manenhan	2	16	0
The 1st Sab. of May at Leacock afternoon			
Friday at Middle town	3	16	0
The 2d. Sab. at Derry	1	10	0
The 3d. Sab. at Hanover			
The 4th Sab. at E. Pensborough	1	17	6
The 5th Sab. at Andrew Brattan's			
Thursday at the same place	3	10	0
Saturday at John Cambel's in Kishocoquillas	1	10	0
Monday at Robert Brotherton's	1	10	0

The 1st Sab. of June in E. Kishocoquillas	3	0	0
The 2d. Sab. together with the friday preceeding and the Monday following at Leader-Spring, Sacrament.	12	0	0
2he 3d. Sab. at upper Paxton	2	14	6
The 4th Sab. at Hanover			

The 1st Sab. of July heard Mr. Linn and on Wednesday set out on my journey for virginia and arrived at Wiliam Ceavens on friday evening Spent 1L 8s

The 2d. Sab. preached at Kittocton	4	18	0
The 3d. Sab. at Turkey Run	10	10	0
Wednesday at Mr. Kamper's			
The 4th Sab. at Mr. George's in Colpepper	1	15	0
Tuesday at Mr. Vandick's in Colpepper	4	10	0
Wednesday at Mr. Woodside's	1	5	0
Thursday at Mr. Barghan's arbor	1	0	0
The 1st Sab. of August at Turkey run	10	0	0
The 2d. Sab. at Gum Spring	8	10	0
Wednesday at Kittocton	6	5	0
The 3d. Sab. at great Canawaga	8	10	0
The 4th Sab. at Hanover			

The 5th Sab. together with the friday proceeding and the monday following at Hanover.

	L	s	d
The 1st Sab. of September at Derry	1	17	6
The 2d. Sab. went to upper Paxton but did not preach			
The 3d. Sab. at Lower Paxton	2	5	0
The 4th Sab. heard Mr. Bard at Hanover			
The 1st Sab. of October together with the Saturday preceding and ye monday following at Brandiwine Sacrament	5	0	0
Tuesday at William Brown's			

The 2d. & 3d. Sabs. Did not preach my time being taken up in preparing to move out to Shirtee.
The 4th Sab. at Rocky Spring in ye afternoon.

The 1st Sab. of November. at ye new erection	0	4	0
The 2d. at Shirtee at Thomas Edgerton's. Psal. 71.16			
The 3d. at Pidgeon Creek. Rev.19.9			
The 4th at Shirtee from—Rom. 5.20			
The 5th at Pidgeon Creek from—Rev. 19.9			
The 1st Sab. of December at Raccoon from—Rom. 8.8 and received	7	10	0
The 2d. at Shirtee from—Song. 3.3			

   Wednesday the 16th of December we moved to our own house.
The 3d. at Pidgeon Creek from—Gen. 5.24
The 4th at Shirtee from Cor. 1.23.24

1779

The 1st Sab. of January. I was to have preached at Pidgeon Creek but was prevented by reason of high water.

The 2d. Sab. at Shirtee from—I Cor. 23.24			
The 3d. Sab. at Pidgeon Creek from—Rev. 19.9			
The 4th Sab. at Shirtee from—I Cor. 1.23.24			
The 5th Sab. at Short Creek received	10.	1.	9.
Wednesday ye 1st of february at Buffelow	12.	15.	8.

The 1st Sab. of February at Pidgeon Creek from—Rev. 19.9
The 2d. Sab. at Shirtee from—1 Cor. 1.23.24
The 3d. Sab. at Pidgeon Creek from—Rev. 19.9
The 4th Sab. together with ye monday following at Oliver Miler's on Peter's Creek received   23.   10.   0.

The 1st Sab. of March to Shirtee from—1 Cor. 23.24
The 2d. Sab. at Pidgeon Creek from—Rev. 19.9
The 3d. and 4th Sabs. was detained at home by sickness.

The 1st Sab. of April at Shirtee from—1 Cor. 1.23.24
The 2d. Sab. at Pidgeon Creek from—Act. 10.29
The 3d. Sab. at Shirtee from—Lev. 26.21
The 4th Sab. at Peter's Creek received   9   18   0

The 7st Sab. of May at Pidgeon Creek from—Mat. 11.28
The 2d. Sab. at Shirtee from—Lev. 26.21
The 3d. at Pidgeon Creek from—Matt. 11.28
The 4th Sab. at Shirtee from—Lev. 26.21
The 5th Sab. at Pidgeon Creek from Matt. 11.28
   Wednesday the wd of June 1779, about seven o'clock poat Meridan William McMillan was born.

The 1st Sab. of June at Shirtee from—Lev. 26.21
The 2d. Sab. at Pidgeon Creek from—Mat. 11.28
The 3d. Sab. at Mr. Marshel's on Cross Creek, together with the monday following recvd.   37   11   6
   Tuesday at Mr. Bailer's place on Raccoon   13   17   3
The 4th Sab. at Shirtee from—Lev. 26.21
   The Thursday following at Mr. Power's

The 1st Sab. of July at Pidgeon Creek from—Mat. 11.28
The 2d. Sab. at Pike run received   15   0   0
The 3d. Sab. at Shirtee from—Phil. 2.12.
The 4th Sab. at Pidgeon Creek from—Song. 3.11

The 1st Sab. of August, together with the monday following at Peter's Creek received   43   15   0
The 2d. Sab. at Shirtee from—Rom. 3.25
The 3d. Sab. at Laurel Hill and the Monday following at Mr. Power's.
The 4th Sab. at Pidgeon Creek from—Song. 3.11
The 5th Sab. at Shirtee from—1 Tim. 4.8

The 1st Sab. of September at Pidgeon Creek from—Song. 3.11
The 2d. Sab. at Shirtee from—Exod. 20. 8-11

The 3d. Sab. at Pigeon Creek from—Mat 22.42
  Monday set out on my journey to see my friends, and on friday came to John Jack's.
The 4th Sab. Preached for M. Lang afternoon.
  Wednesday came to my father's at Leacock.

The 1st Sab. of October. Preached at Leacock   22   13   1
  Monday went down to brandywine.
  Thursday. preached at My Father-in-laws.
The 2d. Sab. at Leacock   22   13   2
The 3d. Sab. at Carlisle   4   17   6
  This week attended the Presbettery and Thursday evening preached at John Jack's.
The 4th Sab. forenoon for Mr. McPheren.
  Friday returned again to my family.
The 5th Sab. Heard Mr. Henderson at Pidgeon Creek

The 1st Sab. of November at Shirtee from—1 Joh. 3.1.
The 2d. Sab. at Pigeon Creek from—Mat. 22.42
The 3d. Sab. at Shirtee from—1 Joh. 3.1.
The 4th Sab. at Pidgeon Creek from Matt. 22.42

The 1st Sab of December at Shirtee from—Exod. 20. 8-11
The 2d. Sab. at Pidgeon Creek from—matt. 22.42
  Wednesday at the same place from—Rev. 3.1.
The 3d. Sab. at Shirtee from—Exod. 20. 8-11
  Tuesday at Ezekel Hopkins from—matt. 24.44   15L
The 4th Sab. at Pigeon Creek from—matt. 22.42

1780

The 1st Sab. of Jan. was to have preached at Shirtee, But the day proving exceeding stormy, only a very few of my near neighbors met at my house with whom I spent the day in a kind of Social worship.
The 2d. Sab. Was to have preached at Pigeon Creek, But was prevented by the deepness of the snow, and the extreme coldness of the weather.
The 3d. Sab. preached at Shirtee from—Exod. 20. 8-11
The 4th Sab. at Pigeon Creek from—Matt. 22.42
The 5th Sab. at Shirtee from Rev. 3.1

The 1st Sab. of February at Pidgeon Creek from—Mat. 22.42
The 2d. Sab. at Shirtee from—Exod. 20. 8-11
The 3d. Sab. at Pidgeon Creek from—Matt. 22.42
The 4th Sab. at Shirtee from—Exod. 20. 8-11

The 1st Sab. of March at Pidgeon Creek from—Rom. 10.21
The 2d. Sab. at Shirtee from—Exod. 20. 8-11
The 3d. Sab. at Pidgeon Creek from—Phil. 1.21
The 4th Sab. at Shirtee from—Mat. 7. 21

The 1st Sab. of April at upper Cross Creek from—Phil. 1.21. received   66L 1s 4d
The 2d. Sab. at Pidgeon Creek from—1 Pet. 1.12
The 3d. Sab. at Shirtee from—Exod. 20. 8-11.
The 4th Sab. at Pidgeon Creek from—Josh. 7.13
The 5th Sab. at Shirtee from—Exod. 20 8-11
   Thursday being a fast day at Thomas Egeton's—Hosa. 13.9

The 1st Sab. of May at Peter's Creek and received   59L 2s 10d
The 2d. Sab. at Pigeon Creek from—Josh. 7.13
The 3d. Sab. at Shirtee from—Josh. 3.5
   Thursday being ye fast day preceeding the administration of the Lord's Supper, at Thomas Egeton's from—Josh. 3.5
The 4th Sab. at Shirtee from—Psal. 63.5 and administered the Sacrament of the Supper, being assisted by the Revd. Joseph Smith, who preached Saturday. Sabbath evening and monday.

The 1st Sab. of June at Shirtee from—Exod. 20.7
The 2d. Sab. at Pidgeon Creek from—Josh. 7.13
The 3d. Sab. at Raccoon. Received   47L 11s 6d
   The monday at Mr. Marshel's on cross Creek   67 16 3
The 4th Sab. at Shirtee from—Exod. 20. 8-11

The 1st Sab. of July at Pidgeon Creek from—Josh. 7.13
The 2d. Sab. at Shirtee from Exod. 20. 8-11
The 3d. Sab. at Pigeon Creek from—Josh. 7.13
The 4th Sab. at Mr. McDonald's on Robinson's run—received   22L 12s 6d
The 5th Sab. at Shirtee from—Psal. 51.5

The 1st Sab. of August at Pigeon Creek from—Josh. 7.13
   Thursday, being a fast, at Mr. Egeton's from—Josh 7.13
The 2d. Sab. at Shirtee from—Rom 8.30
The 3d. Sab. at Pidgeon Creek from—Josh 7.13
The 4th Sab. at Nicholas Depu's at the mouth of Pigeon Creek from—Rom. 3.31 & Isa. 32.2 R.   53L 12s 0d

The 1st Sab. of September at Shirtee from—Rom. 8.30 fol.
The 2d. Sab. at Laurel Hill, received   87L 1s 6d
   Tuesday at Pidgeon Creek from—John. 10. 27,28
The 3d. Sab. at Shirtee from—Rom. 8.30 first 1.
The 4th Sab. at Pidgeon Creek from—Josh. 7.13 & Luk. 22.19
   Thursday at Thomas Edgerton's from—Psal. 26.6

The 1st Sab. of October at Pidgeon Creek from—Isa. 55.1 and administered the Sacrament of the Supper being assisted by the Revd. Mr. Power who preached Saturday and Monday: and by ye Revd. Mr. Dod who preached Sabbath evening.
The 2d. Sab. At Pidgeon Creek from—Act. 16. 29-31

The 3d. Sab. at Shirtee from—John 16.33
The 4th Sab. at Pidgeon Creek from—Act. 16. 29-31
The 5th Sab. together with the monday following at Peter's Creek received   55L 16s 9d

The 1st Sab. of November at Shirtee from—Cant. 2.14
The 2d. Sab. at Pidgeon Creek from—Act. 16. 30
The 3d. Sab. at Shirtee from—2 Cor. 5.20
The 4th Sab. at Pidgeon Creek from—Act. 16. 29-31

The 1st Sab. of December. was to have preached at Mudy Creek, but being prevented, I preached at Patrick Scot's on pidgeon Creek from—Isa. 32.2
The 2d. Sab. at Shirtee from—2 Cor. 5.20. Thursday, being a thanksgiving day at Thomas Edgeton's from—Jer. 9. 23,24
The 3d. Sab. at Pideon Creek from—Act. 16. 31
The 4th Sab. at Shirtee from—Isa. 50.2. Thursday following at Shirtee from Isa. 50.2
The 5th Sab. at Pidgeon Creek from Act. 16.31

1781

The 1st Sab. of Jan. at Shirtee from—Luk. 16.31
The 2d. Sab. at Pidgeon Creek from Act. 16.31
The 3d. Sab. at Shirtee from—Luke. 16.31
The 4th Sab. at little red House   87L 9s 3d

The 1st Sab. of Feb. was to have preached at Pigeon Creek, but was prevented by high waters.
The 2d. Sab. at Shirtee from—Phil. 1.21
The 3d. Sab. at Pidgeon Creek from—Act. 16.31
The 4th Sab. at Shirtee from—Luk. 19.27
   Wednesday at Shirtee being a fast from—Luke. 13.7

The 1st Sab. of March at Pidgeon Creek from—Act. 16.31
The 2d. Sab. at Shirtee from—Luk. 13.7
The 3d. Sab. at Pidgeon Creek from—Act. 16.31
The 4th Sab. at Shirtee from—Isa. 40.1

The 1st Sab. of April at Pidgeon Creek from—Act. 16.31
The 2d. Sab. at Shirtee from—1 Cor. 9.24
The 3d. Sab. at Pidgeon Creek from—Act. 16.31
The 4th Sab. at Shirtee from—I Cor. 16.22
The 5th Sab. at Pidgeon Creek from—Act. 16.31

The 1st Sab. of May at Shirtee from—Phil. 3.8
The 2d. Sab. at Pidgeon Creek from—Rom. 5.20
The 3d. Sab. at lower Cross Creek and the monday following at upper.
   Thursday at Shirtee being the fast from—Hos. 2.19
The 4th Sab. at Shirtee from—Song. 5.1 and administered the Sacrament of the Supper being assisted by revd. Joseph Smith who preached Saturday, Sab. evening and monday.

The 1st Sab. of June at Shirtee from—Hos. 2.19
The 2d. Sab. at Pidgeon Creek from—Act. 16.33. Josh 24.15
The 3d. Sab. at Peter's Creek received   142L   3s   0d
The 4th Sab. at Shirtee from—Rom. 8.6
   Thursday ye 28th of June 1781, Margaret McMillan was born between eleven & twelve o'Clock at night.

The 1st Sab. of July at Pidgeon Creek from—Matt. 16.26
The 2d. Sab. at Shirtee from—Phil. 3.8
The 3d. Sab. at Pidgeon Creek from—Act. 16.33, Josh. 24.15
The 4th Sab. at Shirtee from—Psal. 30.7
The 5th Sab. at the mouth of Pidgeon Creek   18L   7s 10

The 1st Sab. of August at Pidgeon Creek from—Rom. 8.20
The 2d. Sab. at Shirtee from—Phil. 3.8
The 3d. Sab. at Pidgeon Creek from—Act. 16.33, Josh. 24.15
The 4th Sab. at Shirtee from—Song. 5.16 L.C.

The 1st Sab. of September at Muddy Creek   20s
   The Monday following at ten-mile south fork. and the friday preceding being a fast at Pidgeon Creek from—Zac. 7.5
The 2d. Sab. of September at Shirtee from—Rom. 8.7
The 3d. Sab. at Pidgeon Creek from—Act 16.33 & Josh. 24.15
The 4th at Pidgeon Creek, from—Song. 1.2. and administered the Sacrament of the Supper, being assisted by Mr. Power, who preached Friday, Saturday, Sab. evening & monday.
The 5th Sab. at Pidgeon Creek from—Josh. 24.15

The 1st Sab. of October at Shirtee from—2 Cor. 4.3
The 2d. Sab at Pidgeon Creek from—Josh. 24.15
The 3d. Sab. at mount pleasant, assited by Mr. Power at the administration of the Sacrament of the Supper, and preached on friday, Saturday, and Sabbath evening, heard Mr. Clark on Monday. received 41. state P.
The 4th Sab. at Shirtee from—2 Cor. 4.3

The 1st Sab of November at Pidgeon Creek from—Josh. 24.15
   The Wednesday following at Mount Pleasant.
The 2d. Sab. at Muddy Creek.   14L 11s 8d
The 3d. Sab. at Shirtee from—Psal. 81. 10-13
The 4th Sab. at Pidgeon Creek from—Josh. 24.15

The 1st Sab of December at Shirtee from—Psal. 81. 10-13
The 2d. Sab. at Pidgeon Creek from—Josh. 24. 15
   Thursday being appointed by Congress to be observed as a day of thanksgiving, at Shirtee from—Ezra. 9. 13-14

The 3d. Sab. at Shirtee from—John 15.7
The 4th Sab. at Pidgeon Creek from—John. 13. 34,35
The 5th Sab. at Peter's Creek.

1782

The 1st Sab. of Jan. at Shirtee from—Thess. 5.19
The 2d. Sab. at Pidgeon Creek from—1 Joh. 5.4
The 3d. Sab. at Shirtee from—Thess. 5.19
The 4th Sab. at Pidgeon Creek—Rom. 6.23

The 1st Sab. of February at Shirtee from—Luk. 14.17
The 2d. Sab. at Pidgeon Creek from—Joh. 16.8
The 3d. Sab. at Shirtee from—Luk. 14.17
The 4th Sab. at the Fork's meeting house.

The 1st Sab. of March at Pidgeon Creek from—Joh. 16.8
The 2d. Sab. of March at Shirtee from—Luk. 14.18
The 3d. Sab. at Pidgeon Creek from—Luk. 13.24
The 4th Sab. at Shirtee from—Prov. 1.24 &c
The 5th Sab. at Pidgeon Creek from—Joh. 16.8

The 1st Sab. of April at Peter's Creek.
  The Tuesday following at Sewickly
The 2d. Sab. at Shirtee from—Prov. 1. 24 &c.
The 3d. and 4th Sabs. was hindered from preach by sickness.

The 1st Sab. of May at Pidgeon Creek from—Isa. 1.2
The 2d. Sab. did not preach by reason of sickness.
The 3d. Sab. at Shirtee from—Prov. 1.24 &c I Joh. 4.5
  Thursday being the fast before the celebration of the
  Lord's Supper, heard Mr. Smith
The 4th Sab. of May at Shirtee from—Eph. 6.24 and administered the Lord's Supper, being assisted by Mr. Dunlap who preached Saturday, Sab. evening, and monday.
8 tables

The 1st Sab. of June at Shirtee from—Eph. 6.24
The 2d. Sab. assisted Mr. Smith in the administration of the Lord's Supper and preached Thursday, Saturday, Sabbath evening & monday.
The 3d. Sab. at Pidgeon Creek from—Deut. 10.12
The 4th Sab. at Shirtee from—1 Pet. 2.11
  Thursday at Shirtee from—Amos 4.12
The 5th Sab. at Pidgeon Creek from—Isa. 14.5

The 1st Sab. of July at Shirtee from—Isa. 62.5 & Jer. 3.12
The 2d. Sab. at Pidgeon Creek from—Joh. 16.8
The 3d. Sab. at Shirtee from—Jer. 3.12
The 4th Sab. at Peter's Creek.

The 1st Sab. of August at Pidgeon Creek from—Joh. 16.8
The 2d. Sab. of August at Shirtee from—Joh. 16.8
The 3d. Sab. at Muddy Creek
The 4th Sab. at Pidgeon Creek from—1 Pet. 1.8

The 1st Sab. of September at Shirtee from Heb. 3.13
The 2d. Sab. at Pidgeon Creek from—Joh. 16.8
The 3d. Sab. at Shirtee from—Matt. 22.14. forenoon
The 4th Sab. at Peter's Creek.
The 5th Sab. at Pidgeon Creek from—Matt. 20.6
   Thursday being the fast before the celebration of the Lord's Supper preached at Pigeon Creek from 1 Pet. 1.8

The 1st Sab. of October at Pidgeon Creek from—Heb. 12.1 and administered the Sacrament of the Supper being assisted by ye Revd. Joseph Smith who preached Saturday, Sabbath evening and monday
The 2d. Sab. at Racoon, Mr. Smith at Pidgeon Creek.
The 3d. Sab. at Shirtee from—Isa. 32.2
The 4th Sab. assisted Mr. Power to administer the Sacrament of the Supper. preached, friday, Saturday, Sab. evening and monday.
   Tuesday at Mr. Huton's on Monongahale.

The 1st Sab. of November at Pidgeon Creek from—Gen. 6.3
The 2d. Sab. at Shirtee from—Heb. 3.13
The 3d. Sab. at the Ohio court house.
The 4th Sab. at Pidgeon Creek from—Gen. 6.3

The 1st Sab. of December at Shirtee from—Heb. 3.13
The 2d. Sab. at Pidgeon Creek from—Isa. 11.10
The 3d. Sab. at Shirtee from—Matt. 26.45
The 4th Sab. at the Forks meeting house.
The 5th Sab. at Pidgeon Creek from—Isa. 11.10

1783

The 1st Sab. of January at Peter's Creek
The 2d. Sab. at Pidgeon Creek from—Col. 2.6
   The Thursday following at Dover's ferry.
The 3d. Sab. at Shirtee from—Psal. 104.34
The 4th Sab. at Pidgeon Creek from—Prov. 3.17

The 1st Sab. of February at Shirtee from—Joh. 10.27.28
The 2d. Sab. at Pidgeon Creek from—Rom. 14.16
The 3d. Sab. at Shirtee from—John. 10.27.28
The 4th Sab. at Pidgeon Creek from—Heb. 12.1

The 1st Sab. of March at Muddy Creek   1L   2s   6d
The 2d. Sab. of March at Shirtee from—1 Tim. 1.15
The 3d. Sab. at Pidgeon Creek from—2 Cor. 13.5
The 4th Sab. at Shirtee from—Isa. 3.11
The 5th Sab. at Pidgeon Creek from—2 Cor. 13.5

The 1st Sab. of April at Shirtee from—Psal. 101.2
The 2d. Sab. of April assisted Mr. Smith in the administration of the Lord's Supper at Cross Creek, preached Thursday, Saturday, & Sab. evening
The 3d. Sab. at Pidgeon Creek from—Isa. 50.2.

The 4th Sab. at Shirtee from—Hag. 1.7
Thursday being the fast before ye Sacrament at Shirtee from—1 Sam. 16.5

The 1st Sab. of May at Chartiers from—Psal. 116.16 and administered the Sacrament of the Lord's Supper being assisted by Mr. Clark who preached on Saturday, and Sab. evening and by Mr. Smith on Monday.
The 2d. Sab. at Pequea in the forenoon, and on the Saturday preceeding.
The 4th Sab. at New Providence.

The 1st Sab. of June at brandywine.
The 2d. Sab. at Carlisle.
The 3d. Sab. at my own house from—John. 21.15
The 4th Sab. at Pidgeon Creek from—Jer. 13.16
The 5th Sab. at Shirtee from—Act. 13.26

The 1st Sab. of July at Pidgeon Creek from—Hos. 9.12
The 2d. Sab. at Shirtee from—Phil. 4.4
The 3d. Sab. at Pidgeon Creek from—Rev. 3.1
The 4th Sab. at Shirtee from—Rev. 3.1

The 1st Sab. of August at Pidgeon Creek from—Psal. 71.16
The 2d. Sab. at Shirtee from—Rom. 8.1
The 3d. Sab. assisted Mr. Clark in the administration of the Lord's Supper.
The 4th Sab. at Pidgeon Creek from—21 Thes. 1.7
The 5th Sab. at Shirtee from—Rom. 8.1

The 1st Sab. of September at Pigeon Creek from Matt. 11.19
Thursday, September 11th, -83. Mary McMillan was born about eleven o'clock A.M.
The 2d. Sab. at Shirtee from—Rom. 5.20
Tuesday and Wednesday following at Sewickly
The 3d. Sab. assited Mr. Smith in the administration of the Lord's Supper.
The 4th Sab. at Pidgeon Creek from—1 Cor. 11.26
Thursday being the fast preceeding the administration of the Lord's Supper preached at Pidgeon Creek from —Isa. -59.16

The 1st Sab. of October at Pigeon Creek from—Song. 2.16 and administered the Sacrament of the Supper being assisted by Mr. Smith.
The 2d. Sab. at pidgeon Creek from—Prov. 8.4
The Monday following at Sewickly.
The 3d. Sab. at Shirtee from
This week attended the P'b' y at mount pleasant & assist- Mr. Power to administer the Sacrament of the Supper.

The 1st Sab. of November at Pidgeon Creek from—Prov. 8.4

The 2d. Sab. at Shirtee from—1 John. 5.4
The 3d. Sab. at the South fork of ten-mile.   16   8
The 4th Sab. at Pidgeon Creek from—Prov. 6. 10.11
The 5th Sab. at Shirtee from—1 Joh. 5.4

The 1st Sab. of December at Pidgeon Creek from—Heb. 2.3
 The Thursday following being a thanksgiving day appointed by Congress at Shirtee from—Joh. 15.7
The 3d. Sab. at Pidgeon Creek from—Heb. 2.3
The 4th Sab. at Shirtee from—Rom. 16.21

1784

The 1st Sab. of Jan. at Pigeon Creek from—Heb. 2.3
The 2d. Sab. at Shirtee from—matt. 11.28
The 3d. Sab. at Pidgeon Creek from—Heb. 2.3
The 4th Sab. at Shirtee from—1 Pet. 1.12

The 1st Sab. of February at Pidgeon Creek from Heb. 2.3
The 2d. Sab. at Shirtee from—John. 6.37
The 3d. Sab. at pidgeon Creek from—Heb. 2.3
The 4th Sab. at Shirtee from—John. 6.37
Thr 5th Sab. at Pidgeon Creek from—Song. 7.10

The 1st Sab. of March at Shirtee from—Mat. 6.9
The 2d. Sab. at Pidgeon Creek from—Song. 7.10
The 3d. Sab. at Unity congregation—8 12 6
The 4th Sab. at Shirtee from—John 1.12

The 1st Sab. of April at Pidgeon Creek from—Joh. 21.15
The 2d. Sab. at Shirtee
The 3d. Sab. at Pidgeon Creek from—Jer. 3.14
The 4th Sab. at Shirtee from—2 Sam. 12.23 & Jer. 44.4

The 1st Sab. of May at muddy creek received   1   9   0
The 2d. Sab. at Pidgeon Creek from—Jer. 3.14
The 3d. Sab. assisted by Mr. Smith in the administration of the Lord's Supper at lower cross creek
at lower cross creek
The 4th Sab. at Col. Cooks in the forks
The 5th Sab. at Shirtee from—Joh. 15.6

The 1st Sab. of June at Shirtee from—Joh. 10.4 and administered the Lord's Supper being assisted by Mr. Clark, Mr. Smith, and Mr. Dod.
The 2d. Sab. at Shirtee from—Hos. 11.7,8
The 3d. Sab. assisted Mr. Clark at the administration of the Lord's Supper
The 4th Sab. at Pidgeon Creek from—Rev. 22.17

The 1st Sab. Of July at Shirtee from—Deut. 9.24
The 2d. Sab. at Pidgeon Creek from—John 9.35
The 3d. Sab. at Shirtee from—Heb. 12.1 & Joh. 3.14
The 4th Sab. at Pidgeon Creek from—John 9.35

The 1st Sab. of August at Shirtee from—1 Joh. 3.14 & Isa. 1.10
The 2d. Sab. assisted Mr. Clark at ye Sacrament
The 3d. Sab. at Pidgeon from—2 Cor. 5.20
The 4th Sab. at Middle Spring in the afternoon

The 1st Sab. of September at Fag's manor.
The 2d. Sab. at Upper Octorara
The 3d. Sab. assisted Mr. Carmichel at ye Sacrament
The 4th Sab. at Carlisle.   1   17   6

The 1st Sab. of October at mount pleasant
The 2d. Sab. at Shirtee from—Isa. 50.2
The 3d. Sab. at Pidgeon Creek from—2 Cor. 5.20
The 4th Sab. at Pidgeon Creek from—Rom. 6.23 & administered the Sacrament of the Supper being assisted by Mr. Dodd.
The 5th Sab. assisted Mr. Dodd.

The 1st Sab. of November at Chartiers from—Isa. 50.2
 The thursday following at the same place from—Isa. 45.24
The 2d. Sab. of November at Pidgeon Creek from—Isa. 62.5
The 3d. Sab. at Chartiers from—Prov. 3.17
The 4th Sab. at Pidgeon Creek from—Song. 5.2

The 1st Sab. of December at Pike run   1   10   0
The 2d. Sab. at Shirtee from—Eph. 2.1
The 3d. Sab. at Pidgeon Creek from—Joh. 15.2
The 4th Sab. at Shirtee from—Mic. 7.18

1785

The 1st Sab. of Jan. at Pidgeon Creek from—Joh. 15.2
The 2d. Sab at Shirtee from—Mic. 7.18
The 3d. Sab. at Pigeon Creek from—Joh. 15.2
The 4th Sab. at Shirtee from—Rom. 8.26
The 5th Sab. at Pidgeon Creek from—Joh. 15.2

The 1st Sab. of Feb. at Shirtee from—Matt. 6.9
The 2d. Sab. at Pidgeon Creek—Joh. 15.4
The 3d. Sab. at Shirtee from—Matt. 6.9
The 4th Sab. at Pidgeon Creek from—Joh. 15.6

The 1st Sab. of March at Robonson's run
The 2d. Sab. at Shirtee from—Matt. 6.10
The 3d. Sab. at Pidgeon Creek from—Joh. 15.9
The 4th Sab. at Shirtee from—Heb. 2.4

The 1st Sab. of April at ye S. fork of ten mile
The 2d. Sab. at Pidgeon Creek from—Joh. 15.9
The 3d. Sab. at Shirtee from—Song. 7.10
The 4th Sab. at ye lower meeting house in the forks.

The 1st Sab. of May at Pidgeon Creek from—Joh. 15.11
The 2d. Sab. at Shirtee from—Phil. 4.23

The 3d. Sab. at Pidgeon Creek from—Joh. 15.14
The 4th Sab. at Shirtee from—Matt. 22.5
The 5th Sab. at Pidgeon Creek from—Joh. 15.12 & Act. 2.37

    Saturday the 28th of May—85 Catherine McMillan was born about 9 o'Clock A. M.

The 1st Sab. of June assisted Mr. Dunlap at the administration of the Lord's Supper
The 2d. Sab. at Shirtee from—2 Tim. 3.5
The 3d. Sab. at Shirtee from—Luk. 12.32 and administered the Sacrament of ye Supper being assisted by Mr. Dunlap
The 4th Sab. at Pidgeon Creek from—Luk. 16.31

The 2d. Sab. of July at Shirtee from—Rom. 5.1
The 3d. Sab. at Pidgeon Creek from—Luk. 16.31
The 4th Sab. at Shirtee from—Rom. 5.1
The 1st Sab. of this month I preached at Pike run.
The 5th Sab. at Mantures run

The 1st Sab. of August assisted Mr. Dod at ye Sacrament
The 2d. Sab. at Shirtee from—2 Thes. 1.8
The 3d. Sab. assisted Mr. Smith at the administration of the Sacrament
The 4th Sab. at Turttle Creek

The 1st Sab. of September at Pidgeon Creek from—Matt. 13.31
The 2d. Sab. at Ten Mile, Mr. Dod at Shirtee
The 3d. Sab. assisted Mr. Clark at the administration of the Lord's Supper
The 4th Sab. at Shirtee from—I Joh. 4.10

The 1st Sab. of October at Pidgeon Creek from—Psal. 71.16
    Thursday being the fast from—Luk. 22.19
The 2d. Sab. at Pidgeon Creek from—Psal 63.5 and administered the Sacrament of the Supper being assisted by Mr. Clark and Mr. Smith.
The 3d. Sab. at Pidgeon Creek from—Phil. 1.21
The 4th Sab. at Shirtee from—Phil. 2.12
The 5th Sab. at Racoon

The 1st Sab. of November at Pidgeon Creek from—Phil. 1.21
The 2d. Sab. at Shirtee from—Jer. 13.16
The 3d. Sab. at Pidgeon Creek from—Phil. 1.21
The 4th Sab. at Shirtee from—Matt. 3.10

The 1st Sab. of December at Pidgeon Creek from—Mat. 25.11
The 2d. Sab. at Pike run   1   10   0
The 3d. Sab. at Shirtee from—Prov. 3.17
The 4th Sab. at Pidgeon Creek from—1 Cor. 9.24

1786

The 1st Sab. of January at Chartiers from—1 Tim. 4.6
The 2d. Sab. at Pidgeon Creek from—Hag. 1.7
The 3d. Sab. at Shirtee from—Joh. 14.19
The 4th Sab. I was to have preached at pidgeon Creek but was prevented by high waters
The 5th Sab. at Shirtee from—Heb. 9.12

The 1st Sab. of Feb. at Pidgeon Creek from—Col. 3.4
The 2d. Sab. at Shirtee from—Heb. 9.12
The 3d. Sab. at Pidgeon Creek from—Col. 3.4
The 4th Sab. at Shirtee from—John. 7.37

The Lst Sab. of March at Pidgeon Creek from—Ezek. 13.18
The 2d. Sab. at Shirtee from—John. 7.37
The 3d. Sab. at Pidgeon Creek from—Col. 3.4
The 4th Sab. at Mill-Creek   1   10   0

The 1at Sab. of April at Shirtee from—John. 7.37
The 2d. Sab. at Pidgeon Creek from—Isa. 54.5
The 3d. Sab. at Shirtee from—John. 7.37
The 4th Sab. at Pidgeon Creek from—Isa. 54.5
The 5th Sab. at Shirtee from—1 Pet. 1.8

The 1st Sab. of May at Pidgeon Creek from—Col. 3.4
The 2d. Sab. of May at Shirtee from—Song. 5.16
The 3d. Sab. assisted Mr. Smith at the Sacrament
The 4th Sab. at Shirtee from—Song. 5.16
   Thursday being the fast before the Sacrament—2 Sam. 14.32

The 1st Sab. of June at Shirtee from—Song. 1.4 and administered the Sacrament of the Supper being assisted by Mr. Smith who preached Saturday, Sab.-evening & monday.
The 2d. Sab. assisted Mr. Clark at the administration of the Lord's Supper
The 3d. Sab. at Pidgeon Creek from—Eph. 2.1 & Isa. 59.18
The 4th Sab. at Pike run

The 1st Sab. of July at Shirtee from—Song. 5.16
The 2d. Sab. at Pidgeon-Creek from—Gal. 4.19
The 3d. Sab. at Shirtee—from Song. 5.16
The 4th Sab. at Pidgeon Creek from—Col. 3.4
The 5th Sab. at Shirtee from—Song. 5.16

The 1st Sab. of August at King's Creek
The 2d. Sab. at Pidgeon Creek from—Rom. 8.1
The 3d. Sab. at Chartiers from
The 4th Sab. at Long-run

The 1st Sab. of September assisted Mr. Dodd in the administration of the Lord's Supper, and preached on Saturday, Sab.-evening and monday

The 2d. Sab. at Chartiers from—Song. 5.2
The 3d. Sab. was to have assisted Mr. Smith in the administration of the Lord's Supper, but was prevented by sickness
The 4th Sab. attended the administration of the Lord's Supper at Mr. Clark's congregation

The 1st Sab. of October at Pidgeon Creek from—Rom. 8.1
    Thursday being the fast before the Sacrament at Pidgeon Creek from—Jer. 4.1
The 2d. Sab. at Pidgeon Creek from—Hos. 2. 19.20 and administered the Sacrament of the Supper being assisted by Mr. Smith who preached on Saturday and monday.
The 3d. Sab. at Chartiers from—Rom. 3.31
The 4th Sab. assisted Mr. Dunlap to administer the Sacrament of the Supper, and preached an friday, Saturday and monday
The 5th Sab. at Pidgeon Creek from Jam. 1.22

The 1st Sab. of November at Chartiers from—Song. 8.5
The 2d. Sab. at Petato garden
The 3d. Sab. at Pidgeon Creek from—Hos. 13.13
The 4th Sab. at Chartiers from—Song. 8.5

The 1st Sab. of December at Pidgeon Creek from—Psal. 51.11
The 2d. Sab. was to have preached at Mantures but was prevented by the deepness of the snow
The 3d. Sab. at Chartiers from—Luk. 19.42
The 4th Sab. at Pidgeon-Creek from—Micah. 7.18
The 5th Sab. at Chartiers from—Luk. 19.42

1787
The 1st Sab. of Jan.ry at Pidgeon Creek from—Mich. 7.18
The 2d. Sab. at Chartiers from—Luk. 19.42
The 3d. Sab. was to have preached at Pidgeon Creek but was prevented by high waters.
The 4th Sab. at Shirtee from—Luk. 19.42

The 1st Sab. of February at Pidgeon Creek from—Joh. 16.33
The 2d. Sab. at Chartiers from—Luk. 19.42
The 3d. Sab. at Pidgeon Creek from—2 Tim. 1.12
The 4th Sab. at Chartiers from—Ezk. 33.11

The 1st Sab. of March at Pidgeon Creek from—Psal. 96.8
The 2d. Sab. at Pike run
The 3d. Sab. at Shirtee from—Ezk. 33.11
The 4th Sab. at Pidgeon Creek from—Job. 14.14

The 1st Sab. of April at Shirtee from—Rom. 5.18
The 2d. Sab. at Pidgeon Creek from—Job. 14.14
The 3d. Sab. at Shirtee from—Isa. 65.2
The 4th Sab. at Pidgeon Creek from—1 Joh. 3.24
The 5th Sab. at Shirtee from—Isa. 41.1

The 1st Sab. of May at Chartiers from—Song. 6.9 and administered the Sacrament of the Supper being assisted by Mr. Clark, Mr. Smith and Mr. Cornwell.
The 2d. Sab. attended at Pequea and preached on monday.
The 3d. Sab. preached in Philadelphia in the afternoon
The 4th Sab. at Brandywine in the afternoon
The 1st Sab. of June in the great Cove—15s
The 2d. Sab. at Pigeon Creek from—Matt. 3.10
The 3d. Sab. assisted Mr. Clark in the administration of the Lord's Supper
The 4th Sab. at Chartier's from—Jer. 3.22
The 1st Sab. of July at Pidgeon Creek from—Mat. 3.10 & 1 Cor. 2.2
The 2d. Sab. at Chartiers from—Isa. 59.18 1 Cor. 2.2
The 3d. Sab. at Pidgeon Creek from—Rom. 5.10
The 4th Sab. at Chartiers from—1 Cor. 2.2
The 5th Sab. at Pidgeon Creek from—Rom. 5.10
The 1st Sab. of August at Shirtee from—Mark. 16.6
The 2d. Sab. of August at Pidgeon Creek from—Rom. 5.10
The 3d. Sab. assisted Mr. Smith at the administration of the Lord's Supper at Mill-Creek   IL 10s
The 4th Sab. at Chartiers from—Joh. 15.6
The 1st Sab. of September at Pidgeon Creek from—Ezek. 37.1 11
The 2d. Sab. at Chartiers from—Joh. 15.4
The 3d. Sab. at Pidgeon Creek from—Ezek. 47. 1-10
The 4th Sab. at Chartiers from—1 Pet. 2.7
The 5th Sab. assisted Mr. Smith at the Sacrament.

The 1st Sab. of October at Pidgeon Creek from—Gen. 7.1
  Thursday being the fast preceeding the Sacrament preached at Pidgeon Creek from Josh. 3.5
  Tuesday ye 9th of October about half past four O'clock A.M. John McMillan was born.
The 2d. Sab. Administered the Sacrament of the Supper at Pidgeon Creek, and preached from—Psal. 26.6 being assisted by Mr. Smith
The 3d. Sab. assisted Mr. Dodd at ye Sacrament
The 4th Sab. at Chartiers from—Psal. 51.7

The 1st Sab. of November at Pidgeon Creek from—Gal. 2.20
The 2d. Sab. at Washington   1   2   6
The 3d. Sab. at Chartiers from—Hos. 9.12
The 4th Sab. at Pidgeon Creek from—Gal. 2.20

The 1st Sab. of December at Chartiers from—Jud. 1.12
The 2d. Sab. at Pidgeon Creek from—Jer. 23.6
The 3d. Sab. at the three ridges   1   10   0
The 4th Sab. at Shirtee kept society
The 5th Sab. at Pidgeon Creek from—Gen. 6.12.13

1788

The 1st Sab. of Jan. at Shirtee from—Psal. 71.16
The 2d. Sab. was to have preached at Pidgeon Creek but was prevented by a boil.
The 3d. Sab. at Shirtee from—Song. 7.10
The 4th Sab. was to have preached at Pidgeon Creek but was prevented by ye deepness of the snow.

The 1st Sab. of February at Shirtee from—Song. 7.10
The 2d. Sab. at Pidgeon Creek from—Gen. 6.12.13
The 3d. Sab. at Shirtee from—Psal. 119.71
The 4th Sab. at Pidgeon Creek from—Mat. 5.25, 26

The 1st Sab. of March at Chartiers from—Matt. 20.6
The 2d. Sab. at Pidgeon Creek from—Matt. 5.25.26
The 3d. Sab. at Buffalo
The 4th Sab. at King's Creek
The 5th Sab. at Shirtee from—Rev. 2.5

The 1st Sab. of April at Pidgeon Creek from—John. 10.4
The 2d. Sab. at Shirtee from—Rev. 2.5
The 3d. Sab. at Pidgeon Creek from—Prov. 8.17
The 4th Sab. at Shirtee from—Heb. 12.1

The 1st Sab. of May at Pidgeon Creek from—1 Tim. 1.15
The 2d. Sab. at Shirtee from—Heb. 12. 1&2
The 3d. Sab. at Shirtee from—2 Cor. 13.5
The 4th Sab. administered the Sacrament of the Supper at Chartiers and preached from—Rom. 6.22 being assisted by Mr. Smith & Mr. Clark

The 1st Sab. of June at Pidgeon Creek from—1 Tim. 1.15
The 2d. Sab. of June assisted Mr. Smith at the administration of the Lord's Supper at Cross-Creek
The 3d. Sab. at Chartiers from—Isa. 65.2
The 4th Sab. assisted Mr. Clark at the administration of the Lord's Supper at Bethel.
The 5ht Sab. at Pidgeon Creek from—Isa. 43.25

The 1st Sab. of July at Chartiers from—Jer. 44.4
The 2d. Sab. of July at Pidgeon Creek from—I Tim. 6.6
The 3d. Sab. at Chartiers from—Matt. 9.12
The 4th Sab. at Pidgeon Creek from—Deut. 10.12

The 1st Sab. of August at Chartiers from—Matt. 9.12
The 2d. Sab. at Pidgeon Creek from—Deut. 10.12
The 3d. Sab. at Chartiers from—Rom. 8.6
The 4th Sab. at King's Creek and administered the Sacrament of the Supper being assisted by Mr. Dod.
The 5th Sab. at Pidgeon Creek from—Matt. 16.26

The 1st Sab. of September at Chartiers from—Hos. 2.19
The 2d. Sab. at Pidgeon Creek from Matt. 16.26
The 3d. Sab. at Chartiers from—Matt. 11.17
The 4th Sab. assisted Mr. Clark at the administration of the Lord's Supper.

The 1st Sab. of October at Pidgeon Creek from—Isa. 53. 10,11
The 2d. Sab. at Pidgeon Creek from—Matt. 25.5 and administered ye Sacrament of the Supper being assisted by Mr. Clark & Mr. McGready.
The 3d. Sab. at Chartiers—heard Mr. McGready
The 4th Sab. at Pidgeon Creek from—1 Joh. 4.10

The 1st Sab. of November at Chartiers from—Gen. 2.17
The 2d. Sab. at Pidgeon Creek from—Isa. 32.2
The 3d. Sab. at Polk-run   12s   4d
    Thursday being a fast appointed by P.b.y. at Pidgeon Creek from—Zech. 7.5
The 4th Sab. at Chartiers from—Gen. 2.17
The 5th Sab. at Pidgeon-Creek from—Joh. 15.7

The 1st Sab. of December at Shirtee from—Jer. 13.16
The 2d. Sab. at Pidgeon Creek from—John. 15.7
The 3d. Sab. was to have preached at Shirtee but was prevented by the coldness of the weather and spent the day in society with a few that met at my own house.
The 4th Sab. at Pidgeon Creek from—Mic. 6.8

1789

The 1st Sab. of January at Chartiers from—Isa. 11.10
The 2d. Sab. at Pidgeon Creek from—Micah. 6.8
The 3d. Sab. at Chartiers from—Isa. 11.10
The 4th Sab. at Pidgeon Creek Mr. Brice preached

The 1st Sab. of February at Chartiers but did not preach
The 2d. Sab. at Pidgeon Creek from—Deut. 6.5
The 3d. Sab. at Chartiers from—Luk. 10.13,14
The 4th Sab. at Pidgeon Creek from—Psal. 40.14

The 1st Sab. of March at Chartiers from—Isa. 11.10
The 2d. Sab. at Pidgeon Creek from—Psal. 34.19
The 3d. Sab. at Chartiers from—1 Pet. 2.11
The 4th Sab. at Pidgeon Creek from—1 Pet. 1.12
The 5th Sab. at Chartiers from—1 Pet. 2.11

The 1st Sab. of April at Muddy-Creek
The 2d. Sab. at Pidgeon Creek from—Jer. 4.1
The 3d. Sab. at Chartiers from—1 Cor. 1.23,24
The 4th Sab. at Pidgeon-Creek from—matt. 21.19

The 1st Sab. of May at Chartiers from—1 Cor. 1. 23,24
The 2d. Sab. at Pidgeon Creek from—Phil. 3.8
The 3d. Sab. at Chartiers from—1 Cor. 1.23,24
    Thursday being the fast before the Sacrament—1 Cor. 1.23,24
The 4th Sab. at Chartiers from—Phil. 3.8, and administered the Sacrament of the Supper being assisted by Mr. Smith.
The 5th Sab. at Chartiers from—1 Cor. 1. 23,24

The 1st Sab. of June at Pidgeon Creek from—Phil. 3.8
The 2d. Sab. at Chartiers from—Heb. 10. 28,29.
The 3d. Sab. assisted Mr. Clark at the administration of
the Sacrament of ye Lord's Supper.
The 4th Sab. at Unity   1   2   6

The 1st Sab. of July at Pidgeon Creek from—Eccl. 12.1
The 2d. Sab. at Chartiers from—Matt. 20.6
The 3d. Sab. at Pittsburgh   15s
The 4th Sab. at Pidgeon Creek from—Gal. 2.20

The 1st Sab. of August at Chartiers from—Joh. 15.5
The 2d. Sab. at Pidgeon Creek from—Matt. 13. 45.46
The 3d. Sab. at Chartiers from—Heb. 10.29
The 4th Sab. administered the Sacrament of the Supper at
Delap's Creek   1   10   0
The 5th Sab. at Pidgeon Creek from—Matt. 6.10

The 1st Sab. of September at Shirtee from—Col. 1.21
The 2d. Sab. at Pidgeon Creek from—Rom. 8.26
The 3d. Sab. at Shirtee from—Hag. 1.7
The 4th Sab. at Pidgeon Creek from—Matt. 7.21
    Thursday being the fast before the Sacrament preached
    at Pidgeon Creek from—Exod. 19. 10,11

The 1st Sab. of October at Pidgeon Creek from—Prov. 9.5
and administered the Sacrament of the Lord's Supper being assisted by Mr. Clark who preached Saturday and
monday.
The 2d. Sab. at Pidgeon Creek from—Joh. 10. 27,28
The 3d. Sab. heard Mr. Finley in ye Bull Pasture
    This week attended the meeting of Synod at Lexington
The 4th Sab. at Hall's meeting house forks Jame's river

The 1st Sab. of November in the Glades of Sandy Creek
The 2d. Sab. at Chartiers from—Song. 7.10
The 3d. Sab. heard Mr. Porter at Pidgeon Creek
The 4th Sab. at Chartiers from—Song. 7.10
The 5th Sab. at Pidgeon Creek from—Matt. 6.10
    Saturday the 5th of December 1789 Samuel McMillan
    was born about two o'Clock P.M.

The 1st Sab. of December heard Mr. Hindman at Chartiers
The 2d. Sab. at Pidgeon-Creek from—Matt. 6.10
The 3d. Sab. at Chartiers from—Job. 11.20
The 4th Sab. at Pidgeon Creek from—Matt. 6.11

1790

The 1st Sab. of January at Chartiers from—2 Cor. 5.17
The 2d. Sab. at Pidgeon Creek from—Matt. 6.12
The 3d. Sab. at Chartiers from—Jer. 2.17,19
The 4th Sab. at Pidgeon Creek from—Matt. 6.12
The 5th Sab. at Chartiers from—Micah. 7.18

The 1st Sab. of February at Pidgeon Creek from—Col. 2.19
The 2d. Sab. at Chartiers from—Psal. 40. 6, 7, 8
The 3d. Sab. at Pidgeon Creek from—Rom. 8.4
The 4th Sab. at Chartiers from—Psal. 40. 6, 7, 8

The 1st Sab. of March at Pidgeon-Creek from—2 Cor. 4.3
The 2d. Sab. was to have preached at Chartiers but was prevented by a pain in my breast accompanied by cold
The 3d. Sab. at Pidgeon-Creek from—Exod. 20.7
The 4th Sab. at Chartiers from—Psal. 40. 6,7,8

The 1st Sab. of April at Long run 17.4
The 2d. Sab. at Pidgeon Creek from—2 Cor. 4.3
The 3d. Sab. at Chartiers from—2 Cor. 5.20
The 4th Sab. at Pigeon Creek from—Isa. 45.24

The 1st Sab. of May at Chartiers from—Jer. 13.16
The 2d. Sab. at Pigeon Creek from—Isa. 50.2
The 3d. Sab. at Chartiers from—Luk. 12.13
The 4th Sab. at Chartiers from—Luk. 22.19. and administered the Sacrament of the Supper being assisted by Messrs. Clark, Dod, McPherrin and Porter
The 5th Sab. assisted Mr. Clark to administer the Sacrament of the Supper.

The 1st Sab. of June at Pigeon-Creek from—Mark. 10.21
The 2d. Sab. at Chartiers from—Joh. 15.7
The 3d. Sab. at Pidgeon Creek from—Prov. 3.17
The 4th Sab. was to have preached at Long-run but could not get over the river and therefore preached at Lebanon   15s

The 1st Sab. of July at Chartiers from—1 Cor. 1.30,31
The 2d. Sab. at Pidgeon-Creek from—Rom. 3.25 & Isa. 3.11
The 3d. Sab. at Chartiers from—1 Cor. 1. 30,31
The 4th Sab. at Pigeon-Creek from—Act. 13.26

The 1st Sab. of August at Chartiers from—1 Cor. 30.31
The 2d. Sab. at Pidgeon Creek from—L. 13.5
The 3d. Sab. at Chartiers from—Rom. 10.21
The 4th Sab. at Unity, Mr. McPherrin at Pidgeon Creek
The 5th Sab. at Bethel on black lick   2   0   0

The 1st Sab. of September at Chartiers from—Col. 2.6
The 2d. Sab. at Pidgeon-Creek from—Jer. 3.14
   Thursday being the fast before ye Sacrament from—Jer. 3.14
The 3d. Sab. at Pidgeon-Creek from Psal. 116.16 and administered the Sacrament of the Supper being assisted by Mr. Smith
The 4th Sab. at Frank ford in the afternoon

The 1st Sab. of October attended at the administration of the Lord's Supper at Winchester

The 2d. Sab. at Chartiers frm—1 Tim. 1.15
The 3d. Sab. at Pidgeon-Creek from—1 Pet. 2.11
The 4th Sab. administered the Sacrament of the Supper at Buffalo, Mr. Smith being sick.
The 5th Sab. at Chartiers from—2Sam. 7.26
    Thursday being a fast appointed by Synod preached at Chartiers from—Matt. 6.10

The 1st Sab. of November at Pigeon-Creek from—2 Cor. 6.2
The 2d. Sab. at Chartiers from—John. 15.9
The 3d. Sab. at Pidgeon Creek from—2 Cor. 6.2
The 4th Sab. at Pittsburgh   20s

The 1st Sab. of December at Chartiers from—Isa. 1.18
The 2d. Sab. at Pidgeon Creek from—2 Cor. 5.4
The 3d. Sab. at Chartiers from—Isa. 1.18
The 4th Sab. at Pidgeon Creek from—2 Cor. 5.4

1791

The 1st Sab. of Jan.y at Chartiers from—Isa. 1. 18,19
The 2d. Sab. at Pidgeon Creek from—Matt. 12.19
The 3d. Sab. at Chartiers from—Jud. 1.12
The 4th Sab. at Pidgeon Creek from—Song. 8.5
The 5th Sab. at Chartiers from—Joh. 14.19

The 1st Sab. of February at Pidgeon Creek from—Joh. 1.11
The 2d. Sab. at Chartiers from—1 Joh. 3.1
The 3d. Sab. at Pidgeon Creek from—Rom. 8.30
The 4th Sab. at Chartiers from—Mark. 10.28

The 1st Sab. of March at Pidgeon Creek from—John. 3.16
The 2d. Sab. at Chartiers from—Mark. 10.28
The 3d. Sab. at Mingo Creek   1   2   6
The 4th Sab. at Pidgeon Creek from—Eph. 2.5

The 1st Sab. of April at Chartiers from—Rom. 3.25
The 2d. Sab. at Pidgeon Creek from—Prov. 6.10,11
The 3d. Sab. at Chartiers from—Phil 1.21
The 4th Sab. at Pidgeon Creek from—Phil. 2.12

The 1st Sab. of May at Chartiers from—1 Cor. 16.22
The 2d. Sab. at Pidgeon Creek
The 3d. Sab. attended at Pequea at the Sacrament
The 4th Sab. attended in Philadelphia
The 5th Sab. at Marsh Creek

The 1st Sab. of June at Pidgeon Creek from—Song. 5.12
The 2d. Sab. assisted Mr. Peterson at Manutres
The 3d. Sab. at Chartiers from—Heb. 2.14

JOURNAL—PART III [113 Pages]

January, 1820 - October, 1833

1820

The 1st Sab. of January at Chartiers from—Zech. 13.7
The 2d. Sab. at Chartiers from—Ezek. 33. 7-9
The 3d. Sab. at Chartiers from—Matt. 25.3
    In the evening in the College from Matt. 24.44
The 4th Sab. heard Mr. James Scott at Chartiers and baptized one child—a girl.
The 5th Sab. at Chartiers from—Psal. 9.10

The 1st Sab. of February assisted Mr. Ralstone to administer the Sacrament at Mingo Creek—preached on Saturday & Monday from—Luk. 13.23 & 1 Joh. 3.2
    Tuesday attended ye funeral of my brother Thomas he died on Sab. night. Thursday, being the fast, at Chartiers from—Psal. 66.10
The 2d. Sab. at Chartiers from Isa. 33.10,11 and administered ye Sacrament of the Supper, being assisted by Mr. Ralstone who preached on Saturday & Monday
The 3d. Sab. at Chartiers from—Matt. 26. 21,22
    In the evening at the College from—Matt. 24.44
The 4th Sab. at Chartiers from Isa. 45.24 and baptized one child—a girl.

The 1st Sab. of March at Chartiers from—Job. 1.21
    In the evening in the College from—John 8.24
The 2d. Sab. at Chartiers from—Psal. 27.4
The 3d. Sab. at Chartiers from—Isa. 66.4
    In the evening in the college ab cadem and baptized one child—a girl
The 4th Sab. at Chartiers from—Rom. 8.6
    In the evening in the College from—Psal. 126.5 and baptized one adult—a woman

The 1st Sab. of April at Chartiers from—Matt. 12. 43-45
The 2d. Sab. at Washington, and assisted Mr. Brown to administer ye sacrament of ye supper, & preached on Saturday, Sab. evening & Monday from—Luk. 13.23 Prov. 10.24 & Matt & 22,23
The 3d. Sab. at Chartiers from—Song. 8.5
The 4th Sab. heard Messrs. Vaneman & Reed at Chartiers
The 5th Sab at Chartiers from—Psal. 149.2 and baptized one child—a boy.

The 1st Sab. of May at Washington from—2 Cor. 11.2
    Monday at Mr. Howie's from—Prov. 14.32 and baptized 4 children—2 boys and two adults, one male
The 2d. Sab. of May at Chartiers from—John 13. 34,35
The 3d. Sab. at Chartiers from—Luk. 10.21 and baptized one child—a girl
The 4th Sab. at Chartiers from—Psal. 103.19 & Phil. 2.12

The 1st Sab. of June at Chartiers from—Psal. 26.6 and baptized four children—two boys
    Thursday, being ye fast before ye Sacrament—from 1 Thes. 5.11—baptized two children—both boys

The 2d. Sab. at Chartiers from—1 Cor. 11.26
and administered the Sacrament of the Supper being assisted by Mr. Hoge, who preached on Saturday, and by Mr. McClain who preached on Sab. evening & Monday.
The 3d. Sab. at Chartiers from—Rom. 12.1 & Psal. 90.12
The 4th Sab. at Chartiers from—Song. 2.14 and baptized two children—one boy

The 1st Sab. of July at Chartiers from—1 Pet. 2.7 Mr. McMillan preached in the forenoon
The 2d. Sab. at Chartiers from 1 Pet. 2.7 & Psal. 51. 2,3
on this day John Davidson was killed with lightning
The 3d. Sab. at Chartiers from—Eccles. 12.1
The 4th Sab. at Chartiers from—Phil. 3.8
The 5th Sab. at Chartiers from—Prov. 3.33
In the evening in the College from—Eph. 2. 4,5

The 1st Sab. of August, at Chartiers from—2 Thess. 1. 7,8 and baptized one child—a boy
Monday attended the concert of prayer and baptized one adult—a woman
The 2d. Sab. at Chartiers from—Rom. 10.21
The 3d. Sab. at Chartiers from—Joh. 15.7
Monday at Severton Thomas, from—Prov. 14.32
The 4th Sab. assisted Mr. Ralstone to administer the Sacrament at Williamsport, and preached on Saturday, Sab. evening and monday—Eph. 2. 4,5; Matt. 7. 22.23 John 10.16
Thursday being a fast appointed by ye Assembly. Isa. 58.1

The 1st Sab. of September at Chartiers from—Rom. 14.17 and baptized one child—a Girl
The 2d. Sab. at Chartiers from . . . 1 Cor. 2.14 Hag. 1.7. and baptized one child—a boy
Thursday being ye fast before ye Sacrament—from Hos. 14.2, and baptised one child—a boy
The 3d. Sab. at Chartiers from—2 Cor. 5.17
and administered ye Sacrament of the Supper, being assisted by Mr. Brown who preached on Sab. evening & Monday.
The 4th Sab. assisted Mr. Hoge at Claysville

The 1st Sab. of October assisted Mr. Brown at the Sacrament in Washington, & preached on Sat. Sab. evening, Hos. 14.2 & Joh. 1.29
The 2d. Sab. at Chartiers from—Prov. 10.28
The 3d. Sab. at Chartiers from—Jer. 13.16, and baptized one child—a boy
The 4th Sab. at Chartiers from—Jer. 13. 15,16 & Eccl. 2.11
The 5th Sab. at Chartiers from—Col. 2.19

The 1st Sab. of November at Pigeon Creek from—Joh. 1.29 and baptized two children—both Girls
The 2d. Sab. heard Mr. Moore at Chartiers
The 3d. Sab. at Chartiers from—Col. 2.19
In the evening at the College from—1 Cor. 16.22
The 4th Sab. at Chartiers from—Gal. 5.17

The 1st Sab. of Dec. heard Mr. McMillan at Chartiers
   In the evening at the College from—1 Cor. 16.22 and baptized one child
   —a girl
The 2d. Sab. at Chartiers from—Luk. 18.22
The 3d. Sab. at Chartiers from—Rev. 3.1
The 4th Sab. at Chartiers from—Jude 12
   Monday at widow Kerr's from—Prov. 14.32
The 5th Sab. at Chartiers from—Prov. 8.4,5
   In the evening at the College from John. 16.8

1821

The 1st Sab. of Jan. at Chartiers from—Rom. 6.22
The 2d. Sab. heard Mr. Wm. McMillan at Chartiers
   In the evening at the College from—Isa. 1.18
The 3d. Sab. at Chartiers from—Gen. 6. 12.13
The 4th Sab. heard Mr. Wm. McMillan
   In the evening at the College from Act. 13.26

The 1st Sab. of February at Chartiers from—Matt. 20.6
   In the evening at the College from—Joh. 1.29
   Thursday being ye fast before the Sacrament—Hos. 12.10
The 2d. Sab. at Chartiers from—1 John 4.10 and administered ye Sacrament assisted by Mr. Ralstone who preached on Saturday & Monday.
   Tuesday evening at Washington
   Friday evening at Benjamin Williams from—1 Joh. 3.23
The 3d. Sab. assisted Mr. Ralston to administer ye Sacrament, & preached on Sat. & Mon. from—Psal. 96.8 & Joh. 12.35
The 4th Sab. at Chartiers from—Amos. 5.4
   In the evening at the College from—John 12.35

The 1st Sab. of March at Chartiers from—Amos 5.4 and baptized three children—one boy
   In the evening in the College from—1 Joh. 3.23
The 2d. Sab. at Chartiers from—Heb. 9.12 and baptized one child—a girl
The 3d. Sab. at Chartiers from—Heb. 9.12
   In the evening in the College—ab cadem
The 4th Sab. at Chartiers from—Gen. 6.3

The 1st Sab. of April at Chartiers from—Gen. 6.3
   In the evening in the College from—Psal. 89.16
The 2d. Sab. at Chartiers from—Gen. 6.3
The 3d. Sab. at Chartiers from—Phil. 1.21 and baptized one child—a girl
   In the evening in the College ab cadem
The 4th Sab. at Chartiers from—1 John. 5.4 and baptized one child—a girl
The 5th Sab. at Chartiers from—Luk. 12.32 and baptized one child—a boy

The 1st Sab. of May at Chartiers from—1 Tim. 1.15—baptized two children
—one boy
The 2d. Sab. at Chartiers from—Lev. 26.21
The 3d. Sab. at Chartiers from—2 Cor. 61.2
The 4th Sab. at Chartiers from—Act. 16.30, 31 & Heb. 11.6 and baptized one child—a boy

The 1st Sab. of June at Chartiers from—John 15.9
  Thursday, being ye fast before ye Sacrament—at Chartiers Joh. 6.67, baptized one child, a girl
The 2d. Sab. at Chartiers from—Song. 1.2 and administered the Sacrament of the Supper being assisted
by Mr. Brown, who preached on Sat., Sab. evening & Monday.
The 3d. Sab. at Chartiers from—Josh. 24.22 & Jsal. 11.6.12
The 4th Sab. assisted Mr. Ralstone to administer the Sacrament of ye Supper at Pigeon Creek, preached on Sat. & Sab. evening and baptized one adult, a man and three children—two boys

The 1st Sab. of July at Chartiers from—Gal. 3.10
  Mr. McIntosh preached in the forenoon
The 2d. Sab. at Chartiers from—Isa. 45.19 & Psal. 119.57
The 3d. Sab. at Chartiers from—2 Cor. 4.3
The 4th Sab. at Chartiers from—2 Cor. 4.4 and baptized one child, a boy
The 5th Sab. of Chartiers from—Prov. 13.20 & Isa. 8.13

The 1st Sab. of August at Chartiers from—Prov. 8.17
The 2d. Sab. at Chartiers from—Prov. 8.17 and baptized two children—one boy
  Thursday at Chartiers from—Gal. 3.13
The 3d. Sab. at Chartiers from—Prov. 11.18 and baptized one child—a boy
The 4th Sab. at Chartiers from—Rom. 7.9-12 & Jer. 8.20
  Thursday—at Widow Hannah's from—Psal. 89.16

The 1st Sab. of Sept. at Pigeon Creek from Joh. 9.35 & John 1.29 and baptized three children—two boys
The 2d. Sab. at Chartiers from—Matt. 13.30 and baptized three children—one boy
The 3d. Sab. at Chartiers from—Luk. 11.21,22
  Thursday being the fast before ye Sacrament—Jer. 4.3,4
The 4th Sab. at Chartiers from Job. 23.3 and administered ye Sacrament being assisted by Mr. Allen who preached on Sat. Sab. even. & Monday
The 5th Sab. heard Messrs. Mercer & Andrews at Chartiers

The 1st Sab. of Oct. at Pittsburgh
The 2d. Sab. at Chartiers from John 3.18 & John 10.27
The 3d. Sab. assisted Mr. Allen to administer the Sacrament of the Supper at Racoon
The 4th Sab. at Chartiers from—Psal. 97.12 & Phil. 1.23

The 1st Sab. of Nov. at Chartiers John 6.37 & John 15.5 and baptized two children—one boy
The 2d. Sab. heard Mr. Moore at Chartiers and preached in the evening in the College—Zech. 3.2
  Wednesday, being a fast appointed by Synod—Psal. 5. 18,19
The 3d. Sab. at Chartiers from 2 Thes. 3.1
The 4th Sab. at Chartiers from Hos. 4.17

The 1st Sab. of December at Chartiers from—Matt. 16.26
  Spent the week in going thro the congregation in company with Mr. Brown, and baptized five children—two boys.

The 2d. Sab. of December at Chartiers from Matt. 16.26
   In the evening at Benjamin Williams from Rev. 3.20
The 3d. Sab. at Chartiers from Matt. 16.26
The 4th Sab. heard Mr. Smith at Chartiers
   In the evening I preached at the College from—Luk. 14.17
The 5th Sab. at Chartiers from Matt. 16.26

1822

The 1st Sab. of Jan. assisted Mr. Brown to administer the Sacrament in Washington and preached on Tuesday, Wednesday, Saturday, Sab. and Monday
The 2d. Sab. at Chartiers from—Matt. 22.5
   In the evening at the College from—Luk. 8.18 and baptized one child—a boy
The 3d. Sab. at Chartiers from—Micah 2.7 and baptized one child—a girl.
The 4th Sab. at Chartiers from Micah 2.7

The 1st Sab. of Feb. at Chartiers from—John 10.27,28
   In the evening at the College from Act. 16.30,31 and baptized one child—a boy
The 2d. Sab. at Chartiers from—Song. 2.16 and administered the Sacrament being assisted by Mr. Brown
The 3d. Sab. heard Mr. Smith at Chartiers
The 4th Sab. at Chartiers from—Psal. 29.11

The 1st Sab. of March heard Mr. Smith at Chartiers
The 2d. Sab. at Chartiers from Psal. 29.11
The 3d. Sab. heard Mr. Smith at Chartiers
   In the evening preached in the College from—Heb. 4.9
The 4th Sab. at Chartiers from—Psal. 78. 6,7 and baptized one child—a girl.
   In the evening in the College from John 9.4
The 5th Sab. heard Mr. Smith at Chartiers
   In ye evening preached in the College from—Joh. 14.6

The 1st Sab. of April at Chartiers from—Psal. 23.1
   Mr. Smith preached in the afternoon
The 2d. Sab. at Chartiers from—Matt. 15.13 & Joh. 5.6
The 3d. Sab. at Chartiers from—Gal. 4.5 and baptized one child—a girl. In the evening in the College from—- Pet. 4.18
   April ye 27th 1822 William McMillan was born
The 4th Sab. at Chartiers from—Rom. 7.4 & Eph. 1.11

The 1st Sab. of May at Chartiers from—Psal. 51.7
   Mr. Coulter preached in the forenoon
The 2d. Sab. at Chartiers from—Gal. 6.7
   Mr. Leslie preached in the afternoon
The 3d. Sab. assisted Mr. W. McMillan to administer the Sacrament of ye Supper at Miller's run, and preached on Saturday, Sab. evening and monday.
The 4th Sab. at Chartiers from—Psal. 18.2 & Luk. 13.5 and baptized one child—a girl

The 1st Sab. of June at Chartiers from—2 Cor. 4.6 & Hos. 7.9
 Thursday being ye fast before the Sacrament from Matt. 5.23,24 and baptized two children—one boy
 Mr. Smith preached in the afternoon
The 2d. Sab. preached at Chartiers from—Rev. 22.17 and administered ye Sacrament of the Supper being assisted by Mr. Wm. McMillan and Mr. Smith
The 3d. Sab. at Chartiers from—Isa. 44.5
 Mr. Smith preached in the afternoon
The 4th Sab. at Chartiers from—James. 2.18
 Mr. Smith preached in the afternoon
 Monday, preached at Benjamin Williams John 1.29
The 5th Sab. at Chartiers from—Rom. 6. 12,13 and baptized three children, two boys
 Mr. Smith preached in the afternoon

The 1st Sab. of July at Chartiers from—Jer. 13.16 and baptized one child—a girl
The 2d. Sab. at Chartiers from—Song. 8.5
The 3d. Sab. at Chartiers from—Hos. 3. 10,12
The 4th Sab. at Chartiers from—Rev. 21.4
 Mr. Smith preached in the afternoon

The 1st Sab. of August at Chartiers from Psal. 71.16
 Mr. Coulter preached in the afternoon
The 2d. Sab. at Chartiers from—Isa. 66.2 & Song. 3.11
The 3d. Sab. at Chartiers from—Song. 3.11 and baptized one child—a girl
 Mr. Smith preached in the afternoon
The 4th Sab. of August—at Chartiers from Tit. 2.11,12 & Dan. 5.27

The 1st Sab. of September at Chartiers from—Rom. 8.1
 Thursday, being the fast before the Sacrament, at Ch. Matt.10.22,23
 Mr. Gibson preached in the forenoon
The 2d. Sab. at Chartiers from—Song. 5.16 and administered the Sacrament of the Supper being assisted by Mr. Jeffries who preached on Sat. Sab. evening and Monday
The 3d Sab. assisted Mr. Jeffries to administer ye Sacrament at Bethany, & preached on Sat. Sab. evening and Monday
The 4th Sab. at Chartiers from—Song. 5.16 & Gen. 4.4,5
The 5th Sab. at Chartiers from—2 Cor. 5.10
 Mr. Cook preached in the forenoon.

The 1st Sab. of October at Chartiers from—Song. 2.3
 Mr. Brecken preached in the forenoon.
The 2d. Sab. at Chartiers from—Heb. 11.6 & Song. 2.3
The 3d. Sab. at Chartiers from—Psal. 73.26
The 4th Sab. at Chartiers from—Eph. 2.1

The 1st Sab. of November at Chartiers from—Prov. 3.17 and baptized one child—a girl
The 2d. Sab. heard Mr. Smith at Chartiers
 In the evening preached at the College from—Isa. 57.21 and baptized one child, a girl

The 3d. Sab. at Chartiers from—Prov. 3.17
The 4th Sab. at Chartiers from—Isa. 45.24
   In the evening at the College from the same and baptized two children, one boy

The 1st Sab. of December at Chartiers from—Luk. 13.7
The 2d. Sab. heard Mr. Brown at Chartiers
   In the evening at the College from—Prov. 10.24
The 3d. Sab. at Chartiers from—Luk. 16.31
The 4th Sab. at Chartiers from—Luk. 16.31
   In the evening in the College from Joh. 3.3
The 5th Sab. at Chartiers from—Luk. 16.31

1823

The 1st Sab. of Jan. at Chartiers from—Luk. 16.31
The 2d. Sab. at Chartiers from—Matt. 18. 26,27
The 3d. Sab. at Pittsburgh, and assisted Mr. Herron to administer the Sacrament of the Supper.
The 4th Sab. at Chartiers from—John 16.22

The 1st Sab. of Feb. at Chartiers from—Psal. 116.16
The 2d. Sab. administered the Sacrament of the Supper at Chartiers, being assisted by Mr. Herron
   Tuesday evening at Ben. Williams from—Psal. 63.8
The 3d. Sab. at Chartiers from Psal. 116.16
   Thursday evening at Mr. Logan's from—Psal. 63.8 and baptized one child—a girl
The 4th Sab. at Chartiers from—Rom. 7.22

The 1st Sab. of March at Chartiers from—Rom. 5.12
The 2d. Sab. at Nashanock
   Tuesday at Joseph McClain's
   Thursday at Marmeduke Wilson's
The 3d. Sab. at Hopewell—
   In the evening at Mr. Wood's
The 4th Sab. at Nashanock
The 5th Sab. at Mr. Hughs meeting house
   Tuesday at the same place
   Wednesday at Beaver town

The 1st Sab. of April at Chartiers from—Act. 11.26 Eph. 2.4
The 2d. Sab. at Chartiers from—2 Cor. 13.5
The 3d. Sab. heard Messrs. Brown & Allen
The 4th Sab. at Chartiers from—Psal. 81. 10-13 and baptized two children—one boy

The 1st Sab. of May at Chartiers from Rom. 8.7 and baptized one child—a boy
   Mr. Coe preached in the afternoon
The 2d. Sab. Sab. at Washington—Eph. 2.4&5
The 3d. Sab. at Chertiers from Rom. 8.8 & John 3.36 and baptized one child, a girl

The 4th Sab. heard Mr. Hughs at Chartiers
Thursday, being ye fast before ye Sacrament from—Joh. 5.24. Mr. Brown preached in the afternoon

The 1st Sab. of June at Chartiers from—Matt. 12.20 and administered ye Sacrament of the Supper, being assisted by Mr. Brown. Baptized one child —a girl

The 2d. Sab. at Pigeon Creek, and assisted Mr. Wylie to administer the Sacrament of the Supper.

The 3d. Sab. at Chartiers from—Micah 6.8 and baptized one child—a boy

The 4th Sab. of June at Chartiers from—Matt. 11.29

The 5th Sab. at Chartiers from—Rom. 3.31
Mr. Brown preached in the afternoon

The 1st Sab. of July at Chartiers from—Rom. 3.31 and baptized one child —a boy

The 2d. Sab. at Chartiers from Heb. 4.7 and baptized one child—a boy
Thursday evening attended society at Canonsburgh when two adults were baptized—one man

The 3d. Sab. heard Messrs. McMillan & Brown at Chartiers and baptized two children—one boy

The 4th Sab. at Chartiers from—Heb. 4.7

The 1st Sab. of August at Chartiers from—Heb. 4.7

The 2d. Sab. at Chartiers from—Rom. 8.13

The 3d. Sab. was detained at home by sickness

The 4th Sab. at Chartiers from—Rom. 8.13 and baptized one child—a girl

The 5th Sab. heard Mr. McMillan

The 1st Sab. of Sept. at Chartiers from—Rom. 8.9
Thursday, being ye fast—at Chartiers from—Luk. 14.27 and baptized two adults—one young man

The 2d. Sab. at Chartiers from—Prov. 8.31 and administered ye Sacrament of the Supper, being assisted by Mr. Brown

The 3d. Sab. at Chartiers from—Rom. 8.14 and baptized two children— one boy & one adult—a woman
In the evening preached in the College from Isa. 32.2

The 4th Sab. at Chartiers from Rom. 8.14 and baptized one child—a boy

The lat Sab. of October assisted Mr. Ralstone to administer the Sacrament & preached on Sat. Sab. evening & Monday.

The 2d. Sab. of October at Pittsburgh

The 3d. Sab. at Chartiers from—1 Pet. 1.12

The 4th Sab. at Chartiers from—Psal. 4.3

The 1st Sab. of November heard Mr. Tremble at Chartiers.
Thursday, being a fast appointed by ye general assembly—1 Joh. 1.9

The 2d. Sab. in the College hall from—Micah 7.18 and baptized three children, one girl

The 3d. Sab. at Chartiers from Micah 7.18
In the evening at William Howies from 1 Joh. 3.23

The 4th Sab. at Chartiers from—Joh. 8.56
In the evening in the College from—Hos. 10.12

The 5th Sab. at Chartiers from—Joh. 16.8
In the evening at the College ab Codem

The 1st Sab. of December at the College from—Psal. 40. 6,7,8
The 2d. Sab. at Chartiers from—Psal. 40.6,7,8
The 3d. Sab. at the College from—1 Cor. 1. 30,31
   In the evening at the same place from—Jer. 3.12
The 4th Sab. at Chartiers from—1 Cor. 1. 30, 31

1824

The 1st Sab. of Jan.y at the College from—Joh. 15.2
   In ye evening at the same place from the same
   Mr. Brown at Mr. Logan's on friday preceeding and baptized one child—a boy
The 2d. Sab. heard Mr. Kennedy at Chartiers
The 3d. Sab. at Chartiers from—Joh. 15.2
The 4th Sab. at Chartiers from—Joh. 15.2

The 1st Sab. of Feb. at Chartiers from—Joh. 15.8
   Thursday, being the fast before ye Sacrament heard Mr. Borwn at Chartiers
   Saturday—at Chartiers from—Josh. 23.11 and baptized one adult, a woman.
The 2d. Sab. administered the Sacrament
   Monday at Chartiers from—Col. 2.6
   Tuesday evening at Mr. Logan's from—Joh. 3.3 and baptized one adult—a woman.
The 3d. Sab. at Chartiers from—Joh. 15.14
The 4th Sab. in the College from—Eph. 6.24
   In the evening at the same place from—Psal. 56.9
The 5th Sab. heard Mr. W. McMillan at Chartiers

The 1st Sab. of March at the College from—Joh. 1512
The 2d. Sab. at Chartiers from—1 Joh. 4.18
The 3d. Sab. at the College from—Psal. 63.5
The 4th Sab. at Chartiers from Joh. 10.16

The 1st Sab. of April at Chartiers from 2 Cor. 11.2
   Wednesday preached at Mrs. McDowell's from Joh. 3.3 and baptized one adult, a woman
The 2d. Sab. at Chartiers from—2 Cor. 11.2
   Mr. Brown preached in the afternoon
The 3d. Sab. at Chartiers from—Rom. 5.10
The 4th Sab. heard Messrs. Blair & Brown at Chartiers

The 1st Sab. of May at Chartiers from—Matt. 7. 13,14 and baptized one child—a boy.
The 2d. Sab. at Chartiers from—Prov. 18.10
The 3d. Sab. at Chartiers from—Numb. 21.4
   And baptized two children—one boy
The 4th Sab. at Chartiers from—Numb. 21.4
   And baptized one child—a boy.
The 5th Sab. at Chartiers from Gal. 6.14.& Deut. 33.16
   And baptized one child—a boy.

The 1st Sab. of June at Chartiers from—Hos. 11.7
  Thursday being ye fast heard Messrs. Smith & Brown
  And baptized two adults—one man.
  Saturday heard Mr. Jennings at Chartiers
The 2d. Sab. at Chartiers from—Song. 5.1 and administered the Sacrament of the Supper being assisted by Mr. Brown
The 3d. Sab. at Chartiers from—Gal. 6.7
The 4th Sab. at Chartiers from—Prov. 1.7
  And baptized two children—one boy

The 1st Sab. of July—at Chartiers from—2 Cor. 6.2
The 2d. Sab. at Chartiers from—2 Cor. 6.2
  And baptized one child—a Girl
The 3d. Sab. at Chartiers—from—Psal. 5.3
  In the evening in the College from—Psal. 63.8
The 4th Sab. at Chartiers from—2 Cor. 7.10

The 1st Sab. of August—at Chartiers from—Psal. 5.3 & 1 Pet. 2.11
The 2d. Sab. at Chartiers from 1 Pet. 2.11 & Zeck. 13.1
The 3d. Sab. at Chartiers from—Luk. 14.18
The 4th Sab. at Chartiers from—2 Cor. 5.17
  Mr. Todd from Kentucky preached in ye afternoon.
The 5th Sab. at Chartiers from—Isa. 40.31

The 1st Sab. of September at Chartiers—Phil. 2.1,2 & Matt. 9.13
  Thursday, being ye fast heard Mr. Taylor at Chartiers
  Saturday—preached at Chartiers from—Joh. 19.30
The 2d. Sab. Administered the Sacrament of the Supper
  And preached in the evening from Matt. 9.13
  Mr. Brown preached in the morning & Mr. Jennings on Monday.
The 3d. Sab. at Chartiers from—Psal. 76.11
  and baptized one child—a Girl
The 4th Sab. at Chartiers from—Matt. 11.28

The 1st Sab. of October heard Messrs. Brown & Whitney
The 2d. Sab. at Chartiers from—Eccles. 5.2 & Rom. 10.4
The 3d. Sab. at Chartiers from—Isa. 30.10 & Rom. 6.23
  and baptized one child—a Girl
The 4th Sab. at Pittsburgh from John 10 27,28
The 5th Sab. heard Mr. Smith at Chartiers

The 1st Sab. of November at Chartiers—Prov. 10.4
The 2d. Sab. at Chartiers from—Job. 31.3
The 3d. Sab. heard Mr. Brown at Chartiers and preached in ye evening in ye College
The 4th Sab. at Chartiers from—Gal. 6.15
  In the evening in the College from—Joh. 1.29 and baptized one child—a boy.

The 1st Sab. of December at Chartiers from—Song. 3. 7,8 and baptized one adult—a man.
The 2d. Sab. at Chartiers from Heb. 6.19
The 3d. Sab. at the College from—2 Tim. 3.5
  In the evening at the same place from Joh. 6.64
The 4th Sab. at Chartiers from—Jer. 3.14

1825

The 1st Sab. of Jan.y at Chartiers from—Eph. 5.8
The 2d. Sab. at Chartiers from—1 Joh. 2.1
The 3d. Sab. at Chartiers from—Micah 2.13
The 4th Sab. at Chartiers from—Job. 3,17 and baptized one adult, a young woman
The 5th Sab. in College from—Prov. 14.32
   In the evening at the same place ab codem

The 1st Sab. of Feb. y at Chartiers from—Song. 3.1
   Monday attended the concert for prayer and baptized three adults—young women
   Thursday, being the fast, at Chartiers from—Hos. 6.1
The 2d. Sab. at Chartiers from—Isa. 55.3 and administered the Sacrament of the Supper, being assisted by Mr. Brown who preached Sat.y & Monday
The 3d. Sab. at Chartiers from—Isa. 55.3
The 4th Sab. at Chartiers from—Micah 6.9

The 1st Sab. of March at Chartiers from—Job. 40.4
   In the evening in the College from Matt. 9.12 and baptized one child—a girl
The 2d. Sab. at Chartiers from—Prov. 19.21
The 3d. Sab. at Chartiers from—Psal. 96.8 & Rom. 7.21
The 4th Sab. at Chartiers from—Psal. 50.15

The 1st Sab. of April at Chartiers from—Gal. 2.16
   In the evening in College from—1 Pet. 4.17
The 2d. Sab. at Chartiers from—Prov. 30.12 and baptized one child—a boy
The 3d. Sab. heard Messrs. Moore & McMillan and baptized two children—one boy
The 4th Sab. at Chartiers from—Luk. 13.24

The 1st Sab. of May at Chartiers from—Psl. 14.1 & Rev. 20.12
The 2d. Sab. at Chartiers in ye afternoon from Ezek. 16.6
   Mr. Kuntz preached in the afternoon
The 3d. Sab. at Chartiers in ye afternoon from 1 Thes. 4.3
   Mr. Sned preached in the forenoon
The 4th Sab. at Chartiers from—John. 14.6 and baptized three children—two boys
   Mr. Gobmery preached in the forenoon
The 5th Sab. at Chartiers from—1 Joh. 2.20 & Psal. 132.3 & 5

The 1st Sab. of June at Chartiers from—I Thess. 5.23
The 2d. Sab. at Chartiers from—1 Sam. 16.5 and baptized seven children—three boys.
   Thursday, being ye fast before ye Sacrament at Chartiers—Rom. 6.11
   Saturday at Chartiers from—Gen. 7.23
The 3d. Sab. administered ye Sacrament of ye Supper
   D. D. Brown preached in ye forenoon & Mr. Smith in Ye evening.
   Monday heard Mr. Morrow and baptized one child—a boy
The 4th Sab. at Chartiers from—Rom. 5.1

The 1st Sab. of July—at Chartiers from—Rom. 5.1
The 2d. Sab. at Chartiers from—Rom. 5.1 & Isa. 33.14
The 3d. Sab. at Chartiers from—Phil. 4.13
The 4th Sab. at Chartiers from—Phil. 1.21
The 5th Sab. at Chartiers from—Psal. 89. 30-33
    This day my first great grand child was born

The 1st Sab. of August at Chartiers—Song 5.16 & Col. 1.12
The 2d. Sab. heard Messrs. Reed & Abram Scott at Chartiers.
The 3d. Sab. at Chartiers from—Isa. 40.5
The 4th Sab. at Chartiers from—Joh. 1.9

The 1st Sab. of Sept. at Chartiers from—Luk. 13.23
    Thursday, being ye fast heard Mr. Brown at Chartiers and baptized one adult—a black man
The 2d. Sab. at Chartiers from—1 Cor. 11.26 and administered the Sacrament of ye Supper being assisted by Mr. Brown
The 3d. Sab. at Chartiers from—Rom. 10.3
The 4th Sab. at Chartiers from—Psal. 103.1-4

The 1st Sab. of October at Chartiers from—1 Tim. 4.8
The 2d. Sab. heard Messrs. S. Reed & Brown
The 3d. Sab. at Chartiers from—Joh. 5.40 & Prov. 3.33 and baptized one child—a boy
The 4th Sab. attended the administration of ye Sacrament in Washington during ye sessions of ye Synod, & served one table.
The 5th Sab. at Chartiers from—Joh. 4.24

The 1st Sab. of Nov. at Chartiers from—Psal. 89.15
The 2d. Sab. at Chartiers from—Gen. 24.49
The 3d. Sab. at Chartiers from—2 Cor. 2.16
The 4th Sab. heard Mr. Campbell and preached myself at Chartiers from—Song. 2.4

The 1st Sab. of Dec. at Chartiers from—Job. 4.9
The 2d. Sab. at Chartiers from—Matt. 22.42
The 3d. Sab. at Chartiers from—Luk. 15.21
The 4th Sab. at Chartiers from Matt. 11. 29,30
    In the evening in the college

1826

The 1st Sab. of Jan.y at Chartiers from—Rev. 5. 9,10
    Thursday, being a fast appointed by Synod. Jer. 3.22
The 2d. Sab. at Chartiers from—Psal. 111.10
The 3d. Sab. at Chartiers from—Rev. 19.7
The 4th Sab. at Chartiers from—1 Cor. 1. 23-24
The 5th Sab. at Chartiers from—1 Cor. 1. 23-24

The 1st Sab. of Feb.y at Chartiers from—1 Cor. 1. 23-24
    In the evening at John Rankin's from—Joh. 8.24
    Thursday, being the fast, heard Mr. Brown at Chartiers
The 2d. Sab. administered ye Sacrament of ye Supper being assisted by Mr. Brown who preached on Sat. & Sab. morning.
    Monday preached at Chartiers from—Psal. 116.14

The 3d. Sab. at Chartiers from—1 Cor. 1.23,24
The 4th Sab. at Chartiers from—1 Cor. 1.23,24 and baptized one child—a boy
The 1st Sab. of March, heard Mr. Spilman at Chartiers
    Thursday Samuel McMillan died at half past three P. M.
The 2d. Sab. heard Mr. Brown at Chartiers baptized one child—a girl
The 3d. Sab. at Chartiers from—1 Cor. 1. 23,24
The 4th Sab. at Chartiers from—1 Gal. 4.5
The 1st Sab. of April at Chartiers from—1 John 3.9
The 2d. Sab. at Chartiers from—Isa. 26.20
The 3d. Sab. at Chartiers from—2 Cor. 4.6
The 4th Sab. at Chartiers from—Psal. 46.10 & Isa. 3.11
The 5th Sab. at Chartiers from—1 Cor. 6.19,20 & Heb. 4.9 and baptized one adult and three children all families
The 1st Sab. of May at Chartiers from—Prov. 28.1 & Psal. 107.8
The 2d. Sab. at Chartiers from—Psal. 90.12 & Psal. 97.11,12
The 3d. Sab. at Charriers from—John 9.4 & Luk. 13.7
The 4th Sab. heard Messrs. Mercer & Brown at Chartiers and baptized three children—one boy
The 1st Sab. of June at Chartiers from—Psal. 68.18
    Thursday being the fast before the Sacrament from—John 11.5,6, Saturday heard Mr. Brown
The 2d. Sab. at Chartiers from—John 6.55 and administered the Sacrament of the Supper
    Monday heard Mr. Campbell at Chartiers and baptized two children—one boy
The 3d. Sab. at Chartiers from—John 6.28,29 and baptized one child—a boy
The 4th Sab. at Chartiers from—Act. 6.51
The 1st Sab. of July at Chartiers from—Eph. 5.1,2
The 2d. Sab. heard Messrs. Leslie & Brown
The 3d. Sab. at Chartiers from—1 Tim. 4.7
The 4th Sab. at Chartiers from—Rev. 21.7 and baptized one child—a girl
The 5th Sab. at Chartiers from—1 John 5.10
The 1st Sab. of August at Chartiers from—1 John 5.10 and baptized four children—girls
The 2d. Sab. of August 1826 at Chartiers from—Phil 2.12 Psalm 17.1.5
The 3d. Sab. at Chartiers from—Isa. 5.25 and baptized one adult—a woman
    Tuesday morning ye 22nd day Wm. McMillan died
The 5th Sab. at Chartiers from—Prov. 8.17
The 1st Sab. of September at Chartiers from—1 John 3.2
    Thursday ye 7th between 12 & 1 A. M. Wm. McMillan was born
The 2d. Sab. at Chartiers from—Psal 65.3 and baptized one child—a girl
The 3d. Sab. at Chartiers from—Prov. 8.17
    Thursday, being ye fast—at Chartiers from—Prov. 8.17 and baptized three adults, one male, & eight children—4 males
    Saturday—at Chartiers from—Isa. 53.2
The 4th Sab. at Chartiers from—Prov. 4.23 and administered ye Sacrament of ye Supper

The 1st Sab. of October at Chartiers from—Mark 16.7 and baptized two children—one male
The 2d. Sab. at Chartiers from—Matt. 7.22,23 & Phil. 2.13
The 3d. Sab. at Chartiers from—Psal. 71.16
The 4th Sab. at Pittsburgh from—Psal. 71.16
The 5th Sab. at Chartiers from—Joh. 3.8

The 1st Sab. of November at Chartiers from—Rev. 14.13
The 2d. Sab. at Chartiers from—Psal. 38.9 and baptized one child—a boy
The 3d. Sab. at Chartiers from—Isa. 61.1
The 4th Sab. at Chartiers from 2 Cor. 5.4

The 1st Sab. of December at Chartiers from—Isa. 9.13
The 2d. Sab. at Chartiers from—Psal. 85.10
The 3d. Sab. heard Mr. Richard Brown at Chartiers
The 4th Sab. at Chartiers from—Prov. 11.31
The 5th Sab. at Chartiers from—Luk. 10.42

1827

Thursday at my own house from—Psal. 63.8 and baptized two children—one boy
The 1st Sab. of January at Chartiers from—Luk. 15.17-19
The 2d. Sab. at Chartiers from—Psal. 125.1,2
The 3d. Sab. of Jan.y at Chartiers from—Gen. 5.24
The 4th Sab. at Chartiers from—Jer. 3.2

The 1st Sab. of Feb.ry at Chartiers from—1 Cor. 5.8
  Thursday, being the fast, at Chartiers from—Isa. 53. 10,11
The 2d. Sab. at Chartiers from—Song. 5.1 and administered ye Sacrament of the Supper being assisted by Mr. Brown
The 3d. Sab. at Chartiers from—Exod. 19.8
The 4th Sab. at Chartiers from—Psal. 132.3-5
  In the evening at the College from—Rom. 8.30

The 1st Sab. of March at Chartiers from—Amos 3.3
The 2d. Sab. at Chartiers from—Isa. 45.24
The 3d. Sab. at Chartiers from—Matt. 25.3
The 4th Sab. at Chartiers from—Isa 45.24 and baptized one child—a girl

The 1st Sab. of April at Chartiers from—Psal. 9.10 and baptized one child—a girl
The 2d. Sab. at Chartiers from—Ezek. 33.7-9
The 3d. Sab. at Chartiers from—Matt. 24.44
The 4th Sab. at Chartiers from—Rom. 8.6
  Friday June ye 27th about half after 10 o'clock A.M. William McMillian died
The 5th Sab. at Chartiers from—Psal. 27.4

The 1st Sab. of May heard Messrs. McMillan & Brown
The 2d. Sab. at Chartiers from—Psal. 66.18 & Job. 1.21
  ordained three elders & baptized one child—a girl
The 3d. Sab. at Chartiers from—Psal. 126.5 and baptized one child—a girl
The 4th Sab. at Chartiers from Psal. 126.5

The 1st Sab. of June at Chartiers from—Matt. 12. 43-45
The 2d. Sab. at Chartiers from John 13.34,35
   Thursday, being ye fast—at Chartiers from—Isa 66.4 and baptized one adult, a man, & one child, a girl
   Saturday heard Mr. Smith at Chartiers
The 3d. Sab. at Chartiers in ye evening from—Matt. 26.21,22 and administered ye Sacrament of ye Supper being assisted by Mr. Brown who preached on Sab. morning & Monday
The 4th Sab. at Chartiers from—Song 2.14 and baptized one child—a boy
The 1st Sab. of July at Chartiers from—Song 2.14
The 2d. Sab. at Chartiers from—Song 8.5
The 3d. Sab. at Chartiers from—Song 5.16
The 4th Sab. at Chartiers from—Zech. 13.7 & Luk. 10.21
The 5th Sab. at Chartiers from—Rom. 12.1
The 1st Sab. of August, at Chartiers from—1 Thess. 5.17
The 2d. Sab. at Chartiers from—Psal. 51.2,3
The 3d. Sab. at Chartiers from—Prov. 3.33
The 4th Sab. heard Messrs. Fulerton & Espey
The 1st Sab. of September at Chartiers from—1 Pet. 2.7
The 2d. Sab. heard Mr. Brown at Chartiers
   Thursday, being the fast, at Chartiers from—Psal 26.6
The 3d. Sab. at Chartiers from Luk. 22.19 and administered ye Sacrament of the Supper, being assisted by Mr. Brown
The 4th Sab. at Chartiers from—1 Pet. 2.7
The 5th Sab. at Chartiers from—Phil 3.8 and baptized one child—a boy
The 1st Sab. of October at Chartiers from—Psal 103. 19. Eph. 2.4,5 and baptized one child—a girl
The 2d. Sab. at Chartiers from—Col. 2.19
The 3d. Sab. at Pittsburgh—2d. Church
The 4th Sab. heard Mr. Reddel at Chartiers
The 1st Sab. of November at Chartiers from—2 Cor. 5.17
   Wednesday evening at John Hugh's from—Isa. 57. 21 and baptized three children—one male
The 2d. Sab. heard Mr. T. Moore at Chartiers and baptized three children—one boy
The 3d. Sab. at Chartiers from—2 Joh. 15.7
The 4th Sab. at Chartiers from—2 Thess. 1.7,8
The 1st Sab. of December at Chartiers from—2 Thess. 1.7,8
The 2d. Sab. at Chartiers from—Rom. 10.21
The 3d. Sab. at Chartiers from—Rom. 10.21
The 4th Sab. at Chartiers from—Isa. 58.1
The 5th Sab. at Chartiers from—1 Cor. 2.14
   In the evening in the College from—Amos 3.2

1828

The 1st Sab. of Jan.ry at Chartiers from—Rom. 14,17
The 2d. Sab. at Chartiers from—Rom. 14.17
The 3d. Sab. at Chartiers from—Hos. 14.2
The 4th Sab. at Chartiers from—Jer. 13. 15,16

The 1st Sab. of Feb.y at Chartiers from—Jer. 13.16
  Thursday, being ye fast—heard Mr. Brown and baptized an adult, a woman
  Saturday at Chartiers from—Hag. 1.7
The 2d. Sab. heard Mr. Brown & administered the Sacrament
  Monday at Chartiers from—Col. 2.6
The 3d. Sab. at Chartiers from—1 Cor. 16.22
The 4th Sab. at Chartiers from—1 Cor. 16.22

The 1st Sab. of March at Chartiers from—Gal 5.17
  In the evening at the College from—Joh. 1.29
The 2d. Sab. at Chartiers from—Eccl. 2.11
  Thursday ye 13th of March about 8 of'Clock P.M. Robert McMillan was born
The 3d. Sab. at Chartiers from—Luk. 18.22
The 4th Sab. at Chartiers from—Rev. 3.1
  Thursday being a fast, at Chartiers—Psal 51.18 and baptized one child —a boy
The 5th Sab. at Chartiers from—Matt. 20.6

The 1st & 2d. Sabs. of April at Pittsburgh
The 3d. at Bethany and administered the Sacrament
The 4th Sab. heard Messrs. Carrel & Brown at Chartiers and baptized one child—a girl, my great grand daughter

The 1st Sab. of May at Chartiers from—Col. 2.19
The 2d. Sab. heard Messrs. McMillan & Brown
The 3d. Sab. at Chartiers from—Joh. 16.8 and heard Mr. Sickles in the afternoon
The 4th Sab. at Chartiers from—Jude, 12 and heard Mr. Vincent in ye afternoon

The 1st Sab. of June at Chartiers from—Rom. 6.22 and baptized one child—a boy
  Thursday being ye fast, at Chartiers from—Isa. 1.18
  heard Mr. Samuel Jennings in the afternoon
The 2d. Sab. at Chartiers from—1 Cor. 11.26 and administered ye Sacrament of the Supper being assisted by Mr. Brown
The 3d. Sab. at Chartiers from—Act. 13.26
The 4th Sab. heard ,essrs. Allen & Riddle at Chartiers and baptized two children—boys
The 5th Sab. at Chartiers from—Gen. 6.13,14

The 1st Sab. of July at Chartiers from—1 Joh. 4.10 and baptized two children—girls
The 2d. Sab. at Chartiers from—Amos 5.4
The 3d. Sab. at Chartiers from—Amos 5.4
The 4th Sab. at Chartiers from Rom. 8.26 and baptized one adult—Sophia Gwin

The 1st Sab. of August, at Chartiers from—Heb. 9.12
The 2d. Sab. at Chartiers from—Heb. 9.12
The 3d. Sab. at Chartiers from—Gen. 6.3

The 4th Sab. at Chartiers from Gen. 6.3
  Tuesday at Paul Matthew's from—Prov. 10.24
The 5th Sab. at Chartiers from—Phil. 1.21

The 1st Sab. of September at Chartiers from—1 Joh. 5.4 and baptized one child—a girl
  Thursday, being the fast at Chartiers—Luk 12.32 and baptized one adult—a man
  Saturday at Chartiers from—Luk. 12.32 and baptized two children—both girls
The 2d. Sab. at Chartiers from Luk. 12.32 and administered the Sacrament, being assisted by Mr. Smith who preached Sab. morning & Monday
The 3d. Sab. at Chartiers from 2 Cor. 6.2
The 4th Sab. at Chartiers from 2 Cor. 6.2

The 1st Sab. of October heard Mr. Brown
The 2d. Sab. at Chartiers from—Lev. 26.21 and baptized one child—a girl
  Saturday at Pittsburgh 1st Church
The 3d. Sab. attended ye Sacrament at Pittsburgh and served one table
The 4th Sab. at Chartiers from—Acts. 16. 30,31

The 1st Sab. of November at Chartiers from—Acts. 16. 30,31
The 2d. Sab. at Chartiers from—Heb. 11.6
The 3d. Sab. at Chartiers from—Joh. 15.9
The 4th Sab. at Chartiers from—Joh. 15.9
The 5th Sab. at Chartiers from—Joh. 6.67
  In the evening at the College from—Joh. 1.29

The 1st Sab. of December at Chartiers from—Isa. 21. 11,12
The 2d. Sab. at Chartiers from—Gal. 3.10
The 3d. Sab. at Chartiers from—Isa. 45.19
  In the evening at William Horner's from—Joh. 1.29 and baptized one child—a boy
The 4th Sab. at Chartiers from—Psal. 119.57

1829

The 1st Sab. of Jan. at Chartiers from—2 Cor. 4.3
The 2d. Sab. at Chartiers from—2 Cor 4.3
  Thursday preached at ye meeting house from—Isa. 57.1
  In the evening at Mrs. Neil's from—Isa. 48.22
The 3d. Sab. at Chartiers from—2 Cor. 4.4
  Thursday, being a fast appointed assembly—Prov. 23. 29,30 and baptized one adult, a woman
The 4th Sab. at Chartiers from—Psal. 81,11-13

The 1st Sab. of February at Chartiers from—Joh. 12.21
  Thursday, being the fast—at Chartiers from—Psal. 81. 11-13
The 2d. Sab. at Chartiers from—Song 1.2 and administered ye Sacrament of the Supper, being assisted by Dr. Brown who preached on Saturday & Monday
The 3d. Sab. at Chartiers from—Josh. 24.22
The 4th Sab. at Chartiers from—Prov. 13.20
  In the evening in the College from—Isa. 57.21

The 1st Sab. of March at Chartiers from—Isa. 8.13
The 2d. Sab. at Chartiers from—Gal. 3.13
The 3d. Sab. at Chartiers from—Jer. 8.20
The 4th Sab. at Chartiers from—Prov. 11.18
The 5th Sab. at Chartiers from—Prov. 11.18 and baptized one child—a boy

The 1st Sab. of April at Chartiers from—Prov. 8.4,5, Rom. 7.9
The 2d. Sab. at Chartiers from—Matt. 13.30
The 3d. Sab. at Chartiers from—Matt. 13.30
The 4th Sab. heard Messrs. Brown & Hawkins and baptized one adult—a woman

The 1st Sab. of May at Chartiers from—Joh. 4.3,4
   Mr. Ray preached in the afternoon
The 2d. Sab. at Chartiers from—Luk. 11. 21,22
The 3d. Sab. at Chartiers from—John 10.27,28
The 4th Sab. at Chartiers from—Joh. 10.27. Joh. 3.18 and baptized one child—a girl
The 5th Sab. at Chartiers from Psal 97.12 & Joh. 6.37

The 1st Sab. of June heard Dr. Black at Chartiers
   Thursday, being ye fast, heard Messrs. Smith & Campbell
The 2d. Sab. of June administered the Sacrament being assisted by Messrs. Allen & Smith
The 3d. Sab. at Chartiers from—1 Tim. 1.15
The 4th Sab. at Chartiers from—Phil 1.23 and baptized one child—a boy

The 1st Sab. of July heard Messrs. Williamson & Brown
The 2d. Sab. at Chartiers from—Hos. 4.17
The 3d. Sab. at Chartiers from—2 Thes. 3.1 and baptized one child—a boy
The 4th Sab. at Chartiers from—Joh. 15.5

The 1st Sab. of August at Chartiers from—Zech. 3.2 and baptized one child—a boy
The 2d. Sab. at Chartiers from—Zech. 3.2
The 3d. Sab. at Chartiers from—Matt. 22.5 & Luk. 8.18
The 4th Sab. heard Messrs. Campfield and Brown.
The 5th Sab. at Chartiers from—Matt. 16.26

The 1st Sab. of September at Chartiers from—Matt. 16.26 and baptized one child—a girl
The 2d. Sab. heard Messrs. Chestnut & Smith
   Thursday, being ye fast heard Messrs. Smith & Brown
   Saturday at Chartiers from—Job. 23.3
The 3d. Sab. at Chartiers from Matt. 16.26 and administered ye Sacrament, being assisted by Mr. Brown who preached on Sab. morning and Monday
The 4th Sab. at Chartiers from—Micah 2.7 and baptized two children—boys

The 1st Sab. of October at Chartiers from—Micah 2.7
The 2d. Sab. heard mr. Brown at Chartiers
The 3d. Sab. at Pittsburgh second Church
The 4th Sab. at Chartiers from—Song. 2.16

The 1st Sab. of November at Chartiers from—Psal. 29.11
The 2d. Sab. heard Mr. Aldrige
The 3d. Sab. heard Mr. Bracken
The 4th Sab. heard Mr. Coon
The 5th Sab. heard Mr. Rea

The 1st Sab. of December at Chartiers from—Psal. 29.11
    Saturday evening Samuel McMillan was born
The 2d. Sab. at Chartiers from—Joh. 9.4
The 3d. Sab. heard Mr. Coon at Chartiers
The 4th Sab. at Chartiers from—Prov. 10.24

1830

The 1st Sab. of January at Chartiers from—Song. 7.10
The 2d. Sab. at Chartiers from—Song. 7.10
The 3d. Sab. at Chartiers from—Heb. 4.9
The 4th Sab. heard Mr. Coon
The 5th Sab. at Chartiers from—Joh. 14.6

The 1st Sab. of February at Chartiers from—Psal. 23.1
    Thursday being the fast, at Chartiers from—Matt. 25.13
The 2d. Sab. at Chartiers from—Rom. 5.20 and administered ye Sacrament of the Supper being assisted by Mr. Brown who preached Sat. & mon.
The 3d. Sab. at Chartiers from—Joh. 5.6 and baptized one child—a boy
The 4th Sab. at Chartiers from—1 Joh. 3.1

The 1st Sab. of March heard Messrs. W. Hugh's & Coon
The 2d. Sab. at Chartiers from—Rom. 7.4
The 3d. Sab. heard Messrs. Moore & Coon
The 4th Sab. at Chartiers from—Psal 51.7 and baptised one child—a boy

The 1st Sab. of April at Chartiers from—Gal. 6.7 and baptized one child—a boy
The 2d. Sab. at Chartiers from—Luk. 13.5
The 3d. Sab. at Chartiers from—Psal. 51.10
The 4th Sab. at Chartiers from—Eph. 1.11 and baptized one child—a boy

The 1st Sab. of May at Chartiers from—Psal 18.2
    Tuesday May ye 4th Catherine McMillan died
The 2d. Sab. of May 1830 at Chartiers from—Eccles. 12.1
The 3d. Sab. at Chartiers from 2 Cor. 4.6
The 4th Sab. at Chartiers from—Hos. 7.9
The 5th Sab. at Chartiers from—Rom. 6.12,12 Jer. 13.16

The 1st Sab. of June at Chartiers from—Rev. 22.17
    Thursday, being the fast at Chartiers—Jam. 2.18
The 2d. Sab. at Chartiers from Cant. 3.18 and administered the Sacrament of the Supper being assisted by Mr. Ralston who preached Sat., Sab. evening and Monday
The 3d. Sab. at Chartiers from—Song. 3.10 and baptized two children—one boy
The 4th Sab. at Chartiers from—Song. 3.10

The 1st Sab. of July at Chartiers from—Isa. 44.5
    Mr. Nevins preached in the forenoon

The 2d. Sab. at Chartiers from—Psal. 78. 6,7 & Song. 8.5
The 3d. Sab. at Chartiers from Prov. 18.24
 Mr. Eliott preached in the forenoon
The 4th Sab. at Chartiers from Song. 8.5

The 1st Sab. of August, heard Mr. Raney at Chartiers.
The 2d. Sab. at Chartiers from—Song 8.5
The 3d. Sab. at Chartiers from—Isa. 3.10,11
The 4th Sab. at Chartiers from—Isa. 66.2 & Rev. 21.4
The 5th Sab. at Chartiers from—Psal. 71.16
 Friday evening at James Nixon's from—John 1.11 and baptized one child, a boy; and one adult, a girl.

The 1st Sab. of September at Chartiers from—Rom. 8.1
The 2d. Sab. at Chartiers from—Dan. 5.27 & Eph. 2.1
The 3d. Sab. at Chartiers from—Matt. 10.32,33
 Thursday being the fast at Chartiers from—Gen. 4.4,5
The 4th Sab. at Chartiers from Psal 73.26 and administered the Sacrament of the Suppper, being assisted by Mr. McCluskey and Mr. Coon

The 1st Sab. of October heard Messrs. Coon & McAboy
The 2d. & third Sabs. heard Mr. Logan at Chartiers
The 4th Sab. in ye 2d. church in Pittsburgh
The 5th Sab. at Chartiers from—Psal 116.12

The 1st Sab. of November heard Mr. Logan at Chartiers
 Thursday being ye fast appointed by ye G. assem; from Exod. 20. 8-11
The 2d. Sab. heard Mr. Logan at Chartiers
 Thursday at Chartiers from—Song 5.16
The 3d. Sab. heard Mr. Logan at Chartiers
The 4th Sab. at Chartiers from 2 Cor. 5.10

The 1st Sab. of December heard a Union Minister
 Tuesday at Chartiers from—Heb. 11.6
The 2d. Sab. at Chartiers from—Isa. 45.24
 Thursday at Samuel Caldwell's from—Joh. 3.3 and baptized two children—one boy
The 3d. Sab. at Chartiers from—Isa. 45.24
The 4th Sab. at Chartiers from—Song. 2.3

1831

The 1st Sab. of Jan. heard Mr. Wilson at Chartiers
 Thursday at Pittsburgh 2d. Church from—Joh. 1.29
The 2d. Sab. at Chartiers from—Phil. 2.12
The 3d. Sab. was detained at home by a great fall of snow
The 4th Sab. heard Mr. Magaffin
The 5th Sab. at Chartiers from Psal. 103.3

The 1st Sab. of February at Chartiers from—Rom. 7.22
The 2d. Sab. at Chartiers from Luk. 13.7
 Thursday at the same place from—Luk. 13.7
The 3d. Sab. administered the Sacrament being assisted by Mr. Allen who preached Saturday, Sab. morning and Monday
The 4th Sab. at Chartiers from—Prov. 3.17

The 1st Sab. of March at Chartiers from—Song. 5.16
The 2d. Sab. heard McAboy at Chartiers
The 3d. Sab. heard McAboy at Chartiers
The 4th Sab. at Chartiers from—Luk. 16.31

The 1st Sab. of April at Chartiers from—Luk 16.31
  Heard Mr. Leak in ye forenoon
Friday, being ye fast, at Chartiers from—Jer. 3.12
      (Manuscript omitted the rest of the month)

The 1st Sab. of May assisted Mr. Leake at Chartiers
The 2d. Sab. at Chartiers from—Psal. 5.3
The 3d. Sab. at Chartiers from 1 Cor. 1.30
The 4th Sab. at Racoon, assisted Mr. Allen to administer ye Sacrament preached on friday, Saturday, Sab. morning and Monday.

The 1st Sab. of June assisted Mr. Jefferies to administer ye Sacrament at Bethany.
Preached on friday, Saturday, Sab. evening and Monday.
The 2d. Sab. at Bethany in the forenoon.
This week attended P.b.y. and returned to Canonsburgh on Thursday.
Mr. Craig Ritchie died on ye 13th of June 1833
The 3d. Sab. at Chartiers from—2 Cor. 5.8
The 4th Sab. at Chartiers from—1 Cor. 1.31
The 5th Sab. at Chartiers from—Song. 2.4

The 1st Sab. of July heard Messrs. Leake & Wade
The 2d. Sab. at Chartiers from—1 Pet. 1.12
The 3d. Sab. at Chartiers from 1 Pet. 1.12
The 4th Sab. heard Mr. Wallace at Chartiers

The 1st Sab. of August, at Chartiers from—Matt. 11.28
The 2d. Sab. heard Messrs. Pinney & Swift
The 3d. & 4th Sabs. at West Alexandera and assisted Mr. McClusky to administer ye Sacrament

The 1st Sab. of September assisted to administer the Sacrament at Chartiers, and preached on friday the fast day from Joh. 15.2
The 2d. Sab. assisted Mr. Allen to administer the Sacrament at Racoon, and preached on friday, saturday, Sab. morning and monday.
The 3d. Sab. assisted McCurdy to administer the Sacrament at ye Cross Roads and preached on friday, Sab. morning and Monday at Frankford Wednesday.
The 4th Sab. assisted Mr. Scott to administer ye Sacrament at Mill Creek, and preached on friday, Saturday, Sab. morning and evening and Monday
The 5th Sab. at Chartiers from—Joh. 15.2

   *{The Journal ends here and the following notes are added
              in an unknown hand}*
During the 5 following sabbaths, he preached
  5 times at Miller Run
  5 times at Bethany
  2 times at Pittsburgh
  10 times at Wheeling, total 22
    {October, 1833—22 sermons. He died November 16, 1833.}

APPENDIX B
EXPENSE ACCOUNT
Dr. McMillan—Account of expences from 1820 to 1833

	Moneys paid......................
to—Peggy has received cash since 1825	$113.26
to—John has received—do, since do	58.87
to—Polly has received—do—since, do	37.44
to—patty Weaver has received—do—since, do,	7.50
	Total...... 217.07

Peggy & her family have received $2144.75

Expences for the year 1821

Jan. ye	1st. To Thomas Watson for shoing a horse	.25
	15th. To a pound of tobacco	.18
Feb. ye	5th. To shaving soap	.12½
	12th. To John Watson	6.
	13th. To cleaning & repairing watch	.87½
	16th. To Dido for snuff	.25
	22d. To John Watson	10.
March	10th. To John Watson	10.
	16th. To Ritchie for tobaco & paper	.48
	For vaccination	5.
	20th. Gave to Dido for Horner	.25
	22d. paid for sundries at Hamilton's vendue	7.57
	23d. Gave to John Watson	8.
April ye	2d. for advertising the meeting of Trustees	1.
	To Cabbage for brick	5.
	For a barrel of salt	4.50
	5th. Gave to John Watson	9.
	6th. for repairing clock	2.
	9th. Gave to John Watson	10.
	20th. Gave to the commissioner's fund	.50
	23d. Gave to John McMillan	6.
May ye	1st. Gave to Samuel McMillan for cutting horse	.50
	1st. for the Presbyterian Magazine	2.50
	7th. To Dr. Leatherman for Dido	3.
	12th. To John Watson	10.
	15th. To a pound of tobacco	.12½
	29th. for tobacco, powder and lead	.56
June ye	6th. Gave to W. Couch, pump maker	1.
	13th. Gave to John Watson	17.
	13th. Gave to Ritchie for overalls	7.50
	18th. Gave to Sarah McMillan for making overalls	1.10
	Gave to Dido for a gown	1.62½

	20th.	Gave to Isabella McMillan to buy a gown	1.60
		Gave to Baxter for driving horse shoes	.12½
	30th.	Gave to Jane Harper for interest	3.50
July ye	3d.	To Dr. Leatherman for a vomet for Samuel	.20
		To Ritchie for tobaco	.12½
		for taxes to Alexander Scott	6.54
	24th.	for soap & skein of silk for Dido	.20
August ye	6th.	To a quarter of snuff for Dido	.12½
	9th.	for advertising the meeting of Trustees	1.
		to Ritchie for a pound of tobacco for John	.12½
	21st.	to Ritchie for snuf & ribbon for Dido	.50
		to Ritchie for a pound of tobaco	.12½
	24th.	to John Watson	8.
		to one half pound of snuff for Dido	.25
Septembr. ye	13th.	To Natl. Coulter for repairing waggon	.37½
	19th.	To Munroe for a book for Saml. Carmichael	.06¼
	24th.	To the education society	1.
October ye	8th.	for stage fare to & from Pittsburgh	3.
	13th.	for making a pair of shoes	.50
	25th.	for cloth for a coat	10.62½
		for trimmings, tobacco, Rosin, &c|	2.00½
		for snuf for Dido	.12½
	27th.	a pair for shoes for Dido	1.50
		mending shoes for myself	.32
Novembr. ye	2d.	for snuf for Dido	.25
	3d.	to Adam Rice for making cloaths	4.
	10th.	to Adam Rice for making breeches	.50
		To Do. for overalls for Samuel	.50
		To Do. for a coat for John Watson	1.75
		To Do. for a coat for John McMillan	1.75
	19th.	To a Bible for John McMillan Jun.	1.25
	27th.	To two pounds of wool carded for Dido	.75
Decembr. ye	4th.	To Salt, coffee & tobaco	5.
	10th.	Gave to John McMillan Jun.	.50
	21st.	Gave to Dido five yards of blanketing	3.12½
		To Andrew Munroe for Register	5.
	24th.	To Ritchie for two almanacks	.25
	24th.	To cloth for an apron for Dido	.50
		To Wm. Horner for Dido	.12½
	29th.	To Baxter for shoing horse	.37½

Expences for the year 1822

Jan. ye	7th.	For snuff for Dido	.25
		for coffee & snuff for Jane McMillan	.37½
	14th.	for two of the everlasting task	.12½
Feb. ye	8th.	for two yards of flannel to Dido	1.
	16th.	To Samuel McMillan	.50
	20th.	To Samuel McMillan for repairing axes	1.75
		For snuf for Dido	.25
		For an hancerchief for Dido	3.

March ye	4th.	To a spelling book for Hannah	.25
		To Dr. Leatherman for Dido	.25
	18th.	To Ritchie for a pound of tobacco	.12½
		To Ritchie for a pound of coffee	.37½
April ye	2d.	Paid for road taxes	2.50
	15th.	for snuff for Dido	.25
	17th.	for transcribing minutes of P. b. y.	.50
		for a snuff box for Dido	.25
	27th.	for snuff for Dido	.25
May ye	8th.	for the Pittsburgh Recorder	2.
	22d.	for Glass for school-house	.25
	27th.	to Ritchie for a pound of Tobaco	.12½
June ye	1st.	Gave to Isabella McMillan	.50
	3d.	Gave to Peggy Neil	5.
	10th.	Gave to Jane Harper for interest	32.50
	12th.	To Watson for shoing my horse	.25
		To Ritchie for shaving soap	.25
	28th.	for snuff for Dido	.25
July ye	19th.	Gave to McFadden for John Neil	20.
August ye	6th.	Give to James Kerr for taxes	12.75
		to Ritchie for two pounds of lead	.25
		to collection for missionary purposes	4.
	ye 7th.	to ticken for Dido 9 yards	3.37½
	15th.	For Presbyterian Magazine	2.50
		For repairing a watch	1.
	21st.	For snuff &c. for Dido	1.
		To a dress Isabella McMillan	2.25
Septembr.		To two pounds of feathers for Dido	.80
		To a pair of shoes for Dido	1.50
		To collection	.25
Septembr.	26th.	for the Baltimore register	5.
October ye	4th.	for collection and other expenses at synod	.62½
		To W. R. Patterson for no fiction	1.
		To Reed for repairing a watch	.75
		For snuff for Dido	.50
		For a barrel of salt for John	4.
		For a barrel of salt for Samuel	3.50
		Gave to Dido to buy a cap	.50
	ye 8th.	To Baxter for shoing a horse	.62½
	9th.	Gave to Dido two pounds of carded wool	.62½
	22d.	Gave to Ritchie for a pound of tobacco	.12½
	23d.	Gave to Margaret Neil to buy a bonnet	3.
	29th.	To Mr. Ritchie for Coffee and Pepper	.50
Novembr. ye	5th.	Gave to my son William McMillan	2.
	8th.	Gave to McFadden for John Neil	28.50
		Gave to Ritchie for an handkercheif	1.
		Gave to Dido 4 yards of flannel	3.

Decembr. ye	2d.	To James Smith for bridle bits	.25
		To Ritchie for tobaco	.12½
	8th.	To Ritchie for salts and almanack	.37½
	24th.	To Munro for a testament for Hannah	.37½
			56.37½

In account of money expended in the year 1823

Jan. ye	6th.	To Mr. Ritchie for a Gimblet	.06½
	9th.	To Mr. Howey for removing shoes on my horse	.25
	11th.	To Dido for snuff	.25
	16th.	To Mr. Andrews for Recorder	2.
	21st.	To stage fare to and from Pittsburgh	3.
Feb. ye	4th.	Gave to Dido for Sally	.25
	10th.	for collection	.25
	20th.	Gave to John McMillan to buy a cutting knife	2.
March ye	3d.	Gave to William McMillan for carriage	15.
		To Baxter for repairing carriage	.25
	4th.	To Dido for snuff	.12½
		Expenses of a journey to & from Mercer County	6.18
April ye	23d.	paid to Veech for William McMillan for carriage	37.25
		paid for shoes and stockins for Dido	1.87½
		paid to Ritchie for a frock for Catherine	1.
	25th.	Gave to Dido to buy things in Washington	3.
	25th.	Gave to different collections	.75
		Gave to Christian Advocate	2.50
May ye	12th.	for recording a deed	1.
		for snuff for Dido	.25
		for postage to Mr. Munro	14.
		for paper to Ritchie	.34
	21st.	To Ritchie for a jacket pattern	5.37½
	26th.	To Baxter for shoing horse	.37½
June ye	2d.	To James Kerr for taxes	11.56
	3d.	To James Reed for cleaning clocks	3.
	14th.	To James White for repairing carriage	1.
	17th.	To Ritchie for Moses Monmouth	24.
		To Ritchie for tobaco	.12½
	25th.	for snuff for Dido	.12½
July ye	9th.	To Ritchie for a gown for Sally	2.37½
		To Ritchie for a shead	.25
		To Ritchie for a comb for Hannah	.06½
	31	To Ritchie for tobacco & pipes	.25
August ye	5th.	Gave to John McMillan	1.
	9th.	1823. Gave to Seth for Sl. McMillan	3.
		Gave to Dido one pound of wool	.33
		Gave to Dido 2 yards & half of linen	.62½
August ye	19th.	1823 Gave to Dido 5 pounds of feathers	1.56½
	26th.	To Baxter for driving shoes	.12½
		To Dido for seeing Eliphant	.12½

		To Ritchie for fish	.25
		For seeing Eliphant	.12½
		For entering up two Judgments	1.
Septembr. ye	7th.	To Dido three yards of linen	1.12½
	9th.	Gave to Jane Harper—interest	9.
		To Ritchie for tobaco	.12½
	16th.	To snuff for Dido	.12½
	24th.	For the weekly register	5.
Octobr. ye	13th.	for stage fare & in attending synod	2.
		To Munroe for a bible for Hannah	1.
		To Ritchie for silk & twist	.25
	23d.	For a copy of a deed	1.
		To pay of Clerk of Presbytery	.25
		For snuff for Dido	.12½
Novembr. ye	7th.	Gave to Dido to buy things in Canonsburgh	4.
	11th.	Gave to John Clark for making cloaths	2.
		Gave to Ritchie for glass	.50
Decembr. ye	6th.	Gave to James Kerr for John & Samuel's tax	.96
	8th.	Gave to Ritchie for two barrels of Salt	2.
	22d.	Gave to Ritchie for shoes for Dido	1.50
		Gave to Ritchie for almanack, tobacco & glass	.43½
	31st.	Gave to Ritchie for a tin bucket	.75
		Gave to Horner for 100 feet of pine boards	.75

An account of Money expended in the year 1824

January ye	7th.	Gave to Mr. Harbison for a bushel of salt	1.12½
		Gave to Ritchie for shaving soap	.12½
		Sent to Elizabeth Neil	6.
	12th.	To Dido for a pair of shoes	1.75
	15th.	To Dido for five yards of flanel 62½	3.12½
	19th.	To Ritchie for Dido for tea	.25
		To provide venitian blinds for College	1.
	27th.	To Baxter for shoeing my horse	.75
		To snuff for Dido	.25
Feby. ye	12th.	To Dr. Leatherman for Margaret Neil	4.50
		To Ritchie for tobacco	.12½
	13th.	To Widow Campbell for coal	2.
	20th.	To Speers for dressing cloth for Dido	1.
March ye	7th.	For a three quarter Augur	.30
	23d.	To Munroe for Scott's life	1.25
		To Ritchie for tobacco	.12½
April ye	5th.	To the Missionary fund	4.
		To James Hixton for repairing carriage	.75
		To James White for Dido	.12½
		To snuff for Dido	.25
	7th.	To Sally Howey for making a dress for Dido	.25
	15th.	To Munroe for Mr. McMillan's sermons	1.
		To Ritchie for salt & shoes	6.55
		To Widow Cannon	2.
	24th.	To contributions	.81
	26th.	To Thomas Emery for weaving for Dido	.66

	28th.	For snuff for Dido	.25
		For fish for Isabella	.25
		For a bonnet & comb for Dido	7.60
		For the weekly recorder	2.
		For the Christian Advocate	2.50
May ye	5th.	For repairing my watch	.75
	7th.	Paid to John Kerr for taxes	13.61
	26th.	To Baxter for shoing horse	.18
June	5th.	To Mr. Lowry for a hat	6.
	10th.	For a net cap for Dido	.63
		For a bed tick for J. Watson	4.50
June ye	18th.	To Jane Harper interest	9.
		To Ritchie for tobaco	.12½
	30th.	To Hoge for an hancercheif	.07½
		For snuff for Dido	.25
		To Ritchie for shaving soap	.25
July ye	5th.	To Samuel McMillan for shingle nails	4.
	7th.	For repairing a clock for John	1.50
	19th.	To Ritchie for Mrs. Canon	10.
	20th.	To Margaret Neil	5.
August ye	2nd.	To John Grooves for Scholling Catherine	1.50
	4th.	To Craig Ritchie for tobaco	.12½
	20th.	For snuff for Dido & cotton	.43½
		To John McMillan to buy chocolate	.50
	25th.	To Baxter for driving a shoe	.06
	31st.	To John McMillan interest on money lent to Ven.	24.
Sep. ye	8th.	Paid for a watch key	.18½
	9th.	For the Baltimore Register	5.
	30th.	For various collections	.75
		To Dido for tea, etc.	.82
		To Ritchie for Mrs. Canon	10.
Octobr. ye	8th.	Sent to John Watson	12
	19th.	Gave to Dido in money, linnen & wool	1.87½
		Expences in attending Synod	3.75
Novembr. ye	16th.	Gave to Dido for quilting	3.25
	22d.	Gave to Ritchie for tobaco	.10
Decembr. ye	1st.	Gave to Sally Howie for making overhalls	.50
	3d.	Gave for snuff for Dido	.12½
		Gave for pepper for Ibby	.12½
		Gave to Potts for shoes for Dido	1.62½
	23d.	Gave to Dido three yards of flannel	1.31½
	30th.	Gave to poor fund	1.
		Gave to Sally Howie for making bonnet for Dido	.25
		for Miller's lecture	.25

An account of money expended in the year 1825

Jan. ye	17th.	Gave to Coulter for making a slay	5.
		To Dido for snuff	.12½
	22d.	For two alminacks	.25
		To John Grooves for Scholling Catherine	1.50

March ye	12th.	Paid county & poor taxes	12.72
	19th.	Gave to McPeak for Samuel	.25
Apr.	1st.	Gave to John Watson for sole leather	3.07½
		To Dido for snuff	.25
	3d.	Gave to the Missionary fund	4.
	6th.	Gave to Margaret Neil	5.
	18th.	Gave to the commissioners fund	.50
	22d.	Gave to Ritchie for Dido	4.
	28th.	Gave to Ritchie for broadcloth, etc.	25.37
		Gave to Ritchie for Catherine & Jane Weaver	8.50
		Gave to Ritchie for a fine comb	.10
		Gave to Revd. I. D. Baird for a book	.50
		For the Christian Advocate	2.50
May ye	17th.	Gave to Dido to get snuff	.25
June ye	4th.	Gave to Sally Howie for making clothes	2.
		Gave to Sally Howie for Dido	.25
	6th.	Gave to Dr. Leatherman for Dido	.50
		Gave to Dr. Leatherman for Peggy Neil	1.25
		Gave to Ritchie for Casemon	8.12½
	23.	Gave to Dido for snuff	.25
July ye	12th.	Gave to Ritchie for tobaco	.12
	23.	Gave to Peter Ricci	.50
	25.	Gave to James Smith for a girth	.25
August	6th.	Gave to Dido	1.
	16th.	Gave to Dido	1.50
	20th.	Gave to Sally Howey for Dido	.50
		Gave to Sally Howey for making trousers for John	.25
	23d.	Gave to Ritchie for clothes for John	19.50
	30th.	Gave to John McMillan Gloves	2.
Septembr.	7th.	Gave to Ritchie for Dido	4.25
		Gave to Ritchie for John McMillan	1.
		Gave to Munroe for Niles Register	5.
	15th.	Gave to Jane Harper interest	19.
		For snuff for Dido	.25
	28th.	Gave to Munroe for postage	6.50
		Gave to Munroe for ye Pittsburgh Recorder	2.
		Gave to James Reed for a watch key	.25
Octobr. ye	24th.	For stage fare to & from synod	1.
		For Smith's sermons	.50
		For collections	.75
		For a pair of shoes	1.87½
		For snuff for Dido	.25
		For repairing watches	1.37½
		To Mr. Ritchie for bridge	1.
		To Ritchie for two yards of flannel	.50
Novembr. ye	14th.	To Ritchie for Dido	.50
		To Ritchie for tobacco	.34
	18th.	To John McMillan	5.
	20th.	To Samuel McMillan to get whiskey	.50
	30th.	To Potts for shoes for Dido	1.75

Decembr. ye	1st.	For two almanacks	25
	23rd.	For snuff for Dido	.25
		Gave to Dido one pound of wool carded	.37½
	28th.	For subscription for poor fund	1.
		For paying stated Clerk	.25

An account of Money expensed in ye year 1826

Jan. ye	21st.	Gave to Sally Howey for Dido	.50
		Gave to Dido four yards & an half of flannell	2.01
	23d.	Gave to Dido in money	.50
Feb. ye	15.	Gave to James Reed for repairing watch	1.50
		for cleaning a clock for Peggy	1.50
		for recording a Deed	1.94
		for snuff for Dido	.25
		for stage fare to & from Washington	1.
		To Ritchie for tobaco & soap	.25
	23d.	To Ritchie for tea for Dido	.31
March ye	15th.	To Mr. Martin for cleaning clocks	2.75
April ye	8th.	To Nathaniel Coulter for making slay	5.
		Gave to Margaret Neil	10.
		a collection for the commissioners	.50
	17th.	Gave to Dido for past services	1.
	26th.	Gave to John Watson for waggon tire	8.
		To Wm. Donaldson for making wheels	5.25
		To Joshua Weaver for Coffin	6.
		for the advocate	2.50
		for the recorder	2.
		To Harbison	.50
		Gave to Dido for past services	5.
		To Ritchie for a specticle case	.25
		To Ritchie for a tin bucket	.62
May ye	9th.	To Ritchie for writing paper	.25
	23d.	To Mrs. Ritchie for meat for Dido	.50
		To Ritchie for tobaco	.12½
		To Ritchie for Hannah & Catharine McMillan	3.25
June ye	2d.	To McBurney for taxes	13.9
	12th.	Gave to Dido for past services	5.
		To collection	.25
	28th.	To Mr. Ritchie for a pound of salts	.25
July ye	1st.	Gave to John McMillan to buy whiskey	9.
	ye 12th.	Gave to George Weaver for reaping	.75
	ye 29th.	To Joshua Weaver for Coffin	1.25
August ye	3d.	To Andrew Munroe—Bucks Dictionary	2.
		To Mr. Ritchie for tobaco	.12½
August	1st.	To Sally Howie for making a frock	.25
		To Polly McMillan at different times	3.75
	14.	Gave to Margaret Neil	4.
Septembr. ye	5.	Gave to Ritchie for cloth & fish	4.
		To Jane Harper for interest	9.
	11th.	To Dido for past services	3.

	24th.	To Sarah Howie for making a jacket	.50
		To Ritchie for tobaco	.25
		To famile education society	1.
		To Neil's Register	5.
		To Munroe for Postage	3.
Octobr. ye	16th.	To stage fare to Pittsburgh	1.50
		To various collections	.50
		For Ralstone's book	1.00
Novembr. ye	17th.	Gave to Sally Howie for teaching	4.25
		for a quart of tar	.12½
		To Ritchie for tobaco & soap	.37½
		To Ritchie for 24½ pounds of nails	2.20
Decembr.		To Dido for past services	5.

Expenses for the year 1827

January ye	10th.	Gave to get coals for Galbraith	.50
		To Ritchie for tobaco	.12½
		To Dido for past services	5.
Feby. ye	5th.	To Solomon Neil	3.62½
	6th.	Gave to John McMillan	14.
		Gave to Margaret Neil	5.
	28th.	To Ritchie for tobaco & a small bucket	.50
March ye	13th.	Gave to Polly McMillan	1.
	16th.	Gave to James Roney for road tax	5.06
	24th.	Gave to Ritchie for tobaco	.12½
		Gave to Miss Sally Miller for Dido	.50
April ye	2d.	Gave for Missionary purposes	4.
		Gave to James Campbell for Coals	2.40
	7th.	Gave to McElroy for Margaret Neil	3.
		Gave to Margaret Neil	3.
		Gave to James Compbell for coals	2.
		Gave to Andrew Munroe for binding books	.75
	9th.	Gave to James Miller for the Greeks	1.
	10th.	Gave to Coulter for roofing the house	25.25
	13th.	Gave to an Indian	.50
	22d.	Gave to commissioners fund	.75
	26th.	Gave for a pair of wool shears	.87½
		for fish	.25
May ye	10th.	Gave to Ritchie for tobaco	.12½
	13th.	Gave to Munroe for binding books	.75
	29th.	Gave to McBurney for county tax	6.
	30th.	Gave to Horner for gallon of whiskey	.25
June ye	8th.	Gave to Munroe for Mr. Andrews	2.
		Gave to Polly McMillan	1.06
		Gave for fish	.25
	19th.	Gave to McBurney for taxes	7.15½
	27th.	Gave to Margaret Neil	2.50
July ye	2d.	Gave to Munroe for Advocate	2.50
		Gave to Munroe for postage	3.30
		Gave to Ritchie for tobaco & a tin	.18½
		Gave to Ritchie for shoes for Sarah	.50

	19th.	Gave to John to pay reapers	2.50
	20th.	Gave to Sab. School	.25
			106.47½
August ye	17th.	Gave to Ritchie for tobaco & soap	.25
	20th.	Gave to John Rankin for salt	2.00
Septembr. ye	5th.	Gave to Munroe for a spelling book	.18
		For Neils Register	5.
		Gave to Ritchie for tobacco	.12½
	17th.	To a collection	.25
	26.	To Mr. Ralston for Mrs. Guin	1.
		To the famile education society	.25
		To Dido for past services—Ritchie	1.18¾
Octobr. ye	17th.	To stage fare to Pittsburgh	1.50
		To two small books	1.
		for collection	.25
		To Ritchie for glass, putty & tobacco	.40
		Lent to Samuel Caldwell	11.
		To Ann Howie for making a jacket etc.	.75
		To Ritchie for thread, silk & twist	.22
Decembr. ye 10th.		To a pedlar for a black handkerchief etc.	1.
			22.15
			106.47
			128.62½

Expenses for the year 1828

Jany. ye	1st.	Gave to John Watson for repairing of wagon	11.
		To Wm. Donaldson for Do.	5.
		Subscription for the market house	2.
		To Mr. Ritchie for tobaco and box for wagon	.31
	24th.	Gave to Margaret Neil	5.
	31st.	Gave to Ritchie for candles	.50
March ye	5th.	Gave to John Parks for stoves	3.
		Gave to Mr. Ritchie for a shovel & tobaco	.62½
	ye 11th.	Gave to Munroe for getting a book bound	.50
		Gave to Margaret Neil	10.
	ye 14.	Gave to John McElroy	10.
	17th.	Gave to Mrs. Emery of interest	9.
	24th.	To Horner for a gallon of whiskey	.25
	29th.	To N. Coulter for Margaret Neil	17.
	31st.	To Martin for cleaning clocks	2.75
April ye	2d.	To stage fare to & from Pittsburgh	3.
		To Mr. Andrews for Spectator	2.75
		To a dress for Rebecca	2.87½
		To Books	1.75
		To Ritchie for tobacco	.18
	26th.	Gave to Margaret Neil	40.62½
	29th.	Gave to James Speers for dressing cloth	5.13½

May		Gave to the bible society	.50
	29th.	Gave to Jane Harper for interest	9.
June ye	9th.	Gave to James White for Carriage	36.
		Gave for repairing watch	.75
	17th.	for taxes	11.43
		for linnen for a shirt	3.48
		for postage and advocate	5.35
		for a dress for Polly	2.44
		for tobaco & shoes for Cathy	2.4
		for shoes for Jane & tobaco	.50
		for shaving soap	.25
		for a straw hat for John	.25
July ye	30th.	To Ritchie for tobaco	.12½
August ye	2d.	To Ebenezer Howie for making cloaths	2.25
			207.61½
Septembr. ye	1st.	For Niles register	5.
		for a spelling book for Catharine	.12½
		for weaving fine linnen	2.25
		for collections	.50
	ye 27th.	To Thomas Connelly a poor man	1.
Octobr. ye	9th.	To McElroy for Peggy Neil	12.52
		To McElroy for cloath	3.
		To a pedlar for three yards of cotton	.62½
		To stage fare to & from Pittsburgh	2.50
		for Buck's theological dictionary	1.50
		for church in the house etc.	1.
		Gave to John Watson	2.
Novembr.	17.	Gave to McElroy for John McM.	8.50
Decembr. ye	4th.	Gave to Dr. Leatherman for Peggy Neil	1.50
		Gave to Ritchie for an handcerchief	.75
		Gave to Ritchie for John McMillan	2.75
		Gave for mending specticles	.12½
		Gave to John to buy tallow	1.
		Gave to Mrs. Emery for interest	9.
		Gave to Miss Weaver for making shirts	1.
	22d.	Gave for Sunday School	1.
	24.	Gave to two beggars	1.
	31st.	Gave for the Pennsylvanian	2
		To Ritchie for tobaco	12½
			60.77
			207.61½
			268.38½

Expenses for the year 1829

January ye	14th.	Gave to J & L. Weaver for making shirts	1
	19th.	Gave to Peggy Neil	.50
		Gave to John Urie for Mr. Greeg	2.
	28th.	Gave to Ritchie for a bucket of cheese	.81
Feb. ye	9th.	Gave to the collection	.31
	18th.	Gave to J. Speers for Peggy Neil	1.6
March ye	19th.	Gave to J. Speers for John McMillan	5.
	27th.	Gave to Ritchie for testament & trimmings	1.6
		Gave to E. Howie for making a coat	1.75
		Gave to S. Miller for M. McMillan	.50
April ye	3rd.	Gave to Martin for repairing clock	.50
	6th.	Gave to Missionary Fund	4.30
	17th.	Gave to John Kerr for taxes	10.00
		collection for Commissioners' Fund	.50
	28th.	Gave to Dehaven for Christian Herald	2.
		Gave to Munroe for advocate	2.50
		Gave to Ritchie—tobaco	.25
May ye	6th.	Gave to Martha Emery	20.
	21st.	Gave to Peggy Neil	5.
June ye	15th.	Gave to collection	.37½
August ye	5th.	Gave to John McMillan Junr.	.31
		Gave to Peggy Neil	1.
		Gave to Ritchie for Peggy Neil	8.6
		Gave to Ritchie for paper, tobaco & cheese	.75
		Gave to Munroe for postage	4.
		Gave to Colonization society	5.
		Gave to Munroe for binding ye advocate	.50
	26th.	Gave to Polly Weaver	.50
Septembr. ye	8.	Gave to famile education society	1.
	19th.	Gave to assembly's missonary society	5.
	21th.	Gave to Ritchie for Coffee	1.
		Gave for collection	.35
Octobr. ye	14th.	Gave to Ritchie for a cap for Peggy	2.
		Stage fare to and from Pittsburgh	2.50
		Gave for collection in Synod	.25
		Gave to Ritchie for glass and tobaco	.25
	28th.	Gave to Dido in full for past services	8.32
		for the missionary reporter & register	.50
Nov. ye	2d.	Gave to James Miller for E. McClelland	1.
		Gave to Ritchie for cheese	1.18
Novembr.	31.	Gave to Mr. Cloud for S. school library	1.
		Gave to Ritchie for Rebecca McMillan	2.82

Expences for the year 1830

January ye	8th.	Gave to Ritchie for candles, salts etc.	1.37½
		for a dozen of *Butcher's* review	.50
	ye 13th.	Gave to Jane & Catharine Weaver	1.
	ye 28th.	to an hancerchief for Sarah	.87½
		to a primer for Catharine	.06

March ye	11th.	Gave to Peggy Neil	7.
	12th.	To Ritchie for tobaco	.25
	23d.	To Dehaven for ye christian herald	2.
		To A. Short for ye pennsylvanian	2
		To Ritchie for a coffee pot	.50
April ye	20th.	expences going and coming from P. b.y.	.92
		for Green's Exposition	1.
	28th.	to Munroe for the advocate	2.50
		to Ritchie for a dress for Catharine	.50
		to Griffith for a pair of shoes	2.25
		to Ritchie for a bonnet for Sarah	.82
		to Ritchie for tobaco	.12½
May ye	4th.1830	to Martha Emery for interest	7.80
	10th.	to Jane & Catharine Weaver for shirts	1.
	20th.	to Jane Harper—interest	9.
		to a pedlar for pilgrim's progress	.50
June ye	15th.	to Munroe for postage	4.
		to Ritchie for shaving soap	.25
		to John Kerr for poor tax	1.68
	22d.	for a bible for John	1.75
		for a bible for Catharine	.62½
		To Ritchie for tobacco	.12½
		To Mr. Coon for preaching	10.
		To Mary Weaver	10.
July ye	2d.	To McClelland for county & poor tax	13.13
August ye	10th.	Gave to Polly Weaver for making shirts	1.
	13th.	Gave for repairing my watch	.87½
		Gave to Munroe for binding Browns sermons	.50
		To Ritchie for tobaco	.12½
Sep.	2d.	Gave to Mary Weaver	10.
		Gave to ye colonization society	7.50
Septembr. ye	28th.	Gave to Munroe for Neils register	5.
Octobr. ye	2d.	Gave to switser	.50
		Gave Peggy Neil	.56
		to purchase books for Sunday school	.50
		Gave to Polly Weaver	10.
	ye 12th.	Paid for Crocks	.31
	17th.	Gave for collection	.50
	19th.	for stage hire to Pittsburgh	1.25
	26th.	for binding a book	.50
		for a collection in Synod	.25
Novem. ye	24th.	for a cheese	2.50
		Gave for collection	.50

1831

Jan. ye	3d.	to stage fare to & from Pittsburgh	2.50
		To Ritchie for candles & tobaco	.62½
		To collection for sunday schools	5.
March ye	10th.	To Ritchie for paper & tobaco	.50
March ye	19th.	To Ritchie for curry comb	.25
April ye	13th.	To Martha Emery for interest	7.80

Aprl ye	19th.	To stage fare to & from P. b. y.	1.25
		for ye christian herald	2.
		To Ritchie for coffee & tobaco	1.12½
May ye	5th.	To Mr. Perry for county tax	14.70
		To Jas. Reed for repairing watch	1.75
May ye	12th.	for an hatt for little John Mc.	.75
		To Munroe for ye holy war	.50
		To Munroe for postage	4.40
June ye	1st.	To James Reed for cleaning clocks	2.25
		To Watson for Moses Sim	5.
		To Ritchie for Tobacco, cocalote, & water pot	1.12½
		To Ritchie for borrowed money	5.
July ye	28.	To John Walace for S. school library	.50
		To Dr. Leatherman a subscription	10.
August ye	8.	Gave to Munroe for ye christian advocate	2.50
		To Ritchie for an hankercheif & book	1.25
August ye	17.	Gave to Mary Weaver	5.
		Gave to Ritchie for tobaco etc.	.43
Septembr. ye	1st.	Gave to beggar	.50
	11th.	Gave to a collection	.25
Octobr.	8th.	Gave to Jane Weaver for sewing	1.56
		Gave to Ritchie for tobaco	.12½
Novembr. ye	15.	Gave for a cheese	1.12½
		Gave for ye constitution of ye Union	.31
Decembr. ye	7.	Gave to Catharine Weaver	.50
		for tobacco, comb & Almanac	.62½

Expences for the year 1832

January ye	12th.	To Thomas Clemens for Sanduskey	.50
Feby. ye	17th.	To James Hardie for making shoes	.50
		To Smith for sunday school	.50
March ye	20th.	To Matthew Sims for taxes	11.23
	29th.	To Crouch for poor tax	2.94
		To Ritchie for tobaco	.12½
		To Jane Harper for interest	3.
April ye	2d.	To John McMillan interest	5.70
		To Collection for Commissioner fund	.50
June ye	20th.	To Ritchie for tobaco etc.	.18
July ye	8th.	To ye collonization society	1.
Sep. ye	3d.	To the education society	10.
		To the Missionary society	5.
		To collection	.25
Sep. ye	26.	for an hat	6.
Octobr. ye	9.	Gave to McCullouch for tobaco	.12½
	25.	Gave to Munroe for postage	2.90
		for stage fare from Washington	.50
		for collection at Synod	.25
		To Mr. Reed for watch & specticles	.62

Novemb. ye	28th.	To McCullouch for an almanac	.10
		for Coffee and tobacco	1.25
		To Mr. Baird for Herald	1.
		For a dress for Sarah	1.25
Decem. ye	22d.	To Jane Weaver for making clothes	1.50

1833

Feb. ye	4th.	For collection sacramental	.25
	27th.	Gave to John McMillan	40.
		Gave to Catharine Weaver	6.
March ye	29th.	Gave for tobacco, a tin etc.	.25
April ye	17th.	To W. Horner for road tax	10.
May ye	17th.	Gave to Johnstone for a shirt pattern	1.
		for tobacco	.12½
August ye	8th.	Gave to Johnstone for tobacco	.12½
Septembr.	25th.	Gave to Johnstone for cloth etc.	27.50
		for tobacco	.12½
Septembr.	25th.	Gave to Jane Harper for interest	5.50
		to ye foreign missionary society	5.

APPENDIX C

(From "The Pittsburgh Christian Herald and Western Missionary Reporter," December 14, 1833)

THE LATE DR. MCMILLAN

It is with feelings of great regard for his memory, that we record the death of the venerable patriarch of the West, the Rev. John McMillan, D. D. By many of our readers, he is known as the pioneer, who opened the way for the gospel in Western Pennsylvania, and for many years past his still powerful voice thundered forth the truth in the same region. We have the pleasure of presenting a letter from this excellent father in our church, which was written in answer to a request from the President of the College of New Jersey, that Dr. M'Millan, as one of the oldest surviving alumni, would communicate some of his reminiscences. Since the lamented decease of the writer, no reason exists for withholding it from the public.

LETTER FROM THE LATE REV. DR. M'MILLAN TO PRESIDENT CARNAHAN

CHARTIERS, March 26th 1832

Rev. and Dear Sir:—I received your friendly letter, and will endeavor to comply with your request. I was first sent to a grammar-school kept by the Rev. John Blair, where I remained until he was removed to Princeton, to superintend the college there. I was then sent to Pequea, to a grammer-school kept by the Rev. Robert Smith. While there, the Lord poured out his Spirit upon the students, and I believe there were but few who were not brought under serious concern about their immortal souls; some of whom became blessings in their day, and were eminently useful in the Church of Christ, but they are all now gone to rest. It was here that I received my first religious impressions, though, as long as I can remember, I had at times some checks of conscience, and some alarms about the state of my soul, but these seasons were of short continuance. Like the morning cloud and the early dew, they quickly passed away. I now saw that I was a lost, undone sinner, exposed to the wrath of a justly offended God, and could do nothing for my own relief. My convictions were not attended with much horror, though I felt that I deserved hell, and that in all probability it must be my portion; yet I could not feel that distress which I ought to feel, and which I thought I must feel, before I could expect to obtain relief. I feel also much legality mingled with all the duties which I attempted to perform. In this situation I continued until I went to [Princeton] college in the spring of 1770. I had not been long there until a revival of religion took place among the students, and I believe at one time, there were not more than two or three who were not under serious impressions. On a day which had been set apart by a number of the students to be observed as a day of fasting and prayer, while the others were at dinner, I retired to my study, and while trying to pray, I got some discoveries of divine things which I had never had before. I saw that the divine law was not only holy, just, and spiritual, but that it also was good, and that conformity to it would make me happy. I felt no disposition to quarrel with the law, but with myself, because I was not conformed to it. I felt that it was now easy to submit to the gospel plan of salvation, and enjoyed a calm and serenity of mind to which I had hitherto been a stranger. And this was followed by a delight in contemplating the Divine glory, in all His works, and in meditating on the Divine perfections. I thought that I could see God in every thing around me.

I continued at college until the fall of 1772, when I returned to Pequea, and began the study of Theology under the direction of the Rev. Robert Smith, D.D. I had great difficulties in my own mind about undertaking the gospel ministry. I at last came to this determination, to leave the matter wholly with God; if he opened the way, I would go on; if he shut it, I would be satisfied; and I think if ever I knew what it was to have no will of my own about any matter, it was about this. I passed through my trials in the Presbytery of Newcastle and was licensed by them to preach the gospel, October 26th, 1774, at East Nottingham. The first winter I spent in itinerating among the vacant congregations of Newcastle and Donnegal Presbyterias. In the summer of '75 I took a tour through the settlements of Virginia, between the North and South Mountains. In July I crossed the mountains, between Staunton and the head of Tygart's Valley; preached in the various settlements through which I passed until I came to Chartiers; preached on the 4th Sabbath of August, and on the Tuesday following, at Pigeon creek. I then turned my course eastward, and preached in the different settlements as I passed along. In the winter I again visited Augusta county in Virginia, crossed the mountains in January, and preached at Pigeon Creek and Chartiers, until the latter end of March, 1776, when I returned home, and at a meeting of presbytery on the 23rd of April, accepted a call from the united congregations of Chartiers and Pigeon Creek, and was dismissed to join the Presbytery of Donnegal, and on the 19th of June, was ordained at Chambersburg.

It being the time of the revolutionary war, and the Indians being very troublesome on the frontiers, I was prevented from removing my family to my congregations until November, 1778. I however visited them as often as I could, ordained elders, baptized their children, and took as much care of them as circumstances would permit. When I came to this country, the cabin in which I was to live was raised, but there was no roof on it, nor any chimney or floor. The people, however, were very kind, assisted me in preparing my house, and on the 16th of December I moved into it. But we had neither bedstead, nor tables, nor stool, nor chair, nor bucket. All these things we had to leave behind us, as there was no wagon-road at that time over the mountains; we could bring nothing with us but what was carried on pack-horses. We placed two boxes on each other, which served us for a table, and two kegs answered for seats; and having committed ourselves to God in family worship, we spread a bed on the floor and slept soundly till morning. The next day, a neighbor coming to my assistance, we made a table and stool, and in a little time had every thing comfortable about us. Sometimes indeed we had no bread for weeks together, but we had plenty of pumpkins and potatoes, and all the necessaries of life; as for luxuries, we were not much concerned about them. We enjoyed health, the gospel and its ordinances, and pious friends. We were in the place where we believed God would have us to be, and we did not doubt but that he would provide for us every thing necessary; and (glory to his name!) we were not disappointed. My wife and I lived comfortably together more than forty-three years, and on the 24th of November, 1819, she departed triumphantly to take possession of her house not made with hands, eternal in the heavens.

When I had determined to come to this country, Dr. Smith enjoined it upon me to look out for some pious young men, and educate them for the ministry; for, said he, though some men of piety and talents may go to a new country at first, yet if they are not careful to raise up others, the country will not be well supplied. Accordingly I collected a few who gave evidence of piety, and taught them the Latin and Greek languages. Some of them became useful, and others eminent ministers of the gospel. I had still a few with me when the academy was opened at Canonsburgh, and finding that I could not teach and do justice to my congregation, I immediately gave it up and sent them there.

The first remarkable season of the outpouring of the Spirit which we enjoyed in this congregation, began about the middle of December, 1781. It made its first appearance among a few who met together for social worship, on the evening of a thanksgiving day which had been appointed by congress. This encouraged us to appoint other meetings for the same purpose, on Sabbath evenings, and the appearances still increasing, Sabbath-night societies were continued, with but little interruption, for nearly two years. It was then usual to spend the whole night in religious exercises, nor did the time seem tedious, for the Lord was there, and his work went pleasantly on. Many were pricked to the heart with deep convictions, and a goodly number, we hope, were brought to close the happy match with precious Christ. At the first sacramental occasion after the work began, forty-five were added to the church, many of whom continued bringing forth the fruits of righteousness, and filling important offices in the church, until they were removed to the world of spirits. This time of refreshing continued, in a greater or less degree, until the year 1794. Upon every sacramental occasion during this period, numbers were added to the church, who gave comfortable evidence of their having obtained a saving change of heart; but as I neglected to keep a register of their names, I cannot now ascertain the number. The next remarkable season of the outpourings of God's Spirit was in the year 1795. This, however, was not very extensive, nor of long continuance. Yet during this season about fifty were added to the church, most of whom continued to manifest by their walk and conversation, that they had experienced a real change of heart and some of them became successful preachers of the gospel, though there were some lamentable instances of apostasy. In the spring of the year 1799, the Lord again revived his work in this congregation. Many were at once awakened to a serious concern about their immortal souls, and made to inquire the way to Zion with their faces thitherward, weeping as they went. Of those who were thus awakened, about sixty joined the church and made a public profession of religion. This revival, as well as that of 1795, was carried on without much external appearance except a solemn attention, and silent weeping under the preaching of the word. From that time until the fall of the year 1802, religion was evidently on the decline; for, though some were every year added to the church, yet they were generally such as had been brought under serious impressions in 1779, and there were few or none awakened. Sinners became more bold in sin, and floods of vanity and carnality appeared likely to carry all before them. Even the pious themselves became very weak and feeble in the cause of Christ, and much buried in the world, insomuch that when God returned to build up Zion, it might in truth be said, "we were as men that dream." Many stood astonished, not knowing what to make of it; and but few were prepared to meet the Lord, and bid him welcome. This work differed from former revivals only in this, that the body was more generally affected. It was no unusual thing to see a person so entirely deprived of bodily strength, that they would fall from their seats, or off their feet, and be as unable to help themselves as a newborn child. I have seen some lie in this condition for hours, who yet said that they could hear everything that was spoken, and felt their minds more composed and more capable of attending to divine things than when their bodies were not thus affected. As far as I could observe, the bodily exercise never preceded, but always followed, upon the mind's being deeply impressed with a sense of some divine truth. Between fifty and sixty joined the church as the fruits of this revival; a number of whom were students in the college, and now preaching the gospel of Christ to their dying fellow men. Since that time religion has rather been on the decline, though still we are not left without some tokens of the Divine presence. At every sacramental occasion, some have come out from the world and professed to take the Lord for their portion.

The Rev. Joseph Smith settled at Buffalo in the autumn of 1780. His congregation shared largely in the revival that commenced in 1781. I believe that both he and Mr. Power were born in Nottingham. He departed this life April 19, 1792. Thaddeus Dodd settled at Ten Mile, perhaps 1779. He died May 20, 1793. James Powell settled at Mount Pleasant in 1781. He died in 1830. He had not preached for some years before his death. James Dunlap settled at Laurel Hill, I believe in 1781. The time of his death I do not exactly know. He was for some years president of Jefferson college. The Rev. John Clark settled at Bethel in 1772, and died July 13, 1791, in the 79th year of his age. John Watson and Thomas Hughs were licensed to preach in the fall of 1798. Watson, you know, died on the 31st of November, 1802. Hughs yet lives, and was the first who settled north of the Ohio river. Concerning Mr. Strain of Slate Ridge, I knew but little; he died the same week in which I was licensed, 1774. The first presbytery that met on this side of the mountains, was held at Mount Pleasant, on the third week of October, 1783. The first synod met at Pittsburgh, on the last Wednesday of September, 1802.

I forgot to tell you, in the proper place, that I was born on the 11th of November, 1752. I am now in my 80th year, and have outlived all the *first* set of ministers who settled on this side of the mountains, viz: The Rev. Messrs. James Finley, James Power, James Dunlap, John Clark, Joseph Smith, and Thaddeus Dodd; and all the *second* set who were raised in this country, viz: Joseph Patterson, James Hughes, John Brice, James M'Gready, William Swan, Samuel Porter, Thomas Marquis, and John M'Pherrin. Several of the *third* set are already gone to rest, viz: John Watson, William Moorhead, David Smith, and William Wick. I yet enjoy pretty good health, though sometimes troubled with rheumatic pains. I am still able to preach, though my memory has much failed, so that I am obliged to make more use of notes than formerly, yet my lungs are still good, and I can bawl almost as loud as ever.

Thus I think I have fully complied with your request. If in anything I can gratify you farther, you may freely command me. As I have given up my congregation, because I could no longer perform the duties of a pastor, if my life and health be continued, I design this spring and summer to visit some of the old congregations which I helped to collect, and see how they do, and once more blow the gospel trumpet among them.

John M'Millan

BIBLIOGRAPHY

PART I. PRIMARY SOURCES

A. Manuscripts and Transcripts of Manuscripts

RECORDS, DIARIES, LETTERS, SERMONS

1. Subscription List, Academy and Library Company of Canonsburg, 1791. Washington and Jefferson College Library, Washington, Pennsylvania.
2. Account of the Great Revival in Kentucky in 1802. The manuscript of an account given to the *Western Missionary Magazine* by one of its editors, John McMillan. Western Theological Seminary Library, Pittsburgh.
3. Bay, Andrew. "Journal, 1758." Darlington Memorial Library, University of Pittsburgh.
4. Brackenridge, H. H. to Alexander Addison. Letters, 1796. Darlington Memorial Library, University of Pittsburgh.
5. "*Hoc Dievum* or a Daily Journal," a diary of Thaddeus Dod beginning Anno 1740. Washington and Jefferson College Library.
6. Dod, Thaddeus. Autobiography and Memoir (1763-1765). Library of the Presbyterian Historical Society, Philadelphia.
7. Logan, James. "Logan Papers." Library of the Pennsylvania Historical Society, Philadelphia.
8. McGready, James. A letter to John McMillan, November 18, 1802, describing the revival in Logan County, Kentucky. Library of Western Theological Seminary.
9. McGready, James, Notes on the pages of a copy of Ovid's *Metamorphoses*. Transcript in the Washington and Jefferson College Library.
10. McMillan, John. Journal or Diary. The second part of the Journal, 1776-1791, and the third part of the Journal, 1820-1831, are in the possession of Mrs. Helen Wragg, of 1133 Lancaster Street, Pittsburgh, Pa. A copy of the first part of the Journal, 1774-1776, is in the Library of Washington and Jefferson College. The Journal is printed in the Appendix of this book.
11. McMillan, John. One hundred and thirty-five sermons, in the possession of Mrs. Wragg.
12. McMillan, John. Estate, List of Goods, appraised by William Harner and Ira Belant, January 29, 1834. Washington and Jefferson College Library.
13. McMillan, John. Expense Account, 1821-1833. Mrs. Wragg has the manuscript. See the facsimile and Appendix B.
14. McMillan, John. A letter to Albert Gallatin, May 5, 1796. A copy is in the Washington and Jefferson College Library.
15. McMillan, John. A Memorandum Book of such as have been admitted to the Sacrament of the Supper in the congregation of Chartiers from June, 1815, to February, 1830. Mrs. Helen Wragg.
16. McMillan, John. Theology, Natural and Revealed. The original copy of theological lectures given by McMillan is in the Library of the Western Theological Seminary. Mrs. Wragg has a transcribed copy of these lectures made by Moses Allen in 1806.
17. McMillan, John. Notes made on the pages of his Matthew Henry *Commentaries*. Transcription in Washington and Jefferson College Library.
18. McMillan, John. A transcription of McMillan's will. Mrs. Wragg.
19. Nesbit, Charles. Letters to Alexander Addison, 1786-1803. Darlington Memorial Library, University of Pittsburgh.
20. Parkhurst, Jacob. Sketches of the Life and Adventures of Jacob Parkhurst. Washington and Jefferson College Library. Typed copy.

21. Records of the Yohogania County Courts. Sale of land to John McMillan. Darlington Memorial Library, University of Pittsburgh.
22. Treasurer's Book for the Support of Poor Scholars. Account of the distribution of the poor funds from 1805 to 1826. This account was kept by John McMillan. Western Theological Seminary Library.
23. Watson, John. Letter from James Watson to John McMillan, May 13, 1796. Washington and Jefferson College Library.

MINUTES OF CHURCHES, ACADEMIES, AND COLLEGES

1. Minutes of Dunlap's Creek Church, 1787-1804. Transcribed by Jesse Coldren and available at the Library of Western Pennsylvania Historical Society, Pittsburgh.
2. Records of Old Londonderry Congregation, or Fagg's Manor, Chester County. Presbyterian History Department, Witherspoon Building, Philadelphia. Also in *Journal of the Presbyterian Historical Society.* VIII, 342-379.
3. Minutes of Jefferson College, 1802-1864. Washington and Jefferson College Library.
4. Minutes of the Board of Trustees of Washington Academy, 1787-1806. Washington and Jefferson College Library.
5. Minutes of the Academy and Library Company of Canonsburg from January 25, 1796 to the Organization of Jefferson College on January 15, 1802. Washington and Jefferson College Library.

MINUTES OF PRESBYTERIES

1. Minutes of Donegal Presbytery, 1774-1777. Library of the Presbyterian Historical Society. Also a typed copy.
2. Minutes of New Castle Presbytery, 1759-1773, 1774-1795, 1795-1814, 1814-1834. Library of the Presbyterian Historical Society.
3. Records of Ohio Presbytery, 1793-1870. Library of the Western Theological Seminary. Typed transcripts are also available to the year 1835.
4. Minutes of the Redstone Presbytery, 1781-1800, 1800-1814, 1828-1836. Library, Presbyterian Historical Society. The Minutes from 1781-1831 have been printed.

MINUTES OF SYNODS

1. Minutes of the Synod of New York and Philadelphia, 1758-1788. Library of the Presbyterian Historical Society.
2. Minutes of the Synod of Pittsburgh, 1802-1832, 1833-1838. Library of the Presbyterian Historical Society. Also a printed copy, 1802-1832.
3. Records of the Synod of Virginia, 1788-1797, 1798-1806. Library of the Union Theological Seminary, Richmond. Also a typed copy in the Presbyterian Department of History, Witherspoon Building, Philadelphia.
4. Records of the Western Missionary Society, October 5, 1804 to July 24, 1826. This Society was the agency through which the Synod of Pittsburgh functioned. Library of Western Theological Seminary.

B. Published Material

DOCUMENTS

1. *Annals of the Congress of the United States.* Fourth Congress, First Session. Washington, D. C., 1849.
2. *Allegheny County Will Book.* I, III. Allegheny County Court House. Pittsburgh.
3. *Official Records, Borough of Canonsburg, Pennsylvania.* First record book after incorporation in 1802.
4. Pears, Thomas C., Jr. and Klett, Guy S. *Documentary History of William Tennent and Log College.* Philadelphia, 1940.

5. *Laws of the Commonwealth of Pennsylvania, 1700-1802.* 6 vols. Philadelphia, 1803.
6. *Official Records, Washington County, Pennsylvania.* Deed Book (0), 519, Vol. P, 441.
7. *Pennsylvania Archives.* Sixth Series, II, IX. 1906, 1907. Second Series, IV. Harrisburg, 1876.
8. *Treaties of the United States.* Edited by Hunter Miller. I. Washington, D. C., 1931.
9. *Will Book.* III. Mercer County Court House, Mercer, Pa.

AUTOBIOGRAPHIES, DIARIES, MEMOIRS, AND SERMONS

1. Asbury, Francis. *Journal of the Reverend Francis Asbury.* III. New York, 1821.
2. Beatty, Charles. *The Journal of a Two Months Tour* (Bound with J. Edwards' *An Account of the Life of David Brainerd.* 1796). Newark, 1811.
3. Brackenridge, H. M. *Recollections of Persons and Places in the West.* Philadelphia, 1868.
4. Brackenridge, Hugh Henry. *Incidents of the Insurrection in the Western Parts of Pennsylvania in the Year 1794.* Philadelphia, 1795.
5. Brackenridge, Hugh Henry. *Gazette Publications.* Carlisle, 1806.
6. Clarkson, Matthew. *Diary of Matthew Clarkson, 1776.* Printed in *Information Respecting the History, Conditions and Prospect of the Indian Tribes*, pp. 265-278 by Henry Schoolcraft. Philadelphia, 1854.
7. Cuming, Fortescue. *Sketch of a Tour to the Western Country, Through the States of Ohio and Kentucky, 1810.* Edited by Reuben G. Thwaites. IV. Cleveland, 1904.
8. Gratz, Simon. *Autograph Collection American Colonial Clergy.* Philadelphia, 1759.
9. Jennings, S. C. *Recollections of Useful Persons and Important Events Within Seventy Years.* Vancefort, Pa., 1884.
10. McClure, David. *Diary of David McClure.* Edited with notes by Franklin B. Dexter. New York, 1899.
11. McMillan, John. Autobiographical letter to James Carnahan, March 26, 1832. Published in the *Pittsburgh Christian Herald and Missionary Reporter.* V, Nos. 45, 46, 48. 1833. See Appendix C.
12. "McMillan Manuscript, The." An autobiographical account written in January, 1832. It contains several accounts not mentioned in the letter to Carnahan, but it is much shorter. See Appendix, *History of Jefferson College* by Joseph Smith. Pittsburgh, 1857.
13. McMillan, John. "The Duty of Zion's Watchmen" and "Sin Abounding, and Grace Superabounding." In pamphlet form at the Washington and Jefferson College Library. The sermons are also printed in *The Presbyterian Preacher.* II, Nos. 2, 8. IV, No. 6.
14. Mills, Samuel J. and Smith, Daniel. *Report of a Missionary Tour through that part of the United States which lies west of the Allegheny Mountains.* Andover, 1815.
15. Parke, John E. *Recollections of Seventy Years and Historical Gleanings of Allegheny, Pennsylvania.* Boston, 1886.
16. Schermerhorn, John F. and Mills, Samuel J. *A Correct View of that Part of the United States which lies West of the Allegheny Mountains.* Hartford, 1814.
17. Washington, George. *The Diaries of George Washington.* Edited by John C. Fitzpatrick. Boston, 1925.
18. *The Writings of George Washington.* Edited by John C. Fitzpatrick. 35. Washington, 1940.
19. Whitefield, George. *Journal of George Whitefield,* 1739-1744. London, 1744.

PUBLICATIONS OF ORGANIZATIONS

1. *A Digest Compiled from the Records of the General Assembly of the Presbyterian Church in the United States of America.* Philadelphia, 1820.

2. *Minutes of the General Assembly, 1789-1836.* Philadelphia, 1847.
3. *Minutes of the Presbytery of Redstone, 1781-1831.* Cincinnati, 1878.
4. *Proceedings of the Scotch-Irish Society.* 10 vols. Nashville, 1889-1896, 1900-1901.
5. *Records of the Presbyterian Church, 1706-1788.* Philadelphia, 1904.
6. *Records of the Presbyterian Church in the United States of America.* Philadelphia, 1841.
7. *Records of the Synod of Pittsburgh, 1802-1832.* Pittsburgh, 1852.

NEWSPAPERS

1. *The Commonwealth.* IV, Nos. 10, 12 (September and October, 1808). Pittsburgh.
2. *The Pittsburgh Gazette.* 1786-1835.
3. *The Pittsburgh Recorder.* 1822-1827.
4. *The Spectator.* 1826-1829. Pittsburgh.
5. *The Washington Reporter.* September, 1818; March, 1840.

MISCELLANEOUS RECORDS

1. Aitken, C. *General American Register for 1774.* Contains the earliest available list of Presbyterian churches and pastors. Library of the Pennsylvania Historical Society.
2. Copy of the Charter of Jefferson College. Washington and Jefferson College Library.
3. *Charters and Laws of Jefferson College.* Filed in Memorial Hall, Canonsburg, Pa.
4. Records, Franklin Literary Society. Washington and Jefferson College Library.
5. Records, Minutes of the Board of Trustees of Washington College. Washington and Jefferson College Library.
6. Records, Minutes of the Board of Trustees of Jefferson College. Washington and Jefferson College Library.

PART II. SECONDARY SOURCES

A. Periodicals (General)

1. *The American Journal of Education.* Boston.
2. *The Christian Herald.* 1829-1833. Pittsburgh.
3. *Journal of the Presbyterian Historical Society.* Philadelphia.
4. *Leslie's Weekly.* New York, 1902.
5. *Pennsylvania School Journal.* Harrisburg.
6. *The Pittsburgh Christian Herald and Western Missionary Reporter.* V, Nos. 45, 46, 48 (November and December, 1833).
7. *The Presbyterian.* 1831-1834, 1931-1948. Philadelphia.
8. *Presbyterian Advocate and Herald of the West.* 1838-1855. Pittsburgh.
9. *Presbyterian Banner.* 1852-1937. Pittsburgh.
10. *Presbyterian Banner and Advocate.* 1855-1860. Pittsburgh.
11. *The Washington Observer.* September 18, 1941. Washington.
12. *The Western Missionary Magazine and Repository of Religious Intelligence.* Published by the Synod of Pittsburgh, 1802-1805.
13. *Western Pennsylvania Historical Magazine.* 1918, 1935, 1944, 1945. Pittsburgh.

B. Articles and Essays in Periodicals and Annuals

1. Allison, James and Patterson, Robert. "McMillan Centennial," *Presbyterian Banner.* Pittsburgh, 1875.

2. Baxter, Dr. George A. *Presbyterian Advocate*. March 11, 1840.
3. Beam, Jacob Newton. "Dr. Robert Smith's Academy at Pequea, Pennsylvania," *Journal of the Presbyterian Historical Society*. VII, No. 4.
4. Bennett, D. M. "Life and Work of the Reverend John McMillan," *Journal of the Department of History of the Presbyterian Church*. Three installments: September, 1932; December, 1932; March, 1933. Parts I and II of McMillan's Journal appear in these installments. Bennett edited the Journal in places without calling attention to the changes.
5. Dahlinger, Charles W. *Rev John Taylor and His Commonplace Book*. A reprint from the *Western Pennsylvania Historical Magazine*, 1918.
6. Dawson, Mrs. J. L. "Early History and Contrasts," *Presbyterian Banner*. October 15, 1925.
7. Dodd, Cephas. "Memoir of Dr. T. Dodd," written by his son. *Presbyterian Magazine*. IV.
8. Ferguson, Russell J. "Albert Gallatin, Western Pennsylvania Politician," *The Western Pennsylvania Historical Magazine*. XVI.
9. Halsey, L. F. "Great Preachers and Pastors," *North-Western Presbyterian*. 1868.
10. Hamilton, W. F. Address before the Presbytery of Redstone, *Presbyterian Banner*. 1925.
11. "History of Education, Especially in Philadelphia," *Pennsylvania School Journal*. July, 1876.
12. James, Alfred P. "The Significance of Western Pennsylvania in American History." *Western Pennsylvania Historical Magazine*. XVI.
13. Johnson, Jesse. "Early Theological Education West of the Alleghenies," *Papers of the American Society of Church History*. Second Series. V, pp.119-130. New York and London, 1917.
14. Johnson, Roy H. "Frontier Religion in Western Pennsylvania," *Western Pennsylvania Historical Magazine*. 1933.
15. Leake, Lemuel F. "Notes of the Early Life of Dr. J. McMillan," *The Presbyterian Advocate*. VII, VIII.
16. Macartney, Clarence E. "Fagg's Manor," *The Presbyterian*. October 11, 1947.
17. McKinney, W. W. "Eighteenth Century Presbyterianism in Western Pennsylvania," *Journal of the Presbyterian Historical Society*. X.
18. Mellon, Thomas. "Reminiscences of Hon. James Ross, *Western Pennsylvania Historical Magazine*. III, No. 2. 103ff.
19. Moffat, James D. "Pioneer Educators in Washington County," *The Scotch-Irish in America—Proceedings and Addresses of the Eighth Congress at Harrisburg, Pa.,* 1896. Nashville.
20. Patterson, Robert. "Letter to Matthew Brown," *Presbyterian Advocate*. September 1, 1894.
21. Patterson, Robert. "Dr. John McMillan," *Presbyterian Advocate*. III, No. 38.
22. Pears, Thomas C., Jr. "The Foundations of Our Western Zion," *Journal of the Department of History of the Presbyterian Church, U. S. A.* December, 1934.
23. Slosser, Gaius J. "A Chapter from the Religious History of Western Pennsylvania," *Journal of the Department of History of the Presbyterian Church, U. S. A.* September, 1934.
24. Slosser, Gaius J. "Concerning the Life and Work of the Rev. John McMillan D.D.," *Journal of the Department of History of the Presbyterian Church, U. S. A.* XV.
25. Van Rensselar, C. (ed.). *Presbyterian Education Repository, Home, the School and the Church*. VI. Philadelphia, 1856.
26. Veech, James. "Article Written to David Elliott," *The Presbyterian Advocate*. XV, No. 24.
27. Waychoff, Andrew J. "Local History," *The Democrat Messenger*. 1925.
28. Wing, Conway P. *A Discourse on the History of Donegal and Carlisle Presbyteries*. Carlisle, 1877.

C. Theses

1. Hobbs, Jane Elizabeth. "Old Jefferson College." M. A. Thesis. University of Pittsburgh, 1929.
2. Kepner, Charles William. "The Contributions Early Presbyterian Leaders Made in the Development of Educational Institutions in Western Pennsylvania Prior to 1850." Ph.D. Dissertation. University of Pittsburgh, 1942.

D. Letters

1. Ewing, Charles M., Director of Washington and Jefferson College Historical Collections. July 3, 1952 and July 16, 1952.
2. King, Edgar W., Librarian of Miami University, Oxford, Ohio. April 18, 1952.
3. Martin, William T., a retired newspaper man who has recently published a history of the Bethel Church. April 25, 1952.
4. Purnell, W. B., Pastor of the Pigeon Creek Presbyterian Church. August 29, 1952.
5. Smyser, W. C., Registrar of Miami University, Oxford, Ohio. March 18, 1952.
6. Welsh, E. B. Pastor of the Presbyterian Church, New Concord, Ohio. May 1, 1952.

E. Individual Church and Short College Histories and Anniversary Addresses

1. *Addresses and Historical Sketches Delivered at the Centennial Anniversary of the Presbyterian Churches of Upper and Lower Ten Mile* by Doctors Brownson, Allison, and Wilson, and Rev. Messrs. Atkinson and Glen. Washington, Pa., 1879.
2. Allen, Moses R. Centennial Address, "Rev. John McMillan, D. D." by his grandson. 1888. Typed copy in Washington and Jefferson College Library.
3. Baird, C. W. *History of the Bedford Church.* New York, 1882.
4. *Bethel's 175 Years of Christian Service, 1776-1951.* William T. Martin, editor. Pittsburgh, 1952.
5. "History of the Beulah Presbyterian Church from October, 1794." Typed manuscript in the Library of Western Theological Seminary.
6. Brownson, James I. "A History of the Western Theological Seminary." An address delivered in the Third Presbyterian Church of Pittsburgh, April 17, 1872. Library of Western Theological Seminary.
7. Brownson, James I. *Centennial Celebration of the Presbyterian Church of Mount Pleasant, Pennsylvania,* October 9, 1894. Greensburg, 1895.
8. Brownson, J. I. and Moffat, J. D. Addresses on "Presbyterianism in Washington, Penna.," *Proceedings at the Centennial Celebration of the First Presbyterian Church of Washington, Pa.* Washington, 1893.
9. Campbell, Rev. Allen D. "The Founding and Early History of the Western Theological Seminary," *Western Theological Seminary Bulletin.* XX, No. 1.
10. *Canonsburg Centennial.* Addresses, edited by Blaine Ewing. Pittsburgh, 1903.
11. *Centennial Volume of the First Presbyterian Church of Pittsburgh,* 1784-1884. Pittsburgh, 1884.
12. *Centennial of the Western Foreign Missionary Society.* Edited by J. A. Kelso. Pittsburgh, 1931.
13. *Centennial Memorial,* Carlisle Presbytery. I and II. Carlisle, 1889.
14. Class Reunions of Various Classes of Jefferson College. Washington and Jefferson College Library.
15. Collier, Francis J. Address, "Chartiers Church and Its Ministers," *Centennial Celebration of Chartiers Church.* Philadelphia, 1875.
16. Crumrine, Boyd. "The Chartiers Presbyterian Church," an article in D. M. Bennett's *Life and Work of Rev. John McMillan, D. D.* Bridgeville, 1935.
17. Degelman, William C. *Historical Narrative of Bethel Presbyterian Church.* Pittsburgh, 1936.

18. DeWitt, John. "Historical Sketch," *Princeton Sesquicentennial Celebration.* New York, 1898.
19. Dinsmore, John W. "From 1806 to 1865," *The Centennial Celebration of the Chartering of Jefferson College in 1802.* Philadelphia, 1903.
20. Hamilton, W. F. Address, *The Centennial Celebration of the Presbytery of Redstone.* Uniontown, Pa., 1882.
21. Hays, I. N. Address, "The Religious History," *The Centennial Celebration of the Organization of Washington County, Pennsylvania, 1781-1881.* Washington, 1881.
22. Hensel, W. U. *Presbyterianism in the Pequea Valley.* A pamphlet in the Library of the Presbyterian Historical Society, Witherspoon Building, Philadelphia.
23. Holland, W. J. "Historical Address," *University of Pittsburgh 125th Anniversary Celebration.* Pittsburgh, 1912.
24. Jeffers, Eliakim T. *Centennial Address,* 1902. One of the papers of James Moffat in Washington and Jefferson College Library.
25. Johnson, Hubert Rex. *A History of the Neshannock Presbyterian Church, New Wilmington, Pa.* Washington, D. C., 1925.
26. Johnston, James Guthrie, "Early History of Dunlap's Creek Church, Fayette County, Pa.," *A Centennial Address,* August 26, 1914. Carnegie Library, Pittsburgh.
27. *Lebanon Presbyterian Church.* Sesqui-Centennial, 1926.
28. Maxwell, James M. "Clergy and Churches of Monongahela City," *Monongahela City Anniversary.* Monongahela City, 1895.
29. Maus, Charles W. *History of the Long Run Presbyterian Church.* Irwin, Pa., 1931.
30. McCormick, S. B. "One Hundred Years," *Bulletin of the Western Theological Seminary.* April, 1928.
31. McCormick, S. B. "Celebration of the One Hundred and Twenty-fifth Anniversary," *University of Pittsburgh Bulletin.* 1912.
32. Moffat, James D. *Historical Sketch of Washington and Jefferson College.* Washington, 1890.
33. *Old Montour.* The story of Montour Presbyterian Church. 1925.
34. Riddle, Matthew Brown. Address in *Canonsburg Centennial of the Chartering of Jefferson College.* Pittsburgh, 1903.
35. Simpson, James. *History of the Cross Creek Graveyard.* Burgettstown, Pa., 1894.
36. Turner, D. K. *History of the Neshaminy Presbyterian Church of Warwick, Bucks County, Pa.* Philadelphia, 1876.
37. West Alexander Presbyterian Church. *One Hundred Fifty Years,* 1790-1940. West Alexander, 1940.
38. Wilson, Maurice E. *Washington and Jefferson College, the Oldest College West of the Alleghenies.*
39. Wylie, Andrew. *Address in Self-Defense During the College War, 1816-1818.* Library of the Historical Association of Western Pennsylvania.

F. General Church History

1. Briggs, Charles A. *American Presbyterianism.* New York, 1885.
2. Brownlee, John T. *History of the Associate and United Presbytery of Chartiers.* Pittsburgh, 1877.
3. Davis, John R. *Pioneer Presbyterianism in Pennsylvania.* A pamphlet in the Library of the Presbyterian Historical Society.
4. Eaton, S. J. *History of the Presbytery of Erie, with biographical sketches of all its Ministers and Historical Sketches of its Churches.* New York, 1868.
5. Gillett, E. H. *History of the Presbyterian Church in the United States of America.* I. Philadelphia, 1864.
6. Glasgow, W. Melancthon. *History of the Reformed Church in America.* Baltimore, 1888.

7. Hanzsche, W. Thompson. *The Presbyterians.* New York, 1934.
8. Hays, George P. *Presbyterians.* New York, 1892.
9. *History of the Presbytery of Redstone.* Washington, 1889.
10. Hill, William. *A History of the Rise, Progress, Genius and Character of American Presbyterians.* Washington City, Pa., 1839.
11. *History of the Presbytery of Washington in Pennsylvania.* Philadelphia, 1889.
12. *Index of Presbyterian Ministers, 1706-1881.* Philadelphia.
13. Klett, Guy S. *Presbyterians in Colonial Pennsylvania.* Philadelphia, 1937.
14. *Manual of Presbyterian Law for Church Officers and Members.* Philadelphia, 1926.
15. Nevin, Alfred (ed.). *Encyclopedia of the Presbyterian Church in the United States of America.* Philadelphia, 1884.
16. Patton, Jacob Harris. *A Popular History of the Presbyterian Church in America.* New York, 1903.
17. Roberts, William N. *A Concise History of the Presbyterian Church in the United States of America.* Philadelphia, 1917.
18. *A Short History of American Presbyterianism from Its Foundation to the Reunion of 1869.* Philadelphia, 1903.
19. Smith, Joseph. *History of Jefferson College.* Pittsburgh, 1857.
20. Smith, Joseph. *Old Redstone,* or Historical Sketches of Western Presbyterianism; Its Early Ministers and Its Perilous Times. Philadelphia, 1854.
21. Sperry, Willard L. *Religion in America.* New York, 1946.
22. Sweet, William W. *Religion in Colonial America.* New York, 1942.
23. Sweet, William W. *Religion on the American Frontier, The Presbyterians,* II, 1783-1840. New York, 1936.
24. Thompson, Robert Ellis. "A History of the Presbyterian Churches in the United States," *American Church History.* VI. New York, 1895.
25. Webster, Richard. *A History of the Presbyterian Church in America from its Origin until the Year 1760 with Biographical Sketches of its Early Ministers.* Philadelphia, 1857.
26. Wilson, Samuel J. *The Presbyterianism of Western Pennsylvania and Its Influence on the West.* Washington.

G. Western Pennsylvania History

1. *Allegheny County, Its Early History and Subsequent Development.* A. A. Lambing writes of the earlier period to 1790. J. W. White writes of the period from 1790 to 1888. Allegheny, Pa., 1888.
2. Boucher, John Newton. *A Century and a Half of Pittsburgh and Her People.* II. Pittsburgh, 1908.
3. Brackenridge, H. M. *History of the Western Insurrection in Western Pennsylvania.* Pittsburgh, 1859.
4. Buck, Solon J. and Elizabeth H. *The Planting of Civilization in Western Pennsylvania.* Pittsburgh, 1939.
5. *Centenary Memorial of the Planting and Growth of Presbyterianism in Western Pennsylvania and Parts Adjacent* which includes "Life and Labors of the Rev. John McMillan, D.D." by Davis X. Junkin, "The Religious History" by Aaron Williams, "The Educational History" by James I. Brownson, "The Missionary History" by Elliott E. Swift, "The Ecclesiastical History" by Samuel J. M. Eaton, "Pittsburgh in the Last Century" by William M. Darlington, "The Secular History" by James Veech, and "Closing Address" by Samuel J. Wilson. Pittsburgh, 1876.
6. Creigh, Alfred. *History of Washington County.* Harrisburg, 1871.
7. Crumrine, Boyd. *A History of Washington County, Pennsylvania, with Biographical Sketches of Many of Its Pioneer and Prominent Men.* Philadelphia, 1882.
8. Cushing, Thomas, et al. *History of Allegheny County, Pennsylvania.* Chicago, 1889.

9. Ferguson, Russell J. *Early Western Pennsylvania Politics.* Pittsburgh, 1938.
10. Fleming, George Thornton. *History of Pittsburgh and Environs.* New York, 1931.
11. Forrest, Earle R. *History of Washington County, Pennsylvania.* I. Chicago, 1926.
12. Gallatin, Albert. *Speech* of, touching on the important validity of the elections ... held in October 1794. Philadelphia.
13. Macartney, Clarence E. *Not Far from Pittsburgh.* Pittsburgh, 1936.
14. Macartney, Clarence E. *Right Here in Pittsburgh.* Pittsburgh, 1937.
15. McFarland, Joseph F. *20th Century History of The City of Washington and Washington County, Pennsylvania and Representative Citizens.* Chicago, 1910.
16. McKinney, William W. *Early Pittsburgh Presbyterianism, 1758-1839.* Pittsburgh, 1938.
17. Rupp, Israel D. *Early History of Western Pennsylvania.* Pittsburgh, 1846.
18. Starrett, Agnes L. *Through One Hundred and Fifty Years.* Pittsburgh, 1937.
19. Veech, James. *The Monongahela of Old, or Historical Sketches of Southwestern Pennsylvania to the Year 1800.* Pittsburgh, 1858.
20. Walkinshaw, Lewis Clark. *Annals of Southwestern Pennsylvania.* New York, 1939.

H. Miscellaneous Works

1. Adams, Henry. *The Life of Albert Gallatin.* New York, 1943.
2. Alexander, Archibald, Editor and Collector. *Biographical Sketches of the Founder and Principal Alumni of the Log College.* Philadelphia, 1851.
3. Allbach, James R. *Annals of the West.* Pittsburgh, 1856.
4. *Appleton's Cyclopedia of American Biography.* Revised edition. IV. New York, 1900.
5. Baldwin, Leland D. *Whiskey Rebels.* Pittsburgh, 1939.
6. Baldwin, Leland D. *Pittsburgh, the Story of a City.* Pittsburgh, 1937.
7. Bancroft, George. *History of the United States.* II. 1837-66.
8. Bassett, J. S. *A Short History of the United States.* New York, 1914.
9. Beecher, Willis J. *Index of Presbyterian Ministers.* Philadelphia, 1883.
10. Bennett, Daniel M. *Rev. John McMillan, D.D.* Bridgeville, Pa., 1935. This work is a collection of notes, articles by other writers, and extracts culled from many sources.
11. Binney, Horace. *Reports of Cases Adjudged in the Supreme Court of Pennsylvania.* I. Philadelphia, 1844.
12. Birch, Thomas Ledlie. *Seemingly.* Washington, Pa., 1806.
13. Brownson, James I. *The Life and Times of Senator James Ross.* Washington, Pa., 1910.
14. Calvin, John. *The Catechism of the Church of Geneva.* Translated from the Latin by Elijah Waterman. Hartford, 1815.
15. Chambers, George. *A Tribute to the Principles, Virtues, Habits and Public Usefulness of the Irish and Scotch Early Settlers in Pennsylvania.* Chambersburg, Pa., 1856.
16. Chitwood, Oliver P. *A History of Colonial America.* New York, 1931.
17. Cleveland, Catherine C. *The Great Revival in the West.* Chicago, 1916.
18. Collins, Varnum L. *President Witherspoon.* Princeton, 1925.
19. *The Constitution of the Presbyterian Church in America.* Philadelphia, 1941.
20. Croskery, Thomas. *Irish Presbyterianism.* Dublin, 1884.
21. Crumrine, Boyd. *The Courts of Justice—Bench and Bar of Washington County, Pennsylvania.* Washington, Pa., 1902.
22. Dexter, Edwin G. *History of Education in the United States.* New York, 1904.
23. Dinsmore, John Walker. *The Scotch-Irish in America.* Chicago, 1906.

24. Doddridge, Joseph. *Notes on the Settlement and Indian Wars of the Western Part of Virginia and Pennsylvania from 1763-1783.* Printed first in 1824. Pittsburgh, 1912.
25. Eaton, S. J. M. *Biographical and Historical Catalogue of Washington and Jefferson College.* Cincinnati, 1889.
26. Eaton, S. J. M. *Lakeside.* Pittsburgh, 1880.
27. Elliott, David. *The Life of the Rev. Elisha Macurdy,* with an Appendix containing brief Notices of Various Deceased Ministers. Allegheny, Pa., 1848.
28. *Encyclopedia Britannica.* 11th edition. New York, 1910.
29. Fisher, Sidney George. *The Making of Pennsylvania.* Philadelphia, 1906.
30. Ford, Henry George. *The Scotch-Irish in America.* Princeton, 1915.
31. Garland, Robert. *The Scotch-Irish of Western Pennsylvania.* Pittsburgh, 1923.
32. *General Catalogue of Princeton University, 1746-1908.* Princeton, 1908.
33. Gould George M. (ed.). *The Jefferson Medical College of Philadelphia, 1826-1904.* New York and Chicago, 1904. Mrs. John M. Phillips presented to the Library of the University of Pittsburgh the two volumes of this book from the library of her father, Dr. John Milton Duff, a graduate of Jefferson Medical College.
34. Hanna, Charles A. *The Scotch-Irish or the Scot in North Britain, North Ireland and North America.* I. New York, 1902.
35. Hanna, Charles A. *Ohio Valley Genealogies.* New York, 1900.
36. Harkness, Georgia. *John Calvin, The Man and His Ethics,* New York, 1931.
37. *A History of Allegheny County, Pennsylvania.* Chicago, 1889.
38. Hodge, Charles. *The Constitutional History of the Presbyterian Church.* Parts I and II. Philadelphia, 1839.
39. Hulbert, A. B. *Pioneer Roads and Experiences of Travelers.* No. 12 in Series, *Historic Highways of America.* Cleveland, 1902-1905.
40. Hulbert, A. B. *The Old Glades* (Forbes Road). No. 5 in Series, *Historic Highways of America.* Cleveland, 1902-1905.
41. Lankard, Frank G. *A History of the American Sunday School Curriculum.* New York and Cincinnati, 1927.
42. Lecky, William E. H. *History of Ireland in the Eighteenth Century.* New York, 1893.
43. Maxson, Charles Hartshorn. *The Great Awakening in the Middle Colonies.* Chicago, 1920.
44. McAfee, Cleland B. *The Ruling Elder.* Philadelphia, 1936.
45. McCormick, S. B. *History of Western University of Pennsylvania.* Pittsburgh, 1908.
46. McClure, A. K. *Old Time Notes of Pennsylvania.* Philadelphia, 1905.
47. McGiffert, Arthur C. Jr. *Jonathan Edwards.* New York, 1932.
48. McKinney, W. W. *The Challenge of a Heroic Past.* Pittsburgh, 1939.
49. McMaster, John Bach. *A History of the People of the United States.* II. New York and London, 1928.
50. Murphy, Thomas, *The Presbytery of the Log College or the Cradle of the Presbyterian Church in America.* Philadelphia, 1889.
51. *National Cyclopedia of American Biography.* New York, 1893-1945.
52. Paxson, Frederic L. *History of the American Frontier, 1763-1893.* Boston and New York, 1924.
53. Pears, Thomas C., Jr. Unpublished Manuscripts "The Foundations of Our Western Zion, The Pre-Redstone Period," "Barr Chronology," and an unfinished manuscript on Barr. This material was made available by Thomas C. Pears, III.
54. Speer, William. *The Great Revival of 1800.* Philadelphia, 1892.
55. Sprague, W. B. *Annals of the American Pulpit or Commemorative Notices of Distinguished American Clergymen.* III and IV. New York, 1868.
56. Stalker, James. *John Knox, His Ideas and Ideals.* New York, 1904.

57. Tewksbury, Donald G. *The Founding of American Colleges and Universities before the Civil War.* New York, 1932.
58. Van Voorhis, John. *The Old and New Monongahela.* Pittsburgh, 1893.
59. Wertenbaker, Thomas Jefferson. *Princeton 1746-1896.* Princeton, 1946.
60. Wickersham, James Pyle. *A History of Education in Pennsylvania.* Lancaster, Pa., 1886.

INDEX

Academies *see* Canonsburg Academy, Faggs Manor School, Pequea Academy, Pittsburgh Academy, Washington Academy
Academy and Library Company of Canonsburg *see* Canonsburg Academy
Addison, Alexander 135, 141, 143, 172, 193-194
Alexander, Archibald, quoted 11
Allegheny County 41, 48, 57
Allegheny Theological Seminary *see* Western Theological Seminary
Alleghenytown 76
Allen, Matthew, quoted 199
Allen, Moses 47, 54, 66, 71, 147
Allison, James 53, 57-58, 88-90, 95, 139, 141, 147
Amity *see* Dod School
Anderson, Rebecca (Mrs. John McMillan II) 47
Arminians 144
Armstrong, John Francis 12
Associate Presbytery 69, 94
Associate Presbytery pastors *see* Brown, Matthew; Dunlap, James; Henderson, Matthew
Associated Reformed Presbytery 145-146
Augusta and Westmoreland trip 25-29

Back Creek 24, 26
Baptist Meeting House 27, *see also* Monongahela Baptist Center; Pike Run Meeting House
Barr case (Pittsburgh Congregation vs. Samuel Barr, neglect) 49, 106, 118-132, 149
Beasley, Frederick, quoted 12
Beatty, Charles 41, 57
Bedford 33
Bethel Church 63
Bethel Congregation 84, 104, 148
Big Spring 22, 25, 31

Birch case (Thomas Ledlie Birch vs. John McMillan, slander) 134-144, 175, 182
Blair, Betsy (Mrs. Robert Smith) 12
Blair, John 10-11, 66
Blair, Samuel 8, 66, 81
Blessings to pray for 151-152
Bottlecourt Court House 22
Bounty for scalps 109
Bower Hill burned 107
Bracken, Reid 58
Brackenridge, H. M., quoted 87
Brackenridge, Hugh Henry: admires McMillan 87, 168-169; Barr case 121, 130; Birch case 142; Congressional campaign 166-168; Jay Treaty 171-172; Whiskey Rebellion 160
Bradford, David 159-160
Brady (Indian fighter) 110
Brandywine 31-33
Brice, John 81, 86, 103, 107-110, 112, 149
British Treaty *see* Jay Treaty
Brothers Valley 43
Brown, Catherine (Mrs. John McMillan) 31, 47-48, 84, 195
Brown, Matthew 48, 53, 76, 91, 140, 185; quoted 70-71, 74-75
Brownson, James I., quoted 85
Bucks County 82
Buffalo Congregation 51-52, 84
Buflers Creek 23
Burds (in Lyttleton) 25

Caldwell, David 12
Calvin: *Catechism for Children* 9
Campaign for governor 1808, 172-176
Campbell, Alexander 90
Campbell, James 141
Canon, John 53, 63; George Washington visits 61; sponsors Canonsburg Academy 89-90, 92, 95
Canonsburg 39, 46, 182

288

Canonsburg Academy: antecedents 51, 81, 91-92; becomes Jefferson College 95; history 52-53, 75, 89-91, 94-95, 118
Carlisle 22, 25
Carmichael, John 31-32, 34
Carmichael, Pa. 45
Carnahan, James, quoted 65, 179, 186, 197
Cedar Bridge *see* Natural Bridge
Center Presbyterian Church 46
Centre Church 182
Charters *see* Church charters
Chartiers 33-35, 37, 42, 51-52, 57, 62, 151-154, *see also* McMillan School; Smith School
Chartiers Church 53, 58-61, 67-70, 183
Chartiers Congregation 27, 29-30, 33-34, 53, 57-62, 84, 110, 148; divided 182-183; negro members 60; Taylor case 132-133
Chaunceford 22
Church and state: church charters 60; church trials 141
Church buildings 59, 61-62, 183
Church charters 60
Church courts *see* Trials (church)
Church discipline 60-61
Church furniture: McMillan's chair 63
Claim jumping 133-134
Clark, John 88, 103-107, 125, 148
Classical instruction *see* Latin schools
College of New Jersey 11, 17-20, 67, 188, 194; curriculum and student life 19; *see also* Theological Seminary at Princeton
Colleges in Pennsylvania *see* Jefferson College; Jefferson Medical College; Log College; Washington and Jefferson College; Washington College; Western Theological Seminary
Collier, Francis J., quoted 60-61, 84, 88
Collins, Varnum L., quoted 18-19
Commonwealth 173-174
Communion *see* Lord's Supper
Conemaugh 24, 62, 64
Congressional campaign of 1794, 166-167
Conowaga 22
Consubstantiation *see* Lord's Supper

Conversion 66
Cook, Alexander 53, 89, 95
Corbly, John 88
Crab Apple 47
Crawford, Edward 127
Crawford, Samuel, quoted 186
Crawford, William, killed 149
Cross Creek *see* Vance's Fort
Cross Creek Congregation 51, 64, 84, 110, 148, 150
Cross Roads Church 68
Crumrine, Boyd, quoted 143

Dancing *see* Taylor case
Deer Creek 22
Degelman, William C., quoted 63
Dido (slave) 39, 107, 187
Dod, Thaddeus 48-50, 75, 88-89, 102-103, 106-108, 111, 135; *see also* Dod School
Dod School 50-51, 83-88
Dodd, Cephas 50, 85-86, 127
Doddridge, Joseph 90; quoted 6-7
Doddridge, Philip 90
Donegal Presbytery *see* Presbytery of Donegal
Duffield, George 41, 57
Duncan, David 131
Duncan, James 90
Dunlap, James 12, 48, 51-52, 95
Dunlap, John 184-185
Dunlap, William 24
Dunlap's Creek 49, 52
Dunlavy, James 90
Dutch Reformed Churches in Raritan Valley 66
Duty of Zion's Watchmen, excerpts 151-154

East Chester 82
East Nottingham 22
Edgar, Judge 165
Education: Presbyterian attitude 4, 9-11; Western Pennsylvania 10-11, 75, 88, 111; *see also* Log cabin schools; Theological education
Elder, defined 152
Elk Branch 33
Elliott, Dr. (Pastor of Washington Church) 195-196

English schools 80, 85; *see also* Log cabin schools
Episcopal parish taxes 41
Erie Presbytery *see* Presbytery of Erie
Established Church of Ireland 82
Evils *see* Sins
Excise laws revolt *see* Whiskey Rebellion

Faggs Manor 7, 21-22, 31; revivals 66, 69
Faggs Manor School 8, 10-11, 81, 83
Fallen Timber victory 164
Falling Spring Church 31
"Father of education in Western Pennsylvania" 80
"Father Polycarp" 171
Fayette County 41, 48, 57
Federalists of Western Country 159
Ferguson, Samuel 43
Finley, ... 126
Finley, James 31
Finley, John 120
Forks Meeting House 24, 58, 62
Fort Lindley 49
Fort Pitt: John McMillan visits 23-24, 28, 62; other pastors 57; *see also* Pittsburgh
"Four Presbyterian Horsemen of Western Pennsylvania" 48, 74-75
Franklin, Benjamin: interest in Washington Academy 88-89
Frederick 25
Frelinghuysen, Theodorus J., 66
French Revolution influence 163
Frisbee, Levi 41, 57
Frontier congregations: characteristics 62, 113-114, 128-129, 148-150
Frontier life 6-7, 37-42, 59, 133-134, 151
Frontier sins *see* Sins; Taylor case
Frontiersmen: description 42

Galbraith, Robert 120, 127
Gallatin, Albert 160, 166-167
General Assembly *see* Presbyterian Church of America
Georgetown 22
Gilbert, E. H., quoted 65
Grammar schools 75
Great Revival in the West 68-69
Greene County 107

Greensburg (Darlington) 110
Gwinn case (Ohio Presbytery vs. Andrew Gwinn, immorality) 145-148

Hall's Meeting House 23
Hamilton, David 166
Hannastown 24, 41, 62-63
Hanover 22, 25, 31, 33, 43
Hanover County 66
Hanover Presbytery *see* Presbytery of Hanover
Harper, Isabelle (Mrs. Samuel McMillan) 47
Harper, Samuel 45
Henderson, Ebenezer 90
Henderson, Matthew 48, 52-53, 88-90
Herron, Francis 122
Hill Church (near Canonsburg) 45
History of Jefferson College, quoted 85, 91
Hodge, Dr. Charles, quoted 69
Hog Creek 26
Hoge, John 52, 89, 91
Hoge, William 91
Hughes, James 104, 108, 110-113, 145, 149, 193
Hughes, Joseph 111
Hughes, Smiley 110
Hughes, Thomas Edgar 110
Hughs, James 81
Huntingdon Presbytery *see* Presbytery of Huntingdon

Immorality *see* Gwinn case
Indian fighters 109-110
Indian raids 33, 37, 41-42, 93, 109, 149-150, 163-164, 186
Indians: missionary field 41, 113
Intercessory prayer 151-153
Irwin (old woman), quoted 84, 86
Itinerant preachers 62

Jay Treaty 164, 169-172
Jefferson College: antecedents 81, 92-93; chartered 95; emphasis on theology 54, 70, 75-76; funds 46, 106; merger with Washington College 96-98; presidents and trustees 46-47, 52-54, 70, 75, 95-96, 112, 194
Jefferson Congregation 64
Jefferson Medical College 98

Jefferson Township *see* Mifflin Township
Jennings, S. C., quoted 180, 198
Johnston, David 89-90
Johnston, Mary (Mrs. John McMillan II) 47
Johnston, Richard 53
Jones, William 105-106

Kennedy, Catharine (Mrs. William Tennent) 82
Kentucky revival 54, 68-69
Kerr, ..., Washington-Jefferson merger 96
Kerr, James 108
Kerr, Joseph *see* Kerr case
Kerr, Rebecca (Mrs. John Brice) 108
Kerr, William 90
Kerr case (Ohio Presbytery vs. Joseph Kerr, slander) 72, 144-146
King, ... 30-31
Kitchen School *see* Smith School
Klett, ..., quoted 10
Knox, John (1505-1572): advocated education 9; John McMillan compared to 65

Land disputes *see* Claim jumping
Latin School *see* McMillan School
Latin schools 80, 85-88, *see also* Log cabin schools
Laurel Hill Church 49, 59
Leacocks 22, 44
Leake, Lemuel F. 59-60; quoted 178
Leatherman, Dr. Jonathan 187
Lebanon Church 63
Lebanon Congregation 104-105, 148
Lexington Presbytery *see* Presbytery of Lexington
Ligonier 24, 62
Lindley, Demas 49, 109
Lindley, Jacob, quoted 85-86, 89
Lindley's Fort 109
Linn, John 12
Little, Alexander 139
Little Brittain 22, 31
Log cabin schools 75, 80-88
Log College 8, 12, 75-76, 80-83
Long Island Presbytery *see* Presbytery of Long Island
Long Run (near Irwin) 24, 33, 62-63

Long Run Church 64
Long Run Meeting House 58-59
Long's Meeting House 31
Lord's Supper 73
Lower Buffalo 112, 149
Lower Ten Mile 50
Lyttleton 25

Maclagan, James 41
Macurdy, Elisha 68, 147
Mahon, James 138
Mantures Run Church *see* Montour Church
Marquis, Thomas 81, 193; Birch case 139-140; Gwinn case 147; Kerr case 145
Marsh Creek 31, 33-34
McCartney, Dr. Clarence E., quoted 65
McClelland, Sarah (Mrs. William McMillan) 34, 43
McClure, David 41
McConnell, Thomas 138
McDowel, Mary (Mrs. Samuel Barr) 120
McDowell, John 24, 33, 37, 53, 58, 60, 88-90
McElhenny, John 24, 43-44
McElroy-Allison wedding 185
McGready, James 81, 86-87; revivalist 54, 68, 70
McLean, Daniel 90
McMillan, Catherine (Mrs. Moses Allen) *daughter* 46-47
McMillan, James, *brother* 62
McMillan, Janet (Mrs. John McElhenny) *sister* 43
McMillan, Jean (Mrs. William Morehead, later Mrs. Samuel Harper) *daughter* 34, 44-45, 84, 87, 188
McMillan, John—
  appearance and personality 103, 129, 154, 178-199
  called: Father of education in Western Pennsylvania 80; Father Polycarp 171; Patriarch of the Western Church 171-172; Symbol of Frontier Church 131-132
  charities 193
  church organizer 24, 63-64
  consecration 8-9
  conversion 13, 17, 67

291

death 198
early ministry 21-22
education: College of New Jersey 19-20, 111; Faggs Manor 9-10, 81; Pequea Academy 12-14, 20-21, 81; primary 9
educator 80-98: Canonsburg Academy 90-95, 118; Jefferson College 92, 95-98; McMillan School 81; Washington Academy 87-89, 91; Washington and Jefferson College 96
family: parents 5-6, 8-9, 14, 34, 43; wife 31, 47-48, 84, 195 *see also entries beginning* McMillan
farmer 38, 186-187
friends 34, 48-54
homelife 37-40, 111
land grant 45
library 190
military service 186
pastor: Chartiers 33-34, 57-62, 111; Pigeon Creek 61-62; remuneration 34-35, 148-149
political activities 53: influence 171-172; Jay Treaty 169-172; supports Gallatin 166-167; supports Ross 174-175; Whiskey Rebellion 158-166
presbytery affairs 101-108, 112, 117-148 *also* church trials: Barr case 126, 131-132; Birch case 136-144, 175; Gwinn case 146-148; Kerr case 144-146; Taylor case 132-134; *see also entries beginning* **Presbytery of** *and* **Synod of** 191
reading 188-191
retirement 196-198
revivalist 67-68, 70
sermons: *Duty of Zion's Watchmen* 151-154; preparation and delivery 65-66, 153-154, 178-190
teacher of theology: lectures 47, 70-74, 189; methods 74; professor of divinity 70; recognition 76; students 47, 54, 68, 75, 81, 86-87, 107, 110-111, 141, 146, 193; theological library at Jefferson College 76
trustee: Pittsburgh Academy 88; Washington Academy 88, 106

visiting preacher 25, 31, 58, 62-63, 196, 198
will 45, 187, 190
writing 60-61, 71, 194
McMillan, John, *grandson* 47
McMillan, John, *son* 47
McMillan, John, the Covenanter 5-6
McMillan, Margaret (Mrs. John Torbit) *sister* 44
McMillan, Margaret (Mrs. John Watson, later Mrs. John Neill) *daughter* 46
McMillan, Mary (Mrs. John Weaver) *daughter* 46
McMillan, Mary (Mrs. Samuel Ferguson, later Mrs. John McElhenny) *sister* 43-44
McMillan, Samuel, *son* 47
McMillan, Thomas, *brother* 25, 43
McMillan, William, *brother* 27, 43
McMillan, William, *father* 5-6, 34, 42-43
McMillan, William, *nephew* 43, 54, 145
McMillan, William, *son* 45-46
McMillan School, also called School of the Prophets, and the Latin School 75: history 51, 75, 83-88; precursor of Canonsburg Academy 91-92; precursor of Western Theological Seminary 76; teachers and students 54, 86, 141
McMillan's Meeting House *see* Chartiers Church
McPherrin, John 106
Mellon, Thomas 175-176
Mercer, Boyd 135
Mercer County 45
Miami Presbytery *see* Presbytery of Miami
Miami University 112-113
Middle Octorara 22
Mifflin Township 43
Military service 45, 47, 163-164
Miller's Run Church 46
Mingo Creek Society 162
Minister: McMillan defines 152
Moak, Jane (Mrs. Joseph Patterson) 113
Monaughany 22
Monongahela Baptist Center 63
Monongahela Meeting House 24, 62
Montgomery, James 127
Montour Church 64, 115

Morehead, Sara (Mrs. William McMillan) 45
Morehead, William 44-45, 54
Morgan, George 182
"Mothers in Israel" 48
Mt. Moriah 62
Mt. Pleasant 63
Mt. Pleasant Congregation 49, 148
Mountain, James 141
Murdock,.........., Washington-Jefferson merger 96
Murphy, Thomas, quoted 66

Natural Bridge 22-23
Neglect of pastoral duties *see* Barr case
Neil, William 184
Neill, John 46
Neill, William 65
Neshaming 80, 82
Neshannock Church 45-46
Neshannock Congregation 64
Neville, General, home burned 107
New Brunswick Presbytery *see* Presbytery of New Brunswick
New Castle Presbytery *see* Presbytery of New Castle
New London 119-120
New Londonderry *see* Faggs Manor
New Providence Congregation 64
"New Side" 66, 154
New York Synod *see* Synod of New York; Synod of New York and New Jersey; Synod of New York and Philadelphia
North Carolina revival 68
North Mountain Meeting House 22
North Strabane Township 46
Nottingham revival 66

O'Hara, James 124
Ohio Company opens road 40
Ohio Presbytery *see* Presbytery of Ohio
Old Monture Church *see* Montour Church
Old Redstone, quoted 11, 20, 59, 76, 85, 91, 199
Old Redstone Presbytery *see* Presbytery of Redstone
Oxford 52
Oxford Church 113

Park, Sarah, quoted 86
Pastor: McMillan defines 152; relationship to church members 165-166
"Patriarch of the Western Church" 171
Patterson, James 139
Patterson, Joseph 64, 94-95, 104, 106, 113-117, 165, 185
Patterson, Robert 88-90, 193; quoted 48, 86-87
Patterson Creek 50
Pencader 22
Penn, John: land to Pittsburgh Congregation 121
Pennsylvania, Western 23-28, 57, 62-63: education 10-11, 75, 81, 88, 111; Scotch Irish, 37; settling 40-41; yeomanry 128
Pennsylvania colonists, dress and customs 6-7
Pentecost,......... 24, 62
Pentecost, Dorsey 90
Pentecost, Joseph 141
Pentland, Ephraim 173, 175
Pequea 22, 25, 32
Pequea Academy 12, 20, 81, 83
Peter's Creek 33, 43, 63, 104
Peter's Creek Church 63
Petticoat Gap 26
Philadelphia Presbytery *see* Presbytery of Philadelphia
Philadelphia Synod *see* Synod of New York and Philadelphia; Synod of Philadelphia
Pigeon Creek 27, 57-58, 62
Pigeon Creek Church 53, 61-62, 102; Gwinn case 146-148
Pigeon Creek Congregation 27, 33, 57-62, 148
Pike Run Congregation 146
Pike Run Meeting House 63
Pitt Township Congregation *see* Pittsburgh Congregation
Pittsburgh: called "Ungodly city" 115; cultural and social development 124-125; descriptions 123-124; morals 128; Woods plan 124; *see also* Fort Pitt
Pittsburgh Academy 88, 108, 121, 141
Pittsburgh Congregation: Barr case 49, 106, 118-132, 149; incorporated 121; land from Penns 121; visiting pastors 104, 116, 122, 198; worldliness 130

293

Pittsburgh Gazette 159, 168, 171, 199
Pittsburgh Synod *see* Synod of Pittsburgh
Poe, Adam 109-110
Political activity of clergy 107, 165, 172
Political campaigns *see* Campaign for governor 1808; Congressional campaign of 1794
Porter, Samuel 81, 193
Power, James 41, 48-50, 75, 102-103, 148
Power, John 57
Presbyter *see* Elder
Presbyterian Church of America—
  Doctrine 4-5, 71-74: attributes of God 72; baptism 73; Lord's Supper 73-74; miracles 71; original sin 72-73; Trinity 72
  General Assembly: Birch case 137-140; Gwinn case 146-147; Western Theological Seminary 76
  Missionary church 114
  Tenets 74
  see also entries beginning Presbytery *and* Synod
Presbyterians in Ireland 1-5
Presbytery of Donegal 22, 30-31, 33, 41, 101
Presbytery of Erie 75, 104
Presbytery of Hanover 102
Presbytery of Huntingdon 53
Presbytery of Lexington 102
Presbytery of Long Island 101
Presbytery of Miami 113
Presbytery of New Brunswick 83
Presbytery of New Castle 21-22, 25, 51, 101
Presbytery of Ohio 101, 149: Birch case 134-144; Gwinn case 146-147; Jefferson College 95, 118; Kerr case 145; Synod of Pittsburgh 104; Synod of Virginia 103; trial rights 141
Presbytery of Philadelphia 101-102
Presbytery of Redstone 50, 52, 101-103, 114, 148; Barr case 125-128; 1781-1793 known as "Old Redstone" 103; severity toward town congregations 129-130; sponsors Canonsburg Academy and Jefferson College 93-95, 118; Synod of New York and Philadelphia 64; Synod of Pittsburgh 104
Presbytery of Transylvania 102

Princeton *see* College of New Jersey; Theological Seminary at Princeton
Proctor's tent 24, 63

Raccoon Church 47, 64, 115
Ralston, Samuel 145, 147
Ramsey, James, quoted 92
Raritan Valley revival movement 66
Rea, Margaret (Mrs. William McMillan) 5-6, 14
Records of Chartiers Church, quoted 60-61
Redstone Presbytery *see* Presbytery of Redstone
"Religious Agreement" 165
Reno, Francis 86
Revival preachers 51, 54, 66-67, 69, 112
Revivals 8, 18-19, 66-70, 83
Revolutionary War 32-33, 67, 114
Riddle, William 90
Ritchie,..........., Canonsburg petition 95
Ritchie, Craig 90
Robinson, John 59
Rock Creek 33
Rockbridge County, 93
Ross, James 53, 86-87, 111, 141-143, 172-176
Rush, Benjamin, visits John Witherspoon 18

Salaries of clergy 38, 121-122, 148-150; farming to supplement 38, 150; offerings 34, 63-64
School of the Prophets *see* McMillan School
Schools *see* Log cabin schools, *also references under* Academies; Colleges in Pennsylvania
Scotch Irish 1-5, 37, 80, 186
Scott, Abraham 90
Scott, Thomas 166
Seceders *see* Associate Presbytery
Semple, Cunningham 141
Semple, Nathaniel W. 12
Sewickley Congregation 49, 148
Shippensburg 33
Shirtee *see* Chartiers
Short Creek Congregation 112, 149
Sins: Of the frontier 121-122; "Religious Agreement" 165

Slander defined 143, *see also* Birch case; Kerr case
Slate Ridge 22, 31-32
Slavery 39-40, 107
Smiley, William 150
Smith, David 86
Smith, John Blair 12
Smith, Joseph 48, 50-51, 75, 88, 90, 102-103, 106, 112, 114, 125-126, 148, 150; *see also* Smith School
Smith, Mrs. Joseph 48, 84
Smith, Joseph, *grandson,* quoted 11, 20, 59, 76, 85, 91, 199
Smith, Robert 12, 66, 81: influence on McMillan 20, 71, 81, 85; *see also* Pequea Academy
Smith, Samuel Stanhope 12
Smith, Thomas 141
Smith School *also called* the Study, or Kitchen School: history 51, 83-88; students 108, 111
Snodgrass, James 90
Snyder, Simon 173
Social worship 57-58
Socinianism *see* Kerr case
Soldiers Delight 22
Spayd, John 173
Springer, John 12
Staunton 26
Stockton, Jean (Mrs. John Brice) 108
Stockton, Joseph 108
Stockton, Robert 139
Student funds 46, 93-94
Students 40, 81, 84, 86, 106, 193
"Study" *see* Smith School
Swan, William 81
Swearengen, Thomas 90
Swearingen, Andrew 139
Synod of New York 83
Synod of New York and New Jersey 101
Synod of New York and Philadelphia 41, 64, 101-102, 148
Synod of Philadelphia 82-83, 101-102
Synod of Pittsburgh 101, 104, 196: Gwinn case 146-147; theological school 75-76
Synod of Virginia 101-102, 163: Barr case 127; Canonsburg Academy and Jefferson College 93, 95, 118

Tarrytown 25

Taylor, Henry 133-134
Taylor case (Chartiers Congregation vs Henry Taylor, dancing) 132-133
Ten Mile 63
Ten Mile Congregation 84, 110
Tennent, Gilbert 66
Tennent, William 81-82, *see also* Log College
Theological education 75, 83
Theological Seminary at Princeton 75, *see also* College of New Jersey
Theological Seminary in the West *see* Western Theological Seminary
Three Springs revival 68
Tilghman, William, opinion 142
Tinhting Spring 22
Torbit, John 44
Torbit, Sara 44
Transubstantiation *see* Lord's Supper
Transylvania Presbytery *see* Presbytery of Transylvania
Trials (church): freedom of speech endangered 141; *see also* Barr case; Birch case; Gwinn case; Kerr case; Taylor case
Trials (civil) *see* Birch case
Tygarts Valley 23
Tyrone 49

Unity Congregation 49, 148
Universities compared to Log College 82
Upper Buffalo 68, 150, *see also* Smith School
Upper Buffalo Congregation 150
Upper Ten Mile Congregation 50
Urbana 113

Vance's Fort 49, 114
Virginia: McMillan's trips 22-23, 25-26, 28-29
Virginia Synod *see* Synod of Virginia

Wallace (witness) 127
Washington, George: sends troops to Western Pennsylvania 160; visits Col. Canon 61
Washington, Laurence 41
Washington, Pa., indifference of people 89
Washington Academy: antecedents 81; history 88-89; principals and trustees

50, 52-53, 88-89, 106; Washington Academy (re-established) 90-91, *see also* Washington College
Washington and Jefferson College, merger 96-98
Washington College: chartered 91; merger 96-98; *see also* Washington Academy
Washington Congregation 46, 53, 61, 135, 141, 182; Birch case 134-140
Washington County 41, 47, 57, 93, 149, 165
Washington Court House burned 89
Watchman, defined 151-152
Watson, John 40, 45-46, 54, 111, 194
Watson, John II 46
Watson, William Morehead 46
Wayne, General Anthony, at Fallen Timber 164
Weaver, John 46
Weaver, Sara (Mrs. John McMillan II) 47
Welsh, E. B. (?), quoted 7
Welsh, James 135
West Nottingham 22
Western Country *see* Pennsylvania, Western

Western Theological Seminary: antecedents 81; founding 74-76
Westmoreland County 41, 48, 57 *see also* Augusta and Westmoreland trip
Wetzells (Indian fighters) 110
Wheeling, W. Va., 198
Wherry, Joseph 139
Whiskey Rebellion 53, 107, 111-112, 158-165
Whitefield, George 69
Wilkeson, Judge 59
Wilkins (Barr accuser) 127
Wilkinson (Barr accuser) 127
Williams, Isaac (Indian fighter) 110
Williams, John (Indian fighter) 110
Winchester 25-26
Witherspoon, John 17-19, 67
Woods, John 166
Wragg, Mrs. John A. 60, 71
Wyandot Indian massacre 149
Wylie, Andrew 96-97
Wylie, William 90

Yeates, Jasper 141

Zion's Watchmen *see Duty of Zion's Watchmen*

This book was set in Intertype Garamond with heads in Ludlow Garamond Bold and was printed on Warren's Old Style Text by the Herbick & Held Printing Company of Pittsburgh, Pennsylvania. Title page illustration is from a woodcut by Boyd Hanna. Line drawings throughout the book were made by Clarence McWilliams.

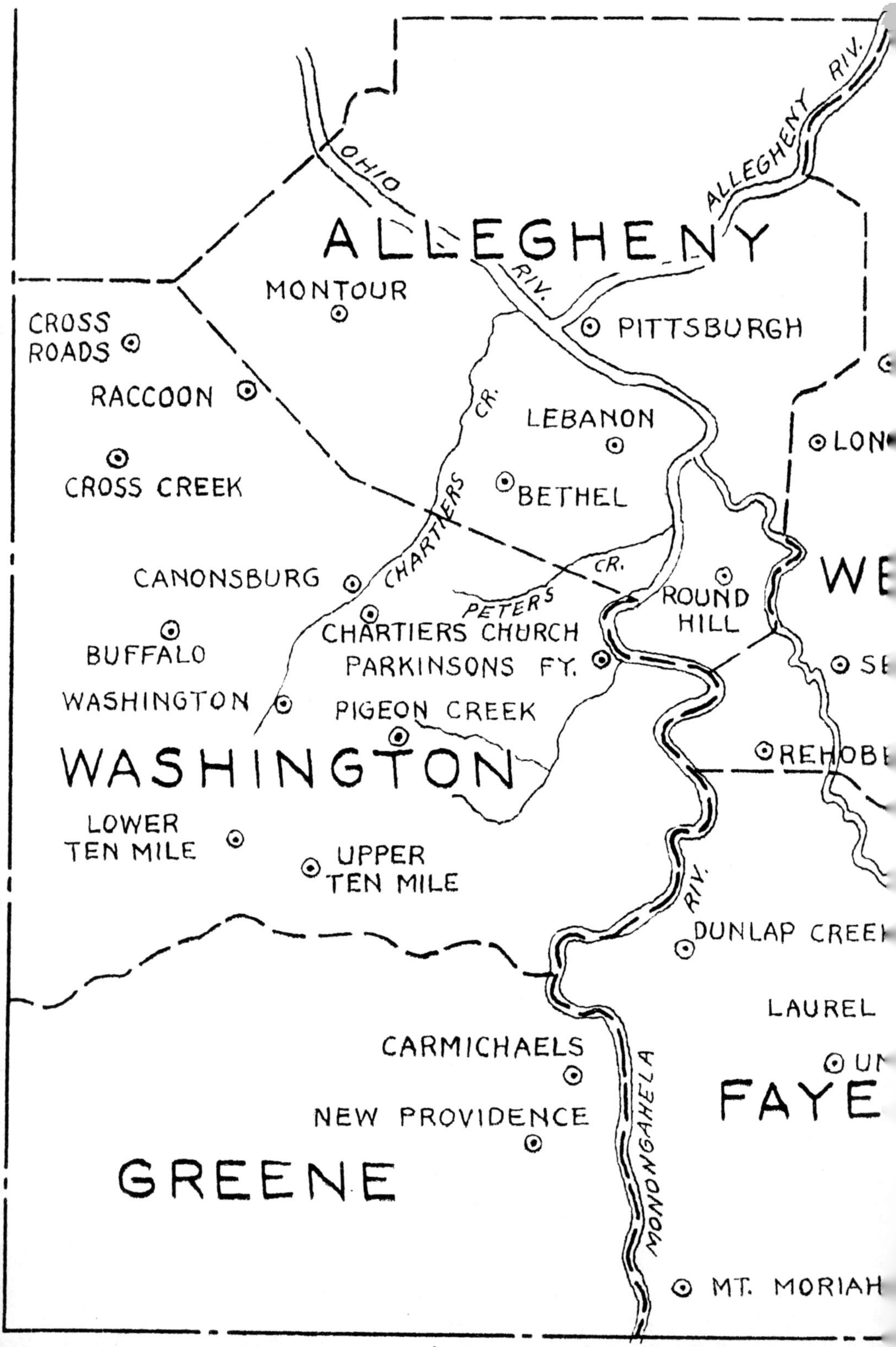

ALLEGHENY
OHIO
ALLEGHENY RIV.
RIV.
MONTOUR
PITTSBURGH
CROSS ROADS
RACCOON
CR.
LEBANON
CROSS CREEK
BETHEL
CHARTIERS
CR.
PETERS
CANONSBURG
ROUND HILL
CHARTIERS CHURCH
BUFFALO
PARKINSONS FY.
WASHINGTON
PIGEON CREEK
WASHINGTON
LOWER TEN MILE
UPPER TEN MILE
RIV.
DUNLAP CREEK
LAUREL
CARMICHAELS
NEW PROVIDENCE
MONONGAHELA
GREENE
MT. MORIAH